THE SOUL'S LONGING

*An Orthodox Christian Perspective
on Biblical Interpretation*

THE SOUL'S LONGING

An Orthodox Christian Perspective on Biblical Interpretation

by Mary S. Ford

*As a hart longs for the flowing streams,
so longs my soul for thee, O God.
My soul thirsts for God, for the living God.
When shall I come and behold
the face of God?*
—PSALM 42:1-2

MONASTERY
P·R·E·S·S

2015

The Soul's Longing:
An Orthodox Christian Perspective on Biblical Interpretation
© 2015, by Mary S. Ford. All rights reserved.

Published by:
St. Tikhon's Monastery Press
175 St. Tikhon's Road
Waymart, Pennsylvania 18472
Printed in the United States of America

ISBN: 978-0-9905029-6-8

This book is dedicated to the memory of William Valerius Sanford, my father. May his memory be eternal!

And

also to Fr. Roman Braga, who first gave me the idea and the encouragement to write a book on this subject.

CONTENTS

FOREWORD

Utilizing all that is valuable in historical-critical and related research, Dr. Mary Ford demonstrates with force and clarity just why biblical hermeneutics needs to return to the perspectives and methods of early Christian interpreters, particularly those of the Eastern Church Tradition.

Since the late Middle Ages, biblical interpretation in Western Christianity has been largely guided by historical-critical methodology. Highly useful for questions of "Introduction" (the "who, what, when, where and why" of biblical writings), it has nevertheless led to a serious "reductionism," represented most flagrantly today by members of the "Jesus Seminar." The indispensable link between exegesis and spiritual life has been largely obscured, with the result that concern for the Gospel promise of salvation has been subordinated to scientific inquiry of the text.

Her focus is consistently on the basic question, "What does the soul long for?" She answers the question by a careful criticism of non-orthodox trends in interpretation (from Spinoza to contemporary exegetes), and by demonstrating how a hermeneutic inspired by the Church Fathers can be faithful to the text, while leading the reader to discover what it means to be "a child of God."

We are greatly indebted to Professor Ford for achieving her intended goal: to demonstrate that authentic and authoritative biblical interpretation is intimately related to the life of faith. This important book is a treasure that will be of special interest to clergy and students of theology, as well as to lay persons who experience the soul's deep longing for God.

Archpriest John Breck, former Professor of New Testament, St. Herman's Seminary (Kodiak, Alaska); former Professor of New Testament and Bioethics, St. Vladimir's Seminary (Crestwood, New York); and Professor Emeritus of Patristic Exegesis and Bioethics, St. Sergius Theological Institute (Paris, France).

To behold the beauty of the Lord, and to inquire in His temple.
—PSALM 27:4

PREFACE

QUITE unexpectedly, in a way only the Providence of God could arrange, more than 25 years ago I found myself teaching Hermeneutics, Introduction to Orthodox Spiritual Life, and (somewhat later) Johannine Writings, at St. Tikhon's Orthodox Theological Seminary, in South Canaan, PA. This book is largely the fruit of those many years of teaching, and of the thoughts and living examples of many people, most especially the old Russian Orthodox emigres whom I was blessed to know in the parishes of London and Oxford, England, as well as at the monastic community of St. John the Baptist, in Essex, England.

Many educated Christians belonging to a wide variety of religious traditions agree that there are serious problems with the way biblical studies is often done currently, as well as the way it has been done in the past several centuries. There have been many attempts to find a better approach, and an increasing number of more traditional Christians are turning to the early Church and the Church Fathers in seeking to recover a "healthier" hermeneutic. Yet, there has not been a book-length study of this problem for a general audience from an Eastern Orthodox perspective, bringing the unique insights of that rich Tradition to bear—especially its emphasis on the inseparability of biblical interpretation and spiritual life. This book also draws out the connections between key theological principles, methods of exegesis, and spiritual life.

It's partly the lack of such a work that led me to write this book for use in my own teaching, and in the hope that it can be of benefit to others. Many of my students have originally come from non-Orthodox backgrounds; many were even pastors and/or missionaries. They, in particular, have urged me to write this book, saying how much this material would have helped them in the past, as well as currently. Whether or not a reader would agree with everything presented here, I believe it's important that the points brought up be part of the broader discussion surrounding hermeneutical questions, including the crucial question of what makes an interpretation authoritative.

Striving to reflect a balanced exegetical approach, this book seeks also to reveal how the strengths of the early Church can be brought into the present, while retaining what is of value from the recent past as well. It's intended to be both an informative and inspirational work, sharing some of the riches of Eastern Orthodoxy with the wider Christian community in an accessible way for those outside, as well as within, that Tradition (hence the decision not to include Septuagint numbering for Old Testament references).

It is amazing to reflect on just how many people have influenced, and are really connected to this, and no doubt, every book and life. My sharing a few of these reflections and offering thanks to some of these people will perhaps give a helpful context for this work. To begin with, I will mention a small part of my journey to becoming Orthodox as it relates to this book. My doctoral supervisor, Dr. Peter Moore—to whom I will always be indebted—sent me (a non-Christian "seeker") to London to experience an Orthodox Church service for the first time. All I knew about it was that the service would not be in English, that they did not have pews, and that it would not matter if I were late (it was more than a three-hour trip from the University of Kent in Canterbury, England, where I was studying).

Those first moments in the Russian Orthodox Cathedral, where Metr. Anthony (Bloom) of Sourozh was serving, were unforgettable. I was overwhelmed by the beauty, the sense of freedom with dignity, and especially, by an extremely powerful sense of the presence of God. I remember thinking, "I don't know what these people believe, but it's obvious that they know God and they know how to worship Him."

And that was what I had been looking for in many wrong places. Though this reality, sadly, is not always so readily apparent in every Orthodox parish, this is the Orthodoxy I grew to love and embrace to the best of my limited abilities. It was foundational for me, as hopefully the last chapter of this book will make clear in a way that may be helpful for others.

Again, only by God's unfathomable Providence, I was immeasurably blessed to live in Britain at a time when Fr. Sophrony (Sakharov), Metr. Anthony of Sourozh, Metr. Kallistos (Ware), Nicolas (and Militza) Zernov, Fr. Lev Gillet, and others were still very active and rather easily accessible. For all their differences, all of them in various ways nevertheless revealed lives powerfully transformed by their personal encounter with Christ, as well as a deep love for and a lived understanding of His Holy Church and Her Tradition that I also aspire to live and to communicate in all that I write and teach. I mention them only to give my profound thanks for their inspiring lives and works, and in several cases, their ongoing personal support of me and my work—especially those at St. John the Baptist Monastery.

However, the first thanks should go to my Southern Baptist father, who introduced me to the word hermeneutics and to that subject—as well as to much else in my life. A prominent lawyer, he also was very much a scholar, and especially a student of the Bible. The use of his extensive library during his lifetime, and after his departing this life, has been of great help. This book is dedicated to his memory—in gratitude for many things, including his continued support of me in every way, even when this interest he inspired led me to a theology and Church which he could not fully accept, though eventually he came to respect it.

The next thanks should go to Fr. Roman Braga, who urged me to put together a book on this topic quite a few years ago, based on some articles I had already published. Though his original idea of a collection of essays has taken a different, and much more difficult, time-consuming form, without his initial encouragement and no doubt prayers, this book probably would not have been written. I hope he will not be disappointed with the final result—even though it has taken so long to complete!

Thanks also to those who hired me at St. Tikhon's, and for all the clear blessings of teaching here—as well as the many struggles, and thanks are due to all the students who encouraged me to write this book. Special thanks must go to our former student, Fr. Matthew Baker, who read much of the book in various phases and had, as always, very insightful and constructive suggestions—as well as photocopies of T. F. Torrance articles (among others) that were most helpful! Many thanks also go to another former student, Abbot Archimandrite Sergius (Bowyer), and the other monastics at St. Tikhon's Monastery, for the many ways we have been supported by them, and for their willingness to publish this book.

I also especially want to thank Bishop Michael (Dahulich), Fr. John Breck, and Dr. Edith Humphrey for carefully reviewing the manuscript and making various helpful suggestions and corrections, as well as our nephew, Chris Liu-Beers (while he was a student at Duke Divinity School), and our friend, Decio de Carvalho, both of whom who gave valuable input from an informed Protestant perspective.

And last, but far from least, thanks to my beloved husband, David, my patient editor-in-chief, without whom I cannot imagine having finished this book, or living my adult life.

Hopefully, it's understood that in spite of help from all of the above and more, any errors are mine. Thankfully also, our Lord is merciful, for He is "the good God Who loves mankind." It's impossible to be adequately thankful for that!

Mary Ford
September 26th, 2014
St. John the Theologian

When You said, "Seek My face," my heart said
to You, "Your face, Lord, I will seek."
—Psalm 27:8

Chapter One

Psyche and Her Sisters: Patristic Interpreters and the Heirs of Spinoza

Faith is the certainty [or proof] of things unseen.
—Hebrews 11:1

I have heard of Thee by the hearing of the ear: but now mine eye
seeth Thee. Wherefore I abhor myself, and repent in dust and ashes.
—Job 42:5-6; KJV

WHAT does the soul long for? How can one pursue that longed for reality? The Bible as a whole could be said to be one long answer to that double question. From the paradise of Eden in the beginning, to the glorious, heavenly, new Jerusalem in its closing pages, it is an eloquent, inspired answer from many authors in many times and places, all revealing in some way how to realize the HEART'S[1] deepest desires. That's why, at the heart of any discussion about the interpretation of the Bible, or HERMENEUTICS, will be found questions about human flourishing and truth—in other words, about spiritual life and what the soul truly longs for, even though these concerns may not be directly mentioned. Questions such as: How can we know what is true? How can we discern if our interpretations are correct, and if what they speak of is true? How does that truth impact my life and the lives of others? Does it lead me to what my soul longs for? Today, one would also have to add the ancient question that has lately received new life: *can* we know what is true?

All interpreters, however much they differ in other respects, share at least some of these basic concerns. Hopefully, some concern for truth, with a desire

---

1. Throughout the book, words in all small capitals are defined in the glossary.

to contribute to human flourishing, to helping souls find what they long for most, is ultimately a large part of what fuels any interpreter's interest in biblical interpretation.

For the past several hundred years, in considering questions about knowledge, truth, and human flourishing in the interpretation of Scripture, the role played by science, and scientific methods, has become central. That there is a conflict between modern science and traditional Christianity, in which science has triumphed, is today such a commonly accepted idea that many professionals in biblical studies, such as Robert Funk of the highly-publicized "Jesus Seminar," feel free simply to assume it as "general knowledge." For example, Funk confidently asserts that

> the Christ of creed and DOGMA, who had been firmly in place in the Middle Ages, can no longer command the assent of those who have seen the heavens through Galileo's telescope. . . . Copernicus, Kepler, and Galileo have dismantled the mythical abodes of the gods and bequeathed us secular heavens.[2]

For Funk and his fellows from the Jesus Seminar, as Richard Hays of Duke University explains, "the Bible's story of the world's history and destiny is a narrative fiction that has lost its credibility and usefulness in late modernity." Funk's view could be summed up by his postmodern statement to his peers about the Bible: "What we need is a new fiction . . ."[3]

Funk and his colleagues represent an extreme which is not the mainstream of biblical studies today. Yet their highly publicized beliefs, reflected in the passages quoted above, have been, and continue to be, very influential on the popular level, and very damaging for many people's spiritual lives. They also highlight key issues facing all those interested in the proper interpretation of Scripture, i.e., interpreting it in a way that encourages and supports people's spiritual lives, helping their souls find what they long for. These issues include:

1. The role of science and the scientific method in biblical studies, and the claim that modern science is necessarily in conflict with traditional Christianity.

---

2. Robert W. Funk, Roy J. Hoover, and The Jesus Seminar, *The Five Gospels: the Search for the Authentic Words of Jesus* (New York: Macmillan, 1993); cited by Richard Hays in a review essay entitled "The Corrected Jesus," in *First Things,* May, 1994, p. 48.

3. Ibid.

2. The role of the literal level of meaning, as well as the role of non-literal levels, including: what did the biblical text originally mean? How was it used? What does it mean for us today? How should we use it?

3. Can the Bible as traditionally understood inspire people powerfully enough that it truly shapes their worldview and enables them to flourish? This is sometimes expressed as a serious question about whether or not the Bible's "story" has lost its ability to *capture the imagination* and thus inspire the will of those in "late modernity," enabling them to forge a way of life based on the biblical *meta-narrative*.[4] In other words, is a traditional understanding of the Bible still credible and effective in the modern world for well-educated people?

4. Most important of all and underlying the first three: is it really possible to know ultimate Truth, and/or to know God, and what does this imply for one's spiritual life in the present, and for salvation, for life eternal? How one answers these key questions will determine the answers to the first three areas of concern. Indeed, these questions about knowing Truth and/or God must be answered before it can be determined if one's fundamental interpretations of Scripture are accurate, and if the fundamental claims of Scripture are true and can be life-giving and salvific, or if "it's all relative" and just a matter for individual interest, as Postmodernism claims.

Indeed, it should be evident from looking at foundational principles of theology and spiritual life, as well as the history of EXEGESIS, described in the pages that follow, that the foundational principles of biblical interpretation are necessarily inseparable from theology and spiritual life. Hence, addressing these four key issues is important for everyone concerned about the spiritual life of all those impacted by contemporary Western culture, as well as for those who love Holy Scripture and Truth—all those who still pay attention to what their soul longs for most deeply.

"What we need is a new fiction" (Robert Funk) or "What is truth?" (Pontius Pilate; John 18:38)

Let us begin our exploration by looking at this declaration by Funk about needing a "new fiction" because "Copernicus, Kepler, and Galileo have dismantled the mythical abodes of the gods and bequeathed us secular heavens." Full of

---

4. A "meta-narrative" is a comprehensive, overarching explanation of various aspects of human reality (the biblical story of the Fall is a prime example of a meta-narrative).

errors, this statement is quite characteristic of the writing of those in the Jesus Seminar and other such extremists, providing an instructive example of the poor scholarship and verbal sleight of hand they often practice.

The idea that the heavens were the "abodes of the gods" was an idea that in fact was "dismantled" in ancient times. Educated ancient Greeks knew such stories to be fictions[5]—hence the telescope and associated ideas cannot rightly be given credit for that "discovery." So Funk's claim that various Renaissance astronomers have "dismantled the mythical abodes of the gods" is completely false.

It is even less true that because of this seeing "the heavens through Galileo's telescope" we need "a new fiction." There is no evidence whatsoever that Copernicus, Kepler, or even Galileo—the scientists Funk mentions by name—had any trouble with "the Christ of creed and dogma,"[6] or that in their minds there was any conflict between their scientific work and traditional Christianity. The reality is quite the contrary, since these great scientists all had strong faith in God.

For example, Kepler, a pious Lutheran and a contemporary of Galileo who knew his work, said, "I wanted to be a theologian. . . . For a long time I was restless. Now, however, behold how through my effort God is being celebrated in astronomy."[7] There is every indication that Kepler was a faithful Lutheran his entire life. Copernicus' religious faith was also central to his scientific work.[8]

---

5. For instance, Theagenes of Rhegium in the 6th century BC—hundreds of years before Christ!—saw the quarrels among Homer's gods as an allegory of natural elements such as heat opposed to cold, etc. (see Manlio Simonetti, *Biblical Interpretation in the Early Church: An Historical Introduction to Patristic Exegesis* [Edinburgh: T&T Clark, 1994], p. 5).

6. Some scholars compellingly claim that modern science is actually a product of the Christian worldview, and that it would not have arisen outside that worldview. For example, see the work of Stanley Jaki. In any case, it did arise within Christianized cultures (see Ch. 6 in this book). To give one example, Kepler reasoned that because the universe was designed by an intelligent Creator, it should function according to some logical pattern. To him, the idea of a chaotic universe was inconsistent with God's wisdom. In contrast, many other earlier scientists had given up searching for a simple logical pattern. The list of important scientists who were serious Christians of some kind is long, including such greats as Isaac Newton, and D. Mendeleev, who was the first to construct a periodic table of the elements.

7. Dan Graves, *Scientists of Faith* (Grand Rapids, MI: Kregel Pub., 1996), p. 49. Kepler studied for years for the ministry, and only the offer of a teaching post in astronomy because of his brilliance in mathematics led to that career. On his deathbed he told the attending minister that he believed "only and alone in the service of Jesus Christ. In Him is all refuge, all solace."

8. See James Hannam, *God's Philosophers: How the Medieval World Laid the Foundations of Modern Science* (Icon Books, Ltd., 2010), Ch. 17, "Humanist Astronomy and Nicolaus

Galileo himself was never condemned or criticized by Roman Catholic authorities for any deviant religious views (he enjoyed papal patronage for some years,
in fact)—only for rejecting the geocentric universe of Aristotle, which was still
accepted without question by most academics of his time. Actually, Aristotelian
professors were the ones who launched the first campaign to discredit Galileo,
not the Church hierarchy. Galileo even wrote a defense of the Copernican theory in which he quoted patristic sources to show that his theories need not
conflict with Scripture.[9]

And these were not the first religiously-oriented astronomers. In the book
that made him famous,[10] a prominent churchman and mystic, Cardinal Nicolas
of Cusa (d. 1464), had written that in order to properly reflect God's majesty,
the universe would need to be limitless: "Therefore, the earth cannot be in the
centre." He also wrote that the earth must be moving, and that it is simply one
of many stars, even if it is the most important one. Copernicus provided the
mathematical proof for this mystic's theory, which was based on his theology,
and Galileo provided the empirical proof. So we see clearly that Funk's claim
could only be made by ignoring the actual facts of history.

On the other hand, the ancient Greek myths that for many centuries have
not been believed to be literally true still have strong evocative power. Even
in today's secular culture, not only are these myths still read, but very popular
contemporary movies and novels are still based on works like Homer's *Odyssey*
(for example, *O Brother, Where Art Thou?* and *Cold Mountain*).

If an ancient fiction that has been known to be fiction for over two thousand
years is still useful, why would we need to *replace* a powerful meta-narrative
like the Bible with "a new fiction"? Clearly, a *story* doesn't need to be literally
true to be useful or effective in contemporary times. Surely Funk knows this.
Something else would seem to be going on.

Copernicus." Also, see his website, "Deconstructing Copernicus" under Articles, jameshannam.
com. Using the style of the Jesus Seminar's *Five Gospels*, one would have to say, "this sure doesn't
sound like people having trouble with 'the Messiah'!"

9. Giorgio de Santillana, "Galileo," in *Encyclopedia Britannica*, Macropedia, vol. 7 (1983), p.
852a. Fear of giving more ammunition to the Reformers to use against the ROMAN CHURCH
seems to have been a major motivation in the effort to prevent Galileo from promoting the
Copernican theory. Luther and other Reformers were strongly against this heliocentric theory
because Scripture, interpreted literally, said that the Earth did not move (e.g., Ps. 93:1), and they
believed this necessarily implied that the earth was the center of the cosmos.

10. Called *On Learned Ignorance*, this book was written after Nicolas returned from
Constantinople. So it would be reasonable to assume that it is based on, or at least influenced by,
the APOPHATIC theology of the Eastern Church (see Hannam, op. cit., p. 198).

And in fact, some of Funk's other statements would seem to indicate that, contrary to what he said above, this search for a "new fiction" is, in a sense, actually a search for truth. At the least, even biblical scholars like those in the Jesus Seminar attempt to *appeal* to those wanting to know the "real truth" about the biblical story and what it claims. Rather than a new fiction, such people want to know what, if any, of the old *is* fiction, and what in the old is true. And judging by the high volume of sales that works purporting to provide this kind of "truth" generally have, there are a lot of people interested in finding and believing what is true.

This search for the "real truth," the "authentic" knowledge "behind" the sources we actually have in the mainstream Christian tradition, is the theme not only of Funk and the Jesus Seminar, but of many such heavily promoted interpreters who frequently come out with sensationalized "hidden gospels," or secret, "true teachings" claiming to reveal how believers have been deceived for centuries. Contemporary examples would be the highly fictionalized *Da Vinci Code*, and the heavily publicized *Gospel of Judas* and other such ancient Gnostic texts. (This basic attitude itself reflects certain gnostic tendencies—wanting to be part of the elite elect who know the "real truth"—as distinct from, and usually opposed to, the generally accepted version which is commonly believed by "most" people.)[11]

Judging by their writings, Funk and those like him unquestioningly accept that any truth to be derived from Scripture must be a truth *behind* its texts, or what the Bible really *should have said*, or what it would have said if it had been written in recent times by those with a more up-to-date understanding of reality, thanks to modern science. In broader terms, this supposed "conflict" between science and religion which Funk says creates the need for searching behind the text of Scripture is really closely related to the age-old questions about truth and about knowledge: "What is truth?" as Pilate asked. Can we

---

11. The term "gnostic" is often broadly used to indicate a dualistic theology characterized by secret teachings/knowledge for an elite, elect few. The "Bauer" thesis is behind many works, such as those mentioned, as well as the works of Elaine Pagels and Bart Ehrman, among others. Bauer's thesis, proclaimed in 1934, basically claims that in the early centuries of Christianity there were many different Christian theologies, including a prevalent Gnostic version, and that somehow, unfortunately, orthodox Christianity managed to crush all this diversity, and that it was especially unfortunate that the Gnostics were crushed. This thesis has been thoroughly discredited and shown to have no solid basis in actual historical data, e.g., in the books *The Heresy of Orthodoxy: How Contemporary Culture's Fascination with Diversity Has Reshaped Our Understanding of Early Christianity,* by Andreas J. Kostenberger and Michael J. Kruger; as well as in *The Bauer Thesis Examined: The Geography of Heresy in the Early Christian Church (Studies in the Bible and Early Christianity)*, by Thomas A. Robinson.

know ultimate truth? If so, how can we know such truth, and that it is true? What kind of knowledge is most reliable?

As this applies to biblical studies, one could also call it a search for a proper hermeneutic—one that will enable its users to ascertain the truth about, and the truths of, Scripture, and especially about Who Jesus is and what that means about human beings, and how we should live. After all, these questions are not just curiosities for the academically inclined, but are crucial for all people in determining how to achieve the most important goals, whether it be to find the greatest happiness possible in this life—to find what the soul longs for—and/or how to have eternal happiness in the next life, or any other such ultimate questions.

Despite their theological and methodological differences, all biblical scholars who use the HISTORICAL-CRITICAL METHOD exclusively (whether they are extremists like Funk, or more balanced like the majority of others) are really heirs of Baruch de Spinoza.[12] This 17th century philosopher is generally considered to be the "father" of HISTORICAL CRITICISM, since he was apparently the first to make the Bible "the object of historical science"—which for him meant that "research into biblical meaning" must be "pursued . . . as if there were no God." Spinoza insisted that the content of the Scriptures must be attributed to "mundane causes, historical conditions, and cultural presuppositions of the times in which they were written"—entirely apart from any dogmatic tradition. Its truth must be only what is "recognizable to unaided human reason," based on "everyday human life."[13]

Spinoza's work was an attempt to develop an exegetical *science*, in contrast to all previous "unscientific" exegesis which claimed as its foundation revealed religion, or at least some kind of divine inspiration. He not only insisted that *human reason is the only foundation for religion and for biblical studies*, but he also insisted that religion and science are so opposed that as one increases the other must decrease.[14]

It is not, then, the telescope that caused the problems of belief that Funk so picturesquely describes. It is rather the adoption of Spinoza's radical new approach to understanding Scripture and its meaning, with all the associated

---

12. Of course, many others influenced Spinoza and were influenced by him. See, e.g., *The Bible in Modern Culture*, by Harrisville and Sundberg, referenced below.

13. Roy A. Harrisville and Walter Sundberg, *The Bible in Modern Culture: Baruch Spinoza to Brevard Childs*, second edition (Grand Rapids, MI: Wm. B. Eerdmans Publishing Co., 2002), p. 42.

14. Ibid., p. 43; see also pp. 39-48. We offer further discussion of Spinoza's ideas and the role of science in biblical studies in Ch. 6 of this book.

ideas and world-view changes this implies, built upon gradually over many years, that has caused the problem.[15]

Following Spinoza's lead, it is no wonder, then, that Funk, speaking for his contemporaries, asserts, "we are having increasing difficulty these days in accepting the biblical account of the creation and of the apocalyptic conclusion in anything like a literal sense." And, he admits, "we are having as much trouble with the middle—the messiah—as we are with the terminal points."[16]

In other words, he is saying the trouble is that because of modern science, we can't believe any of the crucial parts of the Bible's story; we can't believe that the beginning, middle, or end is true "in anything like a literal sense" (though he never explains what he means by "a literal sense," or why he is treating these three very different genres of writing as if they are the same).[17] But then, instead of saying, "so therefore, we need a new story that is rooted in *truth*," he says, "we need a new *fiction*." Now, if what we need, or want, is a *fiction*, then why is it a problem that because of modern science "we" don't believe the biblical story is literally true? If we don't care about what is true, or believe that it is possible to know what is true, why not just stick with the old "fictions," now that we "know" that's what they really are?

It is interesting that Funk and his fellows at the Jesus Seminar do not describe their work to the general public as trying to create the "new fiction" that Funk tells his professional peers we need. Rather, they say that they are trying to create a new, *true* version of the biblical story—one that they believe will be plausible to those who have "seen the heavens through telescopes." As Hays points out in his compelling critique, "*The Five Gospels* deploys the rhetoric of empiricism ('empirical, factual evidence,' gathered by 'independent, neutral

---

15. Of course, Funk can play on popular misconceptions about Galileo, Kepler, and Copernicus to appear to give support to his propositions—but it would perhaps undermine his credibility with many he wished to influence if he acknowledged his much more direct connection with Spinoza. That connection wouldn't be as much fun, because there are no popular misconceptions about Spinoza to play with rhetorically. There is, in fact, a lot of rhetorical sleight of hand going on in the work of the Jesus Seminar, and of many extreme "scholars" like them—yet they are always the most publicized. Their work would seem to reflect either sloppy scholarship, and/or the wolf of aggressive, heavily biased personal agenda masquerading as the "impartial," "scientific" sheep who loves the Truth and hears the "true voice" of the Good Shepherd.

16. Hays, op. cit., p. 48.

17. Lumping the Genesis Creation account, the very historical Gospel accounts, and John's highly symbolic Apocalypse together as if they were all doing exactly the same things, and should be interpreted the same way, should be an obvious tip-off that he is not dealing with these matters in a careful, scholarly, or accurate way. (We'll return to this basic point in a later chapter.)

observers') . . . [it] purports to offer . . . a factual Jesus discovered by scientific methods and disentangled from the fictive Jesus rendered in the gospel narratives."[18]

So it is not, even for the Jesus Seminar, really a question of a new fiction, but of at least making a pretense of finding the truth in, or behind, the Bible—which, as traditionally interpreted, they believe to be in conflict with modern science, and unable to inspire contemporary, scientifically educated people. They do seem to realize, however, that even "modern man," and even most post-modern people, are interested in the truth, and don't really want "a new fiction." Fiction that is only fiction can, at best, only entertain or distract. Only a fiction that reflects truth can inspire and illuminate.

Using An Ancient Fiction

The ancient fiction of Cupid and Psyche, which is also about discerning the truth, provides an illuminating parable for our topic. In the first part of this story, Psyche is given to marry an unknown being. Though fearful at first, she finds herself in a beautiful palace, where everything she needs is provided. Her only restriction is that she is never allowed to see her husband. He behaves in a most loving, kind way—but he is only there in the complete darkness of night.

When her sisters come to visit, they are most impressed by the beautiful palace—and rather envious. They ask Psyche about her husband, and when she explains that she is not permitted ever to see him (an arrangement she has come to happily accept), they are convinced there could only be one possible reason for such a prohibition: he must be a dreadful monster who would terrify and/or completely revolt her if she saw him. They cannot imagine why else he would refuse to let her see him.

They want to convince Psyche of the "real truth" of her situation, and that the beautiful palace is really a cover-up for the terrible monster her husband must be. They fill Psyche with so many doubts that she becomes uncertain—what they say sounds so reasonable! Though she was happy before, now, how can she possibly go on, not knowing whether or not he is a monster? She finally decides to break his commandment: while he is sleeping, she takes in a light to look at him.

And what does she see? Instead of a hideous monster, she sees what was completely beyond the imagination and "unaided human reason" of her sisters: the god of love—an immortal being of inexpressible beauty! This is so completely unexpected, so beyond "the experience of everyday human life,"

---

18. Hays, p. 48.

so *extra*ordinarily wonderful, that in her astonishment she almost drops the oil lamp. From that slip, hot oil spills on Cupid, who wakes up and instantly disappears.

And not only does Cupid disappear, but so does the beautiful palace with everything to meet her needs. Having once seen her Bridegroom even briefly, however, Psyche doesn't care about anything except what seems now to be impossible: to recover her lost love. So, she does the only thing she can do: she sits down and weeps.

Of course, *Psyche* in Greek can mean "soul," and the bridegroom, Cupid, the god of love, can easily represent the true God of Love. Anyone familiar with Scripture knows that the Church as the Bride and Christ as the Bridegroom is a classic biblical analogy[19] continuing imagery from the Old Testament analogy of Israel as the bride (or wife) of God, Who is imaged as the husband (e.g., Hos. 2:2-23, and Is. 54:4-8).

The key point for the analogy in this case, however, is the difference between the kinds of knowledge Psyche and her sisters have. In her first state, Psyche is like many people—including many biblical scholars; they do have some knowledge of God, but it is uncertain, "blind faith" as it is commonly called. So it can be shaken by the speculations of "unaided human reason" and imagination. After Psyche has actually seen her husband, however, she has a far different kind of knowledge. Like Job (as quoted at the beginning of this chapter), once she has seen, once she has *certain* knowledge (Heb. 11:1), everything is different. She truly knows Whom she has lost, and so she weeps and longs for nothing other than to be reunited with her Bridegroom. And in this state, she is an image of the CHURCH FATHERS and SAINTS, as we see reflected in what the Prophet David says in Psalm 42:1-2 (RSV):

> As a hart longs for flowing streams,[20] so longs my soul for thee, O God.
> My soul thirsts for God, for the living God. When shall I come and
>   behold the face of God?

---

19. See, e.g., John 3:29; Matt. 25:1-13, where the bridegroom is usually understood to be Christ; Rom. 7:1-6; 2 Cor. 11:2-3; Eph. 5:23-32; and Rev. 21 (about the marriage of the Lamb, especially v. 9). Also, e.g., Augustine: "In the same way He calls us also the children of the bridegroom, when He says, '*The time will come, when the bridegroom shall be taken away from them, and then shall the children of the bridegroom fast.*' And who is the bridegroom, but Christ the Lord?" (*On the Gospel of John*, Tractate LXXV [NPNF, first series, vol. VII, p. 335]).

20. In the SEPTUAGINT Greek this word is πηγη, which indicates a fountain, or spring of water. See also John 4:14. This also connects with the "living water" and "waters of life" (and the Holy Spirit) in John 4:10; John 7:37-39; and Rev. 22:1.

St. Silouan the Athonite, in the 20th century, similarly cries out:

> My soul yearns after the Lord and I seek Him in tears. How could I do
> other than seek Thee, for Thou first didst seek and find me, and gavest
> me to delight in Thy Holy Spirit, and my soul fell to loving Thee . . . Hadst
> Thou not drawn me with Thy love, I could not seek Thee as I seek Thee
> now; but *Thy Spirit gave me to know Thee, and my soul rejoices that Thou
> art my God.*[21]

Psyche's sisters, however, have only heard about her husband. Their interpretation of him and his palace is based only on this "hearsay"—and what is
"recognizable to unaided human reason" in conformity with "everyday human
life." Being committed to reason alone, they do not approve of "things unseen,"
believing that such things must be lies, and/or certainly something "monstrous."
From their own minds and from what they have heard, the sisters generate
extremely reasonable—but, it turns out, quite false—speculations.

If Psyche, after she has seen Cupid, images the Church Fathers and Saints,
then Funk and the other heirs of Spinoza are, of course, like Psyche's sisters.
They, too, are quite good at generating what seem to be reasonable speculations. They also do not, and never claim to have, direct knowledge of the
divine Bridegroom. Many among them don't even believe such a thing is possible—some even call THE SALVATION ECONOMY of Holy Scripture a "fiction"
that needs replacing by one that is more "reasonable," which presumably they
will create. Not surprisingly, they never mention the source of their authority,
or "wisdom," for making such an assessment (other than vague references to
science), or to justify such a monumentally arrogant undertaking as to imagine
they can create a "story" to replace one which has undeniably inspired millions
of people over several thousand years and been at the core of many contemporary cultures all across the world. For them, the foundation of all knowledge
for biblical studies, just as for every other field of knowledge, must be "unaided
human reason"—especially, it would seem, their own. It would also seem that
they imagine "unaided human reason" is all that is behind the Bible and its
"story."

Since the academics of the Jesus Seminar, and those like them, have decided
that there is no possible direct knowledge of God, no authentic divine revelation, the "fiction" part of the Bible turns out to be anything having to do with
the divine, which, à la Spinoza, they eliminate before they begin their studies.
When they interpret Scripture from this starting point, it should be no surprise

---

21. St. Silouan, in *St. Silouan the Athonite*, by ARCHIMANDRITE Sophrony (Crestwood, NY:
SVS Press, 1999), p. 269 (my emphasis).

(and no proof of anything!) that they find no evidence of divine revelation, but only "ruins" built on the shifting sands of elusive "original historical meanings" and "original historical events"—often imaginative speculations about the largely inaccessible events and ideas that lie *behind* the text.

Tragically, over the past several hundred years, biblical scholarship, even for many who are not extremists and who do believe in divine revelation, has become fundamentally shaped by those who do not. After describing the typical "archeological" approach fostered by the historical-critical method, Cardinal Ratzinger, who became Pope Benedict XVI, said, "No one should really be surprised that this procedure leads to the sprouting of ever more numerous hypotheses until finally they turn into a jungle of contradictions."[22] The highly respected German biblical scholar, Peter Stuhlmacher, referring to the historical-critical method as commonly used, says even more strongly, "New Testament exegesis . . . has made of the biblical canon . . . a ruinous heap of hypothetical possibilities."[23]

But should one expect to see the heavenly Bridegroom with a telescope? Surely even the political masters of reality-altering, the Soviet Communists, could not have seriously thought that God was proven to be non-existent when they proclaimed that their first cosmonaut did not see Him in outer space![24]

Ironically, the real truth is that the heirs of Spinoza, those using the historical-critical method exclusively—both extremists and those more moderate—have themselves created the ruins they find, by insisting on using the wrong instrument for the wrong kind of knowledge, thereby excluding the Bridegroom. This "place" of Scripture is only a beautiful palace, meeting our needs, when we are living in a relationship of love and trust with the Bridegroom dwelling there, and following His commandments which show us

---

22. Joseph Cardinal Ratzinger, "Biblical Interpretation in Crisis: On the Question of the Foundations and Approaches of Exegesis Today," *This World,* Summer, 1988, p. 4.

23. Peter Stuhlmacher, *Historical Criticism and Theological Interpretation of Scripture: Toward a Hermeneutic of Consent* (Philadelphia: Fortress Press, 1975), p. 75.

24. As an interview explains: "But what about the famous phrase attributed to Gagarin: 'I flew into space, but didn't see God'?" "It was most certainly not Gagarin who said this, but Khrushchev! This was connected with a plenary session of the Central Committee addressing the question of anti-religious propaganda. Khrushchev then set the task for all Party and Komsomol [Young Communists] organizations to boost such propaganda. He said: 'Why are you clinging to God? Gagarin flew into space and didn't see God.' However, some time later these words began to be portrayed in a different light. They were cited in reference not to Khrushchev, but to Gagarin, who was beloved by the people. . . . But nothing was ever said by Gagarin about this, nor could he have uttered such things." http://www.pravmir.com/did-yuri-gagarin-say-he-didnt-see-god-in-space/

the life-giving path. In this context, other kinds of knowledge—historical, literary, etc.—can be best used, and can serve a valuable function for Christians.

Hopefully, from even this brief discussion it is clear why the last of the four key issues as given above is the most fundamental: is it really possible to know ultimate Truth, to know God directly? If it is, then that affects everything. Psyche's sisters tell a radically different story from the one Psyche herself tells *after* she has seen her Bridegroom with her own eyes. So whom will we believe?—those like Psyche after she has seen, those who say they have direct knowledge of God?; or those, like her sisters, who merely speculate within the limitations of their own "unaided reason" while denying that the knowledge they lack is even possible?

Many people today do doubt the possibility of direct, real knowledge of God, or of any kind of Ultimate Truth—Psyche's sisters have been whispering in the public's ear for a long, long time. For many, the possibility of direct, certain knowledge of God may seem just as much a "fairy tale" fiction as the Cupid and Psyche story itself.

I have brought in this story to serve as a parable, because a parable is a kind of light that can enable its hearers/readers to see what was previously unseen. Often parables help us to see what we don't want to see: for example, ourselves as we really are, and/or ourselves as others see us—sometimes ugly and revolting. For instance, who wants to see themselves as the rich man who stole the poor man's only sheep (Nathan's parable to King David), or as the jealous elder brother who is angry that his father is celebrating his lost son's return home? (The Prodigal Son).

If a parable is going to be more than just a subjective impression about the feelings of one individual, however, it has to reflect reality. It has to reflect, or in some way reveal, truth. Are the Church Fathers accurately figured by Psyche who has seen, and the heirs of Spinoza by Psyche's sisters who have not? Is it really possible to be in a relationship of love and trust with the divine Bridegroom, so that this "place" that Scripture is becomes for us a beautiful palace, meeting our deepest needs, a palace which we can share with the Bridegroom?

The answer to these questions will determine the answers to many other crucial questions, such as: Who really understands how Scripture should be interpreted? What is a proper hermeneutic? Who are the true authorities in interpreting Scripture? And these answers depend on the answers to even broader questions, such as those we began this chapter with: Who really understands reality? Who really knows the truth—what the soul truly longs for? Can anyone really know ultimate Truth? Who can interpret, or "speak for," God?

Any serious exploration of these issues in a traditional Christian context, in this case that of the Eastern Orthodox Church, will necessarily involve looking at the history of exegesis, the history of the answers given to these questions, and at something of the history of what happened that led to such divergent, even opposing, understandings of reality among those who claim to be Christians.

Through looking at the history of these approaches, one should catch at least glimpses of a better hermeneutic for perceiving the most beautiful truth ever revealed to humanity: the real God of Love, the Bridegroom of *every* soul, overcoming SIN and sorrow, bringing joy, love, and peace in this life, and the eternal transcendence of suffering and death itself in the next life. This is a truth with eternal consequences. What greater tragedy could there be than not to know this truth because one has listened only to those who are like Psyche's sisters—or, because of pervasive cultural influences, one has not even tried to look for it at all?[25]

Seeing the Unseeable?

As a prelude to this history, we will briefly look at what is meant by "direct" or "real" knowledge of God—*seeing God*, in our analogy—since whether or not this is possible is key for all that follows. It will be important to clarify some terms and concepts here at the beginning to avoid perpetuating misconceptions, and to have a better idea what those who answer "yes" to this question actually mean.

Psyche, as we have said, saw her bridegroom with her own eyes, but in Scripture we read, "No one has seen God at any time" (John 1:18; also, e.g., I Tim. 6:16); and even, "no man can see My face and live" (Ex. 33:20). To see the living God "face to face" belongs only to the world to come: "now we see dimly, then face to face" (I Cor. 13:12). The highest good for those who enter the Kingdom of Heaven is that "They shall see His face," as we read in Rev. 22:4; or as we read in I John 3:2, "we shall see Him as He is." (Interestingly, although Psyche sees Cupid, even Psyche doesn't see her bridegroom "face to face" in this world, but only after he rescues her from death and she is given immortal life, i.e., after she becomes godlike herself.)

Traditional Christianity, following Scripture, as seen in verses such as the above, holds that God is not "Someone" Who can be seen in an ordinary way.

---

25. Considering the ultimate, eternal importance of the issue, surely everyone should be willing to give the benefit of the doubt to those who claim to have such experience, and at least to listen to what they say about "having direct knowledge of God," and to listen to how they say one can obtain this kind of knowledge. Can it be wise to reject a possibility out of hand without even knowing what it really entails, or ever trying it out for oneself? It would be like T. S. Eliot's "children in the apple-tree/Not known, because not looked for."

The Judaeo-Christian God was never thought to be like a star up in the heavens which can be gazed upon by anyone with a telescope. Unlike Cupid, whom Psyche could spy on with an oil lamp, the true divine Bridegroom can never automatically be seen, or recognized for Who He truly is, by any merely earthly light, or merely at the whim of any person—even during the Incarnation. If God were like that, if we could completely understand Him, He would not be God; rather, He would necessarily be another creature "on our level"—simply the highest creature.[26] Traditional Christianity understands the radical truth that because we are created and God is uncreated, God is necessarily fundamentally *unknowable*, utterly beyond human comprehension and perception—very much beyond the reach of "unaided human reason" and science.

In the Divine Liturgy of St. John Chrysostom (late 4th century), the usual Eucharistic liturgy for Orthodox Christians, the Orthodox proclaim this emphatically:

> It is meet and right to praise You, to glorify You, to bless You, to give thanks to You, to worship You in all places of Your dominion, for You are God **ineffable, incomprehensible, invisible, inconceivable**, ever-existing and eternally the same, You and Your only-begotten Son and Your Holy Spirit.[27]

Or as St. John of Damascus (8th century) says even more strongly, "God, then, is infinite and incomprehensible, and all that is comprehensible about Him is His infinity and incomprehensibility."[28] And even, as Vladimir Lossky states, in summarizing the thought of St. Gregory of Nyssa (4th century), "The concepts which we form in accordance with the understanding and judgment which are natural to us, basing ourselves on an intelligible representation, create idols of God instead of revealing to us God Himself."[29] Hence, "unaided human reason," according to St. John, St. Gregory, and the Tradition they represent, can only create idols of God (or new fictions) which everyone should rightly reject.

Does this mean that everyone really *is* in the position of Psyche's sisters? If we can't understand or know God through concepts and our "unaided human

---

26. St. Ephrem the Syrian (4th century), in an attempt to indicate a little of what it would mean for God to become man, says, "The Farmer became the grain of wheat." Yet clearly the difference between God and man is much more radical than this, for both the farmer and the wheat are created.

27. From the anaphora section of St. John Chrysostom's Liturgy (my emphasis).

28. On the Orthodox Faith I.4; quoted by Vladimir Lossky, *The Mystical Theology of the Eastern Church* (Crestwood, NY: St. Vladimir's Seminary Press, 1976), p. 36.

29. Lossky, p. 33.

reason," then how else can we know Him? Those heirs of Spinoza who claim that all who have seen the heavens through a telescope—all who believe that human reason and science are the only sure foundation for every kind of knowledge—also claim that there is no heavenly Bridegroom to see—or at best, if such a one exists, He is irrelevant because He is unknowable. The Fathers, following Scripture, agree that "No one has seen God at any time" (1 John 4:12), and that God is incomprehensible, so how can they claim that they know for certain there is a heavenly Bridegroom, and even that they know what He is like? What kind of seeing enables one to see what cannot be seen? How can one know, or have any kind of certainty, about things which are not only "unseeable," but even completely beyond human comprehension?

One crucial implication of saying that God is incomprehensible is that we cannot know anything about Him, or know Him directly, *unless* He reveals Himself to us. And the claim of traditional Christianity is, of course, that out of His infinite love, God has indeed revealed Himself to us, most perfectly in Jesus Christ.

Jesus is the true Bridegroom, the real God of Love, Who holds the lamp Himself so that we may see Him. Jesus is in fact Himself the Light Who makes God visible, Who enables us to see the unseeable. He not only lets us see God, but in His Light we also see ourselves as we truly are. He is the ultimate parable; He is even called the *Word*, the One Who most authoritatively speaks for God, revealing Ultimate Truth. John's Gospel, for example, speaks repeatedly of Jesus as the best, the fullest, the most perfect revelation that God has ever made of Himself: for example, "No one has seen God at any time; the only-begotten Son, Who is in the bosom [or close to the heart of, in the place of greatest intimacy] of the Father, He has made Him known [*exēgēsato* = "revealed," or "exegeted"] Him" (John 1:18); and, "He who has seen Me has seen the Father" (John 14:9).

As St. John makes clear in a multitude of ways in his Gospel account (some of which will be discussed in Chapter 7), Jesus Christ can perfectly reveal God only because He is divine Himself: only God Himself can really know God or reveal Him. St. John underlines the divinity of Jesus in many different ways. To give a few examples: He is God the Father's unique, "only-begotten Son" (John 1:14, 18; 3:16, 18); He is "from above" (3:31; 8:23); He sees what the Father does (5:19; 8:38); He does the work of the Father (5:17-20; 8:28-29); He knows Him (Matt. 11:27) and keeps His word; and both Father and Son have life *in themselves*—something no created being can claim (John 5:26). Jesus can even legitimately use for Himself the name for God from Exodus 3:6, the *egō eimi*, "I am Who I am," as He did repeatedly, but most dramatically when He said,

"Before Abraham was, I am" (John 8:58). At last, here is Someone Who, being divine Himself, can truly "speak for God" (e.g., John 8:38; 17:8).[30]

As truly God and truly man, Christ reveals to us what God is like, and what human beings are intended to be like—their full potential, we could say—as far as it is possible for created human beings to know this.[31] And one of the most important ways that those living after the time of Jesus' earthly life learn about Him is through reading Holy Scripture. St. Augustine (5th century) even says, "For now, treat the Scripture of God as the face of God."[32]

As precious as that is, reading about the most true, best revelation of God in Jesus Christ is not everything that was made possible by the Incarnation. When we read in Matthew 5:8, "Blessed are the pure in heart, for they shall see God," this is indicating more than seeing the HISTORICAL JESUS and/or reading about Him in Scripture in order to have a conceptual understanding of God's love, forgiveness, etc., through that reading. Just as physically seeing Jesus of Nazareth, even seeing His miracles, did not automatically mean one perceived Who He truly is and that He most truly reveals God, so simply reading the Bible does not automatically lead to perceiving "the face of God" in it, or perceiving it truly. It is primarily through the third Person of the Holy Trinity, the Holy Spirit, that we are enabled to perceive and understand these truths most accurately.

For humanity, then, it is equally significant that Christ, Who is the Truth, sends the *Holy Spirit* Who will *guide His followers* into all truth (John 15:26).

---

30. As various people have pointed out, only Christianity, of all the world's religions, claims that the person who founded it is God Himself, and that He enables us to enter into Ultimate Truth. All other religions, founded by mere mortals, are man's attempt to reach up to God.

31. Jesus not only lets us see God, but in His Light we also see ourselves as we truly are, both in our revolting, and at times even "monstrous," sinfulness in contrast to Christ, and compared with the extraordinary beauty of human nature transfigured and restored to its original state in Christ that we are all called to. And this true knowledge of human nature revealed in Christ—the extraordinary beauty which we all have the potential for—is almost as amazing as the knowledge of God that Christ reveals. For according to St. Basil the Great (4th century), among others, it is not only God Who is incomprehensible in His essence, but even people, and all created things, are ultimately unknowable in their essences. As Lossky summarizes, "In contemplating any object we analyze its properties: it is this which enables us to form concepts. But this analysis can in no case exhaust the content of the object of perception. There will always remain an 'irrational residue' which escapes analysis and which cannot be expressed in concepts; *it is the unknowable depth of things, which constitutes their true, indefinable essence*" (*The Mystical Theology of the Eastern Church*, p. 33; my emphasis).

32. Quoted by Robert L. Wilken, *The Spirit of Early Christian Thought* (New Haven, CT: Yale University Press, 2003), p. 50.

It is the Holy Spirit Who makes it possible for believers to be *in vibrant, living communion with Ultimate Truth*—that is, with Christ and the Father Himself. All three members of the Holy Trinity are essential for both true knowledge of God through communion with Him (see, e.g., John 14:23; 14:21; 14:26; 17:20-26), and true knowledge of God through Holy Scripture.

While it is not possible to adequately describe such realities, it is still possible to understand the crucial point: because Jesus Christ is the Truth, Ultimate Truth is *personal,* and not simply statements of facts, or other kinds of ideas or information. Since we are also *persons,* made in the image and likeness of God, we can therefore *participate* in this personal Truth—we can acquire real *knowledge,* not just "feelings," however lofty they may seem. We can truly "see," through this personal communion. Because of the Incarnation, our human nature can actually participate in the divine in ways not possible before. As St. Gregory Palamas (14th century) says, "The divine nature must be at the same time incommunicable and in a sense communicable; we attain participation in the nature of God [2 Pet. 1:4] and yet He remains totally inaccessible. We must affirm both things at once, and **we must preserve the antinomy as the criterion of piety.**"[33]

Saint Gregory of Nyssa, in his homily on the sixth Beatitude (Matt. 5:8), explains the biblical usage of the word "see":

> Remember that 'seeing' in scriptural usage means the same thing as 'possessing.' Cases in point are: 'That you might behold the good things of Jerusalem' [Ps. 128:5], instead of 'that you might find them,' which is what the phrase actually means."[34]

Just as there are different kinds of seeing—a literal seeing with the eyes, and a seeing that is possessing or experiencing—so there are different kinds of knowing. What we want to know determines which "method" should be used to acquire such knowledge. Just as we can't see DNA with a telescope, but we can see it if we use the right instrument, so we must consider the nature of what, or Whom, we want to know, and use the proper means of knowing, the right "instrument," if we want to "see" the heavenly Bridegroom.[35]

---

33. *Theophanes,* PG 150, col. 932; my emphasis; quoted by Vladimir Lossky, *The Vision of God* (Bedfordshire, The Faith Press, 1963), p. 127.

34. J. Patout Burns, ed., *Theological Anthropology* (Philadelphia: Fortress Press, 1981), p. 30. See also St. John Chrysostom, NPNF, second series, vol. XIV, p. 269.

35. In the quotation by Robert Funk on page 1 above, he strongly implies that before science (symbolized by telescopes) came to the rescue, the Christ of creed and dogma was firmly in place in the sky—the physical heavens. Hopefully, it will be clear to all from the very brief overview

According to the Eastern Orthodox Tradition, confirmed by the experience of countless Saints and believers, in addition to "unaided human reason" and the senses, we have *a third means*, or faculty, of knowing. This "organ" of knowing is called the NOUS, or the "eye of the heart." Not the heart as simply the center of our emotions or the pump for our blood, but the heart as *the spiritual center* of each human being, "his deepest, truest self."[36]

The body acquires knowledge through the senses, and a person analyzes the data of sense-experience (and other kinds of information) by means of discursive reason, or the mind (*dianoia*) dealing with abstract concepts. These are the only kinds of knowledge recognized by the heirs of Spinoza, and the only ones generally recognized and cultivated in our culture.

But even if they are not aware of it, through the *nous*, or spiritual intellect, all people have—at least in potential—a faculty for knowing God "by means of direct apprehension, or spiritual perception." This is a special kind of intuition, called by St. Isaac the Syrian (7th century) "simple cognition."[37] The *nous* is regarded as the highest part of the soul, or the purest part; it is sometimes called "the eye of the soul"[38] and "the innermost aspect of the heart."[39] It is to the *nous*, or heart, that the Holy Spirit speaks; it is through the *nous* that we experience grace.

In addition, through this faculty one can understand eternal truths *about* God, and about the *logoi*, or inner essences, of created things—again, not through deductive reasoning, but through "immediate spiritual perception."[40] "The spirit, or spiritual intellect, is thus distinct from man's reasoning powers

---

that follows that Funk's implication is light-years away from the understanding of the Church Fathers who gave us the Creed and our dogmas—those highly educated, extremely sophisticated, brilliant thinkers who combined exceptional intellectual and literary abilities with profound personal spiritual experience and direct knowledge. It is all too common for extremists to take advantage of the general ignorance of history, and combine it with the assumption (generally false) that everyone in the past was simple and credulous, to support the idea that "we know so much better" today.

36. *Philokalia*, vol. I, p. 359.

37. *Philokalia*, vol. I, p. 360.

38. Archimandrite Hierotheos Vlachos, *Orthodox Psychotherapy: The Science of the Fathers*, trans. Esther Williams (Levadia, Greece: The Birth of the Theotokos Monastery, 1994), p. 119; in reference to the teaching of St. John of Damascus.

39. *Philokalia*, vol. 1, p. 360; in reference to the teaching of St. Diadochos of Photiki (5th century).

40. *Philokalia*, vol. I, p. 363. For many examples that are dramatic, clear, and verified in our own day, see, e.g., *Wounded by Love*, the life of Elder Porphyrios; or the lives of any of the many other contemporary Saints who are "wonder-workers."

and aesthetic emotions, and superior to both of them,"[41] since it relies on "direct apprehension" and "perception of the inner essences or principles . . . of created beings . . . [and] divine truth itself."[42]

Thus, while it will always be impossible to fully *understand* God in His essence, now in Christ we can really *know* Him through this experiential knowledge—this simple cognition. This is a direct kind of knowledge not shaped by language, culture, or any presuppositions, although when we begin to try to understand the experience through our reason, and to explain it in words, our culture and language will certainly shape how we speak of it.

These realities should not, however, lead us to overlook another fundamental truth that we can see, for example, in John's Gospel. There we learn that Christ *is* the Truth (John 14:6), but also that He speaks the truth (8:14, 31-32, 45), and does the truth (e.g., 5:19-20). And, in fact, all people need all three of these elements: the foundation is personal communion with Truth Himself, though this may not come first chronologically for everyone, and it must be grounded on the apostolic witness, and usually the witness of others. For this experience is *only safeguarded* by a proper conceptual understanding, by the "RULE OF FAITH," by correct dogma. And the only secure way we can acquire both the full, proper conceptual understanding *and* authentic experience is through *doing* the truth, living the Gospel, ourselves.

In fact, without the proper rational understanding of the experience, it is possible to misinterpret it. Realizing this, St. Paul went to James, the first bishop of Jerusalem, and the apostle Peter, to confirm that his understanding of his experience of Christ on the road to Damascus was correct. So he gives us a great example of not relying solely on our own interpretation even of such a dramatic personal experience.

This NOETIC knowledge, or experience, of God, is profound, and in many ways self-authenticating, like St. Paul's on the road to Damascus; yet it still needs, also like St. Paul's, to be confirmed, or authenticated in some way, by the Church community as a whole. It has to be determined whether or not one's experience is in alignment with Scripture and Tradition in order to be assured that it is not just a subjective impression, or a product of fantasy, or some other kind of deception—for the possibility of self-deception in this area is high.

This kind of noetic knowledge is also different from discursive reasoning, or factual knowledge, in the way it affects us. For example, knowing the names of certain stars does not profoundly change us—this does not affect us *ontologically*, to the core of our being. But when we know God *noetically* (from the word *nous*), meaning experientially through the *nous*, this grace-filled

---

41. Father Kallistos Ware, *The Orthodox Way* (London: Mowbrays, 1979), p. 61.

42. *Philokalia*, vol. I, p. 362.

knowledge is life-transforming communion with Him—or at least, this begins and strengthens the usually long process of transformation.

Such communion with God is inseparable from the process of what many Christians call "sanctification," and what the Eastern Church Fathers, along with the whole Orthodox Tradition, consider even more radically to be "THEO-SIS," or DEIFICATION—becoming like God by grace as much as this is possible for created human beings. As, for example, St. Athanasius (4th century), says, "God became man so that man might become God."[43] Indeed, this "way of the knowledge of God is necessarily the way of deification."[44] For patristic exegetes, and for all those who hold to the traditional Christianity that the Fathers have always lived and written about, the goal of all human existence—the reason God created humanity, and the reason for the Incarnation—is that we might be *deified*, living in constant, intimate communion with Him. The Fathers chose this striking term, no doubt, to emphasize the real ontological change possible in Christ (not that we cease to become human in our nature, but that we become more fully human).

This understanding of deification does not, however, imply a New Age sort of pantheism whereby one's personal identity is lost. Rather, each unique person retains his or her unique personality and personhood while being transformed by God's grace.

But does this, nevertheless, leave us only with some vague sort of spiritual experience added onto a post-modern ignorance, in which all truth is still relative and all speculations about the Truth and about God become equal, because we can't know ultimate reality conceptually? What does all this further imply about the role of Scripture and reason in our efforts to know God and Ultimate Truth?

While strongly insisting that God is incomprehensible and unknowable *in His essence*, the Fathers also emphasize that the KATAPHATIC, or positive things we can say about God based on Scripture and Tradition, are not "wild guesses." They are "a ladder of 'theophanies' or manifestations of God in creation"[45] for us to use to climb towards Him. That is because they are the result of divine revelation, not human reason alone. "God is the Lord and has *revealed Himself* to us" (Ps. 118:27; my emphasis).[46] The reason for having these positive statements about God, including dogmas, and the "guarantee" that they are true, is that they safeguard the real possibility of the fullest possible communion with

---

43. Athanasius, On the Incarnation, Ch. 54.3.

44. Lossky, *Mystical Theology*, p. 39.

45. Ibid.

46. This verse is sung at every Matins service in the Orthodox Church.

God, the participation, or possession, which St. Gregory of Nyssa spoke of—a knowledge through communion meant for everyone.

On another level, the Fathers explain that because God has chosen to reveal Himself, we can have real knowledge *about* Him also through *His* DIVINE ENERGIES—as, for example, St. Basil the Great says, "We know God from His energies . . . but we do not claim that we can draw near to His ESSENCE. For His energies come down to us, but His essence remains unapproachable."[47] Or as Lossky paraphrases St. Basil, "the names which we apply to God . . . reveal His energies which descend toward us."[48]

Metr. Kallistos explains further that

> These energies are not something that exist apart from God, not a gift which God confers upon humans; they are God Himself in His action and revelation to the world. . . .
>
> It is through these energies that God enters into a direct and immediate relationship with humankind. In relation to us humans, the divine energy is in fact nothing else than the *grace of God*; grace is not just a 'gift' of God, not just an object which God bestows on humans, but a direct encounter between creature and Creator. . . . When we say that the saints have been transformed or 'deified' by the grace of God, what we mean is that they have a direct experience of God Himself. They *know* God—that is to say, God in His energies, not in His essence."[49]

As the history of how changes in theology and epistemology have affected exegesis and spiritual life are explored in the rest of this book, the importance of these distinctions will become clearer.

Of course, the truth of the positive statements about God, or their full, proper meaning, and the truth about Scripture or about Who Jesus Christ is, is not automatically obvious to all, or automatically comprehensible. As St. Silouan (20th century), in line with the whole Tradition, states,

> We may study as much as we will, but we shall still not come to know the Lord unless we live according to His commandments, for the Lord is not made known through learning, but by the Holy Spirit. Many philosophers and scholars have arrived at a belief in the existence of God, but they have

---

47. Letter 234.1; quoted by Ware, *The Orthodox Church*, p. 68.

48. Lossky, *Mystical Theology*, p. 33.

49. Timothy Ware, *The Orthodox Church* (London: Penguin Books, 1993), second edition, p. 68 (italics in the original).

not come to know God. . . . Both in heaven and on earth the Lord is made known only by the Holy Spirit, and not through ordinary learning.[50]

It requires God's grace; it requires authentic spiritual experience.

The Lutheran pastor Richard Wurmbrand tells a powerful, true story from his time in a subterranean communist prison camp in Romania that shows one aspect of this reality:

> Let me . . . tell you about another Orthodox Christian. He was not a priest, but a simple farmer. In our country, farmers are almost always illiterate, or nearly so. He had read his Bible well, but other than that he had never read a book. Now he was in the same cell with professors, academicians, and other men of high culture who had been put in jail by the Communists. And this poor farmer tried to bring to Christ a member of the Academy of Science. But in return, he received only mockery.
>
> "Sir, I can't explain much to you, but I walk with Jesus, I talk with Him, I see Him."
>
> "Go away. Don't tell me fairy tales that you see Jesus. How do you see Jesus?"
>
> "Well, I cannot tell you how I see Him. I just see Him. There are many kinds of seeing. In dreams, for instance, you see many things. It's enough for me to close my eyes. Now I see my son before me, now I see my daughter-in-law, now I see my granddaughter. Everybody can see. There is another sight. I see Jesus."
>
> "You see Jesus?"
>
> "Yes, I see Jesus."
>
> "What does He look like? How does He look to you? Does He look restful, angry, bored, annoyed, happy to see you? Does He smile sometimes?"
>
> He said, "You guessed it! He smiles at me."
>
> "Gentlemen, come hear what this man says to us. He mocks us. He says Jesus smiles at him. Show me, how does He smile?"
>
> That was one of the grandest moments of my life. The farmer became very, very earnest. His face began to shine. In the Church today there are pastors and theologians who can't believe the whole Bible. They believe half of it, a quarter of it. Somehow they can't believe the miracles. I can believe the whole of it because I have seen miracles. I have seen transfigurations—not like that of Jesus, but something apart. I have seen faces shining.

---

50. Archim. Sophrony, *Wisdom from Mount Athos* (Crestwood, NY: St. Vladimir's Seminary Press, 1974), p. 21.

A smile appeared on the face of that farmer. I would like to be a painter to be able to paint that smile. There was a streak of sadness in it because of the lost soul of the scientist. But there was so much hope in that smile. And there was so much love and so much compassion, and a yearning that this soul should be saved. The whole beauty of heaven was in the smile on that face. The face was dirty and unwashed, but it held the beautiful smile of heaven.

The professor bowed his head and said, "Sir, you are right. You have seen Jesus. He has smiled at you."[51]

We can even sometimes see Jesus in other people, a little bit like seeing God in Jesus.

But why don't more people have such experiences? As with any instrument, like a telescope, it is not enough just to possess it—one also needs to take proper care of it, so that it is usable; and one needs to know how to use it. And in the spiritual life, even more is needed. Blaise Pascal, the 17th century French mathematician, physicist, inventor, and Christian philosopher, explains what all traditional Christians would agree with:

> Openly appearing to those who look for Him with all their heart, while hiding from those who run from Him with all their heart, God governs human knowledge of His presence. He gives signs that are visible to those who search for Him, yet invisible to those who are indifferent to Him. To those who wish to see, God gives sufficient light; to those who do not wish to see, He gives sufficient darkness.[52]

If we look at Scripture, what do we see about those who have this experience of "seeing" God? Going back to the earlier Scriptures which we quoted (Matt. 5:8, Ps. 11:7, and Ps. 17:15), we see that it is the pure in heart, the upright, the righteous, those who realize that the soul's deepest longing is for God, and who do all they can to be with Him, who can "see God." Indeed, experiencing real communion with God is the primary reason for being righteous!

Returning to the fundamental questions that we posed at the beginning, we now can see that when we ask, "Can we know Ultimate Truth? How can we know what is true, and that it is true? How can we know that our fundamental interpretations of Scripture are correct?" the only way to know "for certain"

---

51. "With My Own Eyes: A Lutheran Pastor's Firsthand Account of Prison Life," *AGAIN Magazine*, Vol. 23, No. 2 (April-June, 2001), p. 24.

52. Quoted by Archim. Tikhon (Shevkunov), *Everyday Saints* (Moscow: Pokrov Publications, 2012), p. vii.

involves purifying the heart. Or we could say, the "instrument" one needs to see God, the heart, the *nous*, doesn't work unless it is cleansed and focused. Logically, then, the next question is, how can one be cleansed, how can one become "pure in heart"?

When St. Gregory of Nyssa asks this question, "How can I become pure, do you say?" he answers: "Well, you can learn almost anywhere in the gospel."[53] But he gives more specific insight into this when he explains in his commentary on *The Life of Moses* why even the great Moses saw only "the back parts of God":

> So Moses, who eagerly seeks to behold God, is now taught how he can behold Him: to follow God wherever He might lead is to behold God. His passing by signifies His guiding the one who follows, for someone who does not know the way cannot complete his journey safely in any other way than by following behind his guide. He who follows . . . always keeps the back of his leader in view.[54]

Again, we can return to the Cupid and Psyche "parable" to give us a glimpse of what this "following" involves. When Psyche realizes whom she has lost, she weeps—she repents. And in order to have a hope of seeing her beloved bridegroom again, to have her longing fulfilled, she must undertake difficult labors—labors that are, in fact, impossible without divine aid. Like Psyche, we need REPENTANCE and asceticism, as well as divine grace. This leads us to a further exploration of fundamental principles in the next chapter: "Loving Difficulties: The Ascesis of Reading Scripture."

---

53. Gregory of Nyssa, "Sermon on the Sixth Beatitude," printed in *Theological Anthropology*, trans. and ed., J. Patout Burns (Philadelphia: Fortress Press, 1981), p. 36.

54. In the *Classics of Western Spirituality* series (New York: Paulist Press, 1978), p. 119.

For in the time of trouble He shall hide me in His pavil-
ion; in the secret place of His tabernacle He shall
hide me; He shall set me high upon a rock.
—PSALM 27:5

CHAPTER TWO

LOVING DIFFICULTIES: THE ASCESIS
OF READING SCRIPTURE

See what love the Father has given us, that we should be called chil-
dren of God; and so we are. . . . it does not yet appear what we shall
be, but we know that when He appears we shall be like Him,
for we shall see Him as He is.
—1 JOHN 3:1

Only affliction can make us see.[1]

AFTER many hundreds of years of different people interpreting Scripture in radically different and divisive ways, it should be very evident today that, contrary to what the acknowledged founder of the Protestant Reformation, Martin Luther, supposed, Scripture is definitely not "most easily accessible, comprehensible, interpreting itself."[2] A text that interpreted itself would certainly be the easiest kind of text to understand—which sounds very appealing. But Holy Scripture has proven to be not like that at all. It has proven to be difficult.

---

1. Alexander Kalomiros, *Nostalgia for Paradise: Guidelines on the Path to the True Fatherland through Our Life in Christ*, trans. George S. Gabriel (Ridgewood, NJ: Zephyr Publishing, 2006), p. 17.

2. Quoted in Hans Frei, *The Eclipse of Biblical Narrative* (New Haven: Yale University Press, 1974), p. 19.

But why? Why is Scripture not clear and simple as Luther imagined, so that all reasonable people would agree about what it means?[3] Why are there so often difficulties that cause us problems of interpretation, that seem to cause so much trouble, and that make it so helpful—at times necessary—to have overall principles of interpretation, to have hermeneutics?

As a part of the foundation for discussing hermeneutics from an Orthodox/patristic perspective, trying to discover what an Orthodox hermeneutic would look like, it will be very useful to consider how those in the Tradition answer these questions. For none of the Fathers had the naive view of language and texts (or human nature!) that Luther's dictum presupposed. Many of the Fathers thought about why interpretation is difficult, and their answers are instructive.

To begin to answer this question, it will be helpful to go back to the real foundations, for there are difficulties in interpreting Scripture for some of the same reasons that there are difficulties in this earthly life as a whole. One of the absolutely foundational principles for Orthodox theology and life is that our God is "a good God Who loves mankind."[4] God has "no pleasure in the death of the wicked, but that the wicked turn from his way and live" (Ezek. 33:11). He "desires all men to be saved and to come to the knowledge of the truth" (1 Tim. 2:4). For God, Who is love, does everything to save us *all*—even to the point of actually sharing His Life with us, and really radically *transforming us at the core of our being*, so that, by grace, we truly become "children of God." As St. Peter says,

> His divine power has granted to us all things that pertain to life and god-liness, through the knowledge of Him who called us to His own glory and excellence, by which He has granted to us His precious and very great promises, that through these you may escape from the corruption that is in the world, because of passion, and become *partakers of the divine nature* (2 Peter 1:3-4; my emphasis).

This is perhaps the fundamental reality—the first light, in light of which everything is, or should be, understood.

---

3. This is not to deny that on some levels and in some ways at least certain people can simply read and understand much of Scripture—by living the Gospel, etc., as will be discussed later.

4. This and similar phrases occur frequently in Orthodox services, e.g., at the end of the "Little Litany" after the Second Antiphon, and in the final blessing of the priest, in the Liturgy of St. John Chrysostom.

The Divine Economy

Not only did God create man out of love in order for mankind to live in a communion of love with Him, but after the Fall, God shaped fallen reality, with all its difficulties, not so much to *punish* mankind, as is often mistakenly thought, but to *help* him.[5] The intent was to set him on the road to that perfect communion of love which will ultimately be made possible in Christ. The "garments of skin" (Gen. 3:21), the very difficulty of life after the Fall—all of this is ultimately a consequence of God's unchanging, limitless Love.[6] As St. Gregory the Theologian (4th century) says, "the penalty becomes an act of compassion."[7] And as St. John Chrysostom (4th century) says of death, the greatest "difficulty" in the fallen world, "even though death entered as a result of sin, nevertheless such is the superiority of God, His lovingkindness, and the excess of His care that He employs even this to the advantage of our race."[8]

Reflecting God's love, there is a certain "economy" to this fallen reality. The Greek word *oikonomia* means the way something is ordered, usually implying that it is in good order. It can refer to the world, or to a well-organized story which flows logically and smoothly, in such a way that the reader can follow it easily and understand the meaning, and experience what the author wishes to convey.[9]

St. Irenaeus (2nd century) and those after him in the Tradition, speak of a "DIVINE ECONOMY," or we could call it "the story" God has written. It also can refer to the good order in which God has arranged the created world, even after the Fall, for the salvation of mankind. In contemporary terms, we can say it means the most true "meta-narrative," which is actually "written" in reality.

To say that humanity is fallen partly means that we do not automatically live "according to nature"—according to our ultimate best interest, which always coincides with how God originally intended us to live. It is clear in the Greek Fathers, and in the Orthodox Tradition as a whole, that even after the Fall all people are still inherently good—the image of God is not destroyed in us, only distorted or tarnished. (This is in striking contrast to the much more negative

---

5. One might distinguish here between "punishment" and "discipline," which is more clearly intended to help us.

6. See Panayiotis Nellas, *Deification in Christ: The Nature of Human Person* (Crestwood, NY: St. Vladimir's Seminary Press, 1987), especially chapters 1 and 2.

7. Oration 45, on Easter, part 8; excerpt given in Nellas, p. 204.

8. *Commentary on the Psalms*, trans. Robert Hill (Brookline, MA: Holy Cross Orthodox Press, 1999), vol. 2, p. 37 (on Psalm 111).

9. John J. O'Keefe and R. R. Reno, *Sanctified Vision: An Introduction to Early Christian Interpretation of the Bible* (Baltimore: Johns Hopkins University Press, 2005), p. 37.

view of Luther, Calvin, and many of their followers who still believe in "total depravity"—meaning essentially that after the Fall, human nature is radically corrupted to such an extent that no one can do anything pleasing to God apart from Christ, and in Calvinism, no "natural knowledge of God" is possible.[10])

Furthermore, by becoming incarnate, Christ has assumed and transformed all of human nature. This is especially the message of the Transfiguration account (Luke 9:28-36)—that on the mountain, in His own Person, Christ showed the disciples "the nature of man, arrayed in the original beauty of the Image."[11] Many of the hymns for this feast explain the implications of this event. For example, "Today Christ on Mount Tabor has changed the darkened nature of Adam, and filling it with brightness He has made it godlike."[12]

This means that after the coming of Christ, all people have the potential once again to become godlike, which is actually to be fully human, to be truly the persons we were created to be. Yet because we are fallen, we must have God's grace to help us. We still have to *learn* the proper way to live in order to fulfill this goodness, to be more than just our animal nature, to be not merely selfish, egotistical individuals. And this, we could say, is also to be saved, to live in a perfect loving communion with the God Who is love. This is to enter again into Paradise. This is what Christ makes possible.

As part of His divine economy, out of His goodness and love, God built right into fallen reality a pedagogy—a spiritual training—to help teach us how to live as He intended, according to our true nature. "God the Artificer of all things sets up the economy of bodies so that we undergo an ascetic training by default. The important question is whether or not we will recognize, embrace, and profit from that discipline."[13]

In other words, if we want to understand the meaning of this life, to know Ultimate Truth, and to experience what God, the Author of Creation, wishes to convey through His creation, we need to be able not only to properly understand the "story" God has written, but we also need to participate actively in the "spiritual training" that He has built into that "story"—the true story of

---

10. See, e.g., the entry in *The Oxford Dictionary of the Christian Church,* eds., F. L. Cross and E. A. Livingstone (Oxford University Press), third edition, 2005, p. 1645.

11. Apostichon for Great Vespers for The Transfiguration of Our Lord (*Festal Menaion*, trans. Mother Mary and Archim. Kallistos Ware [London: Faber and Faber, 1969], p. 476).

12. Apostichon for Small Vespers for The Transfiguration of Our Lord (*Festal Menaion*, p. 469).

13. O'Keefe and Reno, *Sanctified Vision*, op. cit., p. 134.

fallen reality. This is a key aspect of His plan of salvation. "Life itself is a form of ascesis. People just don't recognize it, and lose heart."[14]

The fact that this training, or pedagogy, is ascetic in nature means it necessarily involves ascetic disciplines—including voluntary self-discipline and refraining from self-indulgence and excessive pleasure-seeking (because these things strengthen the selfishness of the ego, and weaken our love for others). It also involves involuntary "difficulties"—trials, afflictions, and suffering (such as illness)—which we are called to experience with the proper attitude. As St. Isaac the Syrian (7th century) says, "Knowledge is the offspring of many temptations and trials"; and, he adds, "the offspring of knowledge"[15] is humility, the greatest virtue along with, and inseparable from, love.

A contemporary theologian explains this as follows:

> He who does not know affliction does not know the truth, for only affliction can make us see. But there is a healthy affliction and an unhealthy affliction, one leading to life and the other to death. The first is tranquil and the other is agitated.[16]

Such a healthy response to affliction is also spoken of in Scripture, where it is also clear that "because God loves us, He allows us to undergo many trials in our lives."[17] For example, St. Paul says, "you became imitators of us and of the Lord, having received the word in much affliction, with the joy of the Holy Spirit" (1 Thess. 1:6, RSV; see also 2 Cor. 4:8-18).

Embracing and profiting from these ascetic disciplines is generally essential for spiritual progress, for purifying our hearts, so that we can see the beloved Bridegroom and receive "the joy of the Holy Spirit." It is also essential for living

---

14. Fr. Maximos, in *Mountain of Silence: A Search for Orthodox Spirituality*, by Kyriacos C. Markides (New York: Doubleday, 2001), p. 60.

15. St. Isaac the Syrian, *The Ascetical Homilies* (Brookline, MA: Holy Transfiguration Monastery, 1984), pp. 295-296; quoted by Archim. Vasileios, *The Saint: Archetype of Orthodoxy* (Montreal: Alexander Press, 1997), pp. 43-44.

16. Kalomiros, *Nostalgia for Paradise*, op. cit., p. 17. It is also important to note that there is a healthy asceticism leading to life, and an unhealthy one. One of the Desert Mothers, Amma Syncletica, explains, for example, that "There is an asceticism which is determined by the enemy and his disciples practice it. So how are we to distinguish between the divine and royal asceticism and the demonic tyranny? Clearly through its quality of balance" (*The Sayings of the Desert Fathers: The Alphabetical Collection*, trans. Benedicta Ward [London: Mowbrays, 1975], pp. 195-196). And from the *Philokalia*: "Anything untimely or pushed to excess is short-lived and harmful rather than helpful" (Evagrios the Solitary, Texts on Watchfulness [*Philokalia*, vol. 1, p. 54]).

17. Archim. Vasileios, *The Saint: Archetype of Orthodoxy*, p. 43.

life fully, as we were intended to live it—a life abundant with joy, peace, and love, even in this fallen world, even with all its difficulties. This is a foretaste of life eternal.

This disciplined way of life that, along with God's grace, purifies our hearts, "is a form of bodily existence that uses the body in the divinely ordained fashion: to induce progress toward the spiritual. . . . [T]he goal is not to flee from or deny these [bodily] realities, but to properly engage or use them so that 'the mind [and especially the *nous*] might be cleansed.'"[18] In addition to bodily disciplines, there are also mental ones, such as prayer and inner attention, repentance, and meditation on Scripture. All of these involve using the mind for a similar purpose, with a similar effect.[19]

As we all know, there are various kinds of "difficulties" or afflictions, including those caused by evil choices people make. It is never God's *will* for anyone to do evil, but in order to give us real freedom, which is essential for real love, God gives us the freedom to do evil. He allows us to choose evil, and most of the world's "difficulties" come about because people have freely chosen wrongly. However, God can bring good even out of such evil. As St. Paul says in Romans 8:28, "All things work together for good to those who love God."

But what about those who don't love God? St. Maximus the Confessor (7th century) says, "As regards all actual and supposed evils, God has made use of them to the good, for the correction and benefit of us and of others."[20] Archim. Vasileios speaks of this even more clearly:

> By opposing or by cooperating, willingly or not, directly or indirectly, everything contributes towards the coming of the One, the True One. . . . All will in the end kneel before what is true. And this is true comfort, giving us power to bear any pain, to understand, to endure in hope every difficulty and everything we cannot comprehend: "That . . . every knee should bow, in heaven and in earth and under the earth, and every tongue confess that Jesus is Lord" (Phil. 2:10-11).[21]

---

18. O'Keefe and Reno, *Sanctified Vision*, op. cit., p. 134.

19. See, e.g., Constantine Cavarnos, *Paths and Means to Holiness*, trans. Abbot Chrysostomos (Etna, CA: Center for Traditionalist Studies, 2000), p. 13.

20. St. Maximos the Confessor, *Scholia* on *The Divine Names* by St. Dionysios the Areopagite (PG 4.305D); quoted by Archim. Vasileios in *Hymn of Entry* (Crestwood, NY: St. Vladimir's Seminary Press, 1984), p. 113.

21. *Hymn of Entry*, p. 113. We can cooperate with God even in an evil situation, e.g., by having the attitude "How can I bring light to this situation?" instead of lamenting, "Why has this happened to me?"

As another part of the pedagogy of this economy, God "organized" fallen reality so that much in the created order exists in analogous relationships—that is, corresponding in some way, such as having a similar structure, or following a similar pattern. Such analogies help us in understanding the realities that correspond to each other.[22] An important example of this analogous structure of reality is that there is "an ascetic economy of Scripture that follows the larger ascetic economy of creation."[23] As life in this world is fraught with various difficulties, so too there are various difficulties in interpreting the Holy Scriptures.

The fact that Scripture is difficult to interpret is, then, actually a manifestation of God's love for mankind, and His desire that all be saved and come to knowledge of the truth. It is part of the ascetic economy of the fallen world. This fact is of fundamental importance for an Orthodox hermeneutic, and for understanding patristic hermeneutics. It is crucial to understand this point, yet it is often hard for us to accept that God has given us difficulties, in life and in Scripture, out of His love for us.

However contrary this seems to the "everyday, common sense" of fallen humanity, it is critical to recognize that these difficulties are necessary for us if we are to be able ultimately to live in a communion of love with the Lord. Therefore, the Fathers and their followers always insist that we should actually love these lovingly given difficulties, and embrace them thankfully—not in themselves, as from some perverse "enjoyment" of suffering, but because they lead us to that blessed end, and are in fact, the only means to it.

Regarding affliction and toil, St. Macarius the Great (4th century) says that the Christian should

> every day have the hope and the joy and the expectation of the coming kingdom and deliverance, and to say, "If today I have not been delivered, I shall tomorrow." As the man who plants a vine has the joy and the hope in himself, before ever he embarks upon the toil, and sketches out vineyards in his mind, and reckons up the income, when there has been no wine yet,

---

22. For example, some have seen an analogous relationship between the structure of humanity and Scripture. As Origen (3rd century) pointed out, "Just as man, therefore, is said to consist of body, soul and spirit, so also does the Holy Scripture, which has been bestowed by the divine bounty for man's salvation" (On First Principles 4.2.4; quoted in *Sanctified Vision*, p. 135). What this correspondence actually means for interpreting Scripture has been understood in different ways, some very different from Origen's understanding, which itself has often been misunderstood. In any case, whether or not one wants to see a relationship between the structure of a person and Scripture, the principle of an ascetic economy for the physical world and for Scripture stands independently.

23. *Sanctified Vision*, p. 135.

and so enters upon the toil—for the hope and the expectation make him labor cheerfully. . . . and in like manner the man who builds a house and the man who tills a field, are at much expense to themselves first, in the hope of the advantage to come; so it is here. If a man does not keep before his eyes the joy and the hope, "I shall find deliverance and life," he cannot endure the afflictions, or the burden, and adopt the narrow way. It is the presence of hope and joy that make him labour and endure the afflictions.[24]

Archim. Vasileios, an important contemporary pioneer for renewal of monastic life on Mt. Athos, can even say this:

In the end, the faithful will thank God only for great sufferings, for complete "perplexities." In other words, everything will be swept away by the fire of praise. And the cooling flame of unbearable fire will leap up from the painful occurrences, the temptations and the thorns that we did not wish to undergo, considering them to be obstacles, a curse making our lives miserable. For we had not realized that for the man who is placed rightly—according to nature—obstacles blocking the road are nothing other than steps which take him upwards and opportunities to give praise. For it is the Lord who is at work in everything.[25]

This understanding is simply the direct continuation of what is very evident in many places in the New Testament. For example, St. Paul instructs believers to be "Always and for everything giving thanks" (Eph. 5:20); and, "Give thanks in all circumstances" (1 Thess. 5:18). And even more explicitly, St. James says, "Consider it *pure joy*, my brethren, whenever you face trials of many kinds, because you know that the testing of your faith develops perseverance" (James 1:2-3; my emphasis). And as Christ Himself says in St. John's Gospel, "In the world you have tribulation; but be of good cheer, I have overcome the world" (John 16:33).

So to interpret Scripture in an Orthodox manner, we must be careful that our hermeneutics—our principles of biblical interpretation—are founded on a proper understanding of difficulties as springing from God's love, so that in response we even embrace these hardships.

An Orthodox approach will not try to erase the difficulties by, for instance, claiming that Scripture is "clear in itself" or "self-interpreting"—as if there were no ascetic effort involved—any more than we would try to live a life of

---

24. St. Macarius the Great, Homily XXVI.11 in the *Fifty Spiritual Homilies*, trans. A. J. Mason (Willits, CA: Eastern Orthodox Books, 1974), p. 190.

25. *Hymn of Entry*, op. cit., p. 105.

pure ease and self-indulgence, and imagine that such a life would lead to spiritual progress. But neither will it pretend that because of the difficulties it is impossible to have that "certainty of things unseen," a genuine experiential knowledge of Ultimate Truth. Rather, an Orthodox hermeneutic will use the difficulties in interpreting Scripture just as we should use all the difficulties in our lives—for spiritual growth, such as helping us to grow in humility, awe, and gratitude, and deepening our ability to love. For "obstacles blocking the road are nothing other than steps which take him upwards." (See the end of this chapter for an example.)

So we recognize and accept the fact that the ongoing struggle to properly understand Scripture, through overcoming the various obstacles that make this difficult, is necessary, and that this effort is an important means of our spiritual growth. Once we recognize and accept this reality, we can then even embrace it joyfully, rather than wishing it would go away, or pretending it doesn't exist.

Other Difficulties: Eve's Error

Yet, there is much more to say about the difficulties in interpreting the Scriptures properly, for there are many different kinds of difficulties. There are various "technical" difficulties, such as questions about vocabulary. For example, which meaning of a word with multiple meanings did the author intend? What meaning did the author have in mind in using a word that has since come to mean something different? Other "technical" difficulties often arise, such as which manuscript tradition is more accurate when the manuscripts disagree? How should we interpret an ambiguous text—one that has two or more possible meanings?

And there are other reasons why difficulties are present in Scripture. For example, St. John Cassian, Origen, St. Augustine, St. Gregory of Nyssa, and many other ancient interpreters agreed that some passages are very clear and straightforward (just as—thankfully!—life is not always difficult or painful), while other passages are difficult, for *a positive reason*: in order to attract some types of people to the challenge of Biblical interpretation, or in order to provide suitable activity for those with particularly active minds.[26]

At this point, however, what is of most importance to consider is a deeper kind of difficulty in interpretation that we see throughout Scripture itself, beginning even in the Beginning. This difficulty reflects perhaps the key obstacle

---

26. These various kinds of difficulties will be discussed later (especially in connection with the discussion of allegorical interpretation, which is particularly concerned with "difficulties" in the text).

people have in interpreting all or any part of reality. We might even say that this same difficulty led to the original Fall. For on one level, what does the story of the serpent tempting Eve deal with but interpretation and epistemology?

As we look at Genesis 2:16-17 and chapter 3, we see that the serpent begins his dialogue with Eve with deception. For while he apparently knows exactly what God had said to Adam and Eve, he asks her,

> "Did God really say you were not to eat from any of the trees in the garden?" The woman answered the serpent, "We may eat the fruit of the trees in the garden. But of the fruit of the tree in the middle of the garden God said, 'You must not eat it, nor touch it, under pain of death.'"[27]
>
> Then the serpent said to the woman, "No! You will not die! God knows in fact that on the day you eat it your eyes will be opened and you will be like gods, knowing good and evil."
>
> The woman saw that the tree was good to eat and pleasing to the eye, and that it was desirable for the knowledge that it could give [or, beautiful to contemplate; to be desired to make one wise]. So she took some of its fruit and ate it. She gave some also to her husband who was with her, and he ate it (Gen. 3:1-6).

In this account, Eve is faced with two interpretations of reality, in particular concerning the one "difficulty" in Paradise—the forbidden fruit. One interpretation of this fruit and why it was forbidden was given by God, Who created Eve and everything else, and another one was given by the serpent, a fellow creature. In his interpretation, the serpent implies that God has lied to Eve out of fear and jealousy to prevent her from acquiring the knowledge she desires—a knowledge which will make her godlike. In other words, he implies that it is a good thing to want to be godlike, so she should seize any means of attaining that—even though in his interpretation God is not a good God Who loves mankind. This becomes the archetypal lie about reality.

Eve, we could say, at this point decides that all that matters is the "text" alone—the two interpretations or statements made—along with how things look on the surface to her own eyes, which is only the superficial, physical reality. Apparently she doesn't stop to consider *who* it is giving each interpretation, and what her relationship is with each interpreter. Like many modern-day commentators, she thinks that interpretation can be impersonal, "objective." "Don't ask God about this," the serpent implies; "He is not trustworthy. He

---

27. Actually, God says to Adam, "You may eat indeed of all the trees in the garden. Nevertheless of the tree of the knowledge of good and evil you are not to eat, for on the day you eat of it you shall most surely die" (Gen. 2:16-17).

doesn't really love you. He doesn't really want the best for you." Then he implies, "And don't ask Adam, either. Judge for yourself—you don't need others to help you discern the truth."

The fruit really is beautiful. It *looks* good to Eve, and what the serpent says *seems* reasonable to her "unaided reason," so she decides to accept the interpretation he offers, and to act on his statement—an action which the serpent implies she can make completely independently. However, Eve doesn't realize that in choosing the serpent's interpretation, and in acting with her supposed autonomy, she in fact chooses communion with the serpent over, and instead of, communion with God and her husband.

While the serpent cleverly gives an extremely negative motive for God's interpretation, Eve foolishly never asks herself anything about the serpent's motive for his. She wanted the greatest good—a knowledge that would enable her to attain the highest level of spiritual life, to be godlike. And here the Orthodox Tradition differs from the understanding commonly held by many other Christians, which usually says first, that it was wrong for Eve to want to be godlike, and second, that her other primary sin was disobeying God's command.

The settled traditional Orthodox understanding can be seen in St. Gregory the Theologian's treatment:

> the tree of knowledge was not planted originally with any evil intent, nor was it forbidden in a spirit of jealousy. Let not the enemies of God make any such suggestion or think to imitate the serpent. On the contrary, it was good if eaten at the right time; for as I understand it, the fruit was contemplation, which is only safely attempted by those who have attained a more perfect state. But it was not good for those at a lower stage of development, . . . just as mature food is not profitable for those of tender years who still need milk.[28]

In other words, it was entirely right for Eve to want to be godlike—that was God's plan all along.[29] What was wrong was wanting this apart from God, and on her own terms and timetable. What was wrong was imagining that judging by appearances with her reason would be a better way to reach the Truth, and that this would be characteristic of the highest, best possible state for a person

---

28. Oration 45.8 on Easter; excerpt given by Nellas, *Deification in Christ*, p. 204.

29. This is indicated in this hymn of the Church: "In times of old Adam was once deceived: he sought to become God, but received not his desire. Now God becomes man, that He may make Adam God. Let creation rejoice, let nature exult" (Stikheron for Matins for the Annunciation; *Festal Menaion*, p. 460).

to be in, rather than being in a loving relationship of communion with God and trusting Him—even if on the surface that approach did not look so promising.

The serpent seemed to offer Eve a "short cut" way to deification—never mind that it was a way without God, and without her husband. Evidently, Eve didn't ask Adam's advice or opinion before following the serpent's advice, and she acted without knowing whether Adam would join her or not. As Fr. Schmemann so eloquently points out in his discussion of this event in *For the Life of the World*, here we have a dramatic breakdown of personal communion and love.[30]

Timothy Patitsas develops this idea further in an illuminating way:

> Eve invents a new kind of epistemology, in which knowledge of isolated things is possible by isolated individuals. After her, knowledge is no longer an automatic synonym for personal communion.[31]

The material world, created to be a transparent means of communion with the living God, intended to be "divine love made food, made life for man,"[32] becomes instead an opaque object. As Dr. Patitsas says,

> Eve's actions in the Garden, then, amount to an act of deep infidelity to God and to Adam. . . . she attempted to conceive the object of knowledge not as being a "Who," or at least as finally always related to some "who," but as a "What," a detachable object. She imagined that God's world, which was given as a medium of communion with God and Adam, could be known as an end in itself.[33]

Genesis itself speaks in this passage of Eve desiring knowledge, and as mentioned above, St. Gregory the Theologian suggests that this forbidden fruit represented the heights of mystical knowledge, which God planned to give to Adam and Eve when they had matured. However, by trying to take it before she was ready to receive this knowledge in communion with God, Eve lost the possibility of having the very thing she desired.

So we see dramatized in Genesis the bitter "fruit" of an approach to the interpretation of spiritual realities that attempts to be "impersonal" and "objective," in the sense that Eve imagines she can discern which interpretation is true

---

30. See chapter 1, especially p. 18 (Crestwood, NY: St. Vladimir's Seminary Press, 1973).

31. Timothy Patitsas, "The Marriage of Priests: Towards an Orthodox Christian Theology of Gender," *St. Vladimir's Theological Quarterly*, vol. 51, no. 1 (Jan.—March, 2007), p. 83.

32. Fr. Alexander Schmemann, *For the Life of the World*, p. 14.

33. Patitsas, p. 81.

without taking into consideration *who* the author of each interpretation is, and what her relationship to each is. Hers is a very individualistic approach. And we see that this approach began with deception and ends in an act of infidelity.

Abraham's Certainty

In Abraham we see a contrasting example of interpretation. Abraham completely believed the first principle we began this chapter with: that God is a good God Who loves mankind, and Who does everything to save us, even though according to surface appearances and "unaided human reason," God's command that Abraham offer his son Isaac in sacrifice seemed to profoundly contradict this understanding of God. Why would God, if He were good, loving, and faithful, ask Abraham to sacrifice, to kill, his only son—the one whom God had promised him as a means of the greatest good, of salvation as he understood it?

In this situation the serpent's lie—that God is not a good God Who loves mankind—certainly seems much more plausible than in Eve's case. But Abraham did not judge by surface appearances, or restrict himself to his own limited reasoning powers. Instead, he trusted that God knew more than he did, that God could even raise Isaac from the dead, and thereby make good His promise. Abraham did not insist on fully understanding why; what mattered was his relationship with God, which gave him true faith.

But what is this faith such as Abraham had? Today, people often use the word "faith" as almost a synonym for "wishful thinking," or as something you need to have when you don't really know for sure, when you are lacking any "certainty" or "hard evidence." As Robert Wilken says, it has been "emptied of its cognitive dimension."[34] This is a radically different understanding of faith from what one finds throughout Scripture, and throughout the mainstream Tradition. In the Book of Hebrews, for example, we read that "faith is the substance [or reality] of things hoped for, the *evidence* [or *proof*] of things unseen" (Heb. 11:1; my emphasis). Along the same lines, St. Irenaeus (2nd century), said long ago: "faith is produced by the truth; *for faith rests on things that truly are*. For in things that are, as they are, we believe, and believing in things that are, and as they are, we keep firm confidence in them."[35] In Scripture and the

---

34. *Remembering the Christian Past* (Grand Rapids, MI: Eerdmans, 1995), p. 56.

35. Demonstration of the Apostolic Preaching.3; quoted by T. F. Torrance, "The Open Texture of 'Faith' and 'Godliness' in the Church's Confession," in *Aksum-Thyateira: A Festschrift for Archbishop Methodios of Thyateira and Great Britain* (London: Thyateira House, 1985), p. 143 (my emphasis).

Tradition, then, "faith is . . . a seeing of what there is to see, and hence a form of knowing."[36]

A contemporary author explains this more concretely:

> A man has faith according to the extent that his mind (*nous*) beholds God, that he touches God and hears Him, and tastes Him, and senses Him through his spiritual senses, as much as this is possible for imperfect humanity. *Faith, then, is a consequence of a man's contact with God.* It is neither an intellectual accomplishment nor a blind acceptance.
>
> No one ever acquired faith because of logical proofs, for these may satisfy the intellect [mind] but they do not convince; they do not give assurance. . . . it is vision by the spirit that assures us. . . . faith alone assures man, it alone illuminates him, it alone makes him a flame of fire. It is a knowledge that does not enclose God or make Him into its object.[37]

Indeed, "the primacy accorded to faith in our knowledge of God reflects the absolute priority of God over all human thought" (which does not imply that rational thought, historical evidence, and similar kinds of knowledge and information are not also used by God to help us—they surely are).[38]

With this kind of faith, Abraham could be certain that God is love, and that all He does is from His love for us, even though the literal interpretation of God's command certainly didn't point to that. Abraham was also certain that it was God Who was giving him this command. His faith was "an act of godliness in humble worship of God and adoring obedience to him . . . [such] godliness is a right relationship to God through faith which *gives a distinctive slant to the mind and molds life and thought*."[39] Such faith and godliness, such fidelity, gave him right understanding, and the certainty which enabled him to do what was "beyond" reason, and obey.

And the result was the opposite of the result for Eve, who could see and hear God, yet did not perceive or understand (as in Mark 4:12) His ultimate goodness and love for her. By accepting the serpent's lie, Eve placed herself "outside" (see Mark 4:10-11). Thus, she lacked faith—this "certainty," or "proof" of things "unseen." As a result, she chose to believe how things appeared on the surface, accepting/assuming that interpretation is impersonal—considering only the words (the text), and ignoring *who* was giving the interpretation.

---

36. Wilken, ibid., pp. 56-57.

37. Kalomiros, *Nostalgia for Paradise*, op. cit., pp. 21-24 (my emphasis).

38. T. F. Torrance, paraphrasing St. Hilary of Poitiers, in *Askum-Thyateira*, p. 144.

39. T. F. Torrance, *Askum-Thyateira*, p. 147 (my emphasis).

But *who* is giving the interpretation makes all the difference in the world. This is a crucial, often overlooked point in biblical exegesis today. Indeed, since the beginning of ill-fated effort to rely on "Scripture alone," and to attempt to let Scripture be "self-interpreting," biblical exegesis has moved farther and farther in the direction Eve chose. Though trying to include inspiration by the Holy Spirit, and a relationship with God, the path of "Scripture alone" led to an emphasis on the "impersonal" interpretation by the isolated individual depending on his or her own reason and good judgment.

Interpretation, especially of spiritual realities, is fundamentally and inescapably *personal*—whether we acknowledge this or not. We should be able to trust the person who gives the interpretation, to be confident that he or she knows from personal experience what he speaks of, or that at least he is depending on those who know for the correct interpretation; hence it is also necessarily *communal*. Trying to be "totally objective"—which is impossible anyway (see chapter 6)—to isolate the text from persons, and only look at it "in itself," to claim a "direct reading of the plain text," leaves us open to every serpent that slithers along.

* * * * *

A Brief Example of Seeing Difficulties in a Positive Light

One aspect of the New Testament that has been considered a difficulty by some since the time of the early Church, something even criticized by educated pagans like Celsus (late 2nd century), as well as some today, is the fact that the Church accepted four somewhat different Gospel accounts.[40] Why might the Church have canonized this "difficulty" rather than creating one harmony? Or in the early days, why did the Church not ensure that only one—the best and most authentic "original"—account would be accepted as canonical?

There is, of course, no way to "prove" any speculation about this, and there could well be a number of valid reasons or explanations. At this point, I would simply like to consider something important that we can learn from accepting this "difficulty" as something intended, meaningful, and completely appropriate.

We could begin by asking, why do we have Gospel accounts at all? Why do we have Peter's and Paul's speeches quoted, and their activities recounted in

---

40. For a very interesting discussion of this issue which considers many theological, "cultural, political, economic, and technological presuppositions undergirding and shaping the debate in every historical period," see *A History of the Synoptic Problem*, by David Laird Dungan (New York: Doubleday, 1999), p. 2; see especially Part 2, which is less speculative.

the New Testament and preserved there? Why do we have personal letters to specific congregations of people? We might ask: Why don't we simply have a good, clear, straightforward summary of all the key teachings of Christ and His Apostles? Why is our Scripture in the form of these very personal, and therefore fluid and even "messy," accounts and letters, full of difficulties for interpreters?

I would submit that in the New Testament itself, in both the style and the content, we can see that what matters most is not some objectively obtained information, some unambiguous, straightforward statements about the faith—Who Jesus is, what He taught, etc.—but *personal* witnesses authenticated by the *community* of the Church. All the writings eventually accepted into the New Testament canon were composed by those who not only saw Him in the flesh (or were close to those who did) (see, for example, 1 John 1:1-2; John 1:14), but who also truly "perceived and understood," whose lives had been transformed through and through by Christ. They were living the new life in Christ fully, shining as radiant examples of the life we too are meant to seek through many spiritual disciplines, including reading the Scriptures.

In John's Gospel Christ tells us, "I am the truth" (14:6). So, as mentioned in the previous chapter, Ultimate Truth is a Person. This means that knowing Ultimate Truth is being in communion with that Person, rather than knowing certain facts (though this does not mean that conceptual knowledge is unimportant!). It also indicates what the style of the New Testament as whole implies: that language can only point to, or witness to, truth, more or less effectively—*it cannot contain it.* Having multiple personal Gospel accounts reflects and communicates this understanding. Because language can only point to truth, and truth of this kind can ultimately only be known through personal communion, it is most appropriate to have multiple accounts about Christ, and about the Faith, told by those who were in closest communion with Him.

Because they know from their own experience, these people are in the best position to judge which ways of speaking about the truth point to the truth most effectively on the basis of their personal *and communal* spiritual experience. The disagreements among the Apostles which are reported, for instance, in the Book of Acts, and how these disputes are resolved by, and in, the Church, demonstrate that individual experience and the understanding based on it are not enough to ensure correct interpretation. Rather, it is *the consensus* of the Church community—the oneness of mind on essentials; the communal, ecclesial dimension—that is essential to confirm the authenticity of the equally crucial individual experience and interpretation. Those confirmed as authorities by the Church (because of their manifest living in communion with Christ) are in the best position to say what language, what images, etc., best safeguard the experience of life in Christ, which it is the purpose of Scripture to nurture.

This is why the Apostles and those close to them were the ones whose words and lives were chosen to be remembered and studied, to help those who come afterwards to draw closer to Christ, and to enable all of us to live the new life that He came to bring. These works, and the works of the Fathers (whom the Orthodox consider also "God-inspired," though, of course, their works are not as authoritative as Holy Scripture) and other Saints, have been preserved and passed down because those in the Church found that these writings were the most helpful for safeguarding the experience of life in God made possible by Christ.

And this reality continues from the early times until today. We could say that traditional Christianity learned from Eve's mistake—realizing that it is vitally important to consider *who* gives an interpretation, *what sources* the interpretation is based on, why the interpretation is given, and finally, based on all these factors, why any particular interpretation might be considered to be authoritative. In the case of the Church, a crucial part of that consideration is whether or not any particular interpretation is in harmony with the centuries of wisdom confirmed in and by the Church.

Having multiple Gospel accounts, and knowing who gave the various interpretations of them, also enables us to see that there is often a range of meanings in interpretation (though there is also a clear "rule of faith"), that texts are not always easily understood, or "self-interpreting," and that this is not a bad thing, but part of reality as God made it, out of His love, to help us. All of this pushes us to look for a patristic consensus, to consciously understand important texts as being representative of a community in direct continuity with those faithful who have gone before—in other words, being part of a living Tradition.

This is also a way of not erasing the difficulties in Scripture. It shows that personal engagement, even struggle, is necessary. For there are not always easy answers.[41]

So Orthodox Christians are reading and quoting these authorities, these Fathers and Saints, not because they can't, or are afraid to think for themselves, or because they don't highly esteem Scripture itself, but because they are part of the ongoing communion of believers continuing the same basic approach to communicating the truths we find in the New Testament itself. They can be confident that these "witnesses" to the living Tradition, which has been passed

---

41. In emphasizing different specific personal examples of those living the Faith and considering their testimony as being authoritative, the Orthodox are actually following ancient Jewish tradition—"Rabbi so and so said, . . ."—as well as early Christian methodology of interpretation, which always meant looking to the ones who went before, those who knew from their own experience and were faithful to the original experience of the Apostles.

down from Christ through the Apostles and their successors, are the surest guides to the new life that it's the purpose of Scripture to bring us to.

At times, the difficulties in interpreting Scripture can perhaps seem like the powerful enemy army which the Israelite spies saw in the Promised Land—an army that, humanly speaking, appeared impossible to defeat. Even though God had done the impossible for the Israelites repeatedly, as a whole they still did not believe that "with God all things are possible" (Matthew 19:26).

All of the many interpreters of Scripture who have ever decided to follow Spinoza, accepting the path of doing only what is humanly possible, have been forced to wander—and it has been a very long "forty years" that biblical critics have been wandering in the wilderness of spiritually unhelpful hermeneutics. Many have been wandering so long they don't even know that they are in a desert, much less that there is anything beyond it.

But an increasing number of interpreters have awakened to the fact that the steps they have been taking with their hermeneutics will not bring them out of the desert, or even any closer to the Promised Land—however this is defined. The way out, I would suggest, lies partly in going back to look at a time when things were radically different, and in realizing that ultimately it is only with God's help that any real victory over the difficulties of interpreting Scripture can occur.

The Lord is my light and my salvation—whom shall I fear?
—PSALM 27:1

CHAPTER THREE

BEFORE THE FALL:
EXEGESIS IN THE EARLY CENTURIES

*The ignorance of Scripture is a great cliff and a deep abyss;
to know nothing of the divine laws is a great betrayal of
salvation. This has given birth to heresies, this has introduced a corrupt way of life, this has put down the things
above. For it is impossible, impossible for anyone to depart
without benefit if he reads continually with attention.[1]*
—ST. JOHN CHRYSOSTOM (ANTIOCH AND
CONSTANTINOPLE; D. 407)

Ignorance of the Scriptures is ignorance of Christ.
—ST. JEROME (ROME AND THE HOLY LAND;
D. 420)

T HE history of the reading and use of the Holy Scriptures is not only
interesting, but also of great value for the light it can shed on the search
for a better hermeneutic, helping people's spiritual lives. This history also
illuminates a number of common misconceptions about how Scripture was
used and understood in the early centuries of Christianity, misconceptions that
perpetuate divisions among Christians to this day. Key common misunderstandings are that until the Reformation, there was never a time when Scripture
was read by the laity, and that not too long after the Apostles' era it was even
forbidden for the laity to read it, or for it to be translated into the vernacular.

---

1. Third Sermon on Lazarus and the Rich Man, in *St. John Chrysostom: On Wealth and
Poverty* (Crestwood, NY: St. Vladimir's Seminary Press, 1984), p. 60.

Those who hold such misconceptions will be quite surprised, however, by what even a brief look at the actual history reveals.

Part One: Literacy among the Early Christians

Both Hellenism and Judaism promoted literacy, and the use of books was widespread during the early period before and after Christ. Already by 75 BC in Judah, elementary education was available for *all* boys—the world's first public school system, one could say. A significant number of people, at least in cities, could read, and "writing was an essential accompaniment of life at almost all levels to an extent without parallel in living memory."[2]

There are even indications that during this time "a basic level of literacy was probably more widespread than in any period prior to the twentieth century."[3] This general cultural reality, in addition to the exceptionally high veneration the Jews had for their Bible, prepared the way for early Christian attitudes toward and use of their own Scriptures.

This partly explains why Manlio Simonetti, a historian of early biblical interpretation, can say of Christians in the first few *centuries* (not decades!), "the whole life of the community was conditioned by the interpretation of Scripture."[4] He also writes, "the study of Holy Scripture was the real foundation of Christian culture"—including DOCTRINE, worship (liturgical life), organization (the structure of the Church), and discipline.[5]

From almost the beginning, then, "Christian culture and education were bookish through and through . . . . This ensured that the specifically Christian preaching would be transmitted in writing at an early date."[6] Much good work today is being done by scholars like Richard Bauckham who are providing compelling evidence that the Gospels were, in fact, based on eyewitness accounts, in direct contrast to what many scholars claimed in the previous century.[7]

---

2. C. H. Roberts, "Books in the Graeco-Roman World and in the New Testament," in the *Cambridge History of the Bible*, edited by P. R. Ackroyd and C. F. Evans (Cambridge: Cambridge University Press, 1970), vol. 1, p. 48.

3. Frances M. Young, *Biblical Exegesis and the Formation of Christian Culture* (Peabody, MA: Hendrickson Publishers, 2002), p. 12.

4. Manlio Simonetti, *Biblical Interpretation in the Early Church*, trans. John H. Evans (Edinburgh: T & T Clark, 1994), p. 1.

5. Ibid., p. 2.

6. Roberts, op. cit., p. 66.

7. For instance, *Jesus and the Eyewitnesses: the Gospels as Eyewitness Testimony*, by Richard Bauckham (Grand Rapids, MI: Eerdmans, 2006).

Papyrus fragments of St. Matthew's Gospel have even been found that a leading papyrologist, C. P. Thiede, has dated to around 70 AD—a time when many eyewitnesses of Christ were still alive, including perhaps even the Evangelist Matthew himself.[8] Indeed, "On the rapid circulation of literature among the churches and on its regular and public reading, much of the coherence of the early Church must have depended; libraries and archives would have been as essential an element in them as they were in the synagogues."[9]

The public reading of Scripture was always an important part of worship, enabling even those who couldn't read to become familiar with the Scriptures.[10] But it also provided a communal context for hearing and interpreting the sacred texts, which made it very clear that the Scriptures belonged to the Church community, which was called upon to safeguard, and to initiate others into, the new life in Christ.[11]

The New Testament was written in *koine* Greek—a common form of spoken Greek (not an elevated literary style) which was the dominant international language in the Mediterranean world and all the Middle East from about 300 BC to 300 AD. Also, most Jews at the time of Christ, and most of the early Christians, read the Hebrew Bible in the popular Greek translation called the Septuagint. Thus, translating Scripture into a vernacular language was not a concern. Even in Rome, Greek was the language for business, etc., and the early Roman biblical commentators wrote in Greek up until the early 3rd century.

Many people today are not aware that even in the 7th century and beyond, Scripture was not usually circulated as a complete book containing all the books we find today in our Bibles in one volume. Rather, the four Gospels, or

---

8. C. P. Thiede and Matthew d'Ancona, *The Jesus Papyrus* (London: Weidenfeld & Nicolson, 1996); commented upon by Constantine Siamakis, *Transmission of the Text of the Holy Bible*, trans. Andrew Hendry (Belmont, Mass.: Institute for Byzantine and Modern Greek Studies, 1997), p. 16. Finding such fragments indicates that the text was at least fairly widespread before this date.

9. Roberts, op. cit., p. 64.

10. It should be remembered that people who are illiterate, especially if they are part of a largely oral culture, generally have much better memories, and much more practice remembering large amounts of material, than literate people have.

11. It is interesting, though not relevant for this brief summary, that oral tradition, the voice of a living witness, was highly valued, even over written texts, in Jewish tradition at the time of Christ. This, combined with the Jewish reluctance to write down their tradition of oral interpretation except as notes, may have delayed the writing and publication of Christian writings such as the Gospels. Jesus' teachings themselves could be seen as an oral interpretation of the Hebrew Bible, and therefore, not to be published as a book (but only notes kept to aid the memory).

the epistles, or the Psalms, or perhaps the first five or eight books of the Old Testament, would be bound and sold separately.

The Creation of the Canonical New Testament

Fairly quickly after the deaths of the Apostles, many books were written which falsely claimed that they were written by an Apostle, in order to attempt to use apostolic authority to promote very different teachings from those of Christ, leading to a very different sort of spiritual life. Because there wasn't one official single volume containing all the approved writings, there was a great need for the Church to discern which of the various existing writings were authentic, especially in terms of the "rule of faith,"that is, the principle guiding truths revealed by Christ and passed on the Apostles (that are the foundation of the later Creeds).

And even for the books containing authentic teaching, there was a long, gradual process to discern which ones should be considered normative for guiding the Church—in other words, which ones should be included in a New Testament "canon," meaning a "rule," or even "guide," to be considered canonical Holy Scripture. This long process was basically completed by the early 5th century. However, even in the late 6th century or early 7th century, St. Andrew of Caesarea, for example, felt the need to write a commentary on the Revelation of St. John to defend its inclusion in the New Testament, since some still challenged its being accepted as canonical. Still today there are minor differences in the Old Testament canons of the Roman Catholic and Orthodox Churches.

So, after the deaths of all the Apostles, great care was taken by those in the Church gradually to create a canon of sacred writings in order to safeguard for all times and all peoples the new life that Christ had made possible. Two of the most important factors determining whether or not a book would be included in the Bible were whether or not a book or letter was "read in all the churches," and whether or not it was often quoted by well-respected Church authors.

There were also other early works by traditional Christians that were highly valued then and now (for example, the seven epistles written in about 107 AD by St. Ignatius, the third bishop of Antioch; and the *Didache*, a compendium of Christian teachings dating from the last half of the first century). But over time, the Church determined that these books, though valuable to be read by Christians personally, should not be part of the New Testament canon which would be read in the churches until the end of time.

Bishop Eusebius of Caesarea (c. 260—c. 340), the first great Church historian, gives a list of books that by the early 4th century were widely accepted in the churches as written by Apostles or other eyewitnesses, and were so clearly faithful to Christ's teachings and to the entire early Apostolic Tradition as to be universally included in the canon of Holy Scripture. He also listed seven books that were still "disputed" in his day, largely because there was some dispute over whether or not the author was an Apostle—though the teachings in these books were not in dispute: 2 and 3 John, the Revelation of John (because of the difficulty in interpreting it), James, Jude, 2 Peter, and Hebrews. As we know, all seven of these books eventually—by the end of the 4th century—did gain full acceptance by the entire Church.

Eusebius also gives a list of other books that were considered "rejected"—including the Shepherd of Hermas, which had been considered by some churches during the second and third centuries to be of such spiritual value as to be included in the New Testament canon. By the early 4th century, however, this book had been rejected from the canon of Scripture simply because it was not apostolic. Still, it was considered very worthy of being read by Christians for personal edification. Other books, such as the Gospel of Thomas, Eusebius mentions as being unworthy even of being considered "rejected"!

In explaining why he made these lists, Eusebius states:

> we have nevertheless felt compelled to give a catalogue of these [disputed and rejected books] also, distinguishing those works which *according to ecclesiastical tradition* are true and genuine and commonly accepted, from those others which, although not canonical but disputed, are yet at the same time *known to most ecclesiastical writers.* We have felt compelled to give this catalogue in order that we might be able to know both these works and those that are cited by the heretics under the name of the apostles, including, for instance, such books as the Gospels of Peter, of Thomas . . . or of any others besides them . . . *which no one belonging to the succession of ecclesiastical writers has deemed worthy of mention in his writings.* And further, the *character of the style is at variance with apostolic usage, and both the thoughts and the purpose of the things that are related in them are so completely out of accord with true orthodoxy* that they clearly show themselves to be the fictions of heretics. Wherefore they are . . . all of them to be cast aside as absurd and impious.[12]

The earliest extant list of exactly the 27 books of the New Testament that we have today appears in St. Athanasius's annual Paschal Letter of 367 AD, reflecting the usage of his church in Alexandria. This list was generally accepted by all the churches by the early 5th century.

---

12. Quoted by Frank Sadowski, *Church Fathers on the Bible* (Staten Island, NY: Alba House, 1987), p. 143 (my emphasis); *Ecclesiastical History*, 3.25.

This long process clearly shows the Church's determining role in deciding that more than the Hebrew Bible was needed as Her Holy Scripture, and also in establishing which writings should be included in it. The Bible is the Church's book—not just the Church of the Apostles and the first century, but the Church of the first four centuries at least (which already had a fully developed hierarchical structure [bishop, priest, deacon], liturgical life, and sacramental worldview, to mention some of the key aspects).

Production of the Scriptures

The importance of the Scriptures for early Christians meant that great care was taken to produce accurate copies of them (though the Christians were not as scrupulous about every detail of transmission as the Jews were),[13] in sufficient quantities to meet the growing need for them. So copies of the Scriptures, made by the community for the members of the community (rather than produced privately or for the commercial book trade), gradually became increasingly available. There is evidence of central *scriptoria*—groups of scribes who would copy biblical manuscripts—beginning from the early 2nd century. Eusebius even tells us that Origen's scriptorium (early 3rd century) employed some women stenographers who knew both shorthand and calligraphy.[14]

At least by the 4th century in the East, biblical manuscripts were mass produced by groups of up to 100 scribes who would write down what a reader dictated. One such group of scribes could produce about 1000 copies a month in this way. Obviously, such large numbers of copies would not have been regularly made unless there were many people who were able to purchase and make use of them.

Martyrdom on behalf of the Scriptures

As another indication of the incalculable value that early Christians placed on Scripture, during times of persecution Christians could and did lose their lives protecting their copies of Scripture. For example, on Feb. 23, 303, the Roman emperor Diocletian (r. 284-305) decreed that all Bibles and liturgical materials

---

13. Roberts, op. cit., p. 66. The Christians were not as scrupulous about every detail of transmission as the Jews were. For example, the Jews did not allow copies to be made from dictation, but the Christians did. Evidently the need for many copies outweighed the concern that some minor errors might creep into copies produced by dictation.

14. Roberts, op. cit., p. 65.

were to be surrendered, with the Bibles to be burned. All church buildings were to be destroyed, and all meetings of Christians were forbidden. Those who did not cooperate were to be imprisoned, and/or tortured and killed.[15] Many were martyred at this time, such as St. Irene, who ended her life being burned in the same flames used to destroy the copy of the Scriptures she was trying to protect. And many manuscripts of the biblical books were lost during the nine years of the Diocletian Persecution.

Extant Copies of New Testament Manuscripts

Thanks to the careful efforts in producing and preserving good manuscript copies, and to the demand for many copies, despite the efforts of Diocletian and other persecutors we have by far more extant copies of the Christian Bible than any other ancient manuscript, along with far more papyrus fragments. And we have far more of both forms that are far older than any other manuscripts. They are also, along with the Jewish Scriptures, the most reliable of all ancient manuscripts.

One biblical historian writes,

> If we arranged all the complete manuscripts in the world in chronological order, for the first seven centuries (2nd—8th centuries) we would have only manuscripts of the Bible; then, during the next four centuries (9th—12th centuries), manuscripts of Greek, Latin, Hebrew, and eastern Christian authors would begin to appear; later, from the 12th century onwards, Arabic and Islamic ones would begin to make their appearance; and only from the 13th century on would Indian, Chinese, paleo-American, and other manuscripts appear.[16]

---

15. In the East, where the persecution was much worse, all clergy were arrested, and only freed if they offered sacrifice to the idols. And in 304 *all* citizens were required to sacrifice to idols, or they would be killed. Again, this was mainly enforced in the East, and many martyrs come from this period. This longest period of persecution was ended in 313 by the Edict of Milan, which proclaimed tolerance for all religions *(not,* as many think, making Christianity the one official religion).

16. Siamakis, op. cit., p. 20. He gives more details: "The works of Homer and all other authors before and after Christ exist in manuscripts dating [only] from the 9th century onwards (10th—17th cent.). The only exceptions are half of Aristotle's *Constitution of the Athenians* in a manuscript of the 1st century AD, and Menander's comedy *Dyskolos* in a manuscript of the 3rd century. [In contrast,] the Bible has 20 complete manuscripts with both Testaments, 80 of only the New Testament, and another 180 with half of the New Testament—a total of 280

This would hardly be the case if Christians in these early centuries had not given an extremely high priority to the reading of Scripture.

Interpretation of the Scriptures

Many people also heard a great deal of Scripture and its interpretation in long homilies given in church. A striking example of this is reported by the famous Spanish pilgrim Egeria at the end of the 4th century. She recounted that while she was in the Holy Land during Great Lent, the bishop spent three hours each morning gradually explaining the entire Bible, beginning with Genesis, giving first the literal and then the spiritual meaning of the passages.

Early Christians not only read and prayed Scripture, using it in their liturgical worship, and oftentimes preaching extensive homilies with many references to the Scriptures, but they also studied it intently. Some highly educated Christians wrote biblical commentaries on various books, often showing great interest in both the exegetical and interpretive levels of the literal sense.[17] The earliest commentaries were apologetic in nature, but more systematic biblical studies began in earnest with St. Hippolytus of Rome (c. 170—235) in the West, and Origen (185-254) in the East.

Origen is generally known for his extensive use of allegorical interpretation, but he also did much scholarly work on the literal level of Scripture, considering both the "exegetical" and the "interpretive" levels. He even did some biblical archaeology—for instance, he speaks of finding a translation of the book of Psalms in a jar in the desert. He compared different manuscript versions, did word studies, considered the historical context of various passages, etc.—all things that we would now refer to as aspects of BIBLICAL CRITICISM.

Origen was the first person we know of to interpret in written form many of the books of the Bible. He systematized and built on the work of previous interpreters as well. A wealthy benefactor paid for scribes to take down his works by dictation—so that many copies could be produced (which surely indicates that

---

manuscripts—older than the 9th century, i.e., older than the manuscript traditions of all ancient Greek authors, from Homer to the last of this group, all Latin authors, and, indeed, of any book, of known or unknown authorship, in the world" (p. 20).

17. Fr. Stylianopoulos correctly gives three levels of interpretation: 1), the exegetical, which is simply determining the basic sense of the words; 2), the interpretive, which involves theological interpretation; and 3), the transformative level (which is discussed later in this chapter). See his *The New Testament: An Orthodox Perspective* (Brookline, MA: Holy Cross Press, 1997), especially Ch. 3.

a significant number of people wanted to read such works). To give an example of how prolific he was: he wrote 32 books on St. John's Gospel alone.

Popular Study of the Scriptures

At the end of the persecution that began under Diocletian, especially after Constantine issued the Edict of Milan (313 AD) requiring toleration of *all* religions—including Christianity—there was a great flowering of biblical study in both the East and the West which continued through the 5th century. To give a few indications of this: St. John Chrysostom (late 4th century) assumes that all of his parishioners in Constantinople, except the very poorest, will own at least a copy of the four Gospels and Acts, and he strongly recommends that they read Scripture at home in the evenings.[18] Even the poor, he says, can hear Scripture read in church. It is characteristic for him to tell his flock:

> I often tell you many days in advance the subject of what I am going to say [preach on], in order that you may take up the book in the intervening days, go over the whole passage, learn both what is said and what is left out, and so make your understanding more ready to learn when you hear what I will say afterwards.
>
> I also always entreat you, and do not cease entreating you, not only to pay attention here to what I say, but also when you are at home, to persevere continually in reading the divine Scriptures. When I have been with each of you in private, I have not stopped giving you the same advice.[19]

He says in another homily, with some typical rhetorical exaggeration, but nevertheless showing how important he believed it was for his parishioners (not just the clergy) to know Scripture: "This is the cause of all evils—not knowing the Scriptures."[20]

In the West, St. Jerome (c. 342—420) translated the Old Testament from Hebrew into Latin, which was the vernacular of that time and place, at the request of the Pope of Rome, Damascus. Damascus wanted a much better translation made so that more Latin-speaking Christians could—and would—read the Bible. (The early translations into Latin were very poorly done.) Jerome also translated the Psalms from the Septuagint Greek, and improved existing

---

18. First Sermon on Lazarus and the Rich Man; *On Wealth and Poverty* (Crestwood, NY: SVS Press, 1984), p. 27.

19. Third Sermon on Lazarus and the Rich Man; *On Wealth and Poverty*, p. 58.

20. Ninth Homily on Colossians (NPNF 1, vol. XIII, p. 301).

translations of, or translated afresh, all of the New Testament. His entire Bible in Latin became known as the "Vulgate," which was widely used in the Western Church until recent times, even though it was not made the "official" Latin version of the Scriptures by the Roman Church until 1546.[21] Jerome also wrote many biblical commentaries, and had serious Bible studies with pious women—a number of whom were later canonized as Saints.

In making the following complaint, Jerome shows just how widespread reading and interpreting Scripture was for those in the Roman Church:

> On the Scriptures, everyone quite indiscriminately undertakes some enterprise on his own account . . . the old gossip, the old fool, the wordy sophist, all of them take it up and tamper with it, teaching others before they learn themselves.[22]

Even in Gaul in the 6th century, far away from the great centers of civilization like Rome and Constantinople, St. Caesarius of Arles urged his parishioners, who would have included farmers and tradesmen, to buy copies of the Bible and read it at home— especially in the long, dark, winter months![23]

Study Helps

During this period, various study helps were produced—from biblical dictionaries to Greek/Latin interlinear Bibles. Tyconius (d. c. 400) wrote the first Christian treatise of biblical hermeneutics, called *Book of Rules*.[24] The Church historian Eusebius wrote a dictionary of all the place names in Palestine which Jerome later translated from the Greek into Latin. And in addition to his translations and commentaries, Jerome created other reference books, including a catalogue of Christian writers up to 393 AD.

---

21. Jerome was first asked to improve the Latin translation of the New Testament. Then he decided to translate the Psalms from the Septuagint—though he decided to translate the other books from the Hebrew.

22. Epistle 53.7; quoted by Simonetti, op. cit., p. 88.

23. One of the rules he drew up for the women's monastery he established was that every nun be taught to read and write (and that the nuns should have the right to choose their own abbess).

24. Since much of Tyconius's exegetical work was correct, it was often used by those in the canonical Church, even though Tyconius was a member of the schismatic group called the Donatists, who believed, for instance, that the efficacy of the sacraments depended on the personal holiness of the priest.

In fact, there was generally in the culture a great interest in history during this time, and Eusebius not only wrote a Church history, but also published a work on the history of ancient Israel. And when he wrote commentaries on the Old Testament books, he developed the historical setting, as did Cyril of Alexandria (d. 444). St. Cyril even said that

> Those who reject the historical meaning in the God-inspired Scriptures as something obsolete are avoiding the ability to apprehend rightly, according to the proper manner, the things written in them. For indeed spiritual contemplation is both good and profitable; and, in enlightening the eye of reason especially well, it reveals the wisest things. But whenever some historical events are presented to us by the Holy Scriptures, then in that instance, a useful search into the historical meaning is appropriate, in order that the God-inspired Scripture be revealed as salvific and beneficial to us in every way.[25]

Thus, in the first five centuries after Christ, we see that all Christians were encouraged to know the Scriptures. By the 4th and 5th centuries, many laypeople, encouraged by the clergy, were reading the Bible in a language they spoke. And far more were quite familiar with it from hearing it read in Church, and hearing long sermons explaining it. Serious study of the literal level of the Bible, at least in educated circles, was also happening. All this went on in spite of—and sometimes in response to—waves of persecution, martyrdom, and the determined efforts of various heretics (such as Arius) to overthrow traditional, apostolic Christianity and the authentic life in Christ which the Scripture safeguards and nurtures.

Part Two: But Why?

But why? What did these Christians of the early centuries understand the purpose of all this reading and study of Scripture to be? Why would St. John of Damascus (d. 749) even say that believers should "revel insatiate" in Scripture?[26] It is not enough to understand that early Christians thought knowing Scripture was important. What is most critical is to understand *why* they thought it was so important.

---

25. Commentary on the Prophet Isaiah 1.4; PG 70.192A-B.

26. St. John of Damascus, Exact Exposition of the Orthodox Faith IV.17 (NPNF, second series, vol. IX, p. 89).

A glimpse of the answer to that important question can be seen in the light of the fuller context for St. John of Damascus's remark:

> Let us draw from the fountain of this garden [the Scriptures] perennial and purest waters springing into life eternal. Here let us luxuriate, let us revel insatiate: for the Scriptures possess inexhaustible grace.[27]

Clearly for St. John, whose words here are characteristic of the entire patristic and Orthodox understanding, the purpose of reading Scripture is inseparable from the ultimate goal of Christian life: eternal life through union with God—*deification,* being changed by grace, being transformed into what we were originally created to be. As we noted St. Ephrem saying so beautifully about God, "He clothed Himself in language [of Scripture] so that He might clothe us in His mode of life." The reason God revealed Himself to the authors of Scripture, the reason God "clothed Himself in our language," was precisely so that He could make us "partakers of the divine nature" (2 Peter 1:4).

The Transformative Power of the Scriptures

The Gospel accounts—and the New Testament as a whole—are full of exhortations about the need for positive change, the need to "bear fruit," to *keep* Jesus' words/commands—to "do the truth" (John 3:21), to live the Gospel life. And we are called to do this, not because these are arbitrary rules like the speed limit, but because this is the only way to achieve the most profound personal transformation—a transformation which will be life-giving for ourselves and others, leading to true health, to "life in abundance," to eternal life in Christ. That's why this level of interpretation has been called "transformative."[28] This transformation always begins with a specific kind of change, often misunderstood today, called *repentance.*

Jesus' preaching often called for repentance. His first word in Matthew's Gospel account is "Repent," and His first words in Mark's account concern the same theme (Matt. 4:17; Mark 1:15). In the Greek of the Fathers, repentance (*metanoia*) "signifies primarily a 'change of mind' or a 'change of the intellect' (*nous*): not only sorrow, contrition or regret, but more positively and fundamentally the conversion or turning of our whole life towards God."[29] According

---

27. Ibid.

28. Again, see Stylianopolos, Ch. 3.

29. *Philokalia,* vol. 1, pp. 363-364.

to St. John of Damascus, "Repentance is the returning from the unnatural into the natural state, from the devil to God, through discipline and effort."[30]

The Gospels tell of the movement from darkness to light, from blindness to sight, from seeking to finding, from captivity to freedom. They tell that this movement, this change, is necessary, and now is possible because the Kingdom of Heaven, God's Reign, is at hand, is drawing near in the Person of Jesus Christ. Christ makes God—and thus His Reign, or Kingdom—present, because He is God Incarnate. Those who have been sitting paralyzed "in darkness . . . in the region and shadow of death" (Isaiah 9:1, 2; Matt. 4:16) are finally free to move, to be in a truly *natural* state, because now the Light is shining in the darkness, showing the way—and the darkness cannot overcome It (cf. John 1:5).

Indeed, Scripture as a whole, both the Old and New Testaments, tell of a journey from slavery to freedom, from exile to home in the Promised Land. They tell of mankind's movement—made possible by the coming of the Light—towards *entering again* into Paradise, the new Paradise of the End Times, also called the Kingdom of Heaven (not that it is simply "near") through Christ's victory over death. As one of the hymns of the Church says, "The fiery sword no longer guards the gate of Eden [or Paradise], for in a strange and glorious way the wood of the cross has quenched its flames."[31] The salvation *economy* (the way God has "organized" fallen reality for our salvation) realized in Jesus Christ makes possible the coming of the Holy Spirit, Who brings deifying grace to believers, making possible this journey, this personal transformation for every believer.[32]

Acquiring this grace of the Holy Spirit which enables us to have life eternal is, thus, the ultimate purpose of *all* Christian disciplines—whether fasting, prayer, worship, reading Scripture, or any others. And this transforming grace provides us at last with the right instrument for "seeing God" (Matt. 5:8), enabling our purified hearts to "behold the beauty of the Lord" (Ps. 27:4).

Elder Aimilianos, the well-known former abbot of Simonopetra Monastery on Mt. Athos, widely recognized as a living Saint, gives a brief account of one example of this grace-filled, life-transforming vision as he describes a powerful experience of St. Basil the Great (as recounted by Basil's brother, St. Gregory of Nyssa):

---

30. Exact Exposition of the Orthodox Faith, Ch. XXX (NPNF, second series, vol. IX, p. 43).

31. This hymn is the kontakion from Matins for the Sunday of the Cross (*Lenten Triodion*, p. 342). The rest of it goes, "The sting of death and the victory of hell are now destroyed, for Thou art come, my Savior, crying to those in hell: 'Return again to Paradise'" (pp. 342-343).

32. This *economy* includes forgiveness of sins, healing, purification, spiritual growth: all aspects of personal transformation, through the uncreated energies of God, or grace.

One night, shortly after midnight . . . there appeared to him an "outpouring of light, and, by means of divine power, the entire dwelling was illuminated by an immaterial light, having no source in anything material." In his small hut, St. Basil was visited by God. Divine lightning flashed forth, the darkness became like day, and Basil himself became like the sun. All was a single light, shining from a place nowhere in the world. Just as Christ entered the upper room, although the doors and windows were shut (John 20:26), so too did He enter into the room of St. Basil the Great. And Basil saw Him with the spiritual eyes of his soul and said: "What is more marvelous, more worthy of love, than the beauty of God?" On the basis of this divine illumination, he wrote the masterpieces which he left behind to illuminate us.

This is more or less how all the Fathers of the Church wrote their books.[33]

Fr. Aimilianos can speak of this with confidence, because he himself had such transforming experiences of grace.[34] And this transforming experience of grace is at the heart of the use of Scripture in the patristic approach, and why knowing Scripture is considered so important. All patristic exegesis flows from and supports this spiritual life, rooted in this kind of experience.

The well-known patristic scholar, Frances Young, rightly observes that "the use to which a work of literature is put surely influences the way it is understood. . . . The Bible's principal function in the patristic period was the generation of [or more accurately, the support of] *a way of life, grounded in the truth about the way things are,* as revealed by God's Word [in the living Tradition]. Exegesis served this end."[35]

Scripture helps us acquire the grace of the Holy Spirit partly because it shows us *how to live based on the truth*—the way things really are—and not on how things may appear on the surface in the fallen world, or according to false world-views and theologies. Archim. Vasileios, another well-known holy man from Mt. Athos, describes such false theologies:

---

33. Abbot Aimilianos, *The Church at Prayer: The Mystical Liturgy of the Heart* (Athens: Indiktos, 2005), p. 130.

34. Naturally, those familiar with the New Testament will be reminded of Christ's appearing to St. Paul on the road to Damascus in unearthly, blinding light; and the Transfiguration of Christ as described in the Synoptic Gospels. And Christ is called "the light of the world" in John 1:4-9 and 8:12.

St. Gregory of Nyssa's Homily on the Sixth Beatitude was already quoted at the end of Chapter 1 explaining more of what this kind of "seeing" means: "possessing," making it possible for human beings truly to know Ultimate Truth. Also, e.g., cf. Isaiah 26:10 LXX).

35. Frances Young, *Biblical Exegesis and the Formation of Christian Culture* (Peabody, MA; Hendrickson Publishers, 1997/2002), p. 215; my emphasis.

I listen to some theories or "theologies" which are like airports with no runway for takeoff. These are the things which restrict man and abuse the aeroplane. The aeroplane has to take off—it is not a push-cart you can use to sell tomatoes from in the market. It has a different destiny. And man too has a different destiny.[36]

Images/Analogies for Scripture

Our life, then, is about acquiring the Holy Spirit, so that we can be trans- formed, and we could say that in these early centuries, Scripture's intended role is understood to be ultimately to provide us with "glasses" permitting us to see more and more clearly the way things truly are—so that we can move forward on our journey, so that we can move forward and eventually "take off."

Archim. Vasileios continues his image from above:

Before the runway ends, it [the airplane] has found a different means of support, and so it doesn't have a crash. Before this life ends, man has to find a different means of support. And by the time death comes, he no longer treads this earth.[37]

We could also say that Scripture is intended to be a light—"Thy word/law is a lamp unto my feet" (Ps. 119:105)—that illumines a way of life which, when we follow it, enables us to see the Beloved Bridegroom, and to know that He is Jesus Christ, the God-Man, Who most perfectly reveals the one true God—and to know that this God is the good God Who loves mankind.

It is clear not only from explicit statements, but also from the images fre- quently used by the Church Fathers to describe Scripture during these early centuries, that personal transformation through grace—growth through tak- ing in nourishment, obtaining "glasses," a light shining in the darkness—how- ever we choose to describe it—is key in the Patristic understanding of the pur- pose of reading Scripture.

The Scriptures are described by the Fathers as being like wells (holding the water of the Holy Spirit, Who transforms our lives); water; living water; suc- culent food; medicines; healing plaster for wounds; tree leaves that heal; yeast (that transforms the whole lump of dough); a weapon; armor; leaves that pro- tect and shield; a beacon light, guiding us safely; and a counselor, keeping us

36. Archimandrite Vasileios, *The Christian in a Changing World* (Montreal: Alexander Press, 1997), p. 50.

37. Ibid., p. 49.

on the right path, protecting us from error, so we can grow in the new life. Scripture is understood, then, to support and encourage movement and positive change: nourishment for growth (and growth is change), movement from sickness to health, while also providing safety and protection for both growth and good health.

These images also strongly imply that part of what it means to say we live in a fallen world is that people are in a weakened state, in poor spiritual health, likely to stray from the good path, to be tempted to leave the path that leads to fullness of health, and that therefore we all *need* the healing, nourishing, guiding, and protecting that the Scriptures provide. These various images also imply that entering into the new life in Christ isn't just a matter of mentally accepting some ideas as true. If we need protection, then it isn't an easy process; it involves struggle, *deep* change, a cross.

Proper Interpretation Depends on the Good Spiritual State of the Interpreter

If we are weak and sick with sin, we need corrective lenses, a light to illumine the darkness we find ourselves in. And if we need to be transformed or purified, that means that fallen humanity unaided and untransformed *cannot* properly see or perceive, hear or understand true reality (see Mark 4:12), especially spiritual realities, as one can notice many times in the Gospel accounts. Certainly we cannot see the Beloved Bridegroom, and, as indicated in Chapter 1, we may even believe Him to be a monster, or not to exist at all.

Hence, spiritual transformation through the grace of the Holy Spirit is necessary for true seeing, true understanding. This is a fundamental principle in the patristic approach, central in the writings of all the Fathers in all times, based on their shared experience: that what one is able to see, to discern—one's ability to interpret—depends directly upon one's spiritual state.

After the most fundamental principle for exegesis and spiritual life discussed already in Chapter 2, that God is a good God Who loves mankind—and that He has most fully and truly revealed Himself in Jesus Christ—this is the next most important principle. It is indicated in the following words of Christ:

> "a tree is known by its fruit. Brood of vipers! How can you, being evil, speak good things? For out of the abundance of the heart the mouth speaks. A good man out of the good treasure of his heart brings forth good things, and an evil man out of the evil treasure brings forth evil things" (Matt. 12:33-35).

We remember that the context for these words is the Pharisees' misinterpretation of a miracle that Jesus works—when He healed a demon-possessed man who was both blind and mute "so that he both spoke and saw" (Matt. 12:22). In response to this amazing event, the Pharisees give an evil interpretation of it—that Jesus works miracles not because He has come from God, but because He is in league with the ruler of the demons! (v. 24). This evil interpretation has come forth from the "evil treasure" of their hearts.

There is no sense here, or elsewhere in the Gospel accounts, that one can be an "objective" observer and interpret Jesus' actions and words accurately from a detached position. Again, how one interprets, one's very ability to interpret, or "see," depends directly upon one's spiritual state.

This also means that many of the key aspects which Scripture is primarily concerned with (including, as in Matthew 12, Who Jesus truly is) can only be fully, properly understood by being in a good spiritual state—by having a pure heart, or at least being repentant and striving for a pure heart. As St. Athanasius says in concluding his classic work *On the Incarnation*,[38]

> For the searching of the Scriptures and *true* knowledge of them, *an honorable life is needed*, and a pure soul, and that virtue which is according to Christ. So that the intellect, guiding its path by it, may be able to attain what it desires, and to comprehend it, in so far as it is accessible to human nature to learn concerning the Word of God. For without a pure mind and a modeling of one's life after the saints, a man could not possibly comprehend the words of the saints. For just as, if a man wished to see the light of the sun, he would wipe and brighten his eyes, purifying himself in some way like what he desires, and then he may see the light of the sun . . . thus he who would comprehend the mind of those who speak of God must begin by washing and cleansing his soul, by his manner of living, and approach the saints themselves by imitating their works. So that, associated with them in the conduct of a similar way of life, he may understand also what has been revealed to them by God. And thenceforth, as being closely knit to them, he may escape the peril of the sinners and their fire at the Day of Judgment, and receive what is laid up for the saints in the kingdom of heaven, which "Eye hath not seen, nor ear heard, neither have entered into the heart of man" (1 Cor. 2:9), whatsoever things are prepared for those who live a virtuous life, and who love the God and Father, in Christ Jesus our Lord, through Whom and with Whom be to the Father Himself, with

---

38. See also, e.g., St. Ignatius Brianchaninov, *The Arena*, the chapter on carnal zeal; St. Symeon the New Theologian, *The Discourses*, Chapter XXIV.

the Son Himself, in the Holy Spirit, honor and might and glory forever and ever. Amen.[39]

This reality—that you must live the Gospel to fully/properly understand it, that you must be like the Saints in order to fully understand their words—has even been called by others "the fundamental rule" of traditional patristic exegesis.[40] This principle has also been called "the desert hermeneutic,"[41] though actually it is emphasized in all times and places by those following the apostolic and patristic Tradition.

This transformative level—living the Gospel—is available to all who are simple, humble lovers of Christ, who strive to live the Gospel, who read it with openness and prayer. Thus, anyone with such faith and life who can read the Scriptures, or can hear them read in Church, or even can have others read them to him or her at home, even those with little or no education, can interpret effectively in this primary way in which the Scriptures were intended to be used. And everyone, including those who are not spiritually advanced, if they are trying to grow spiritually, can understand many important things about God and the spiritual life communicated through Scripture! By living what you do understand, you keep making real progress.

A striking example of a living commentary on Romans 12:15—"Rejoice with those who rejoice"—comes from the life of a 70-year-old Romanian priest named Surioanu while he was held captive in a subterranean Communist prison camp:

> This priest had a son who had died in a Soviet jail. His daughter was sentenced to twenty years. Two of his sons-in-law were with him in jail—one with him in the same cell. His grandchildren had no food, they were forced to eat from the garbage. His whole family was destroyed. He had lost his church. But this man had such a shining face—there was always a beautiful

---

39. Part 57; NPNF 2, vol. IV, p. 67 (my emphasis).

40. St. Justin Popovich, a contemporary Serbian Orthodox Saint and scholar, says "the fundamental rule of Orthodox exegesis" is that you have to live the Gospel in order to fully, properly understand it (see, e.g., his "How to Read the Bible," which can be found at http://www.sv-luka.org/library/howtoread_jp.htm.). And that is why, for those in the patristic Tradition, and for those who follow them, Jesus Christ is the only true 'exegete of God.' Because He is God, He alone fully lives that reality (see John 1:18).

41. Douglas Burton-Christie, "Scripture and the Quest for Holiness in the *Apophthegmata patrum*" (Ph.D. dissertation, Graduate Theological Union, 1988); quoted by Paul Blowers, *Exegesis and Spiritual Pedagogy in Maximus the Confessor: An Investigation of the Quaetiones ad Thalassium* (Notre Dame, Indiana: University of Notre Dame Press, 1991), p. 38.

smile on his lips. He never greeted anyone with "Good morning" or "Good evening," but instead with the words, "Always rejoice."

One day we asked him, "Father, how can you say 'Always rejoice'—you who have passed through such terrible tragedy?"

He said, "Rejoicing is very easy. If we fulfill at least one word from the Bible, it is written, 'Rejoice with all those who rejoice.' Now if one rejoices with all those who rejoice, he always has plenty of motivation for rejoicing. I sit in jail, and I rejoice that so many are free. I don't go to church, but I rejoice with all those who are in church. I can't take Holy Communion, but I rejoice about all those who take. I can't read the Bible or any other holy book, but I rejoice with those who do. I can't see flowers [we never saw a tree or a flower during those years. We were under the earth in a subterranean prison], but I can rejoice with those who see the rainbows and who see the multi-colored butterflies."

In prison, the smell was not very good. But the priest said, "Others have the perfume of flowers around them. And others have picnics and others have their families of children around them. . . . And he who can rejoice with all those who rejoice can always rejoice. I can always be glad." That is why he had such a beautiful expression on his face.[42]

It is very important to recognize the fundamental role of this transformative level of interpretation, because the primary reason Holy Scripture was kept and considered "holy" and so valuable in these early centuries, the primary reason we should read it today, is to acquire this kind of understanding—an understanding/knowledge that is life. After all, St. John the Evangelist explicitly tells us that he wrote his Gospel account so that we might "have life in His name" (John 20:31)—that we might know Christ and live as He has told us and shown us to live in Him, so that our lives will be transformed through our communion with Him.

In Scripture itself, and in the patristic understanding of it, "hearing" and understanding, seeing and perceiving" (see Matt. 13:13-15; Mark 4:12; Isaiah 6:9-10) involve both conceptual understanding, which concerns the exegetical and interpretive levels (defined above), *and* a living out of what is understood—the transformative level, which involves an experience which necessarily precedes real understanding. When this is grasped, one can see why the holiness of the text demands the holiness of the interpreter to make possible a

---

42. "With My Own Eyes: A Lutheran pastor's Firsthand Account of Prison Life," AGAIN Magazine, vol. 23, No. 2 (April-June, 2001), pp. 23-24; this is the account given in an interview with the well-known pastor, Richard Wurmbrand, who wrote *Tortured For Christ*.

full and proper interpretation—or in other words, why the fact that Scripture is inspired means *you* have to be inspired in order to truly understand it.[43]

Hence there is also great emphasis on the necessity to pray in order to understand Scripture. There is a very instructive prayer which the celebrant says before the Gospel is read every time the Divine Liturgy of St. John Chrysostom is served. It begins:

> Illumine our hearts, O Master Who lovest mankind, with the pure light of Thy divine knowledge. Open the eyes of our mind to the understanding of Thy Gospel teachings. Implant also in us the fear of Thy blessed commandments, that trampling down all carnal desires, we may enter upon a spiritual manner of living, both thinking and doing such things as are well-pleasing unto Thee.[44]

At the beginning of this chapter, we indicated that the Fathers understood the importance of the exegetical and interpretive levels of Scripture, but it should be evident by now why they were most interested in the transformative level[45]—and why they were not interested in the first two levels as ends in themselves, but as important because they can lead to the transformative level. Jesus' preaching indicates that He also was most interested in this transformative level, as is the rest of the New Testament.

St. John Cassian (early 5th century) gives a beautiful analogy for this basic approach, as summarized by Robert McNally:

> He who knows the spiritual sense of Holy Scripture becomes, in the fixed humility of his heart, like the ark of the covenant, filled with spiritual understanding, imbued with divine memories, guarded by two cherubim, [who represent] the fullness of the spiritual and historical interpretation of Scripture.[46]

---

43. Once, when I asked Archim. Zacharias (Zachariou) at the monastery of Archim. Sophrony (Sakharov) in England what he thought it meant to say the Scripture is inspired, he immediately replied, "It means *you* must be inspired to understand it properly." This is fundamental to an Orthodox understanding of what it means to say Scripture is inspired.

44. *The Order of the Divine Liturgy According to St. John Chrysostom,* fourth edition (South Canaan, PA: STS Press, 2013), p. 44.

45. See Fr. Stylianopoulos, op. cit., Ch. 3.

46. Robert E. McNally, S.J., *The Bible in the Early Middle Ages* (Atlanta, GA: Scholars Press, 1959/1986), p. 56.

St. John Cassian also reports about some monks asking Abbot Nesteros, one of the Desert Fathers in Egypt, the following problem which they saw with this fundamental principle—that some heretics, and some immoral men, know the Scriptures inside out, and can speak very eloquently about them, so how can you say that they don't know the meaning—while some holy men have only a very elementary faith and don't know the Scripture nearly so well. The abbot says that the heretics and the immoral and those who are not striving for all the virtues can't possibly understand "the very heart of Scripture and the mysteries of its spiritual meanings." They can only know the surface. Don't be confused by eloquence and skill in disputation, for these are worthless if the person's life is not right. Cassian says this is in fact "like a gold ring in a swine's snout"![47]

Because the ultimate purpose of Scripture, and thus its interpretation, is deification through God's grace, the person who can best interpret Scripture in the way that is most important for the believer—the transformative level—is, then, someone who is very knowledgable in terms of this kind of spiritual experience, as confirmed by the Church and her long Tradition. That is why knowledge of spiritual realities is essential for proper Christian exegesis, and ultimately why the Saints, and especially the Fathers who have been confirmed by the Church, are the ultimate authorities, at least for the most important, transformative level of the text.

As the contemporary Saint Silouan (20th century) says from his own experience, "We may study as much as we will, but we shall still not come to know the Lord unless we live according to His commandments, for the Lord is not made known through learning, but by the Holy Spirit. . . . To believe in God is one thing, to know God another. Both in heaven and on earth the Lord is made known only by the Holy Spirit, and not through ordinary learning."[48]

It is the universal experience of countless holy men and women in a wide variety of times, cultures, and places that seeing God and understanding spiritual realities properly involves living the Gospel and experiencing purification and spiritual transformation—making spiritual progress—which that Gospel life and God's grace enables, so that one acquires a likeness to Christ and His Saints. This understanding is reflected in the New Testament itself, e.g., 1 John 3:2—"we know we shall be like Him, for we shall see Him as He is."

---

47. The Conferences of St. John Cassian, First Conference of Abbot Nesteros, ch. XVI (NPNF 2, vol. XI, p. 443).

48. Quoted by Fr. Theodore Stylianopoulos, *Bread of Life: Reading the Bible* (Brookline, MA: Department of Religious Education, Greek Orthodox Archdiocese of North and South America, 1980), p. 37.

Scripture as Witness: Like Water from the Desert Rock

The fact that we are weak, that we need transforming and purifying before we can have "true knowledge," or can both "see and perceive," has other important implications that profoundly affect the exegesis of the Scripture. As St. Gregory of Nyssa says,

> I have heard the divinely inspired Scriptures disclose marvelous things *about* the transcendent nature—yet what are such things compared to the Nature *itself*? For even if I were capable of grasping all that the Scripture says, yet that which is signified is more. . . . So it is with the words said about God in Holy Scripture, which are expounded to us by men inspired by the Holy Spirit. If measured by our understanding, they are indeed exalted above all greatness; yet they do not reach the majesty of truth. . . . what are they compared with the reality?[49]

St. Gregory also says,

> The Prophets, the Evangelists, and the Apostles . . . all of them have become rivers for us, drawing their waters so far as they could from dark, hidden, and invisible treasuries. Even though every one of these is full to overflowing with the vastness and depth of doctrine, yet they are merely *drops* of dew in comparison with actual Truth.[50]

As these passages make very clear, it was understood in the patristic era that human minds, human reason, and human language are all inadequate for understanding God and expressing Ultimate Truth. Therefore Scripture can only be *a witness* to Truth.

The well-known patristic scholar Thomas Torrance uses St. Hilary of Poitiers' writings (4th century) to explain this important fact more fully: "the positive things we can say about God, the analogies made to attempt to describe Him—which have been revealed to us by God—are only 'helpful to man,' not really portraying God in any full way." Even for the language of Scripture, any statement or analogy about God (such as 'God is love') "points out the meaning rather than exhausts it. . . . [Yet] in spite of its inadequacy, . . . *analogy is*

---

49. From *On the Beatitudes*; quoted by Fr. Thomas Hopko, *All the Fulness of God* (Crestwood, NY: St. Vladimir's Seminary Press, 1982), p. 63 (my emphasis).

50. From St. Gregory's *Commentary on the Song of Songs*; quoted by Fr. Hopko, ibid. (emphasis in the original).

necessary because of the weakness of the human understanding."[51] God is incomprehensible—utterly beyond our understanding; and He is so beyond our understanding that there can be no real comparison between God and earthly things.[52] We can only know about God what He Himself reveals to us, in the various ways that He makes this possible.[53]

Because of this inadequacy, it is impossible to argue *from* the analogies, or the language, *to* the divine reality that it indicates. Rather, as Torrance says, we must "look in the direction they point, rather than trying to read the truth off the language itself."[54] This, of course, implies that there actually is a divine reality which we can experience, which language and analogies point to.

We can't chose appropriate analogies for God ourselves, therefore, because choosing a good analogy involves thoroughly understanding the reality first. "We can but make use of the analogies and terms God himself provides [in Scripture] as he condescends to speak to us in our own language, enlightening our understanding by using terms commonly understood, while making them suggest, or hint, or point to, what they are incapable of indicating themselves."[55]

St. Ephrem of Syria (4th century) expresses this fact as follows:

> I considered the Word of the Creator,
> > and likened it
> to the rock that marched
> > with the people of Israel in the wilderness;
> it was not from the reservoir
> > of water contained within it
> that it poured forth for them
> > glorious streams:

---

51. Thomas Torrance, *Divine Meaning: Studies in Patristic Hermeneutics* (Edinburgh: T&T Clark, 1995), p. 406 (my emphasis).

52. Ibid.

53. As said in Chapter 1, the closest we can come to understanding what God is like, or Ultimate Truth, is to know Christ through living communion with Him. After that, it is to look at Christ as depicted in the New Testament—Who, because He is "in the bosom of the Father," because He is one with God, is the One Who can best *exegete* (i.e., interpret or explain) God in the various ways He chooses, including His language, His actions, and His own Person. After that, we look in the Scriptures as a whole to see "the face of God for now," as St. Augustine said (see Robert Wilken, *The Spirit of Early Christian Thought*, p. 50).

54. Ibid., p. 408.

55. Ibid.

there was no water in the rock,
*   yet oceans sprang forth from it.*[56]

As Torrance explains, such analogies are "steps or instruments we have to use, because of our lowliness and infirmity, in order to be directed beyond the reach of our words and their power of expression or description."[57] This means one can only indirectly communicate to others knowledge of God.[58] Any language—even that revealed by God's self-revelation—must and can only *direct* others to the truth, to encourage others to look beyond what we say and throw themselves on the truth which is "its own sufficient witness."[59] In other words, we have to rely "upon the action of God Himself . . . for it is His action alone that spans the chasm between our language and His own Truth, and He alone who creates in us the capacity to partake of God's knowledge of Himself."[60]

As St. Ephrem says in another hymn:

Let us give thanks to God
   who clothed Himself in the names of the body's
   various parts...
It was just the names of such things
   that He put on,
and—although in His true being
   there is no wrath or regret—
yet He put on these names
   because of our weakness. . . .
By means of what belongs to us did He draw
   close to us:
He clothed Himself in language
   so that He might clothe us
   in His mode of life. . . .

---

56. St. Ephrem the Syrian, *Hymns on Paradise*, Hymn V; trans. Sebastian Brock (Crestwood, NY: St. Vladimir's Seminary Press, 1990), p. 102 (my emphasis).

57. Torrance, op. cit., p. 409.

58. Ibid., p. 410.

59. Ibid., p. 411. The Fathers' "poetic" view of language, and their extensive use of poetry, should not be seen as opposed to exact, or factual, scientific language, but is partly the result of recognizing the inadequacy of language to convey ultimate truth, or anything about spiritual life adequately. Understanding language as a witness to truth, rather than as "containing" it, leads to highly valuing poetry.

60. Ibid., p. 412.

the fact that He strips off
> and puts on all sorts of metaphors
tells us that the metaphor
> does not apply to His true Being:
because that Being is hidden,
> He has depicted it by means of what is visible.[61]

St. Maximus the Confessor (7th century) gives another very helpful analogy for Scripture when he says that we can "call the words of holy Scripture the garments of the Logos [at the Transfiguration], and interpret its ideas as His flesh."[62] In other words, the garments alone don't/can't convey a vision of the UNCREATED LIGHT—but the Logos can make any garments shine with that revealing, transfiguring light. Any garments worn by the Logos, Christ, would be transfigured, of course—but they would also be appropriately chosen by Him.

Not only was the realization of the inadequacies of the human mind and of human language regarding ultimate truth foundational for patristic exegesis, but also in that era when hand-copied manuscripts were the only means of reproducing a text, everyone was very aware of the inadequacy of the means of transmission. Even the most carefully copied manuscripts almost always seemed to have some minor differences, and having some scribal errors was accepted as completely normal. Yet the Christians from this era are the ones who not only chose the books that would comprise the New Testament, but they are also the ones who first considered the New Testament Scripture to be *holy*—to be, indeed, "God's perfect word," in the words of St. Irenaeus (2nd century).

It would seem that this is because, even though we are inadequate beings, with inadequate reason and inadequate language which is inadequately transmitted, God can overcome all these inadequacies in order to achieve His primary goal for us: to bring us to His idea of perfection—new life in Him. Scripture—written by people in human language and transmitted inadequately—can still be considered to be *perfect*, because it is exactly in the linguistic form that people in all times and places need for reaching this primary goal of personal sanctification in and through Christ.

All of the above should be kept in mind in order to understand what is meant when various Fathers speak of the "sufficiency" of Scripture "to affirm the fullness of saving truth." St. Athanasius, for example says, "The Sacred and

---

61. *Hymns on Paradise*, quoted in the Introduction by Sebastian Brock, op. cit., pp. 45-46 (my emphasis).

62. *Ambigua* 10; given in Blowers, op. cit., p. 105.

inspired Scriptures are *sufficient* to declare the truth."[63] Yet, as can be seen in part from the long quotation from him above, the Scriptures are not sufficient automatically, or by themselves. Not only must one live a virtuous, holy life, and be enlightened by the Holy Spirit, as he explains, but the very writing of *On the Incarnation* demonstrates the necessity to interpret Scripture according to the correct "rule of faith" and the Tradition of the Church, which he therefore spells out in some detail in his work. The recurrent problem of heretics misinterpreting and misleading the faithful—and in this way causing great spiritual damage—demonstrates the need for the "rule of faith" and an expanded Tradition to clarify it, so that the fullness of life in Christ (our salvation and deification) will be safeguarded. Indeed, as Fr. John Breck suggests, it is not a question of Scripture *and* Tradition, but a question of Scripture *in* Tradition.[64]

Looking to the Things that Are Unseen (cf. 2 Cor. 4:18): Allegorical Interpretation in the Tradition

Reality in the fallen world often has more to it than the "surface level"—more than meets the eye, and fallen humanity often can't see those other levels of reality. That means, with God's help, we often must look beyond, or beneath, the surface to see all these levels, or "true reality." As St. Paul says in the context of patiently, bravely, and even cheerfully enduring afflictions in this life because of our hope for the next, "we look not at [to] the things that are seen, but at [to] the things which are not seen" (2 Cor. 4:18).

This basic understanding and experience of reality sets the foundation for the widespread use of one of the most misunderstood and puzzling aspects of the exegesis of Scripture in these early centuries: the extensive use of allegorical interpretation. St. Basil the Great (4th century) elaborates the fundamental principle:

> You will finally discover that the world was not conceived by chance and without reason, but for a useful end and for the great advantage of all beings, since it is really a school where reasonable souls exercise themselves, the training ground where they learn to know God: *since by the sight of visible and sensible things the mind is led, as by a hand, to the contemplation of invisible things.* "For," as the Apostle says, "the invisible things of

---

63. Cited in Theodore G. Stylianopoulos, *The New Testament: An Orthodox Perspective*, vol. 1 (Brookline, MA: Holy Cross Orthodox Press, 1997), p. 41.

64. See his *Scripture in Tradition: The Bible and Its Interpretation in the Orthodox Church* (Crestwood, NY: SVS Press, 2001).

Him are clearly seen from the creation of the world, being understood by the things that are made" [Rom. 1:20].[65]

This means that because God is invisible, beyond the capacity of our reason to understand, and beyond our language to adequately communicate, and yet He wants not just to communicate with us, but even to share His eternal life with us, the only way that could happen (apart from the Incarnation!) is for Him to provide analogies, images, pointers, and other various indications in human language, and within the grasp of human reason, to witness to, and to indicate enough of, Who He is, to enable us to enter a loving communion with Him.

So in a real sense, all of reality, including physical nature, has an allegorical character. It is not just "itself," since the visible and sensible lead the mind, "as by a hand, to the contemplation of invisible things," as St. Basil says. Through the visible, the surface, the literal level, we can move to the invisible, the spiritual. As used within the Christian Tradition, this kind of allegorical interpretation, or way of seeing things, can rightly be called INCARNATIONAL ALLEGORY, that is, two realities are considered together and seen as analogous, in order to give new insight while both maintain their importance. Applied to Scripture, this means that the spiritual level is seen *through* the literal, while both levels are kept together, and, as said, considered important, in a roughly analogous way to Christ being perfect God and perfect man in the Incarnation.[66]

From the 20th century, St. Nikolai of Zicha and South Canaan quotes St. Maximus the Confessor (7th century) saying,

---

65. Hexameron, Homily 1.6 (NPNF 2, vol. VIII, p. 55; my emphasis). St. Basil also says, "I want creation to penetrate you with so much admiration that everywhere, wherever you may be, the least plant may bring to you the clear remembrance of the Creator. If you see the grass of the fields, think of human nature and remember the comparison of the wise Isaiah, 'All flesh is grass' [Is. 40:6]" (Hexameron, Homily 5.2; NPNF 2, VIII, p. 76). And as we quoted St. Ephrem above, "because that Being is hidden, He has depicted it by means of what is visible."

66. This is in contrast to gnostic allegorical interpretation, which reflects its dualistic worldview by regarding the literal and the visible as essentially containers that have little or no importance once the meaning, or content, has been removed/extracted. The term "incarnational allegory" was coined by Graham Hough, a literary critic, in "The Allegorical Circle," *Critical Quarterly* 3 (1961), pp. 199-209. As Francis Young has said, "The categories usually used to discuss patristic exegesis are inadequate to the task" (*Biblical Exegesis and the Formation of Culture*, p. 35).

To those who have eyes to see, all the invisible (spiritual) world is mysteriously presented in symbols of the visible world; and all the natural world
depends on the supernatural world.

Then he comments,

It is clear from this that whoever reads the natural without knowing the
spiritual content and significance of what he has read, reads death. . . . Also,
whoever considers visible nature as the only reality and not as a riddle in
the mirror of the spirit, does not know more than the child who may recognize letters but is far from understanding written words.[67]

Everything in the fallen world has the potential to lead the mind to God, to
encourage us to move toward that communion of love which alone is true fullness of life. St. Maximus even speaks elsewhere of "traces of God's own majesty
intermingled with sensible things . . . These traces of God's majesty are able to
transport the human mind, which uses them as a vehicle."[68] Thus, it is not just
human imagination or human projections of itself making God after our own
images, but God Himself has set up reality so that people can really know Him,
and know about Him, through creation.

This traditional patristic understanding also reflects another extremely
important attitude, or approach to life, for traditional Christians on a personal
level, which the following story from the life of St. Macarius the Great (4th
century), one of the Desert Fathers, illustrates:

One day he [St. Macarius] went up from Scetis to the mountain of Nitria.
As he approached the place he told his disciple to go on ahead. When
the latter had gone on ahead, he met a priest of the pagans. The brother
shouted after him saying, "Oh, oh, devil, where are you off to?" The priest
turned back and beat him and left him half-dead. Then, picking up his
stick, the priest fled.

   When he had gone a little further, Abba Macarius met him running and
said to him, "Greetings! Greetings! You weary man!" Quite astonished, the
other came up to him and said, "What good do you see in me, that you
greet me in this way?" The old man said to him, "I have seen you wearing

   67. *The Universe As Symbols and Signs: An Essay on Mysticism in the Eastern Church*
(Libertyville, IL: Serbian St. Sava Monastery, 1950), pp. 2-3.

   68. Quaestiones ad Thalassium 51; quoted by Paul M. Blowers, *Exegesis and Spiritual
Pedagogy in Maximus the Confessor: An Investigation of the Quaestiones ad Thalassium*, p. 110.
This language is meant to indicate that real knowledge of God is possible in this way.

yourself out without knowing that you are wearing yourself out in vain." The other said to him, "I have been touched by your greetings and I realize that you are on God's side. But another wicked monk who met me insulted me, and I have given him blows enough for him to die of them."

The old man realized that he was referring to his disciple. Then the priest fell at his feet and said, "I will not let you go till you have made me a monk." When they came to the place where the brother was, they put him on their shoulders and carried him to the church in the mountain. When the people saw the priest with Macarius, they were astonished, and they made him a monk. Through him many pagans became Christians. So Abba Macarius said, "One evil word makes even the good evil, while one good word makes even the evil good."[69]

Here is another, contemporary example:

At school, of course, they used to make fun of the Religious Education teacher. But then that teacher left, and there was to be a replacement. Soon they discovered it was to be a woman! They thought they would really have fun stirring her up. They prepared to receive her with provocative, ironic, and impertinent questions.

The day came and she entered the classroom filled with smirking children who rained down on her the questions they had prepared. She remained unmoved, however, and taught the lesson. The same thing happened the next day, and the next. The teacher calmly continued her work, and the children started to become curious. Our young man began to ask himself: What is going on here? If you shoot at someone and your bullets pass through them and do them no harm, then either they must be a ghost, or they are receiving power from somewhere else. Something is happening here. And indeed, the children's behavior quickly changed. The young man began to see the teacher as the only really genuine human being he had ever met—she became a mother to him, and he was able to open his heart to her. It was she who led him to the Orthodox Church. . . .

She showed her pupils what a saint is. She demonstrated in action how Christ behaved during His Passion.[70]

---

69. Benedicta Ward, trans. *The Sayings of the Desert Fathers: The Alphabetical Collection* (London: Mowbrays, 1975), p. 116.

70. Archim. Vasileios, *The Saint: Archetype of Orthodoxy*, pp. 45-46. For another striking example see the life of Papa-Nicholas Planas, *Papa-Nicholas Planas, 1851-1932: The Simple Shepherd of the Simple Sheep;* especially his encounters with the Communist who hated priests.

These are living demonstrations of what St. Ignatius Brianchaninov (19th century) speaks about in *The Arena*. Although he speaks of monks since he was writing for them, his advice applies to all:

> Holy monks constantly remembered Christ's words: *Truly I tell you, when you did it to one of the least of these My brethren, you did it to Me* [Matt. 25:40]. They did not stop to consider whether their neighbor deserved their respect or not; they paid no attention to his numerous and obvious defects. Their attention was taken up with seeing that they did not somehow fail to realize that our neighbor is the image of God, and that Christ accepts what we do to our neighbor as if it were done to Him.
>
> The proud fallen angel hates this notion and does all in his power to filch it from the Christian. This notion is foreign to the carnal and animal outlook of fallen human nature, and special attention is required to retain it in the memory. It requires considerable spiritual effort, and it requires the cooperation of divine grace for the heart damaged by sin to grasp this notion so as to have it constantly in mind, in our relations with our brethren. But when by the mercy of God we grasp this notion, it becomes a source of the purest love for our neighbor, a love for all equally. Such love has a single cause—the Christ Who is honored and loved in every neighbor.[71]

This fully Christian way of living requires a kind of allegorical approach to life and to people: believing and seeing that there is a deeper, spiritually important meaning beneath what's on the surface, and understanding that everything that happens can be used for our spiritual profit, and that every person has a purpose, that all those we encounter have, or can have, a purpose in our own lives that we can benefit from. "Inquire more deeply into everything, and don't judge things superficially," as St. Porphyrios (20th century) says.[72] Or as St. Symeon the New Theologian (late 10th and early 11th centuries) says, "We need to regard all of the faithful as one and think that each one of them is Christ."[73] Indeed, Christ Himself tells us, "Do not judge according to appearances, but judge with righteous judgment" (John 7:24).

But thinking of everyone as Christ, seeing the image of God in your neighbor who has many obvious faults and who perhaps treats you badly; seeing that difficulties can be, and are intended by God to be, blessings and helps in our spiritual lives; seeing all the evil in the world and realizing that God is actually

---

71. *The Arena* (Jordanville, NY: Holy Trinity Monastery, 1983), pp. 62-63.

72. *Wounded by Love*, p. 183.

73. Quoted by Elder Porphyrios, ibid.

a good God Who loves mankind—all this requires seeing more than just the surface level of things. It requires judging "not according to appearances," for things are not always as they appear on the surface. Indeed, true reality very often is not as it appears on the surface.

Finally, this approach requires seeing things from a *spiritual* perspective. And when we do this, many positive, even astonishing, things are possible—like the pagan priest becoming a Christian monk and bringing many others to Christ. This kind of seeing deeper is a critical part of love, as in 1 Cor. 13:7—"love hopes all things"—which is very positive. It is a fundamental principle in how Christ taught and responded to people. And because this is so fundamental to an authentic, fully Christian mind—such as we see in the Saints—I believe this is the fundamental reason why allegorical interpretation has always been so popular in traditional Christianity: it reflects and reinforces this same basic Christian understanding of and approach to things.

Recognition of the need to "see deeper" than the surface, understanding the inadequacy of language, along with the fact that the more one purifies one's heart and draws closer to God, the deeper one's understanding of Scripture will be—all these aspects are reflected in the other main emphasis in the analogies for Scripture: its endless depths and riches. Hence, to add to the list of images for Scripture that we gave above, Scripture is also compared to a vine with endless fruit; endless wealth; a never-failing spring; a meadow with diverse flowers and copious fruit; abundant fragrance—a paradise of flowers and fruit; a fair garden with varied sounds; a treasure chest with inestimable riches and precious stones; a rock with oceans of water springing from it; and something possessing inexhaustible grace.

Ironically, the very inadequacy of human language and human reason enables Scripture to be more than adequate, because this allows it to have multiple levels, and multiple meanings, endless riches. Generally in the Tradition, this polysemous quality is seen as very positive. St. Augustine, for example, says,

> For what could God have more generously and abundantly provided in the divine writings than that the same words might be understood in various ways, which other no less divine witnesses approve?[74]

This very positive traditional understanding of the polysemous quality of biblical language was rejected, along with much else of the Tradition, by many Christians beginning before, but especially after, the Reformation. By the time

---

74. Augustine, On Christian Doctrine III.38; cited in Stephen L. Wailes, *Medieval Allegories of Jesus' Parables* (Berkeley, CA: University of California Press, 1987), p. 11.

of the late 19th and early 20th centuries, it was standard in most biblical scholarship to say that allegorical interpretation reflects a Platonic world-view that
does not adequately value the material world, or the literal level of Scripture.
However, the fact is that allegorical interpretation can, and has been, used to
reflect a number of very different world-views. And in the case of traditional
Christianity, this accusation is completely wrong—for allegorical interpretation indeed reflects an authentic Christology, the same Christology we see in
the New Testament.

In the Christian Revelation, we are shown *true* reality; surface appearance,
the literal level, is not the whole story. In Jesus of Nazareth, the people of His
time saw only a human being, but in reality He is both God and man. In the
Eucharist, we see bread and wine, but in reality they are not just bread and
wine; for they also communicate to us the Body and Blood of Christ. We see
a fallen world, but that is not the whole picture; for it is also a world which
is being transfigured by the creative love of God. It is a world in which the
Kingdom, our real participation in the divine life, is already present (though
future in its fulfillment), a world in which persons can begin to be freed from
the distortions of sin and the dominion of death. It is a world that is not static,
fixed, isolated, or unconnected to its source and meaning, but a world that is
open, dynamic, loved, and being redeemed in a process with which we can
freely choose to cooperate.

As stated above, this world, by its very nature, is one in which *true* reality
is often not apparent on the surface. It is a world which is influenced by and
called to cooperate with its source and "meaning," namely, God. Thus, it is a
world admirably reflected in, and completely consonant with, much allegory
and allegorical interpretation. Indeed, many uses of allegory are particularly
Christian in the world-view they reflect. They have long been used effectively
not only as a method of interpretation, but also as a means of instruction, contemplation, and prayer.[75]

* * * * *

Although there was always some variety among all the patristic interpreters
in the early centuries in terms of how much they included the more technical,
scholarly aspects of interpreting the literal level of Scripture, and how much
allegorical interpretation they used, on the whole, the methods of interpretation

---

75. Parts of this final section, and a fuller discussion of these issues, appeared already in
my article, "Towards the Restoration of Allegory: Christology, Epistemology, and Narrative
Structure," *St. Vladimir's Theological Quarterly*, Vol. 34, No. 4 (1990); and in my doctoral dissertation, "'How Do You Read?': Theology and Hermeneutics in the Interpretation of New
Testament Parables," The University of Kent, Canterbury, England (1985).

were fairly standard in the entire Christian Tradition, both in the East and in the West, until what is called the Middle Ages in the West (from the 7th to the 14th century).[76]

In light of all of this very positive history in the early centuries in both East and West, a major question would seem almost inevitably to arise: What went wrong?

---

76. See Appendix I for a more comprehensive list of key principles of an Orthodox/patristic approach to interpretation of Scripture.

Do not hide Your face from me; Do not turn Your servant away in anger; You have been my help; Do not leave me or forsake me, O God of my salvation.
—Psalm 27:9

Chapter Four

What Happened?
The Middle Ages in the West

The course of history is in itself a cleansing process . . . Every age is an age which opens up new paths, which offers new potentials . . . for knowledge of the Truth, because it brings new crises.[1]
—Archimandrite Vasileios (20th century)

Part One

WITH such a promising beginning, what went wrong? What happened that led to the Reformation, the Enlightenment, and the problems with exegesis of Scripture today?[2] Today we have not only an extreme manifestation like the Jesus Seminar being taken seriously by some, but even more so, there are many traditional Christians finding their methods of interpretation largely bankrupt, or at least problematic.

---

1. Archim. Vasileios, *Hymn of Entry*, p. 98.

2. The history of anything significant is so involved and complex that it would be almost impossible to follow, even if one could succeed in capturing most of it in writing. Nevertheless, it is extremely helpful and even necessary to make such simplifications in an attempt to understand, as long as one bears in mind the incomplete and provisional nature of what one selects to focus on. The goal here is to simplify things, not in order to misrepresent and condemn, but in order to try to achieve a compassionate, better understanding of the past, especially so that hopefully one can take some positive action in the present—or at least inspire others to do so. The following historical account should be read with this in mind.

People commonly speak of the Middle Ages as if things stayed basically the same throughout that long period of time. That this is far from the case will be seen in the discussion below. It would be impossible to discuss all the many radical changes happening during this roughly 1000-year period in western Europe. Thus, it will be necessary to simplify matters and omit many nuances in all the history that follows in order to keep to a reasonable length. However, it is very instructive to look at some highlights and follow a few themes that are especially helpful for understanding the changes in the attitude toward Scripture and its role in the lives of believers—changes that helped lead to today's many problems.

Some of the key areas affecting how the role of Scripture was understood were education; the relationship, or lack thereof, with the Eastern, Byzantine Churches; and the lack of knowledge of Greek and the early Greek Fathers. There are also broader areas of change that it is helpful to be aware of to get a better sense of what led to the Reformation, as well as what has come after it, even though these areas do not directly touch on biblical studies. In addition, this background helps to clear up some common misconceptions, and therefore should also help with better mutual understanding among Christians within different traditions. For organizational purposes, we will first look at some of the political and cultural historical background, and then in a separate chapter, consider key theological changes during this period.

The Early Medieval Period

One can say that the problems began in 476, when the western half of the Roman Empire fell to the barbarians. As a result, education and scholarly labors went into a severe decline in Western Europe, especially after the fall of Emperor Justinian's reconquests that came shortly after his death in 565. No longer were a significant number of people highly educated, with some having the leisure to pursue studies not directly practical or even essential for defending the Faith. In this context, the more scholarly kinds of study of Scripture were often largely, or even completely, ignored, especially in the early Middle Ages in the West, when secular learning was at its lowest point.

Everything said here about the Middle Ages applies only to the former western part of the Roman Empire. In the eastern part, which did not fall until 1453, education and scholarly pursuits were still flourishing, except during a few periods—the two eras of Iconoclasm in the 8th and 9th centuries, when the iconoclastic rulers discouraged literary activities of all kinds, and the period of the captivity of Constantinople by the knights of the Roman Catholic Church's Fourth Crusade in the 13th century. But even in these periods, things were never nearly as bad in the eastern part of the empire (until after 1453) as in the western.

Overall, biblical interpretation in the eastern, Byzantine world seems to have continued largely as it had in the earlier centuries. Although there had always been a concern to be in harmony with, and to be guided by, the ancients—even in Judaism—perhaps the only noticeable difference in exegesis during this period was more of an explicit emphasis on what the earlier Fathers had said, including in hymnography.[3] We see this interest, for example, in the patristic *catenae*, or chains—commentaries that often give verse by verse exegesis by providing excerpts from various Fathers—as well as in the many references to earlier Fathers given in the writings of later ones.[4]

Many do not realize that in the early Middle Ages, after the barbarian invasions, education was so lacking in the West that it was common for even the nobility to be unable to read—which was a radically different situation from that in the first centuries of Christianity. Learning was kept alive only in the monasteries. There was no point in mass producing copies of Scripture, or encouraging lay people to read Scripture, as had been widely done up into the 6th century, because almost no one outside the monasteries could read anything during this period. This is why the monks focused on painstakingly producing single copies of *illuminated manuscripts*, with beautiful illustrations and calligraphy, commonly associated with this whole era.

Thus, there was no deliberate attempt to suppress the reading of the Scriptures, which had been encouraged in the earlier centuries, or to restrict it to clergy and monastics during this period. These things happened simply as a result of the difficult political, economic, and social conditions which made widespread education impossible. However, this situation did begin to create a division between the clergy and the laity in a way that had not been present before.

Because of such factors, biblical exegesis was at a very low point in the 7th and 8th centuries in the West, with only a few exceptions—like the work of Venerable Bede in the north of England. Apart from these few exceptions, the lack of general education, as well as the lack of knowledge of Greek and the

---

3. Much of the Orthodox hymnography used today was written in the 8th and 9th centuries, though it often includes passages from much earlier works, such as parts of a sermon of St. Gregory the Theologian (4th c.) being used in the service celebrating the Nativity of Christ. The oldest hymn still in use, called "O Gladsome Light" *(Phos Ilarion)* comes from the late 3rd century, and is sung at every Orthodox vespers service.

4. See Christos A. Arabatzis, *Patristic Hermeneutics: 4th-14th Century*, trans. and ed. Fr. George D. Dragos (Columbia, MO: Newrome Press, 2012), throughout.

Greek Fathers, meant that exegesis had become "divorced from the true spirit and method of the patristic tradition."[5]

In spite of all these difficulties, however, there was always a great reverence for Scripture and "the Gospel message." And even in this period of so little education, people still heard Scripture read in church (though by the 7th or in some cases the 8th century, not necessarily in a language they readily understood). People still heard sermons in a language they could understand, although the educational level of the clergy was usually quite low—not at all what it had been before the fall of Rome. The common people also had biblical scenes in stained glass windows in the churches to gaze and meditate upon, though these were more reminders of biblical events, Saints' lives, etc., than real instructional tools for the ignorant.

The extremely poor state of education on the continent slowly began to improve under Charlemagne (late 8th and early 9th centuries), who implemented some serious educational reforms. He wanted "to develop literary education for the preservation and interpretation" of the Scriptures.[6] He made creating good copies of the Bible and the writings of the Fathers a top priority, because the manuscripts available, as he explained, were "'full of an infinite number of errors.'"[7] One reason for the poor state of the copies was that before his reforms, monks (sometimes young boys) often couldn't read what was written in their copies, yet they tried to copy them anyway![8]

Alcuin, whom Charlemagne brought from York, England, in 781, to be his theological advisor, developed a simplified script—known as the Carolingian script—which is much easier to copy, and is the basis of our English letters today. Alcuin made it easier to have good copies not only by simplifying the script in which they were written, but also by insisting on many practical improvements which most people today take completely for granted—such as using capital letters at the beginning of a sentence, putting spaces between words (no more texts written like GODISNOWHERE, as in ancient manuscripts), dividing a text into sentences and paragraphs, and having standard punctuation and uniform

---

5. Robert E. McNally, S.J., *The Bible in the Early Middle Ages* (Westminster, MD: The Newman Press, 1959; Atlanta: Scholars Press, 1986), p. 38.

6. Ibid., p. 20.

7. Ibid., p. 41.

8. Hand-copied manuscripts generally have some errors even if copied very carefully, so it was necessary to compare new copies to ones known to be reliable. In the case of the Scriptures, which were so carefully copied, errors tended to be very minor, such as misspellings, until the Middle Ages in the West—even though the manuscripts had no spaces between words, no punctuation to speak of, no paragraphs, etc.

spelling! He also corrected the grammar in the Latin translations, and in some instances improved the Latin.

This serious effort in the early 800s to create accurate copies of the Scriptures and the writings of the Fathers led to something of a patristic renaissance and a renewed interest in biblical studies, as well as positively impacting liturgical, ascetical, and pastoral areas of life.[9] But because of political, economic, and military disasters in the 900s, this new intellectual life couldn't really flourish for long during that later period.

Another crucial area of change was the relationship between the eastern and western parts of the Roman Empire. Because of the unstable political situation since the fall of Rome in the West, western Europeans were largely isolated from the rest of the Christian world in the East. Charlemagne, with his claim to be the *Holy Roman Emperor*, certainly didn't want to acknowledge that the Byzantine Empire was actually the direct continuation of the Roman Empire in its eastern part. (The later Roman popes, who wanted supreme authority over the Church both in the West and in the East, also were not eager to recognize this fact, or the fact that historically, the other patriarchs were considered as equals, with the pope of Rome being considered as the first among equals.)

Even more importantly, there was little knowledge of the Eastern Fathers, the Eastern Church, or even the Greek language during this period in the West. Scholars estimate that from the 7th to the 11th century, probably only six theologians in the whole of western Europe knew Greek well—and all of these, except Venerable Bede, lived in the mid to late 800s! This meant that during those four or five centuries, only those six scholars could read the New Testament, or the Greek Fathers' commentaries, in the original Greek. And only three of those six used Greek seriously for exegesis—Bede (d. 735), John Duns Scotus (d. 877), and Christian of Stavelot (d. 900).[10] Perhaps partly because of this, Venerable Bede had greater authority in the scholarly world than any of his contemporaries.[11]

Since Britain and Ireland were islands, they were not quite as negatively affected by the barbarian invasions, at least until the end of the 8th century; hence, knowledge of Greek continued longer there—it was even called an "Irish monopoly."[12] Yet even among Irish manuscripts, the evidence shows only

---

9. Ibid., p. 42. Over and over again, periods of increased education have led to renewal in monasticism and in spiritual life generally, and to other positive developments.

10. Ibid., p. 50.

11. Ibid., p. 45.

12. G. W. H. Lampe, *The Cambridge History of the Bible*, vol. 2: *The West from the Fathers to the Reformation* (Cambridge: Cambridge University Press, 1969), p. 130.

a very elementary knowledge of Greek. And apparently some Irish monks even invented "Greek" words![13]

All of this meant that beginning even as early as the 6th century, there was little or no solid influence of Greek theology in the West. This, then, was another contributing factor in the widening gulf between the Latin and Greek parts of Christianity,[14] and a cause of many problems for the Latin West.

This situation also meant that the biblical study that was done tended to be primarily compiling patristic exegesis, especially from the Latin Fathers (and there were fewer great Latin than Greek Fathers), as well as from those parts of the writings of the Greek Fathers which had previously been translated into Latin. However, there was no library in all of Europe that possessed all the available translations of the Greek Fathers (although there were forty authors translated at least in part in various libraries), and the existing translations were often defective—poorly done and/or poorly copied. This was all in addition to the difficulties that are likely to arise in understanding a translation when one does not have access to anyone with knowledge of the original language.

By the 10th century, the Roman Church had grown even more isolated from the Eastern Orthodox Churches, not only because of the already mentioned theological, political, and language barriers, but also because of the Arab incursions in the Mediterranean. The Great Schism in 1054, when the Roman Church broke communion with the Orthodox and vice versa, largely over the issues of papal supremacy and the use of the FILIOQUE clause in the Nicene Creed, deepened and formalized an already existing divide.[15]

---

13. McNally, op. cit., pp. 50-51.

14. By the 5th century Latin came to dominate in the West to such an extent that even such a highly educated person as Augustine did not know Greek well, though other scholars such as Ambrose did. Nevertheless, Augustine and others show great concern to have unity with the Greek-speaking Church; see, for example, his letter to Jerome (Letter 71), in which he urges Jerome to translate the Old Testament from the Septuagint, lest there be "grievous . . . differences . . . between the LATIN CHURCHES and the Greek churches" (excerpt given in Frank Sadowski, ed., *The Church Fathers on the Bible* [New York: Alba House, 1987], pp. 152-153).

15. After the Great Schism, various attempts at reconciliation were made over a long period of time. But after the barbarous sack of Constantinople by the knights of the Fourth Crusade in 1204 and the establishment of a Latin kingdom there that lasted 57 years, as well as the increasingly numerous differences in theology and practice, reconciliation proved impossible. The final breach came in 1484 when a Church council in Constantinople officially renounced the Council of Florence (1439) which had proclaimed reunion. (This reunion had been supported by the Byzantine Emperor and numerous Church hierarchs almost entirely for political reasons—in hopes of military aid against the Turks). This division between the Eastern and

Later during the 11th century, the division was deepened even further by the significant increase of papal insistence that the pope had authority over the whole Church—including over the other patriarchs—claiming that the pope of Rome was no longer the first *among equals*, but simply first. Pope Gregory VII, who had been prominent in the papal administration since 1048 before ruling as pope from 1073 to 1085, was one of the most powerful popes in history. He succeeded in greatly strengthening papal authority over the western churches. He did this partly by supervising such a major reorganization and centralization of the western church that some call this "the first reformation." By the beginning of the 14th century, a shared Latin-speaking culture had been created in western Europe, with the Roman Papacy understood by many in the Latin Church as a "God-given universal monarchy in the world as the vicar (substitute) of Christ on earth."[16]

The distance between the Eastern Church and the Roman Church continued to increase, until a point of no return was reached in the early 13th century when the Latin knights of the Fourth Crusade, with the encouragement of the clergy who were with them, got involved with Byzantine politics, and ended up attacking the Christians of Constantinople, whom they were despising as heretics. Even though the brutal, sacrilegious sack of Constantinople (1204) by the Crusaders was condemned by Pope Innocent III,[17] the damage was done, and the Crusaders went on to establish their own kingdom there that lasted 57 years. During what the *Cambridge History of the Bible* calls "this barbaric episode," many manuscripts were lost, and the work of the scriptoria, which had been producing so many copies of the Scriptures, also ceased.[18]

Even though the Byzantines regained their beloved capital city in 1261, they never fully recovered from this devastating conquest and captivity. At least, after the Byzantines regained control, another period of producing good quality manuscripts began. This lasted up until the fall of Constantinople to the Ottoman Turks in 1453.

Western Churches continues to this day, although the anathemas from the 11th century were officially lifted in 1965.

16. Diarmaid MacCulloch, *The Reformation* (New York: Viking Press, 2003), p. 26.

17. Pope Innocent wrote, e.g., "How . . . will the church of the Greeks return into ecclesiastical union . . . when she has seen in the Latins only an example of perdition ["who made their swords drip with Christian blood"] . . . so that she now, and with reason, detests the Latins more than dogs?" (David B. Hart, *The Story of Christianity* [London: Quercus Books, 2008], p. 147).

18. P. R. Ackroyd and C. F. Evans, eds., *The Cambridge History of the Bible*, vol. 1: *From the Beginnings to Jerome* (Cambridge: Cambridge University Press, 1970), p. 313.

The Mid-Medieval Period

In the period after the Great Schism, there were even more radical changes on many levels than in the early Medieval period. By the mid-11th century, we find significant new growth of prosperity and literacy. There were also political changes occurring from the 11th century onwards which contributed to an increasingly well-educated laity, many of whom were part of the new middle class (which included bankers and skilled craftsmen as well as merchants).

This was the period of the rise of universities and "independent" scholars, who often had quite different goals from those of the early Church Fathers. Most of the earlier theologians were highly educated ascetics or monks who were very advanced spiritually and who were often bishops as well. Thus they combined holiness of life and powerful personal spiritual experience with brilliant minds, the best education of their day,[19] as well as important official teaching roles in the Church.

In contrast, scholars at universities did not need to be ascetics, or even to have personal virtue, or powerful spiritual experience. Nor did they have any kind of official, or formal, teaching roles in the Church, or even at times, any commitment to the Church. No longer did they have as their fundamental purpose salvation, union with God, and the welfare of their flocks. This opened the way for much greater interest in a purely speculative exploration of ideas—more knowledge for knowledge's sake. This was all happening just at the time when reason was being given a much more dominant role in theology at the expense of *noetic* knowledge—a crucial point to which we will return in the next section.

Though there were always exceptions, from at least the 11th century onwards, starting with Anselm, theology increasingly came to be seen as the province of reason *apart* from spiritual experience. There developed in many circles what some have called a split between the head and the heart[20]—a rejection of noetic knowledge as "real" knowledge—by those who imagined that all mystical experience is merely subjective feelings, and therefore not relevant for theology. This led to an even greater overemphasis on reason, and a split between

---

19. See, for example, St. Gregory the Theologian's Panegyric on St. Basil, section 11 (NPNF 2, vol. VII, p. 398): "I take it as admitted by men of sense, that the first of our advantages is education."

20. For example, Andrew Louth, *Discerning the Mystery* (Oxford: Clarendon Press, 1985), pp. 5-6.

spiritual experience and theology—as well as between spiritual experience and biblical studies—that persists for many to this day.[21]

This split between head and heart was part of an increasingly more dualistic understanding in many areas, including the way that the literal and spiritual levels of Scripture are related. In the traditional "allegorical" way of seeing reality, both the literal and spiritual levels are kept together as valuable (this can rightly be termed "incarnational allegory," as stated previously). This equal valuing of both the literal and spiritual levels begins to change already in the 12th century, with a greater emphasis being placed on the literal level.[22]

This emphasis was very much encouraged by Francis of Assisi (1181-1226) and his followers. This was no doubt related to Francis' much greater emphasis on the humanity of Christ, and on His suffering seen apart from His Resurrection, although this emphasis was already a tendency in the Roman Church of his time. This split strongly affected Church art—with Christ no longer being depicted as the Lord of Glory on the cross, but a bloodied, suffering, ordinary-looking man. We can see in this Franciscan approach a loss

---

21. By the 13th century, the era of Aquinas and full-blown Scholasticism, there was great optimism about human reason. This was a period of a strong economy, more political stability, and therefore more literacy. Such times tend to be more optimistic about human reason and fallen humanity.

22. There was a lot of confusion during the early part of this period over what exactly were the literal and spiritual levels of meaning, for the balance in the early centuries had been lost. For example, in contrast to the earlier usage, now the spiritual level—largely allegorical interpretation—was sometimes used to try to "prove" certain points of dogma. For instance, it was said that "the creation of the sun and moon as the greater and lesser lights . . . and the two swords of the apostles signified that secular government was inferior to or dependent upon ecclesiastical" authority! (Lampe, op. cit., pp. 214-215). And it was asserted that these Scripture verses "proved" this was so.

Thomas Aquinas (1225-1274), writing at the height of the Scholastic era, redefined these two levels of interpretation. He declared that "the literal sense was the sacred writer's full original meaning. . . . The spiritual sense was defined as the meaning which God, the chief author of Scripture and of the events it describes, had put into sacred history. . . . The spiritual could be used for edification of the faithful, but not for proof" (ibid., pp. 215-216). By saying that the spiritual level could not be used for proving points of doctrine, he returned to traditional usage.

This definition/clarification gained general acceptance, and happily lessened the use of the spiritual meaning to try to prove political issues, etc., as in the example above. In this context, it also resulted in more focus being placed on the human author's original meaning. Unfortunately, the tendency toward extreme, arbitrary forcing of three or four levels of meaning in passages continued; this was one reason the Reformers turned so much against allegorical interpretation later on.

of balance—partly to counter an overly rationalistic and complex approach in theology—no longer holding together the cross and the Resurrection, the literal and the spiritual. This imbalance will become more extreme with some of his later followers.[23]

Not surprisingly, a strong reaction against this unnatural divide between the head and the heart, and the barren theology it led to, occurred in the form of other, new kinds of affective, or more emotional, mysticism. Much good arose from this, but since it was an unbalanced reaction without roots in the continuous Tradition of the Church, it was unable to heal the split that still exists to this day in many Christian circles, and which is at the root of the problems with contemporary biblical studies.

Some groups of laypeople influenced by this new mysticism, such as "the Friends of God" (inspired by Meister Eckhart and his disciples), joined together regularly to practice contemplative prayer. Others, such as the "Brethren of the Common Life," developed devotional practices, known as "Devotio Moderna," or "Modern Devotion," that greatly impacted biblical studies and the role of Scripture in the lives of believers, since these practices involved deepening one's spiritual life through methodical meditation on the life and Passion of Christ (hence on the Gospel accounts). The Brethren were founded by Gerhard Groote (1340-1384), who was influenced by the mystic John of Ruysbroeck, among others. Groote was a brilliant, highly successful and worldly scholar, who, after undergoing a powerful spiritual change of heart at the age of 34, became a dynamic preacher in the Netherlands. He emphasized acquiring true inner peace through silence and prayerful meditation, simplicity of life, moral purity, and general faithfulness to the Gospel life.

Many of his followers were laypeople working in the world, who lived together in simplicity and celibacy, and who used their combined resources to do good works—giving to the poor, and especially teaching. Groote became a deacon after his spiritual conversion, and was very outspoken against various clerical abuses of the time. While a number of clergy whom he openly criticized for their laxity opposed him, he was protected by his own bishop, and he was able to continue teaching, preaching, and influencing literally thousands.

---

23. He and his followers attempted to imitate the life of Christ in a very literal way, hoping thereby to return to a more authentic and primitive Christianity —even to the point of bearing the stigmata, like the wounds Christ received while on the cross; Francis was the first such case on record. This started a general trend toward seeing the Christian life more in terms of a literal *outward imitation* of the life of Christ rather than emphasizing *participation in* Christ. This new, much greater emphasis on Christ's humanity also caused a greater emphasis on His mother and especially her mother, St. Anne, as well as St. Joseph—as seen in the fact that the first outdoor Christmas scene—the crèche—was designed and carried out by Francis.

He only lived ten years after his conversion, and a good part of that time was spent in prayerful seclusion, yet he and his followers had tremendous influence in much of western Europe. In many ways they laid the foundations for the Reformation, as well as the system of elementary and secondary education that would come to prevail throughout Europe. Eventually his brotherhood, and its monastic counterpart, were approved by Pope Gregory XI.

Thus we see that the Brethren of the Common Life did not react to the overly rationalistic Scholasticism of their day by rejecting education, but quite the opposite: they sought to correct that imbalance by emphasizing deepening one's spiritual life through personal meditation on and study of the Gospel, as well as through doing good works and the other things mentioned above. They had many schools which provided high quality, free general education throughout the Netherlands, and later in Germany. Their schools also emphasized careful study of the Bible, and began using vernacular translations of the Scriptures, one of which was available in the Netherlands shortly after 1360.[24] To provide books for their schools, many members copied manuscripts or later were involved with printing. They also used the linguistic techniques of the Humanists (see below) in their studies.

The Brethren of the Common Life movement was so popular that there was even a monastic counterpart which at one point had 82 priories. Both Erasmus and Luther were educated at their schools (though unfortunately, Luther only briefly); and Thomas à Kempis, who wrote the tremendously popular *Imitation of Christ*, was a monk of that order (he also wrote Groote's life), as was Nicolas of Cusa. Hence in many ways, the attitudes toward Scripture of the Reformers were a continuation of a strong movement within the late medieval Roman Catholic Church that had been growing for about 150 years.

---

24. This translation, done by a learned monk, was commissioned by a wealthy benefactor of his monastery. Some clerics did not approve, while others did. William François, in his review of Mikel Kors' *De Bijbel voor Leken: Studies over Petrus Naghel en de Historiebijbel van 1361*, says: "It is known that the Brethren gathered students and other residents of the town in their houses on Sunday and Feast day afternoons to deliver 'collations' or *admonitiones*, which were often based on the reading of the Scriptures of the day. Even Erasmus, who grew up in a spiritual milieu marked by the *Devotio Moderna*, witnessed that, when he was a boy, the Scriptures were being read in French and 'German translation (*Ep.* 1581). Hence, in the Low Countries, particularly in the northern part, vernacular Bible reading established for itself a legitimate place in the spiritual life of the population and remained above suspicion or imputation of heresy (although hesitation on the part of some part of the clergy remained). . . . it was basically also Naghel's text which was printed in Delft in 1477, gaining the honour of being the ever first Bible printed in the Low Countries" (*The Medieval Review*, 08.11.15; https://scholarworks.iu.edu/dspace/bitstream/handle/2022/4147/08.11.15.html?sequence=1 ; accessed 9-9-2014).

Scripture in the Vernacular

This brings us to the important topic of Scripture in the vernacular. A common misconception today is that Scripture in the vernacular was never encouraged, or even permitted, until the Reformation. Already we've seen that this was far from the case in at least the first six centuries of Christianity. But what about during the Middle Ages?

Translation of the Scriptures into the vernacular language was a central part of the missionary work of the Eastern Church, as seen, for example, in the work of Saints Cyril and Methodius in Moravia in the 9th century. But in western Europe, Latin, which was still the vernacular until about the 7th or 8th century, prevailed as the language of worship and the Scriptures until the late Middle Ages—though this was far from inevitable.

The push toward the dominance of Latin probably began in the early 9th century when Alcuin, in the very influential court of Charlemagne, was emphasizing the Vulgate and the Latin heritage in general.[25] Alcuin also believed that the Bible had been *fully* interpreted by the Fathers, even though the Fathers themselves frequently emphasize the inexhaustible nature of Scripture, and that it is impossible for anyone, or any group, to exhaust its valid meanings.

Alcuin's understanding meant that there was almost no point in reading Scripture itself unless one has studied the Fathers—something that was not a possibility for the laity of the time. So Alcuin, through Charlemagne's court, gave a major push away from encouraging the laity to read the Scriptures in the vernacular—though in his time, very few of the laity could read in any case. By the 12th century, for this and other reasons, all serious scholarly work on Scripture had come to be done in Latin—and even in Italy Latin was no longer the vernacular.[26]

---

25. Alcuin replaced Jerome's translation of the Psalter from the Hebrew with Jerome's Gallican Psalter based on the Greek Septuagint; this became the form of the Vulgate which prevailed. In fact, it was essentially Alcuin's version of the Vulgate that prevailed; yet this version was not officially declared to be of special importance for doctrine, etc., until the Council of Trent in the mid 16th century! Thus, what is basically Jerome's Vulgate—though others worked on it—was not given special status or made the "official" Bible of the Roman Catholic Church until the mid 1500s. Ironically, this was at a time when scholarship was revealing more of the weaknesses of this version of the Scriptures (Lampe, op. cit., p. 108).

26. According to the *Encyclopedia of the Middle Ages*, vol. 2, edited by André Vauchez, Richard Barrie Dobson, and Michael Lapidge (London: Routledge, 2001), the process of change begun in the 5th century culminated in the 8th century with spoken Latin no longer being "identical with itself," but at that point being proto-French, etc. (p. 1506).

The overemphasis on reason, along with the attitudes and changes mentioned above, led biblical scholarship to become "specialized and technical to an unprecedented degree."[27] Many resources such as dictionaries, concordances, etc., became available, but most of these materials were suitable only for the very learned—rather like a lot of what goes on today in certain circles. Roger Bacon (1214-1291), the English Franciscan who wanted to reform theology by returning Scripture study in the original languages to its central place, even said that one *had* to know Greek and Hebrew in order to be able to understand the Bible, and that all theology should be based only on Greek and Hebrew versions of Scripture—not on Latin—so certainly not on a vernacular translation!

Ironically, the rise of the universities also led to increased reluctance to support vernacular translations. This was a "self-imposed censorship" by the intellectual elite, following the same kind of reasoning used by Bacon. By the 14th century, many scholars felt that the knowledge needed to understand Scripture was so complex that only a highly trained person could and should attempt it directly. It was believed that one needed to know Aristotelian philosophy, natural science, and detailed philological and linguistic information, among other things. Since "it took fifteen years of hard study by the keenest minds to become a doctor of theology, . . . the unlearned had plainly no place in this work."[28]

It was also generally believed that it wasn't necessary for the "unlearned" to read the Bible anyway. Good works were all that mattered for them—it was assumed they had faith in Christ.[29] Of course, there were still sermons, confessional practices, wall-paintings, plays, etc., to teach the common people basic Bible stories and central concepts of the faith, knowledge of which was always encouraged when possible.

Nevertheless, at the same time, beginning already in the 11th century, many laypeople *could* read once again, and they were generally not persuaded by the intellectual elite's opinions. There was, therefore, a growing "demand for precise translations of the Bible" for the laity,[30] especially in connection with Groote's *Devotio Moderna*, and the Brethren of the Common Life, in the 14th century. This is one of many examples of the strong contradictory currents at work throughout this long period.

Apart from Alcuin's influence, one might well ask why the process of Scripture translation into the vernacular was so slow in the West. Actually, the

---

27. Lampe, op. cit., p. 380.
28. Ibid., p. 385.
29. Ibid., p. 376.
30. Ibid., p. 431.

history of Scripture in the vernacular is different for each western European country, and the whole topic of translation is far more complex than is generally believed.[31]

First of all, there were serious practical considerations that slowed the translation of Scripture into the various vernacular languages. One consideration was financial: there is documentary evidence that when St. Ceolfrith commissioned three copies of the Vulgate Bible in Northumberland, England, in the 7th century, he requested a land grant to raise 2,000 cattle from whose skins the vellum pages would be made! Obviously, not many could afford such a project. An additional complication was that in most of these countries during this period there were many frequently changing, very distinct dialects (for example, people in the north and south of England could not understand one another). It would be difficult to translate into all those dialects, and the translations would be outdated relatively quickly. This was an especially serious concern when all new copies of the Scriptures were handwritten.

Secondly, recall that the books of the Bible were often bound in small groups, such as only the Psalms being bound in one volume. Sometimes, as was the case in some districts in the Netherlands in the 14th century, for example, the authorities were not really concerned about translations of the Gospel accounts, or the Psalms, into the vernacular, but only the translation of what they considered to be the more difficult books to interpret, such as the historical books of the Old Testament (some of which depicted episodes that included immoral behavior, or practices no longer permitted for Christians, such as polygamy), or the Pauline epistles, as well as an obviously difficult book like the Revelation of John.[32]

---

31. This history is complex for the East as well. While using the vernacular was the early model for the Orthodox, it was not always followed in practice, especially in more recent times, though never with the intent of keeping the laity from understanding either Scripture or the liturgical services. For a variety of reasons, in recent centuries both the Russian and Greek Churches have resisted translating services into the vernacular in their own countries, though Russian Orthodox missionaries to Alaska in the 19th century did not hesitate to translate the Bible and the liturgical services into the native tongues. A problem with using the vernacular has been a greater temptation to nationalism. The positive side of only using Latin was the greater ease in producing a trans-national culture. Again, this is a complex subject and much more could be said, but the main point here is to show that many vernacular translations were done and laity were encouraged to read them well before the Reformation.

32. William François, in his review of Mikel Kors' *De Bijbel voor Leken: Studies over Petrus Naghel en de Historiebijbel van 1361,* also writes, concerning the right of the members of the Brethren to read the Scriptures in the vernacular, "In the second part of *De libris teutonicalibus,* . . . Zerbolt seems to restrict this right to the reading of the Gospels and the Acts of the

Later on, occasionally there were even political motivations for not using the vernacular. For example, concerning the Moravian church, German-speaking barons, along with the pope, opposed using the vernacular because that was associated with the Orthodox Church. They felt that by insisting on Latin, they would keep the Moravians closer to themselves, and separate them from the Orthodox. It is ironic that the Church which itself used a translation of the Bible did not encourage new translations, while the Church of the original language did![33]

Below are a few of the most relevant highlights for specific countries.

England

In England as early as the 9th century there were some vernacular translations of parts of the Scriptures. Around 893 King Aelfred instituted a program of education in the vernacular for all free men, and if one were called to the priesthood, he would go on to learn Latin. This certainly shows that King Aelfred had an ideal of not just the clergy, but also all laymen, being educated and reading Scripture. And as has often been the case, this emphasis on learning led to a monastic revival, which in turn led to a spiritual revival.

By the 10th century in England, "the vernacular was reaching out to grasp at the sacred text. Kings and bishops and men of state cared for vernacular

---

Apostles, adding the Psalms in the second appendix of his work. It is thus clear from the censuring part that Zerbolt himself was quite reserved when it came to reading more 'obscure' books, such as Paul's Epistles, the Books of the Prophets and the Apocalypse. He even appears to have doubts about the reading of the historical books of the Old Testament, because the writings in question, when taken in their literal meaning, contain apparently improper morals and practices. In the first appendix to his work, in contrast, Zerbolt argues that the ban against reading certain books of the Bible could be dispensed with for people who live a continuously spiritual life and can achieve a 'spiritalis scientia' through a profound reading of and meditation on Scripture. . . . In 1401 Frederick of Blankenheim, the Bishop of Utrecht, approved the way of life of the Brethren and Sisters of the Common Life and thus the reading of the Bible in the vernacular. In addition, and perhaps more importantly, vernacular Bible reading did not remain confined to the members of these devout communities" (*The Medieval Review*, 08.11.15; https://scholarworks.iu.edu/dspace/bitstream/handle/2022/4147/08.11.15.html?sequence=1 ; accessed 9-9-14).

33. Though, of course, Jesus primarily spoke Aramaic. Some have observed how providential it is that we do not have the exact words of Jesus in the language in which He spoke, for if we did, most likely there would not have ever been any translations. But this way, since all versions of His words are translations, we are free to translate into every language!

writings."[34] There was a translation of the four Gospels into the West Saxon dialect by this time, which was used until the 13th century. But the greatest blow to the vernacular Bible in Britain was, in fact, the Norman conquest in 1066. The Norman invaders and their descendants were generally of the upper classes, who were more literate, and more proud of their Latin heritage, than their English neighbors were. They had no use for any English vernacular culture. As a result, nearly all learning in English was lost by the 12th century.

Germany

German Psalters existed as early as the 9th century, but the rest of Scripture was not translated for the surprising reason that the Germans of that time thought their vernacular language was only suitable for poetry! In the 11th and 12th centuries paraphrases of parts of the Bible in the form of poetry were made in the vernacular. The entire Bible may finally have been translated by around the year 1300, for we know that the first printed Bible in German, published in 1466, was based on a version at least 150 years old—long before the Protestant Reformation broke out in 1517. Indeed, between 1466 and 1522 there were twenty-two editions of the Bible in High or Low German, and ninety editions of the Gospels in one of the vernacular German languages.

Martin Luther is often thought of as the one who first translated the Bible into German. However, what he actually did was to produce an extremely popular and influential new translation of the Bible into High German directly from the Greek and Hebrew texts, rather than from the Latin Vulgate version. Greek and Hebrew had only begun to be taught again in Western Europe at the very end of the 14th century, so very few people in Germany before Luther's time even had the possibility of making such a translation. Luther learned these biblical languages when he studied at a Brethren of the Common Life school. His goal in making his translation was to make sure the language of the Bible would be comprehensible to people of all levels of education. Clearly, he was very gifted as a translator, and his translation is said to have impacted the German language much like the King James Version of the Bible did the English language. However, it was definitely based on earlier vernacular German versions.

---

34. Lampe, op. cit., p. 377.

France

In France, the royal house encouraged translation of the Bible into French. This was first accomplished by 1280. At this time, usually only the wealthy could afford copies of these Bibles, aside from those used in the monasteries. The Latin Bible, which would sell many more copies, was, however, mass-produced. As usual, there were more Psalters and New Testaments available in French than complete Bibles, but "Scriptural knowledge was never censored, merely rationed by the purse."[35]

Various Others

In contrast to what is often believed, at least before the Reformation, there was never any "absolute prohibition of the translation of the Scriptures into the vernacular, nor [was a prohibition] of the use of such translations by clergy or laity . . . ever issued by any council of the Church or pope."[36] Some papal *letters* condemned vernacular translations, but these were directed against translations made by heretics such as the Waldensians, who were against the Church as an institution; they were not general, or formal, prohibitions. One such letter in 1375 forbade Bibles in the German language, but as indicated above it had little, if any, effect, as is evident from the fact that this was the period when the Brethren of the Common Life and other such movements, which promoted study of the Bible in the vernacular by the laity, were flourishing with the support of local bishops and many members of the clergy. Elsewhere, printed vernacular editions were published in Italian in 1471, in Dutch in 1477, and in Spanish in 1478.[37]

Banning and Spreading the Vernacular

It was not until the 14th century that England became the first *country* officially to ban all versions of the Bible in the vernacular. This happened because John Wycliffe, who had made a new translation, was not simply translating the Bible, but was also attempting to use the vernacular Bible to undermine the authority of the Roman Church. He claimed that the true Church is invisible (comprised of all believers and known only to God), and not the visible Roman Catholic

---

35. Ibid., p. 451.
36. Ibid., p. 391.
37. Diarmaid MacCulloch, *The Reformation: A History* (New York: Viking, 2003), p. 71.

Church. He also declared that everyone should read and interpret Scripture for himself, and that the Scriptures should be the ultimate authority in spiritual affairs, rather than the hierarchy of the Roman Church. However, owning earlier copies of the Bible in the vernacular was *not* banned, and often Bibles were simply given an earlier date so they would not be seized. In general, this ban was not strictly enforced.

The ban on the vernacular by England did not start a trend, however. The vernacular translation in Spanish was not banned by the Inquisition in Spain until 1513 (partly for fear of Christianized Jews reverting back to Judaism because of it). And the vernacular was not banned in Italy—where the pope lived—until 1559, so this was clearly done *in reaction to* the Reformation; it was not *a cause of* the Reformation.[38]

Technological changes also greatly impacted the spread of Scripture in the vernacular in this era—especially the printing press. Gutenberg finished printing his first copy of the Bible in 1455; hence that's the date given for the invention of printing. Astoundingly, already by 1500 about six million copies of various books had been published in Europe. One scholar has written, "Without the printing press it is impossible to conceive that the Reformation would ever have been more than a monkish quarrel, or that the Scientific Revolution, which was a cooperative effort of an international community, would have occurred at all. In short, the development of printing amounted to a communications revolution of the order of the invention of writing . . . it transformed the conditions of life."[39]

As more and more books were printed, more and more people wanted to read, more and more people learned to read, and more people valued book learning for profit and pleasure. This also led to more people adopting a more inward-looking, personalized style of devotion, such as the *Devotio Moderna*, which included Scripture reading at home. Such readers were urbane, and generally sophisticated—such as merchants, gentry, lawyers—who would not be content with the simple faith and customs of the rural people. They were becoming a large group—and "a ready audience for the Protestant message."[40]

----

38. See *Church, Censorship and Culture in Early Modern Italy*, edited by Gigliola Fragnito, translated by Adrian Belton (Cambridge: Cambridge University Press, 2001), p. 115.

39. Donald Weinstein, "Renaissance," in *Encylopedia Britannica*, 15th edition, Macropedia, vol. 15, p. 670.

40. MacCulloch, op. cit., p. 73.

The Later Middle Ages: The Humanists

Another powerful multinational movement, directly linked to the *Devotio Moderna* and greatly aided by the invention of the printing press, was Humanism (so-called because of its focus on the liberal arts—grammar, poetry, rhetoric, moral philosophy, and history, as well as usually music and mathematics). The technical aspects of the Humanists' work were foundational for much that has been good in biblical studies during their time and continuing even today; the work of Erasmus is particularly instructive.

The Humanists began by "rediscovering" the ancient classics—which were, of course, actually medieval copies preserved by educated monks. There had been two previous revivals of interest in classical antiquity in the Middle Ages. The real difference at this time was that so many more laypeople were educated and interested in literary culture; thus many more people were affected. Nobles and commoners who hoped for careers in the government or diplomacy—a new field begun by the popes (sending what were essentially spies to foreign nations)—sought the linguistic and rhetorical skills that Humanism could provide.

It was the Humanists, beginning with Petrarch (1304-1374)—often called the Father of Humanism[41]—who emphasized the importance of learning the classical languages—not just Latin, but also Greek and Hebrew. In 1397 Greek began to be seriously studied again in the West when a Greek scholar was invited by Humanists to teach in Florence.

In addition to insisting on the crucial importance of *learning the original languages*, the Humanists also insisted on *reading the original works* of the classical authors. This resulted in a greatly increased demand for copies of their works, which was eventually met by the printing press. It also resulted in the development of a high level of classical scholarship involving "searching out and authenticating ancient authors and works," as well as

> editing—comparing variant manuscripts of a work, correcting faulty or doubtful passages, and commenting in notes or separate treatises on the style, meaning, and context of an author's thought. Obviously, this demanded not only superb mastery of the languages involved and a

---

41. Petrarch was taught Greek by Barlaam of Calabria, the opponent of St. Gregory Palamas. Barlaam's position that it is not possible to truly, directly know God was rejected by the Orthodox Church, which supported the traditional understanding of Palamas that while we cannot know God in His essence, we can truly know Him through real, direct participation in His uncreated energies—often experienced as uncreated light. Imagine if Petrarch's teacher had held the traditional view!

command of classical literature, but also a knowledge of the culture that formed the ancient author's mind and influenced his writing. Consequently, the Humanists created a vast scholarly literature devoted to these matters and instructive in the critical techniques of classical philology, the study of ancient texts.[42]

Once the languages and other technical elements were mastered, it was held that one should cultivate eloquence, which was actually intended to be "the union of elegance and power [to persuade] together with virtue."[43] The purpose of all this study was to excel in persuading men to live virtuously—which was understood to be synonymous with living the good life.[44]

By the 16th century, in part because of the printing press and the work of the Brethren of the Common Life schools, classical languages, including Greek and even Hebrew, were being learned by a growing number of people—not just a few scholars. Also, the printing press meant that lexicographical and grammatical handbooks were available as never before, and for the first time it was possible to try to determine a "normative" biblical text by comparing different manuscripts and versions of the Bible. Not only was this possible, but the fact that now many copies guaranteed to be the same could be printed greatly increased the need to determine a normative version.

All these practices of the Humanists directly impacted biblical studies when Humanists like Erasmus began to apply the same scholarly approach to Scripture. As part of his effort to produce a better Latin translation of the Bible, Erasmus also produced the first printed critical edition of the New Testament in the original Greek. This was published in 1516.[45] It was Erasmus's Greek text

------

42. Weinstein, op. cit., p. 664.

43. Ibid.

44. This goal could be in harmony with the patristic approach, or it could become a merely human substitute for the truly Christian ultimate goal of sanctification.

45. In the whole period before the printing press, people generally had a much freer attitude toward translations and versions of Scripture, in the sense of not being concerned to use only one "critical edition"—which is produced by considering the various best manuscripts of a text for which there is not an "original" and trying to determine which variations are most likely the original. Usually this would include the "critical apparatus" indicating which manuscripts, and in the case of Scripture, which early Church Fathers, have which variations—almost all of which are minor in the case of Scripture, and do not affect any important Christian teaching. Before the printing press, it was not really feasible to attempt this.

Most missionaries and even scholars were primarily concerned with the "SKOPOS" of Scripture—with teaching people the Gospel life and the basics needed for coming to know and live in Christ. The Psalter and the Gospel accounts, being the most important books, were what

that became the version used by Martin Luther, the King James translators, and others.[46]

Erasmus also worked to put into print reliable editions of the works of the early Church Fathers by comparing different manuscripts and working to try to determine the most authentic versions—that is, to produce a critical edition. He had a whole team of scholars helping with most of this work. Listed in chronological order, these writings included those of St. Jerome (in nine volumes, 1516), St. Cyprian of Carthage (1520), St. Hilary of Poitiers (1523), St. John Chrysostom (various times), St. Irenaeus of Lyons (1526), St. Ambrose of Milan (1527), St. Basil the Great (1532), and even Origen. A strong motivation for all this work was his belief in the importance of looking for a patristic consensus, rather than using primarily only one figure, such as Augustine, as the ultimate authority.[47]

Erasmus had a great love for the Greek Fathers, especially St. Gregory the Theologian, and, according to the well-known French scholar Louis Bouyer, his theology was much closer to that of the Greek Fathers than that of other medieval writers. And like the Greek Fathers, Erasmus's scholarly interest in Scripture was not just academic; he believed that theology required the inspiration of the Holy Spirit to be done properly, and its ultimate goal must be to

---

most people were really familiar with. People were happy to "mix and match" different translations and manuscript traditions to suit their practical purposes. This was further encouraged by the fact, as mentioned above, that single-volume Bibles were rare even still in the 7th century. This situation continued into the late Middle Ages, and to a lesser extent even after the printing press was invented.

A great scholar like St. Gregory the Great (late 6th century) even "stated explicitly that he would use Jerome's text as his basis, but would not hesitate to adopt the Old Latin whenever it lent itself better to his own emphasis on moral and ascetic interpretation" (Lampe, op. cit., p. 109; see pp. 109-131 for an extended discussion of these topics).

46. This caused some problems later, because Erasmus's text was based on only six manuscripts (his second edition added a seventh), yet it quickly became the standard version (the "received" text); therefore the many scholars who carefully pointed out the hundreds of differences with a large number of manuscripts were hotly criticized by many churchmen, who felt that the very authority of the Bible was thereby being seriously undermined (see David Laird Dungan, *A History of the Synoptic Problem* [New York: Doubleday, 1999], especially pp. 192-193, and chs. 14, 15, and 19. He mentions that John Mill found "nearly *thirty thousand* words and phrases differing from Erasmus' text"). It should be understood that all these differences are minor in terms of doctrine, or anything that might affect one's understanding of the Christian life.

47. Bouyer, "Erasmus in Relation to the Medieval Biblical Tradition," *Cambridge History of the Bible*, vol. 2, edited by G. W. H. Lampe, p. 493.

help Christians become Saints. He really hoped for "the revival of traditional patristic *culture*, made new again, so that Scripture too should be rediscovered, and be at the heart of a reform of the Church entirely from within."[48] His scholarly work was closely linked to the devotional practices that he was steeped in from being educated in the *Devotio moderna* movement, with its emphasis on deepening spiritual life in part through *personal meditation on the Gospel*. Thus, Erasmus would have understood reading the Gospel to be something of value for all believers, even those without all the additional knowledge provided by Humanist studies, valuable as that was.

The spiritual level of the text was included as part of a careful study of Scripture itself. Erasmus rightly insisted that how biblical authors use other biblical authors presupposes the "possibility of layers of different meanings for a single text, within the whole compass of revelation." Still, he also advocated seeking interpretations that *suggest themselves* when one looks at Scripture as a whole,[49] in an effort to get away from the forced allegorical interpretations common in the Latin Church after the early Medieval period.

Combining the devotional dimension with a Humanist interest in textual criticism and philology—and hence, a concern with both the spiritual and literal levels of interpretation—Erasmus developed what Bouyer calls his "balanced view of exegesis": "Philological study of the text prepares the way for a meditation drawing together all that he found most sure in the spiritual exegesis of the Fathers."[50]

The overall program espoused by Erasmus was "to reform the Church from within by a renewal of biblical theology, based on philological study of the New Testament text, and supported by a knowledge of patristics, itself renewed by the same methods. The final object of it all was to nourish . . . chiefly moral and spiritual reform . . . For him, rigorously scientific biblical study must sustain an effort to renew the interior life, and the interior life must itself be at once the agent and the beneficiary of a renewal of the whole of Christian society."[51]

The Humanists were strongly opposed to much in late medieval Roman Catholicism which they rightly saw as running counter to the Gospel. Erasmus was one of many Humanists who wanted to reform Christianity from within—especially through education, emphasizing the Gospel which they understood as focused on love, peace, and simplicity, and to have these as the heart of Christian piety. They emphasized morality over dogma, and encouraged religious tolerance. They had no idea of leaving the Roman Church. How

---

48. Ibid., pp. 504-505 (my emphasis).

49. Ibid., p. 504.

50. Ibid., p. 497.

51. Ibid.

different—and how peaceful—the history of western Europe would have been had most western Christians of this era followed this more gradual, non-revolutionary path of reform!

Further Changes

The time of the Humanists is also the period known as the Renaissance (the 14th to 16th centuries, although many of the ideas and tendencies of this era began earlier). This was generally a time of skepticism, with widespread anti-scholastic, anti-Aristotelian sentiments—hence, against the ancients and tradition as it was understood generally, with a growing emphasis on the importance of the individual. Not only was this a time of many major changes, but also a number of very significant things happened to shake people's confidence specifically in the Roman Catholic Church and her tradition (which by this time had diverged significantly from that of the early Church and the ongoing Orthodox Tradition). As would be expected, all of this directly affected biblical studies as well.

During these centuries there were hosts of problems with corruption and chaos in the hierarchy of the Roman Church—including various notorious popes. In many places, the Roman Catholic Church had acquired tremendous wealth, and quite a few nobles entered clerical office primarily to acquire power and a share of that wealth. The pope of Rome had his own lands and armies, and was engaging military power struggles in Italy and beyond.

There had been disputes about papal authority beginning from the 9th century onwards, and from the 11th century, there were serious attempts to restrict papal supremacy—which was far from universally accepted even in the West during this period. In the late 14th century and into the 15th century, there were several competing popes—all claiming supreme authority—which was at best a very confusing situation for the laity, and which undermined Papal claims. And one of the Humanists, Lorenzo Valla, proved that the "Donation of Constantine," a key document for supporting papal supremacy in the Middle Ages, was actually an 8th century forgery. Another blow was the failure of the Crusades to permanently retain control of the Holy Land.

Much of the medieval understanding of the physical world was based on Aristotle, Ptolemy, and the medicine of Galen, and this was increasingly challenged and even overthrown by discoveries of previously unknown ancient sources that critiqued Aristotle, et al., as well as by new scientific discoveries. One striking example was the complete overthrow of the ancient certainty that there were only three major land masses on the face of the earth when a fourth—the New World—was discovered. By 1521, Magellan's ship had sailed around the globe.

All these and many other discoveries in various fields tended to shake people's confidence generally in the ancients and tradition, as well as specifically in the Church in the West. This was especially the case because the Roman Church had put Aristotle, Ptolemy, and other ancient pagans almost on the same level as Scripture and the Fathers. During the Inquisition of the late Middle Ages, for example, one could be condemned for heresy for disagreeing with Aristotle! (That's partly what happened to Lorenzo Valla, and also Galileo.)

In addition to these serious problems in the Church, in the mid to late 14th century, there was also the Black Death, which killed one third of the population of western Europe, and a little ice age that was disastrous for the agrarian economy which was the foundation of feudalism.

All this set the stage for several reactions, one of which was the late medieval nominalists' emphasis on God's omnipotence as His defining characteristic. No longer could one say that God is good, they claimed, or that He loves mankind—only that He is omnipotent; and some even claimed this meant that He *could not* respond to people's prayers, because that would limit His omnipotence!

In the light of so many problems, and such confusion, it is not surprising to find a growing distrust of the hierarchy and the Church among a growing number of people. Throughout these centuries there was a lot of criticism of the problems in the Church and attempts to reform it (for example, the Conciliar Movement, climaxing at the Council of Constance in 1414 to 1418, which directly and powerfully countered the idea of papal supremacy), though none were ultimately very successful. It is generally agreed that the papacy, and perhaps the Latin Church as a whole, was at its lowest point around the time of Luther, and it may well have been at its worst in his region of Germany in particular.

What is also seldom realized is the significant influence of Muslim activity during this period. A considerable impact was made by Muslim commentators and translators from the 13th century onwards who made available scores of ancient Greek works which had been lost to the West, especially some of the works of Aristotle. Almost all the theologians of the western Church were either influenced by these works, trying to come to terms with them (like Aquinas and the Dominicans), or reacting against them (as did Franciscans like William of Ockham). The Crusaders' efforts to reclaim the Holy Land from the Muslims had failed completely by 1293, and aggressive Islamic policies, especially in the late 15th and 16th centuries, shook western leaders. In 1453, the fall of Constantinople to the Ottoman Turks, seriously frightened leaders in the West. And in Spain, which the Muslim Moors had invaded beginning back in 711, the so-called *Reconquista* was not able to drive the Muslims back across the Strait of Gibraltar until 1492.

Fear of the Ottoman Turks only deepened in the next century. One scholar of the period can even say that in 1500 Europe's biggest fear was that it would "disappear."[52] In 1526 the King of Hungary and Bohemia (brother-in-law to the Holy Roman Emperor) was killed, along with many nobles, clergy, and 16,000 soldiers, as Ottoman Turks occupied and wrecked his capital city. In 1529 they besieged Vienna, which triggered a great fear that they would overrun all of Europe. This ended up helping Luther and his cause, for it distracted Charles V, the Holy Roman Emperor, who otherwise could easily have crushed Luther's movement early on.

Also adding to the fear, it is estimated that Islamic raiders enslaved around one million western European Christians between 1530 and 1640. Interestingly, this was about the same number of West Africans who would be taken as slaves by Europeans across the Atlantic. So, as one historian says,

> The fear that this Islamic aggression engendered in Europe was an essential background to the Reformation, convincing many on both sides that God's anger was poised to strike down the Christian world, and so making it all the more essential to please God by affirming the right form of Christian belief against other Christians.[53]

Having considered at least briefly the relevant political and cultural historical background, we can now move on in the next chapter to the most significant theological changes.

---

52. MacCullough, op. cit., p. 55.

53. Ibid.

Teach me Your way, O Lord, and lead me in a
smooth path, because of my enemies.
—Psalm 27:11

Chapter Five

Radical Changes and New Divisions: the Late Middle Ages and the Reformation

The whole of history, everything that happens—new theories, revo-
lutions, movements, prophecies, and people killing one another—all
this goes to make up an extended Holy Week, which is a judgement
on the world and reveals the degree of our own maturity. The danger-
ous thing continues to be His great respect for man, and the weight
of responsibility that man shoulders with the freedom given him.[1]
—Archimandrite Vasileios
(20th century)

Summary of Key Theological Points for This History

D URING the middle and late Middle Ages, there were many theological changes which contributed significantly to the political and cultural changes described in the previous chapter. Since the period dealt with here is so long, only a sort of "cross-section" study can be made, focusing on just a few keys areas which are most significant for biblical studies. This also means that significant simplification will be necessary. However, in this way the key points will stand out more clearly.

---

1. Archim. Vasileios, *Hymn of Dismissal* (Montreal: Alexander Press, 2012), p. 115.

But first, it will be helpful to discuss briefly the single most important theological difference between the Latin West and Greek East. This single difference is, I believe, at the root of all the important theological changes that occur during this period in the Latin Church—changes which led to the Reformation and what followed, changes which are the theological underpinnings of the problems in biblical studies today. This key difference can be phrased as a question: is salvation extrinsic and juridical, or is it intrinsic, involving an ontological change in our human nature? The answer to this all-important question depends on one's Christology.

Some may imagine that Christology is largely an academic issue relevant only for specialists in theology, even though in the Gospel accounts themselves, one can see that the key question is: Who is Jesus Christ? There have been a number of significant variations in the ways that people have answered this question throughout history, as will be indicated below. From this history one can clearly see that the proper understanding of Who Jesus is, one's Christology, is essential not only for all the rest of one's theology to be true and life-giving, but also for all that springs from one's theology to be likewise true and life-giving. Even though individuals within a given theological tradition may not understand the fine points of these differences, their spiritual lives will be very much impacted by them; a proper Christological foundation, therefore, is essential.

The best brief discussion of this topic, I believe, is found in an article on the Atonement by the highly respected patristic scholar, Thomas Torrance, who, since he was a Presbyterian, can hardly be accused of "denominational bias" in his critique of his own western tradition. Torrance states that

> by and large in Western Theology, Roman and Protestant alike, . . . [one finds] a dualist way of understanding and interpreting the message of the Gospel according to which, as it became very clear to the Nicene Fathers in their struggle with Arianism, the relation between the incarnate Son and the Father was merely one of *an external and moral kind contingent upon the divine will, and not a relation internal to the being and life of the Godhead . . . so that His atoning sacrifice was expounded merely in moral and juridical terms.*[2]

As Torrance explains:

---

2. Thomas Torrance, "The Atonement, the Singularity of Christ and the Finality of the Cross: The Atonement and the Moral Order," in *Universalism and the Doctrine of Hell: Papers Presented at the Fourth Edinburgh Conference in Christian Dogmatics*, Nigel Cameron, ed. (UK: Paternoster Press, 1992), pp. 249-250 (my emphasis throughout).

Latin theology took the view that in becoming flesh the Son of God took, *not our actual nature*, but a human nature untouched by sin and guilt, which gave rise . . . *to a doctrine of atoning transaction expounded in terms of moral and juridical external relations between Christ and ourselves.*[3]

Hence, as he says,

The crucial question was whether Christ took upon himself our fallen humanity with its alienated mind, and thereby laid hold of the root of our sin lodged in it, in order to redeem, heal and sanctify it *in himself within his own holy life* and activity as the incarnate Mediator, *or* whether he acted redeemingly upon our fallen existence through *some kind of external activity* [such as "paying a debt" taken too literally, as some see His death on the cross], as if he were merely an instrument or intermediary in the hands of God effecting our salvation. Thus the issue at stake was whether in his incarnation Christ took some neutral humanity upon himself, or whether *he actually became what we are* [he earlier quotes 2 Cor. 5:21 and Gal. 3:10, 13] *in order to make us what he is.*[4]

Torrance further explains:

Eastern theology . . . rejected that anti-Pauline dualist approach [i.e., of the Latin West] and insisted that in the incarnation the Son of God took

---

3. Ibid., p. 238. This approach also led to idea of the Immaculate Conception of Mary, which was finally made dogma by the Roman Church in 1854. The Orthodox do not believe in "inherited guilt," so there is no need for a special "Immaculate Conception" of Mary so that she would not pass on "inherited guilt" to Christ. In the Orthodox understanding, there is no "inherited guilt," so it could not have affected Christ, or any other person.

This also means that for the Orthodox, Christ took our actual fallen nature. For example, St. Gregory of Nyssa says, "the apostolic word testifies that the Lord was *made into sin for our sake* by being invested with our sinful nature" (*The Life of Moses*, p. 62; cf. 2 Cor. 5:21). St. Gregory the Theologian says, "And so the passage 'The Word was made flesh' seems to me to be equivalent to that in which it is said that he was made sin or a curse for us; not that the Lord was transformed into either of these—how could he be? But because by taking them upon himself he took away our sins and bore our iniquities" (Letters on the Apollinarian Controversy.101; LCC 3:222; in *Ancient Christian Commentary on Scripture*, Thomas C. Oden, gen. ed. [Downers Grove, IL: InterVarsity Press, 1998f.], New Testament, vol. VII, on *I and II Corinthians*, Gerald Bray, vol. ed., p. 253). St. Ambrose says, "This proves that His body and soul are of the same substance as ours" (The Sacrament of the Incarnation of our Lord 7.76; FC 44:248; in ACCS, ibid., p. 251).

4. Ibid., pp. 237-238.

upon himself our actual sinful existence subjected to his own judgment, but in such a way that his assumption of that was also and *from the very beginning* a redeeming, healing and sanctifying of it.[5]

Here is one example confirming that this is so from St. Gregory Palamas (14th century), who says in a homily on the Transfiguration, "The apostles . . . saw that transformation which *our human clay had undergone,* not at that time, but from the moment in which it had been assumed, when it was deified through union with the Word of God."[6] Torrance concludes, following Palamas and the Orthodox Tradition, "*In Christ our fallen Adamic humanity was recreated* and through his vicarious obedience as the Son of God become man it was restored to perfect filial relation to the Father."[7]

Orthodox hymnography is full of language like this. For example,

> The Creator, when He saw man perishing, whom He had made with His own hands, bowed the heavens and came down; and from the divine and pure Virgin did He take all man's substance, being made truly flesh.[8]

> Beyond all thought and without measure is Thy poverty, O Word of God! I know that, for my sake who am fallen, Thou hast from pity clothed Thyself in Adam, and all the posterity of Adam Thou makest new again.[9]

> Thou hast put Adam on entire, O Christ, and changing the nature grown dark in past times, Thou hast filled it with glory and made it godlike by the alteration of Thy form.[10]

The difference between the later Latin and Eastern approaches "is considerable," as Torrance puts it. This will be evident in the comparison made below between the understandings of four key areas, an understanding that was largely shared both East and West during the first six centuries (representing

---

5. Ibid., p. 238.

6. St. Gregory Palamas, Homily 34.14, "On the Transfiguration," in *The Homilies of St. Gregory Palamas,* Christopher Veniamin, ed. and trans. (Waymart, PA: Mount Thabor Publishing, 2009), p. 272.

7. Torrance, op. cit., p. 238.

8. Canticle One, First Canon, Matins for the Nativity of Christ (*Festal Menaion,* p. 269).

9. Fourth Stikheron, Matins for the Forefeast of Holy Theophany (*Festal Menaion,* p. 311).

10. Canticle Three, First Canon, Matins for the Transfiguration of our Lord (*Festal Menaion,* p. 483).

what Torrance calls the "Eastern" approach), and the changing ideas in these four areas in the mid-medieval and late medieval periods in the West.

These four areas are:

A. the basic understanding of God and how we know God—our relationship to God;

B. the fundamental understanding of the Incarnation and the goal of Christian life which Christ makes possible—which then determines one's understanding of salvation;

C. the understanding of difficulties in general, and in particular, as they relate to language and the interpretation of Scripture; and

D. some specifics concerning Scripture and its interpretation.

Although much of the material for the first six centuries has already been covered, we'll begin with a brief summary of these four areas for this time period to make it easier to compare this period with the later years.

The First Six Centuries

A. The fundamental characteristic of God revealed by Christ is that He is good and loves mankind. God truly reveals Himself in Christ, in Scripture, and indirectly through nature. Jesus Christ, by His Incarnation, life, death on the cross, Resurrection, and ascension, overcame sin and death by recreating and redeeming "our fallen Adamic humanity"—i.e., our actual human nature. This makes it possible once again for human beings to freely choose to truly know God through a real communion with His uncreated energies (GRACE) through the *nous*, or spiritual intellect, to be sanctified and to live eternally in a communion of love with the Triune God.

Noetic, experiential knowledge is primary, though the authenticity of any individual's experience must be confirmed by the Church as being in conformity with Scripture as understood within the ongoing authentic Tradition of the Church.[11] Noetic knowledge is potentially available to everyone, regardless of one's level of formal education, or lack thereof. The training required for this kind of knowledge is largely ascetic—purifying the heart by keeping

---

11. For a thorough and helpful discussion of this topic, see Edith Humphrey, *Scripture and Tradition: What the Bible Really Says* (Grand Rapids, MI: Baker Academic, 2013).

the Gospel commandments/living the Gospel life (hence also knowing/under-standing Scripture); striving for virtue by means of various spiritual disciplines such as fasting, prayer, and almsgiving (all part of the Gospel life); and partic-ipation in the sacraments and the ongoing life of the Church (also indicated in Scripture)—all necessitating one's cooperation with God's grace. Sin, which these practices, in conjunction with God's grace, help to overcome, is most often imaged as *an illness* preventing fullness of health.

Human reason, highly valued as a great gift from God, is used along with rhetorical skills, technical study of language, etc., in Scriptural exegesis and theology. But awareness of the limitations of reason, especially regarding spir-itual matters, is never lost sight of. The Fathers are not merely "authorities" from an inaccessible, grace-filled past whose interpretations and ideas are to be mechanically and blindly followed; they are, rather, trustworthy witnesses witnessing to and helping others to access for themselves what is primary: an ongoing experience of life in Christ available to all people in all times through the Holy Spirit. The Fathers teach not only about a right way of thinking, or correct ideas, but also about a right way of *living* that leads to the acquisition of the Holy Spirit and new life in Christ.

Divine justice is radically different from human justice. There is no equal exchange remotely possible; as Torrance observes, "the whole moral order as we know it in this world needed to be redeemed and set on a new basis."[12] Divine justice is more like what Lewis Hyde calls a "gift economy" (posses-sion and the highest place of honor go to the ones who give the most without expecting anything in exchange, or at least nothing of equal value)—with God giving far more than we could ever imagine, especially in the Incarnation and Crucifixion.[13] As Torrance explains, "if the atonement is [rightly] understood in terms of [both] the inner ontological relation between Christ and God, on the one hand, and in terms of the inner ontological relation between Christ and mankind, on the other, then no account of it can be offered merely in terms of a moral or legal framework external to the incarnation."[14]

---

12. Torrance, op. cit., p. 252.

13. The well-known contemporary holy elder Fr. Paisios gives the following simple example of a person following either human or divine justice. Following human justice, if there are two people and ten peaches, each one gets five. But following divine justice, if there are two people and ten peaches, the one, if he knows the other loves peaches, will take only one of them and then say to the other, "Please, you have the rest, I don't like them very much." "This person has divine justice; he prefers to be unfair to himself by human standards and be rewarded for his sacrifice by God's grace" (*Elder Paisios of the Holy Mountain* [Thessalonica: Holy Mountain, 1998], pp. 61-62).

14. Torrance, op. cit., pp. 250-251.

B. The goal of the Incarnation and the Christian life that Christ makes possible—as well as the goal of exegeting Scripture—is *deification*, meaning real, personal transformation in this life, leading to fullness of eternal life (life in God) in the next. An "incarnational allegorical"[15] view of reality is held; the spiritual and literal are both are kept in balance, because both are highly valued (e.g., always keeping the cross and the Resurrection together, always seeing the Resurrection even in the cross). This reflects Nicean Christology, that Jesus Christ is both fully God and fully man.

As indicated in the New Testament, people are expected to "repent"; to "do the truth" (John 3:21); to show their love for God and His Son by keeping the Gospel commandments (John 14:15, 21), which is the only way to fullness of health and wholeness/holiness. This includes being baptized (e.g., Matt. 18:19; John 3:5) and partaking of Christ's body and blood (John 6:53, 57); giving alms; praying and fasting (Matt. 6:5-18); and performing other ascetic practices as much as is in each person's power. In other words, we are all called to do everything in our power to purify our hearts so that we are open to being transformed by the Holy Spirit—to drawing closer to God, and thereby to receiving more grace (e.g., John 14:15-17), bringing us an ever deeper experience of true life and love.

All these "ascetic" practices are not considered to be "good works" which we must do to *earn* salvation. There is no sense that we must, or even can, "earn" our salvation, for salvation involves our *ontological* transformation—it is intrinsic to our being. Only God can transform us in this way; only He can save us by transforming us and uniting us with Christ through the grace of the Holy Spirit. Nevertheless, God asks that we do what we can; and since we can trust in His infinite and perfect goodness—including that He wills for everyone to be saved and come to the knowledge of the truth (1 Tim. 2:4)—there is no great, anxious uncertainty about salvation that will plague a later era. Neither is there a doctrine of "once saved, always saved," or of "eternal security," since one needs to struggle to grow spiritually until the end of one's earthly life, all the while trusting in the goodness and love of "the good God Who loves mankind."

C. In this context, difficulties are seen in a positive light. In fact, the whole of reality is seen very positively. Since God is good and loves us, everything He has created must be of benefit in some way. So the difficulties of Scripture, and the ambiguous and inadequate character of human language, are understood, accepted, and seen as positive, because for one thing, they force us to rely on the Church, and on both personal and communal witness. There is no automatic, infallible criterion of truth. Rather, the most secure criterion

---

15. See footnote 66, Ch. 3.

is the consensus of personal witnesses (what Tradition preserves) in line with Scripture and Tradition, and the possibility for everyone of what the contemporary holy elder, Fr. Aimilianos, calls "complete assurance" through experiential knowledge.[16]

D. Everyone, including the laity, are encouraged to study Scripture, and it is available in vernacular translations (which Latin originally was). In exegesis, one finds a balanced allegorical approach along with the study of the literal level, and respect for the text as it stands. The ambiguity of human language and the reality of divine inspiration mean that Scripture is inexhaustible—no one will ever be able to completely interpret it. Inspiration is also ongoing: new Fathers can be raised up in every generation.[17] To say that Scripture is inspired also means you have to be inspired to properly understand it. The ultimate authorities on Scripture in its most fundamental meanings (the "rule of faith"), and comprehensive purpose, or *skopos,* are those with mature, personal experience of God and spiritual realities, as verified by the community of the Church and Her Tradition (i.e., Fathers and Saints in line with ECUMENICAL COUNCILS; see Ch. 8 for further discussion), and in line with Scripture. The Fathers add to such spiritual experience brilliant, highly educated minds, and usually a special teaching role in the Church (often as bishops).

The Mid-Medieval Age in the West (roughly 600-1300)[18]

In contrast:

A. In the work of Anselm of Canterbury (11th century) we see a new fundamental characteristic of God being emphasized: divine justice. This characteristic was not absent previously; rather, it is a question of *how much* this, and later on other images, qualities, etc., are emphasized, and how much other aspects are consequently minimized, or even ignored. With this overemphasis on divine justice, the substitutionary theory of atonement is developed. In the Latin Church, following this thinking, it was believed that divine justice can be understood in terms of this *fallen* world's moral order—in other words, that divine justice is like human justice (based on exchanges of equal value. Torrance says this root understanding is true of both Protestants and Roman

---

16. *The Way of the Spirit* (Athens: Indikos Press, 2009), p. 136.

17. E.g., First Letter to Akindynos; quoted by Fr. John Meyendorff, *A Study of Gregory Palamas* (London: The Faith Press, 1964), p. 44.

18. The summary below deals mainly with the latter part of this time period.

Catholics; see above). Very ironically, the Protestant Reformers kept this false understanding, which was at the heart of so much of what they rightly objected to in the Roman Church of their day.

Anselm's theory involves the necessity of "satisfaction"—as in the medieval feudal code: for every crime committed, an equal payment, or *satisfaction*, must be made. For example, if you break a window, you cannot simply say you are sorry; you must pay for it. This was applied to God and our spiritual state and life by claiming that an equivalent "payment" or satisfaction is due to God as a penalty on account of everyone's sin. Anselm said that the debt[19] due for one's sins was far too great for any human being to pay. But Christ's death, since He is the Son of God, was a sufficient vicarious *satisfaction* for all the sins of all of humanity. Actually, it was considered to be more than enough to cancel the debt that mankind owed.

This basic idea is then extended to claim that every sin committed must have a penalty on earth—*or* in Purgatory. So sin is understood as primarily a kind of illegal action—more like a crime one must make reparation for than an illness one needs to be cured of. This meant that one owed a debt to God for every sin (like a boy breaking a window). The belief was that even after repentance, confession, and forgiveness (absolution), you *still* have to pay this debt, and the main way you pay is having years of suffering in Purgatory, though ways were developed to get the time in Purgatory reduced.

This juridical, extrinsic understanding of salvation affected many aspects of church life. It is not hard to understand why many of the Reformers reacted so strongly against the "Mass" and prayer for the departed which were so closely connected to this understanding of sin as primarily a debt, especially when you realize that false ideas about this topic profoundly altered church architecture, the role of the clergy, monasticism, and virtually everyone's spiritual life. Already in the 9th century we see the idea not only that masses should be said for the dead, but that the more masses said, the better—so churches were being built with multiple altars, or multiple altars were added to existing churches. By the 12th century, a whole speculative "geography of the afterlife" had developed,[20] and the early general idea of being purified in the next life by the fire of

---

19. Again, it is not that the idea of a "debt" is absent before—it is found in St. Paul and many other places. It is, again, a question of emphasis, or overemphasis, and a question of this becoming the dominant analogy, instead of one of many other analogies. It is also a question of the whole work of salvation being considered from the standpoint of human justice, as Torrence notes.

20. MacCullogh, op. cit., p. 11.

God's love, found, for example, in St. Isaac the Syrian,[21] was developed in a very literal, detailed, systematic—and obviously wildly speculative—way. And all of this was based on the ideas of "satisfaction" being necessary, and that divine justice is just like human justice—that the moral order of fallen humanity was untouched by Christ.

These ideas are really what even led many who became Protestants to reject all sacraments—at least as they were understood in the early Church, or in the medieval Roman Catholic Church. Most did keep some form of baptism—and some kind of Eucharist, or "Lord's Supper," although in reaction to the medieval Roman Catholic doctrine of transubstantiation, when the Eucharist was retained, it was often considered only a symbol for remembering Christ's self-sacrifice.

However, as Torrance explains—and this is critically important for understanding the differences between the Orthodox and the Latin churches,

> The whole moral order as we know it in this world needed to be redeemed and set on a new basis, and that is precisely what the justifying act of God in the atoning sacrifice of Christ was about. . . . Such is the utterly radical nature of atoning mediation perfected in Christ, for it might well be called 'a soteriological suspension of ethics' in the establishing of *a new moral life that flows from grace in which external legal relation is replaced by inner filial relation to God the Father*. . . .
>
> Thus we are made to live in union with him and in the communion of his Holy Spirit who sheds the love of God into our hearts, and informs our life with the very mind of Christ the obedient Son of the Father. ***This does not represent merely a conceptual change in our understanding of the moral order, but a real ontological change resulting from the interlocking of incarnation and atonement in the depth and structure of our human existence and the translation of the Son/Father in Christ into the daily life of the children of God.*** The atonement is so profound that it transforms the fundamental moral framework of thought and constitutes the very parameters within which it is rightly to be understood. Hence we go back on the atonement if we seek to understand and interpret it within the parameters of the unredeemed moral order.[22]

---

21. Vladimir Lossky, *Mystical Theology of the Eastern Church* (Crestwood, NY: St. Vladimir's Seminary Press, 1976), p. 234.

22. Torrance, op. cit., pp. 252-254 (my emphasis).

Absolutely key here is the fact he mentions that Christ does not merely bring a "*conceptual* change in our understanding of the moral order," but a "*real onto-logical* change," and real knowledge through communion with God.

Unfortunately, interpreting the atonement "within the parameters of the unredeemed moral order," or "going back on the atonement," was exactly what was happening in the Roman Church during this time; and it was happening to an extreme. By the 12th century, this place of purgation, called Purgatory, had been mapped out in great detail, and there developed a whole "purgatory industry."[23] There was even a special place, called limbo, for unbaptized infants, and a separate limbo for the Old Testament patriarchs (since this extrinsic juridical approach prevented the great Old Testament patriarchs from being fully recognized as Saints, as they are in the Orthodox Churches).

Purgatory had a time limit—unlike heaven and hell—so gradually people came to think about it in terms of years. If saying a Mass could prompt God's mercy on a departed soul, then couldn't the degree of mercy be figured out in years? Then why not figure out how many years off Purgatory each mass was worth? Altars or side chapels called chantries were established specifically for masses to be said for the dead. This was, in fact, how the universities of Oxford and Cambridge got started.

These ideas about Purgatory also led from the 12th century on to more and more monastics being ordained as priests, so that they could say as many masses as was devotionally possible (earlier, and still in the Orthodox Church, most monastics are not ordained). This seems to have reinforced the idea that all clergy should be celibate. Clerical celibacy was officially required beginning in 1139 (though there is evidence of tendencies in the Latin Church towards mandatory clerical celibacy from at least the beginning of the 4th century).[24]

Saying the Mass was not the only thing that could get you time off Purgatory. Doing works of mercy, such as almsgiving, giving to hospitals, building a bridge, or paying the town's tax bill even in your will, would also reduce your time. Something positive could result in the midst of all this strangeness, however: the beggar would pray for the soul of the one who gave him alms, the sick would pray for the benefactors of the hospital, and the dead in Purgatory

---

23. MacCullogh, op. cit., p. 15.

24. Before 1139 in the Roman Church, clergy could live with their wives, but they were expected to refrain from marital relations. For some time after this decree, many priests and even some bishops openly had mistresses and children, causing scandal to the faithful. It is also interesting that when most of the male monastics came to be ordained clergy, the women's monasteries, with their often very influential abbesses, lost a lot of their significance and intellectual importance in comparison with their influence in earlier centuries. Probably this unintentionally further divided the clergy from the laity and lessened the importance of the laity in general.

would pray for the living who paid for masses to be said for them. So a greater sense of community and oneness in Christ could develop in spite of this false theology.

B. Concerning the goal of the Incarnation and the Christian life: towards the end of this period, the dominant understanding was an extrinsic, juridical view of salvation, as said, like a legal transaction, with the focus on Christ paying our debt(s) on the Cross (with the Cross split from the Resurrection—and both from the Incarnation itself), so that one will suffer as little as possible in the afterlife.

Torrance points out another serious Christological problem with this basic idea:

> Whenever the Incarnation and the vicarious act of Christ on the cross are held apart, the atonement is inevitably thought of as an external transaction between God and man and between Christ and man, in which divine and human agency in Christ are held apart, which inevitably calls in question the inseparable conjunction in him of the divine and human natures.[25]

Torrance identifies other problems as well:

> In the Latin view the atoning sacrifice on the cross deals only with *actual* sin, so that in addition to the expiatory sacrifice offered on the cross, although on the ground of what it accomplished, infusions of grace are provided to deal with *original* sin. In the Greek view, however, it is the *whole incarnate life of Christ* vicariously and triumphantly lived out from his birth to his crucifixion and resurrection in perfect obedience to the Father *within the ontological depths of his oneness with us* in our actual fallen existence, that redeems and saves us and converts our disobedient alienated sonship back to filial union with the Father. That is the grace of the Lord Jesus Christ.[26]

And he concludes,

> The cardinal issue here, then, is the all-important truth of the *vicarious humanity* of Jesus Christ as Lord and Saviour of mankind. This carries with it a rejection of any idea that the humanity of Christ played a merely instrumental role in some kind of external legal transaction in the hands of Almighty God [as Anselm and those after him in the Latin Church

---

25. Torrance, op. cit., p. 239.

26. Ibid., p. 238 (my emphasis).

implied], and gives it an essential and integral place in indivisible oneness of agency with that of the Father and the Holy Spirit.[27]

Hence, the mistaken understanding in Latin Christology leads not only to a false understanding of salvation, but it also implies a subordinationist Christology, meaning that Christ is seen as not having a divine nature equal to God the Father—that Christ is not "of one essence with the Father" as the Nicene Creed states. For Christ is seen *primarily* as the Perfect Man paying the debt to satisfy and appease the wrath of God the Father; the understanding that it is God Himself, God the Son, Who is "paying the debt" for us, is almost entirely lost. And the full deity of the Holy Spirit is also diminished, for if salvation is accomplished *primarily* by Christ paying a debt, there is not much of a role left for the Holy Spirit in the life of believers. This diminished role of the Holy Spirit is also reflected in the *filioque* clause,[28] which was officially promoted in Rome by Pope Benedict the VIII in 1014. The understanding of salvation as being a dynamic process of ongoing personal transformation/ sanctification/deification is almost totally lost, especially in much of Protestantism.

C. Difficulties began to be seen negatively, even as punishments. For with this mistaken Christology, God comes to be seen as a punishing God demanding restitution. This negative view is moderated, however, by the understanding that since it is God the Father Who sends Christ to pay our basic debt to Him, God is still a "good God," though not in the fuller sense of the early Church, or of the Orthodox Tradition. As Archim. Vasileios, a contemporary Orthodox theologian and well-known holy monk says, "We do not understand or experience salvation in legal terms of procedures." He also says,

> You feel that the difference between East and West is theological. . . . The author of our faith is not known to us as the strict Judge who threatens us with punishments in order to bring us to our senses. Nor does He sentence us to torments in order to save us. Rather, He is the craftsman of love and compassion: "He who is surpassing goodness has fulfilled the whole

---

27. Ibid., pp. 238-239 (his emphasis).

28. This refers to the clause about the Holy Spirit ("Who proceeds from the Father *and the Son*") added to the Nicene Creed in the West (first used in 589 in Spain to counteract Arianism there, it was later strongly promoted by Charlemagne and the Franks). The Orthodox objected to this for two reasons: that it makes the Holy Spirit not an equal member of the Holy Trinity, and because the Creed had been decided by consensus at two Ecumenical Councils and thus could not be changed by any individual, including the pope of Rome, or even by a local council.

dispensation for the salvation of mortals" [from the service on the eve of Pentecost].[29]

We also see in the West the beginning of a serious search for an *infallible* criterion of truth. This seems to be linked to no longer understanding God as primarily the good God Who loves mankind, doing all He can to save us while still respecting our free will to respond positively to His love towards us (or not), but rather primarily to seeing God in a negative light, e.g., as the punishing God, or later, the God about Whom we can only know that He is omnipotent.

D. Already with Alcuin, in the early 9th century, we've seen the idea that Scripture has been fully explained by the Fathers, so that equal inspiration is not ongoing; hence some seemed to believe that there can be no new Fathers, or at least none even close to the level of the early Fathers. The patristic period is over (in contrast to the Orthodox Tradition, which understands that there can be new Fathers in every age, although, in virtue of their closeness to the time of Christ, and their being part of basically the same culture, these early Fathers will always have a certain priority for the Orthodox). Also growing is the idea that there is no point in the laity reading Scripture, for only the highly educated, those who can research the Fathers—and who can acquire all kinds of other technical information—can possibly understand it. And the Holy Spirit's role is changed and limited, as was noted. Such ideas were increasingly accepted as time went on.

As mentioned, the immensely influential Francis of Assisi (1181-1226) further overemphasized the cross separately from the Resurrection, the humanity of Jesus separately from His divinity, and the literal level of Scripture separately from the allegorical level.

This is a period characterized by an increasingly rationalistic approach that continues into the next period. An opposition has begun between theology and mystical experience, a split between the head and the heart, between faith and reason. As an attempt to counteract this imbalance, a highly emotive, affective mysticism that is skeptical of study and theology arises. Yet during these same years we find the rise of universities, and in many people's minds (especially the scholars'!) the ultimate authorities are the highly educated "academic" experts who may have little or no spiritual experience, and no special teaching role in the Church.

---

29. *Hymn of Dismissal*, op. cit., p. 92.

The Late Medieval Period, Especially Late Medieval Nominalism (roughly 1300—1500)

A. For the Nominalists of this period, such as William of Ockham (c. 1287—1347), the fundamental characteristic of God is *omnipotence*, defined as having *no limits*—doing what He wills with no concern for the consequences. The "essence of omnipotence in [the Nominalists' view] . . . was an absolute freedom that was indifferent to its object. God wills what he wills and wills it only because he wills it."[30] Making God's omnipotence His fundamental characteristic, instead of His goodness, or love, etc., leads to a very dark view of God—a God Who does not reveal Himself, a God Who is so far removed from people that the Nominalists believed we can't know anything else about Him at all. So this becomes really a kind of agnostic position, such as that apparently held also by Barlaam the Calabrian, the opponent of St. Gregory Palamas. Luther will continue this view of regarding omnipotence as the most important characteristic of God, while Erasmus will insist on the traditional view that it is His goodness that is most fundamental.[31]

The Nominalists went so far as to say that we can't know anything about God even by analogy. For example, if we say God is good—that is, if we say He always acts in a way analogous to what human beings would consider to be good, loving, etc.—then first of all we have no way to know this *for certain*; and second, if we claim this, then we are *limiting God*, and making Him in our image.[32] But limiting God is the key thing they will not accept, because they believe the most important thing is His omnipotence as they have defined it. Obviously, they do not get these ideas from the Gospel accounts, from the revelation in Jesus Christ of Who God is. Theirs is indeed "a different gospel" (cf. Gal. 1:6-8).

Insisting that the main characteristic of God is ultimately His omnipotent will is perhaps the final extreme of the faulty Christology that Torrance points out. We recall how he says, "it became very clear to the Nicene Fathers in their struggle with Arianism, [that for the Arian heretics] the relation between the incarnate Son and the Father was merely one of *an external and moral kind contingent upon the divine will*, and not a relation internal to the being and life of the Godhead. . . . so that His atoning sacrifice was expounded merely in

---

30. Michael Allen Gillespie, *The Theological Origins of Modernity* (Chicago: University of Chicago Press, 2008), p. 134.

31. Ibid., pp. 149-150.

32. Without the traditional understanding of the analogical relationship between God and man, it is not surprising that allegorical interpretation gets rejected.

moral and juridical terms."[33] Again, it is a matter of the will only, rather than ontology.[34]

B. The goal of the Incarnation and Christian life is still an extrinsic kind of salvation, but not always even juridical. The Nominalist William of Ockham even said that God can put Saints in hell and sinners in Heaven. Clearly, in this view, salvation is not about ontological personal transformation. Ockham's idea would be impossible with deification as the goal, because when that is the goal, salvation means ontological transformation through *real participation in the divine life*, and hell is understood as rejecting communion with God.

With the Nominalists, individualism is emphasized even more, for they do not believe that natures—including human nature—exist; only individual things are real. Such an idea makes a traditional understanding of the Gospel and Who Jesus is impossible, since that view presupposes that Christ transformed human *nature*—that a deep, radical, ontological change occurs to human nature through the Incarnation, Crucifixion, Resurrection, and Ascension of Jesus Christ.

An elaborate system of works was still in place that was supposed to lessen the suffering of the saved in purgatory.[35] A "works" approach was also extended to salvation. For some, like Luther before his "tower experience," it seemed that no matter how much you did, it was never enough to be sure you were saved. And when this is combined with a theology that denies we can be sure of God's

---

33. Torrance, op. cit., pp. 249-250.

34. Perhaps this emphasis on the divine will here, and in Luther, and in general what seems to be the western fear of any talk of the importance of our free will for our salvation (often labeled semi-Pelagianism), can be explained by this misunderstanding. In those views, the relationship between the Father and Son is focused on the Father's *will*, and if our salvation is a fruit *only* of the Father's will, how can one then allow for *synergy*—the need for the human will to cooperate with the divine will? Or how can one have an emphasis on *participation in Christ*, rather than simply *imitating* Christ?

35. "Consider an example. The monastic Order of St. Bridget was founded by a fourteenth century Swedish noblewoman who was also an outstanding mystic. . . . The Bridgettine Abbey of Syon, . . . devised the Fifteen Odes of St. Bridget for the use of the general public. This devotion . . . was based on a systematic use of a physical object, a set of five beads, the ancestor of the later rosary . . . The user would meditate on the Passion mysteries, but would also have to repeat every day for a year the Lord's Prayer 15 times and the Hail Mary 15 times. That would ensure 5,475 years off one's time in purgatory, since 15 times 365 days of the year adds up to 5,475. Some advertising blurbs attached to the prayer promised that this action would also liberate 15 deceased relatives from purgatory, convert 15 living sinners to a good life, and sustain 15 other relatives' virtue—altogether it was value for effort" (MacCullogh, op. cit., p. 23).

goodness, it is easy to see how this could lead to great anxiety (e.g., Luther's famous *angst*), due to the uncertainty about one's salvation.

By Luther's time, the system of indulgences that greatly strengthened an extrinsic, juridical view of salvation was firmly in place, as well as further corruptions issuing from it. In this system, since Christ's merit is infinite, there were "extra" merits or graces beyond what was needed to pay the debt mankind owed to God—very much like money "in the bank." In fact, all these extra merits were called the "treasury of merits." These extra merits could be given by clergy, but especially by the pope (giving him another source of power and funding), to the faithful to help them pay what they owed for their sins. Likewise, it was understood that Christ's mother and the Saints have extra merit, which could be drawn upon for the use of the faithful or the departed. Ordinary people also could do things to earn extra merit to give to others to help them pay what they owed.

This is where the indulgences come in that Luther objected to so strongly. Indulgences meant that less of a penalty needed to be paid, because one is being given some of these "extra" merits. A *plenary indulgence* meant that no satisfaction/penalty needed to be paid at all—you go straight to heaven. These only began to be issued in the late 11th century, to encourage people to go on the First Crusade. All this flows directly and logically from the Latin understanding of salvation as extrinsic and juridical (though not inevitably).

Luther initially objected to this system because it made a mockery of the sacraments: if you can pay money to the pope to give you an indulgence that will get rid your debt for all your sins so that you go straight to heaven, then why do you need any sacrament except baptism? And especially, what is the point of the Sacrament of Confession? Ironically, this became the view of many Protestants—that there is only one sacrament, baptism (though it was often understood as merely a symbol); and for many of them, the Eucharist became only a memorial. But actually, certain elements of the Roman Catholic theology of the time led almost inexorably, even though unintentionally, to these novel ideas.[36]

---

36. If sin is seen in terms of a kind of legal transaction, then the salvation economy can be depersonalized and become mechanical. The focus can easily shift from personal transformation to being more like an economic exchange—I give *x* (money, services), and I get *y* in return (years off purgatory, less punishment)—even if this was not the original intent.

One might well ask, what does all this have to do with a person's relationship with God in the here and now, and with the state of his/her soul? The focus can become not personal transformation in this life, and being "partakers of the divine nature" (2 Peter 1:4) in order to be closer to God in this life, and to have a blessed state in the next in even closer communion with God, but simply doing good in this life—or acquiring indulgences—in order to avoid punishment in the

There was, then, no understanding of deification, of Christ healing and transforming human nature through the whole economy of salvation. Nor was there focus on the spiritual life being a seamless whole: sacraments, including Confession, as well as prayer, ascetic practices, "good works," etc., all leading to personal transformation on an ontological level, bringing one closer to God in this life and the next. There was still an overly rationalistic approach to theology, and the more rationalistic it became, the more emphasis was placed on the juridical and extrinsic character of salvation. It is important to remember, however, that there were always people who did not agree with these developments, and there were always people in the Latin Church who were trying to bring reform—sometimes a lot of people, sometimes in high places.

C. Difficulties are seen as negative: if God cannot be relied upon to be faithful, loving, and good, He will be understood to be unpredictable (this becomes extreme in a later thinker like Descartes, who believed that God really might design reality so that it tricks us!), and the search for an infallible criterion, or standard, of truth intensifies (in a later time, this desire also helps to lead Descartes to the scientific method).

D. Some claimed that equal inspiration is not ongoing, so there are no new Fathers—the patristic period is over. Barlaam apparently held this, for example. With such a view, the Holy Spirit's role is changed and limited on some level. As discussed in Chapter 4, there were many changes and discoveries undermining trust in Tradition in general, especially when traditions from ancient Greek pagan ideas about geography, physics, and other sciences had been given so much authority and supported by the Roman Catholic Church, but then were undermined by the many new discoveries.

Barlaam and many Nominalists (unlike Luther) did believe that God especially inspired the early Fathers, so they should be relied on as authorities. But St. Gregory Palamas (14th century), and the Eastern Orthodox Tradition as a whole, have said that if God revealed Himself to the early Fathers, "why should He not reveal Himself today [meaning in every era] to the Church through the theologians called to elucidate the mystery of the Trinity with the aid of the

---

next. This is what Luther called "works righteousness," which doesn't have to involve personal transformation at all.

Also, when all these sorts of ideas became widespread, different aspects of the spiritual life and the salvation economy came to be separated and isolated, so one finds the appearance of strange new devotions. For example, even the wounds of Christ were separated and venerated in isolation (this apparently was begun by Bernard of Clairvaux in the 12th century, and promoted by Francis of Assisi in the 13th).

Holy Spirit?"[37] This is not meant to imply a kind of "progressive revelation," but that new Fathers are inspired to *clarify* the perennial, unchanging truths for their own times. This is really the main issue St. Symeon the New Theologian (d. 1022) was concerned with as well: the ongoing work of the Holy Spirit in the life of the Church—that there is a living Tradition passed down and continuing through the grace of the Holy Spirit, with grace being understood as the uncreated energies of God, the actual life of God, continuing for as long as there is a Church on earth.

If we can experience the uncreated energies of God—or grace, as the Eastern Orthodox have always affirmed—this means it is possible to have a kind of "sure knowledge of God" through the Holy Spirit.[38] However, in order to be certain that it *is* the Holy Spirit Whom one is inspired by, this needs confirmation by others in the Church, and must lead to a life and understanding in line with Scripture and Tradition. Thus, we do not only have the possibility to speculate about God, or know about Him through revelation, but because we have a *nous*, a spiritual intellect or *heart* in the patristic sense, we can really know God through real communion with Him.

But Barlaam and the Nominalists do not know of, or even admit, that there is a possibility of, any noetic knowledge. For them, the sacraments, mystical experience, etc., do put man in contact with divine realities, but only as intelligible symbols—and such symbols for them meant something merely *representing* divine realities, not giving real access to divine realities. In other words, "Union with God could not, in the last resort, be anything but intellective or symbolic." So, for example, the light of Christ's Transfiguration on Mt. Tabor was believed to be just a symbol perceived by the mind.[39] Fr. Meyendorff points out that this is a kind of Nestorianism, or a move in that direction: "humanity and divinity" are "inalienable natures impermeable one by the other, . . . in a purely external relation of juxtaposition."[40] Hence, there is no *perichoresis* (real interpenetration; reciprocal inherence) between the divine and human natures of Christ, as traditionally affirmed. (In fact, for the Nominalists, there are not even any natures, only separate individuals.) In this view, "deification" is not a true union with the divine, for grace is a created entity, and "for that reason it is essentially different from the divine nature, and belonging to the domain of symbols."[41]

---

37. First Letter to Akindynos; quoted by Fr. John Meyendorff, *A Study of Gregory Palamas* (London: The Faith Press, 1964), p. 44.

38. Meyendorff, p. 45.

39. Ibid., p. 187.

40. Ibid., p. 181.

41. Ibid.

Barlaam and the Nominalists denied that Christ brought a radically new way of knowing God, not available to the ancients, however brilliant and virtuous they may have been. Partly because Barlaam, et al., had no essence/energies distinction, they are driven to say there is no possibility for real, positive, or *kataphatic,* knowledge of God through His Energies in order to safeguard the unknowable quality of God's Essence (for if we could know His Essence, we would have to be God). Their rejection of the understanding that there is an analogical relationship between God and man since we are made in His image and since He made this world, etc., also played a part in the origination and spread of these false ideas. And these ideas are not merely curiosities from the past, but their repercussions are still profoundly affecting many people today.

Belief in this terrible God of Nominalism generates, at least in some people, a lot of fear and anxiety.[42] For in this view God is unpredictable and may even be capricious from a human point of view, so there is consequently a search for certainty in something besides God. No longer do they have Jesus Christ as Ultimate Truth Incarnate revealing that God is a good God Who loves mankind. No longer do they have a personal relationship, a real communion, with Christ in the Holy Spirit; therefore, real communion with Christ is no longer the key to ultimate knowledge. In fact, Christ as the most true revelation of God seems entirely absent from all this. It is not surprising, then, that some other "infallible criterion of truth" is sought, and this is, ironically, in part the origin of both Christian Fundamentalism and its opposite—the historical-critical method.

Late medieval Nominalism and reactions to it led directly to the Protestant Reformation.

The Reformation

Adding all the theological changes outlined above to all the radical political, economic, and technological changes that went on in the late medieval and "Renaissance" periods understandably led to a situation characterized by the break-up of all kinds of traditional patterns, with a resulting lack of confidence in tradition in general, and in the Church in particular. A central problem in

---

42. Some versions of "Humanism seemed to suggest that there might be no life after death, and Nominalism [seemed to be saying] that even if there were an afterlife there was nothing we could do to insure or even improve our chances of salvation" (Gillespie, op. cit., p. 104). All this tended to create an extreme focus on the uncertainty of salvation. For many, like Luther, this generated great anxiety and fear; as Gillespie says of Luther, "He thus lived in terror of a wrathful God" (p. 105).

the West had become: whom can we trust to reveal the truth? Who should be the ultimate authority? If the Church's hierarchy, her Tradition, and the ancients were all unreliable, how can we discern the truth?

Within this context and atmosphere arose the Reformers, chief of whom were Martin Luther, who is generally viewed as the one who began the Reformation in 1517 (he died in 1546), and John Calvin (d. 1564). This, and the Post-Reformation era, are especially important periods to cover, even if briefly, because as a number of scholars have noted, all the key aspects of the non-traditional, non-patristic biblical interpretation typical in our own time were in place by around 1680. This means that most of the problematic things in biblical interpretation happening today, no matter how "cutting edge" they claim to be, are essentially a continuation of what was happening during that period. The main focus in this brief overview will be on Luther and Erasmus as representative of two very different general paths that could, and still can, be taken in the three areas of: their basic understanding of Scripture, the role of the Fathers (and Tradition), and the best way to reform the Church (though it should be noted that Luther is widely recognized to be quite unsystematic in his thought and writings).

One can see some of Luther's thought as being a reaction against certain aspects of late Medieval Nominalism, while he continued to accept other aspects—certainly the influence of Nominalism was very strong. Luther attended a Nominalist university, and later entered a monastery that was a center of Nominalist thought.[43] He at one point viewed William of Ockham "as his master"[44]—the very one who insisted on God's omnipotence to the point that He could put Saints in hell and sinners in heaven. This God of the Nominalists, and of Luther, cannot respond to people, for that would limit his omnipotence, so he becomes an undependable, capricious God Who does not just permit, but ultimately for Luther, even must be the cause of evil. Gillespie makes a strong case that Calvin's theology was also influenced by the dark theology of Nominalism about Whom one can only know that he is totally omnipotent. It would seem that this negative view of God, at least in part, led to an intense search throughout this period and beyond for an infallible external criterion of ultimate truth (recall that in the Tradition, Ultimate Truth is a Person, namely Christ; and thus personal communion with Christ is the only way of knowing Ultimate Truth).[45]

---

43. Gillespie, pp. 103-104.

44. Ibid., p. 104.

45. For a more thorough discussion of this, see Gillespie's *Theological Origins of Modernity*. René Descartes provides a vivid example of this in a later period.

Although at first Luther wanted to work within the Roman Church, he and the other Reformers and their followers concluded that the institutional Roman Catholic Church of their day, with its novel, unbiblical doctrines (like papal supremacy, indulgences, purgatory, etc.) and the obvious immorality within it of various kinds, was beyond repair. Thus, that Church, her clergy and her traditions, could no longer be considered a reliable authority. Luther, along with many others, therefore, chose to assert a new authority, a new criterion of truth: Scripture alone (*sola scriptura*), as interpreted by the individual, whom, it is assumed, will be inspired by the Holy Spirit.[46]

It became evident almost immediately how problematic this is in practice. Although Luther had a profound spiritual experience and was convinced the resulting insights he had about spiritual life were inspired, and although he claimed to be using only Scripture with no allegorical interpretations, his key insights, ironically, were yet more novel, unbiblical doctrines. These novel ideas became, in effect, his new "rule of faith." Michael Gillespie, in his fascinating study *The Theological Origins of Modernity*, says, for example, that Luther's God, at least in this life, is "not a personal God at all, but resembles the Greek concept of fate governing and determining all things."[47] Luther compares the human will to a beast of burden that will either be ridden and guided by God or by Satan: "nor can it choose to run to either of the two riders or to seek him out, but the riders themselves contend for the possession and control of it."[48] In fact, Luther could only support his claims about the "bondage of the will"—the lack of free will in fallen humanity, so that "all things occur by absolute necessity"—by quoting John Wycliff, whom the Roman Church had condemned as a heretic, and Virgil, a pagan poet! As Gillespie points out, his view "puts him outside the previous Christian tradition altogether. It has no basis or support in Scripture, the church fathers, or scholasticism."[49] In this way, Luther provides an example of a very individualistic model of interpretation that many later Protestants took even further.

Erasmus, in an effort to draw Luther into discussion about his new approach of "Scripture alone" that he claims as support for his novel doctrines, asks him why anyone should trust his subjective impression of what Scripture means, or for that matter, *anyone's* subjective impression, more than that of others?—"One might claim that such certainty is warranted because it comes from God, but this claim is complicated by the fact that others make similar claims that do not agree with your own." This question of how to discern which

---

46. Dungan, op. cit., pp. 157-158.

47. Ibid., p. 114.

48. Cited in Gillespie, op. cit., p. 154.

49. Ibid., p. 145.

interpretations are authoritative will be one of the most significant problems for the Reformers, and especially for those who come after them. Erasmus continues very perceptively, asking

> Furthermore, how do you know that it is God rather than Satan who fills you with this sense of certainty? And if you do have the truth, why are there so many great men who stand against you and only three who agree with you—Valla, Hus, and Wycliff—the first in trouble and the latter two already condemned as heretics?"[50]

Clearly, this is the very opposite of a consensual approach. As Gillespie paraphrases Erasmus, it is as if Luther is saying, "I have the Spirit of Christ, which enables me to judge everyone but no one to judge me; I refuse to be judged, I require compliance." Gillespie goes on to explain that

> Erasmus in this way sees Luther, like the Stoics, relying on an absolute standard or criterion [of truth]. He knows that Luther believes that Scripture is such a criterion, but he knows it cannot serve this function. . . . different people read Scripture differently depending on the goal they have in view. Many of the apparent contradictions in Scripture are thus not in the text but in the exegesis of the text. Coming to terms with Scripture requires not the uncompromising assertion of what one believes Scripture to mean, but *a broad, communal discussion that reflectively compares multiple views of one's contemporaries and one's predecessors.*[51]

Important implications for practical virtue also come out of these two opposing views on interpreting Scripture and related ideas. Erasmus's goal in his discussion is to emphasize Divine goodness and human responsibility, and to encourage virtue. He believed there was time to develop "a program of education . . . that would bring about a gradual improvement in both morality and piety" in the Roman Church. In contrast, since Luther believed that "God's triumph . . . eliminates all our doubts, for when he rules in our souls, *we cannot err*,"[52] he is so concerned to assert his "infallible" views that he insisted, as Gillespie points out, "immediate reformation was necessary *regardless of the cost*."[53] He even responds to "Erasmus's concerns that his bellicose dogmatism

---

50. Ibid., pp. 148-149 (here Gillespie is summarizing Erasmus's thought).
51. Ibid., p. 149 (my emphasis).
52. Ibid., p. 155, Gillespie paraphrasing Luther.
53. Ibid., p. 151 (my emphasis).

would allow evil to triumph" in the following words: "As to your saying that a window is opened for impiety by these dogmas, let it be so."[54]

Luther also accuses Erasmus of Pelagianism,[55] and is so concerned to avoid that heresy himself, that he goes to an opposite extreme. Erasmus, anticipating this criticism, carefully explains why his view is instead, like that of Augustine (the premier opponent of Pelagianism): yes, grace is required for salvation, but we have free will and need to exercise it in cooperation with God. (This is really the early Augustine's view, as well as essentially that of the whole Orthodox Tradition; this *cooperation* with grace is called "synergy.")[56] Luther, however, never answers most of Erasmus' points—he simply resorts to *ad hominem* attacks.

One's understanding of free will and synergy has important implications for biblical interpretation; if one believes that we have free will, and that we need to work *with* God's grace, then one will be much more likely to embrace an understanding that proper biblical interpretation involves "a broad communal discussion [or a consensual approach] that reflectively compares multiple views of one's contemporaries and one's predecessors."

Actually, the Reformers were not a new phenomenon. What was new was the failure of the Roman Catholic Church to limit the influence of these Reformers, and to prevent such a large number of people from completely breaking with her. Another path is represented by Erasmus, and those like him, who saw the same problems with the Roman Church that the Reformers did, but who believed these problems were the result of fallen human nature (not inherent in the institution of the Roman Catholic Church), and that thus they could take time to work within the Roman Church to reform it. They proposed careful study of Scripture, *and* careful study of both the Greek and the Latin Fathers, to discern the *consensus* uniting all of them—something which had not been possible in a significant way for centuries in the West—thereby to renew the Church from within. (The Reformation created such a strong reaction within the Roman Church that it is impossible to know how much success "Erasmus'

---

54. Ibid., p. 161.

55. Ibid., p. 151. Gillespie succinctly describes Pelagianism as the belief that "extraordinary works of virtue can win salvation without grace" (p. 150).

56. In his later writings, written specifically against the Pelagians, Augustine rejects his earlier view on free will, now stating that affirming free will lessens God's omnipotence—which he evidently thought must be safeguarded in the face of Pelagianism, even if it meant affirming double predestination, limited atonement, and irresistible grace—none of which were affirmed by any of the Greek Fathers, and all of which would very much seem to make God no longer primarily "the good God Who loves mankind."

path" would have had in reforming the Roman Church if it had been taken by the majority of reformers).

It is interesting that many of the early Protestant Reformers also looked to the Church of the first centuries, and especially the first four Ecumenical Councils, as well as to a number of the most prominent Church Fathers, to guide their "reformation" of the church of their own time. One could say their main objection was more to the pope of Rome being given so much authority (something the Orthodox would agree with!), as well as to the moral corruption that was so evident, rather than a rejection of the Church as it had developed in the first centuries. Both Calvin and Philip Melanchthon (Luther's primary, though much more moderate, theologian) — to give two examples — were, like Erasmus, trained as Humanists and had studied Greek. Interestingly, the Church Father whom Calvin quotes most often after St. Augustine is St. John Chrysostom. Thomas Torrance even summarizes Calvin, stating that his intention was "to restore the face of the ancient Catholic Church."[57]

However, there was not a lot of knowledge about the early Church in their day, and they were, at least from an Orthodox Christian standpoint, cut off from the living Tradition of that Church. They were also in a serious quandary: how could they justify leaving the Roman Church and setting up an alternative ecclesiastical structure, unless there were radical differences between themselves and the Roman Church, especially concerning how to determine dogma — which meant how to determine authoritative interpretations of Scripture?

In the matter of the Ecumenical Councils, for instance, while Calvin says "I venerate them from my heart and desire that they be honored by all," he also says "we have been amply equipped by the Word of the Lord for the *full proof* of our teaching and for the overthrow of all popery, and consequently there is no great need to require anything additional" — thus, in effect, making the Councils optional. He does say that if required, the Councils would "provide us enough evidence" both for his teachings and the "overthrow of popery."[58] But this begs the questions: *whose* interpretation of Scripture does the "Word of the Lord" provide the "full proof" of, and how? Why does Calvin think that they needed to have those Councils in the early centuries if "the Word of Lord" could really, *by itself*, provide "full proof"? Nothing the Reformers say really

---

57. This is how Thomas Torrance summarizes Calvin's intent in his *Kingdom and Church: A Study in the Theology of the Reformation* (Edinburgh: Oliver and Boyd, 1956), p. 73.

58. Calvin, *Institutes*, Book IV, ch. ix; p. 1166 in the second volume of the Westminster Press edition of 1960; my emphasis.

answer this question: on what basis can Calvin, Luther,[59] and the others claim *their* interpretations of Scripture are authoritative? Their approach, and the dilemma it springs from, will lead many to take "Scripture alone" much more literally and consistently than the early Reformers like Calvin and Luther did.

A classic example of a doctrine that both Luther and Calvin (as well as many later followers) came to assert which is completely alien to traditional Christianity, and which seems to come more from Nominalist ideas of God than from the New Testament, is double predestination. This is the idea that God creates certain people not only definitely to go to heaven, but also He creates some in order for them to be tormented eternally in hell for doing things and being a certain way they had no control over—He created them to be that way. And there is nothing they can do about it, for they are *predestined* to this. A God who would do this is a God who looks nothing like Jesus Christ Who is the "express image" (Heb. 1:3) of the good God Who loves mankind, but rather a lot like the devil (as even Luther apparently admitted). Luther even said that "the highest degree of faith" is "to believe that He is merciful, Who *saves so few and damns so many; to believe Him just, Who according to His own will, makes us **necessarily** damnable*"![60] Here we can also note a very different understanding of faith, one that underlies the popular view today: rather than the "certainty" or "*proof*" of things *unseen* (Heb. 11:1), faith becomes trusting in what you have no basis in reason or reality for trusting!

So, in spite of a desire on the part of a number of the Reformers to try to be in line with the early Church (and to prove that the Roman Catholic Church was not), Scripture alone as interpreted by the individual (following that initial model of Luther) becomes the ultimate authority. In any case, especially for many of those in the post-Reformation, the individual self is in effect substituted for the interpretive context provided by Tradition. This was not really a new idea (Wycliffe and Hus had promoted a similar idea two centuries earlier), but rather an idea whose time had come—it took on new power in the cultural/theological framework of the day.

One important result for biblical studies of this novel claim that "Scripture alone" can be authoritative is that those following the original Reformers had to focus much more on trying to *prove* the authority of "Scripture alone," as well as the unity of Scripture. This in turn led eventually to a new, much greater

---

59. Luther even more openly chose to adopt this new criterion of truth—this new authority: Scripture alone (*sola scriptura*), as interpreted by his own conscience (Dungan, op. cit., pp. 157-158).

60. Martin Luther, *The Bondage of the Will* (Grand Rapids, MI: Baker Book House, 1976), pp. 70-71.

focus on hermeneutics within this tradition in an attempt to find a way to determine which interpretations are, in fact, authoritative.

Contrary to what is often assumed, the Reformers' insistence on Scripture alone, Scripture as the only and ultimate authority, was not *primarily* the result of a greater love of Scripture as the Word of God than previous Christians had had (though the Reformers' love of Scripture is not in question).

The emphasis on the importance of Scripture was not at all original with the Protestant Reformers. As mentioned, a renewed emphasis on personal and group Bible study and personal meditation on the Gospel, and an emphasis on living the Gospel, was very popular within the late medieval Roman Catholic Church—about 150 years before Luther or Calvin—e.g., Groote's Brethren of the Common Life was a large, very influential movement. Also, by the 15th century, the parish clergy were much better educated (from one third to one half of all the clergy in southern Germany had some university education). Well before the Reformation, therefore, people expected the clergy to really preach and not just "say mass," and we have evidence that there were long sermons. There were textbooks on preaching, and even illustrated Bible picture books for clergy who were barely literate, so even they could preach using the Bible!

What was original was the Reformers' radical solution to the problem of how to discern the truth when your previous authority has gone awry, and this was primarily the result not only of the whole historical situation outlined above, but also of their acceptance of a new worldview which enabled them to believe, among other things, that Scripture could be *self-interpreting* (although Wycliffe was already espousing a similar view in the late 14th century). That is, the literal sense of its words (as defined by Thomas Aquinas, the original human author's *full* meaning) was the true meaning and was clear in itself. Since Scripture was "self-interpreting," and because "the Word of the Lord" provided "full proof," as Calvin had said, one did not then *need* Tradition (or the Church hierarchy) to provide an interpretive context for understanding the Bible. Indeed, the implication was that one did not need an interpretive context at all.

The Reformers did admit that some passages were obscure, and Luther and Calvin said that sometimes you first need to know the historical context, etc.—and they said that uneducated people might need extra help in understanding such passages. But once you had that kind of information, those biblical passages become perfectly clear, and the obscure ones could rather easily be interpreted in the light of clearer ones. This belief was expressed in Luther's oft-quoted remark that Scripture is "through itself most certain, most easily accessible, comprehensible, interpreting itself, proving, judging all the words of all."[61] With this attitude, it also became natural and even necessary to focus on the "original meaning" of the words—and hence almost exclusively on the literal level of meaning. In any case, things had been gradually moving in the direction of focusing on the literal level since the 12th century in the West.

Since those in the Reformed tradition effectively rejected Tradition—or tried to—there was also the strong push to try to allow as direct and unmediated a link as possible between the reader and the biblical author, in order to have the closest possible access to the inspired original meaning.[62] This is part of the reason for so much emphasis on finding the original words of the historical Jesus, and the original historical meaning also. This becomes, in effect, an effort to *get behind the text* we have (passed down through the Church) to the original events. Trying to determine for sure the exact words of Jesus was something new, since it was not practical before the printing press, or of great importance for those who understood and trusted the basic transmission process for canonical Scripture, and the Church in which this process took place. For if you trust your witnesses and understand what they say, you have no need to try to "recreate" the original event from the text.

It is very important to understand that the only way anyone could even think of claiming that Scripture could be "alone authoritative" was by believing that it was truly "self-interpreting"—that the Councils, the Tradition of the Church, etc., however much they might be honored, were not necessary for later Christians in order to be able to determine authoritative interpretations. When they said it was "alone authoritative" as interpreted by the individual, they were assuming that the interpretations people would find would basically all agree, since Scripture—at least under the inspiration of the Holy Spirit—would actually somehow be interpreting itself.

It is obvious how inseparable the rise and continuation of the theology of the Reformed movement was from the belief in the "direct authority" of Scripture, and therefore, from the belief that language can be, and that biblical language is, self-interpreting. Yet from the beginning, this premise was often ignored. It was ignored when practices and teachings not explicitly mentioned in the Bible were kept (such as decisions of the Ecumenical Councils about Christ and the Holy Trinity), and when extensive biblical commentaries were written (for if Scripture is self-interpreting, why would these long biblical commentaries

---

61. Quoted by Hans Frei, *The Eclipse of Biblical Narrative: A Study in Eighteenth and Nineteenth Century Hermeneutics* (New Haven, CT: Yale University Press, 1974), p. 19; also quoted by Roy A. Harrisville and Walter Sundberg, *The Bible in Modern Culture: Theology and Historical-Critical Method from Spinoza to Kasemann* (Grand Rapids, MI: William B. Eerdmans Publishing Company, 1995), p. 18; second ed. (2002), p. 17.

62. Harrisville and Sundberg, p. 47; second ed., pp. 44-45.

be needed?). This key doctrine was also ignored in specific interpretations of Scripture.

Luther, for example, held that *only parts* of Scripture were "genuinely true and authoritative"— those parts "which proclaimed or clearly implied this awesome tension between law and gospel"[63] which he felt was the primary characteristic of the relationship between God and man. Thus, he effectively made a new "rule of faith," or interpretive key. This was surely an overreaction to the overemphasis on law and works (the teaching that that's all laypeople need—to do good works) in the Roman Catholic Church of his day, as well as a misunderstanding of the law in Judaism and early Christianity (as many scholars today point out). Needless to say, he did not see his interpretation as merely subjective. The telling point is that he was willing to invalidate anything expressed in canonical Scripture which did not agree with his theology, and his own "conscience" was the primary basis for making such critical decisions.

Conveniently, Luther "never equated the gospel with the written scriptures," but believed it was "essentially oral." He "contrasts Moses as a writer of 'doctrine' [having a negative view of doctrine, which is understood radically differently from the traditional Orthodox way] with Christ Who commanded that His teaching 'should be orally continued, giving no command that it should be written.'" To Luther, the existence of the New Testament itself was evidence of "a serious decline and a lack of the Spirit which necessity forced upon us,"[64] So he definitely did not believe in the inerrancy of the biblical text. Rather, we can say that for him, it was his "rule of faith," and the *skopos* of the Gospel, that was inspired.

This idea allowed him, for example, to disparage (even to the point of sarcasm) the injunction in Acts 15:29 not to eat blood, since the German people loved to eat blood sausages![65] Much more seriously, this approach allowed him to reject parts of canonical Scripture. For example, he considered the Epistle of James (since it is filled with positive remarks about doing good works) to be worthless—an "epistle of straw," as he wrote in his introduction to the book in his German translation of the Bible. He also wanted to relegate Hebrews and the Revelation to a lower status, and to eliminate the Book of Esther altogether since it doesn't mention God. So, in effect, he was making his own canon of Scripture! And in practice, he largely ignored even the synoptic Gospels, since they give so many "moral injunctions"—all the many teachings given by Christ about Christian behavior. As David Dungan observes, Luther "refused

---

63. Frei, op. cit., p. 20.

64. Harrisville and Sundberg, second ed., p. 15, citing a passage in Luther's *Church Postil* of 1522.

65. Ibid., p. 15.

to use the teachings of Christ in the Gospels as a guide to Christian holiness,"[66] because that seemed to go against "faith alone." Calvin and other Reformers, however, did not follow him in being that extreme.

There were multiple reasons why the Reformers and their followers largely rejected allegorical interpretation. One reason was the Reformers' need to focus so much on the literal level and the original historical meaning of the biblical authors in order to support the inseparable doctrines of "Scripture alone" as authoritative, and the doctrine of Scripture as interpreting itself. Another reason was the Roman Catholic hierarchy's use of very arbitrary allegorical interpretations to try to prove that their novel practices and dogmas were biblical, as well as a general tendency toward very arbitrary allegorical interpretations in the Middle Ages for those in that Church. Hence, Luther was largely opposed to allegorical interpretations, and misunderstood their use by the Fathers. He even said he had

> wasted and lost much time on Gregory, Cyprian, Augustine, and Origen. For the Fathers, in the their time, had a remarkable attraction to and liking for allegories; they used them constantly, and their books are full of them . . . the reason is this, that they all followed their own conceit, mind and opinion, as they thought right, and not St. Paul, who wanted to let the Holy Spirit act there from within.[67]

Luther does not seem to notice the irony that this is exactly what he openly claims to do: to follow his own "mind and opinion"—though he believes he is inspired by the Holy Spirit, unlike the Fathers (whom Luther by implication believed were not nearly so inspired as himself). The Fathers, in fact, aim to follow one another, looking for consensus; or as St. Basil said, "But as for us, what our fathers said, we repeat. . . . But we are not content simply because this is the tradition of the Fathers. What is important is that the Fathers followed the meaning of Scripture."[68]

When Luther toured around the villages of his area as an "inspector" and found out what the minimally educated people reading Scripture on their own were getting out of it, he was apparently quite dismayed, for they were getting out of it quite different ideas from those he had gotten! "Scripture alone" was definitely not working in these circumstances. He decided "the Church would have to push the [Gospel] message more systematically," and to help matters

---

66. Dungan, op. cit., p. 178.

67. Quoted by Pope Benedict XVI, *Principles of Catholic Theology: Building Stones for a Fundamental Theology* (San Francisco: Ignatius Press, 1987), pp. 140-141.

68. On the Holy Spirit, ch. 7; SVS Press edition, p. 34.

along, he wrote several catechisms—a shorter one for "ordinary people," and a longer one for teachers and pastors.[69] Thus he began a serious campaign of education, in order to provide *a new interpretive context to replace the Tradition of the Church*—without, apparently, his ever noticing the full implications of these inconsistencies.[70]

So from the beginning, even the first Reformers could not really put into practice what they were claiming: that the Bible is self-interpreting, and therefore alone authoritative. Although a useful concept to defend the basic Protestant position, *sola scriptura* was impossible for even the original Reformers to follow thoroughly in practice, since it is impossible for any text to be self-interpreting (which is not to deny that some passages are clear to most readers, at least on the surface). An interpretive context is both unavoidable and essential, as even Luther's recognition of the necessity for education in order for people to have a proper understanding of Scripture shows, as does the continued emphasis in Protestant circles on Sunday Schools and Bible Studies to help people *learn* how Scripture should be interpreted.

All of the above should make it less surprising that *sola scriptura*, the attempt to use only the Bible as an ultimate authority, leads us to the historical-critical method.

From Sola Scriptura to Pseudo-Science: A Brief Overview of the History Behind the Historical-Critical Method

Before it is possible to adequately understand the historical-critical method and why it so often seems to be the enemy of the Faith—yet an "enemy" which serious scholars of Scripture in some ways seem to be unable to do without—it is important to be aware of its historical context: why it arose when it did, and why it became so dominant. Having considered the pre-history, we can now look at an overview of the immediate history of this method.

Despite the fact that so many serious, reasonable Christians praying for the guidance of the Holy Spirit were getting different—and even

---

69. MacCulloch, op. cit., pp. 160-161.

70. Calvin agreed with Luther "in affirming the right of scripture to interpret itself over against the ecclesiastical ideology of allegorical exegesis." But in other important ways, he had quite a different approach, for he was even more extreme than Luther in emphasizing the literal level. Calvin allowed no allegorical interpretation of anything in the New Testament, and only a little of the Old. He even rejected some standard Christological interpretations (such as the "her seed" in Genesis 3:15 bruising the serpent's head, which was from very early times seen as a prophecy of Christ).

radically conflicting—interpretations of Scripture, all Protestants in the Post-Reformation period clung to the claim that Scripture is "self-interpreting." Their experience does not seem to have led them to ask what seems to be such an obvious question to many today: can Scripture really be "self-interpreting" if so many serious, prayerful, educated Christians are getting such radically different interpretations?

In spite of the growing evidence to the contrary, the Reformers had to insist on Scripture being "self-interpreting" because only if this claim were true could Scripture be "alone authoritative." Only if this claim were true could they succeed in establishing a new, alternate "authority" instead of the Roman Catholic Church, her hierarchy, and her Tradition as they understood them. Thus, although the Reformation era discussion of Scripture was largely concerned with its authority and unity, Protestant interpreters from the post-Reformation era onwards needed to find a way to solve this most serious problem: *how* to enable Scripture to be "self-interpreting" *in practice*, so that it could effectively be "alone authoritative." This is the main reason why the hermeneutical question—the emphasis on principles of interpretation and methodology—came to be of such importance.

Just as the Roman Church had been moving away from the traditional conciliar approach in her government (to the idea of the pope of Rome being the Supreme Pontiff over all the churches), so also the Roman Church had been moving away from the traditional consensual approach[71] to biblical interpretation. Although Erasmus and others advocated for a version of this, by the time

---

71. This consensual approach meant that on matters of doctrine, the "rule of faith," the *skopos*, and a consensus of past and present witnesses recognized as authoritative by the Church (usually Church Fathers and Saints, and including the witness of Scripture itself), would be authoritative. In cases where there was still disagreement over matters crucial to the Faith, Ecumenical Councils, attended in principle by all the bishops representing all the churches, would come together, pray, discuss—following the model in Acts 15—and decide. But if enough people (including laity!) disagreed with the decisions of a Council, its authority could later be revoked (e.g., the "Robber Council" of 449, and the Iconoclastic Council of 754). There was also a sense of defining only what was absolutely essential for maintaining "access" to the new life in Christ. See Ch. 8 for further discussion.

The Roman Church at the time of the Reformation, and well afterwards, emphasized instead that the pope and bishops were the "supreme" interpreters, expanding in an exclusive way the teaching office traditional for bishops. And before and during that period, they were using allegorical interpretations of Scripture to try to prove that their innovations (such as papal supremacy) were biblical and hence part of the authentic Tradition—a use of allegory that was never made in the earlier Tradition (but was common in Gnostic circles). This approach was not seriously looking for a consensus with a majority of witnesses from the past, nor did it include even

of the Reformation, in the minds of many, this approach was evidently either too closely connected with the corrupt Roman Catholic hierarchy, or misunderstood, and Protestants in the post-Reformation era searched for another way.

The Reformation, the Post-Reformation, and the Scientific Revolution all arose in the same historical context and were influenced by the same worldviews. Each of these large-scale movements seems to have supported and furthered the development of the others. So, it is quite in keeping with their historical context that many of those in the Post-Reformation who needed to find a way to discern the truth in Scripture which would enable it to remain "alone" (i.e.,"disentangled" from any tradition or church hierarchy—at least the Roman Catholic hierarchy) eventually turned to applying a "scientific" method to Scripture.

Many problems still today in biblical scholarship and in spiritual life result from a misunderstanding of science, including that it is necessarily opposed to religious faith, and a misunderstanding of what a scientific approach actually involves. This has led to a misuse of the idea of using a "scientific" approach in interpreting Scripture. Thus, it is important to look briefly at this background to more completely address this first of the four key issues in biblical interpretation mentioned in Chapter 1.

The Scientific Revolution is generally understood to have begun around 1550 with the work of Copernicus, and to end around 1700 with the work of Isaac Newton. However, as mentioned in Chapter 1, it was the Roman Catholic Cardinal Nicolas of Cusa (d. 1464) who, in addition to his works on the mystical life and the real possibility of directly knowing God, had written that the earth must revolve around the sun and upon its own axis, as well as that the universe was infinite and ruled by mathematically derived laws.[72] What Copernicus (1473-1543), another faithful churchman, did was to provide mathematical proof for Cardinal Nicolas's theory about the earth. That is why he is credited by most as beginning the Scientific Revolution.

Copernicus intended only to "purify" classical Aristotelian cosmology. Instead, his work led to its being overthrown, which served as another blow to the trust the people in the medieval West placed in the basic idea of Tradition and the "authority of the ancients" (never mind that these were pagan

---

recognized Saints and earlier Church Fathers, whether clergy or lay (such as St. Maximus the Confessor, one of the greatest Orthodox Fathers, who was not ordained).

72. Dungan, op. cit., p. 150. Nicolas of Cusa's mathematical and astronomical ideas were based on speculation (and also on theology and number symbolism) rather than direct observation, which was technologically impossible in his time; but his ideas were later proved to be correct.

ancients!).[73] Less than one hundred years later, Galileo (d. 1642), with his telescope, was able to provide empirical evidence for Cardinal Nicolas's theory.

The scientific method itself developed over many centuries, actually beginning in ancient Greece, being further developed in the Muslim world and the medieval West, until the Scientific Revolution in Western Europe. The classic scientific method of that later period, simply put, was understood to be first of all a gathering of information from nature through direct observation (i.e., empirical data), by an objective observer who would carefully and systematically study the data by means of repeatable experiments—carefully and thoroughly testing all hypotheses and conclusions, until finding a hypothesis that best accounted for all the results of the experiments.

The fact that the data was gathered by an objective observer with supposedly no preconceptions, and that the experiments were repeatable by anyone with the proper equipment, was seen to guarantee the certainty of the results. The traditions of the pagan ancients had been proven wrong on many counts during the late Middle Ages and after; thus it made sense to forget about these traditions and have any such matters under consideration examined directly. Again, the assumption was that the person, with his or her personal biases, prejudices, and other kinds of "traditions," could then be bypassed—and surpassed.

So, since Scripture alone as interpreted by the individual was not working in practice, it is not surprising that many of those in the Post-Reformation era eventually wanted to apply a "scientific" method to Scripture. They reasoned

---

73. Though he did not intend it, Copernicus' work can easily be seen as beginning an ever-growing trend to emphasize empirical observation, individual experience, rational argument, and sensory information as the surest ways to *all* true knowledge of reality—not just being dominant over, but even *replacing*, all Tradition, including the path of noetic knowledge through prayer, asceticism, etc.

As the theories of Copernicus, and of many other scientists and mathematicians, came to influence the overall world-view of western society, we see reality coming to mean exclusively what is physical (as the pure Nominalists asserted) and quantifiable—that is, only what can be measured. As a result, when reality is thus defined, empirical observation and mathematics become the dominant forms of knowledge.

In a traditional and biblical view, the cosmos is a harmonious, hierarchically ordered whole, created and *sustained* by God for His purposes. Therefore, He can "overrule" the usual order of nature whenever this is according to His purpose (we often hear this in our hymns), producing what we call miracles, etc. But this new emphasis on mathematics led to the world being viewed as always strictly uniform, and organized according to unbreakable natural laws. So in this view, God just gets the world started, but then the unbreakable laws He created in the beginning keep it working (Dungan, pp. 150-151). This was also thought to hold true for "natural laws" of language, just as much as for natural laws in physics and other natural sciences.

that since the scientific principles and natural laws would be "natural"—a "built-in" part of language—they were not technically something *additional* to Scripture; thus, in using them they would not be violating the principle of "Scripture alone." And since it was "objective," the scientific method could provide what Luther had, in essence, claimed that Scripture alone could be: an "infallible criterion of truth" that all reasonable people would have to agree with.[74] This "infallible criterion of truth" was not something sought for in the early Tradition, but it begins to be seriously sought for in connection with the late medieval Nominalists and their radically non-Christian understanding of God and reality.

An important element in this new approach to finding the truth in Scripture begins indirectly with Francis Bacon (1561-1626), who is credited with beginning truly modern science based on scientific empiricism (direct observation and/or experience); indeed, the scientific method is also known as the Baconian method.[75] One result of his approach was to emphasize the importance of methods—the idea that the most important element needed to discover the truth in science is *the correct method*. In this view, any errors made are the result of using a wrong, or a defective, method.

In a sense, exegetes were right in following Bacon's fundamental principle: the problems in exegesis did arise because the "correct method" was not being used. Unfortunately, however, the dazzling successes of the scientific method in the natural sciences, coupled with the attempt to reject Tradition and a failure to realize that different kinds of knowledge require *different* methods, depending upon what it is that one desires to know, led them away from the truly "correct method" for discerning the truth in the spiritual realm—"the method" which the Church Fathers and their followers have always used to interpret Scripture.[76] Many were led, instead, to believe that the best, and

---

74. We note here the belief in the possibility of complete objectivity, and that this is the ideal even with regard to spiritual matters.

75. To be termed scientific, a method of inquiry must be based on **empirical** and **measurable** evidence subject to specific principles of reasoning. The *Oxford English Dictionary* says that the scientific method is "a method or procedure that has characterized natural science since the 17th century, consisting in systematic observation, measurement, and experiment, and the formulation, testing, and modification of **hypotheses**" (my emphasis).

76. During the Middle Ages, many exegetes had already moved away from the "correct method" of the Fathers. For they focused on an overly rationalistic approach, emphasizing reason as the highest from of knowledge, rather than noetic knowledge. Now, to this overly rationalistic tendency was added the supremacy of empirical and deductive knowledge. (At first, of course, this attitude applied only to knowledge about nature, but gradually it was then extended to all kinds of knowledge, even knowledge about spiritual realities.)

indeed, the only "correct method" for every kind of knowledge is the scientific method. Many people during this time (and still today) had an almost blind faith in the reliability—and seeming inevitability for success—of anything discovered with the scientific method, or as we will see, of anything even labeled as being "scientific." Again, this did not just apply to knowledge in the natural sciences about the material world, but also for an increasing number of people, it referred to *all* knowledge.

Another unforeseen result of the claim of "Scripture alone" was, then, that in attempting to make this approach possible by looking for "natural laws" and principles by means of the scientific method, what Scripture *itself* says about interpreting spiritual realities was ignored. The very foundation of biblical hermeneutics was altered from noetic knowledge (and apostolic witness based on that knowledge—as well as later witnesses) to knowledge determined by reason alone, through a secular methodology. (Of course, the validity of noetic knowledge for knowing truth had already been minimized by many in the Middle Ages, and this had already resulted in an overly rationalistic approach in many quarters.) In fact, in the Post-Reformation, we are dealing with the first of many deceptions: for if Scripture needs *help* to be self-interpreting, then it is not really self-interpreting at all, despite Luther's claim that it was clear "in itself." And ironically, what is added—the interpretive context chosen to enable it to "interpret itself"—comes from the secular world-view of that era.

With this huge change from the traditional approach, it was perhaps inevitable that biblical studies would gradually become more and more secularized, and ironically, more and more seen as the province of a highly educated elite, rather than the Bible being seen as a holy text which everyone can read directly and thereby benefit from on some level—which was a hallmark of both traditional and Reformation theology.

Another key reason for the special appeal during this period of an objective, scientific approach that all reasonable people would have to agree with, becomes very clear if one looks even briefly at what was going on in Europe after the Reformation. This is a very important part of the story of the rise of the historical-critical method (as well as the rise of the negative attitude towards dogma that persists to this day in many quarters).

It could be said that one of the results of the widespread acceptance of the idea that Scripture is self-interpreting and alone authoritative was, ironically, the so-called Wars of Religion in the late 16th and 17th centuries. These wars involved Spain, the Netherlands, France, the German states, Denmark, Sweden, and England—in short, almost all of western Europe. The situation was worst in Germany, where the wars lasted 30 years (1618-1648), and some claim the population was reduced from 21 million to 13.5 million. In some cities over half the population were killed or had to abandon their homes.

As would be expected, this terrible time had a tremendous influence on the culture at many levels, including biblical studies. It wasn't just Roman Catholics and Protestants fighting against one another, but Lutherans against Calvinists, and one kind of Lutheran against a different kind of Lutheran. There were fierce battles over doctrine; inflammatory pamphlets and sermons were read and heard by all classes of people, many with little understanding of the dogmas involved, but all claiming the absolute authority of Holy Scripture for their varying interpretations. And the new ease of printing and distributing information due to the invention of the printing press contributed significantly to the conflicts.

As usual, these wars were only partly—or even superficially—about religion. In the Wars of Religion, "religious questions, more often than not, merely provided ideological and propagandist grounds for very secular war aims and peace proposals."[77] The Hapsburgs' hope of reestablishing the empire of Charlemagne—with one united Roman Catholic empire, ruled by the Hapsburgs—and the other European rulers' determined desire to prevent this (and/or sometimes with their own desire to rule all of Europe themselves) was at the root of the violence. The Reformation just added fuel to the already burning fire.[78]

This was not only because many princes had long wanted to take back power from the Roman Church—and in the new Protestant areas, the local governments were directly linked with the Protestant churches—or because inflammatory tracts which heightened the level of passion and lessened the level of understanding could be mass-produced easily and cheaply with the printing press. But also the doctrine of *sola scriptura* itself supports the idea that every individual is capable of interpreting Scripture correctly, regardless of

---

77. S. H. Steinberg, "Thirty Years' War," *Encyclopedia Britannica* (Chicago: Encyclopedia Britannica, Inc., 1983 [15th edition]), Macropedia, vol. 18, p. 334.

78. This was also the time when the witch hunts reached a peak. As the Protestant authors of *The Bible in Modern Culture* point out, "The radical dislocation of beliefs, practices and institutions that marked the Reformation unleashed dark forces of superstition and chaos" (p. 34). In one Swiss canton, between 1581-1680, 3,371 people were tried for witchcraft, every one of whom was killed (the usual pattern was that once you were accused you would automatically be found guilty, and would then be executed). This was just a little earlier than the Salem witch trials in the U.S. in 1690. This era of "religious" warfare in western Europe was similar to the period in France after the French Revolution with its Reign of Terror, and in Russia under the Soviets, and especially under Stalin (when millions were killed by the atheistic government). In both of these cases, the massacres were conducted by fiercely *anti-religious* rulers (giving the lie to those who claim that all the world's atrocities have been committed by those holding a form of monotheistic religion).

one's spiritual state, or even one's level of education. One can see that from this idea, a power struggle analogous to that of the independent European states struggling over who would control Europe, could easily arise over who would control the interpretation of Scripture. For again, out of the many conflicting interpretations of this supposedly self-interpreting text, without Tradition and a Church hierarchy, how could one determine, in an authoritative way, which interpretations were correct? No wonder the idea of an objective, "infallible criterion of truth" that all reasonable people would have to accept was so appealing.

This approach also sets the stage for great individualism and arrogance. For instead of humbly following the Church Fathers, and being actively, consciously part of the communion of believers in all times and places, each person is supposed to be capable of interpreting Scripture by himself or herself—because the claim really ends up being that one doesn't need help interpreting Scripture, since it interprets itself. Even if people claim that they are asking the Holy Spirit for guidance in their efforts at interpreting the Scriptures, how can one be sure it is really the Holy Spirit doing the inspiring, as Erasmus wisely asked Luther? Traditionally, there were two ways of being sure one's interpretation was correct: if it was in line with the consensus of the Tradition and the whole of Scripture, and by the positive fruits of living according to the interpretation, both of which were now being ignored.

From our perspective today, we can see that the violence was largely politically motivated, fueled by deep-seated PASSIONS thinly justified by appeals to upholding religious truth. As Charles Dickens insightfully observed of the analogous No Popery riots in London in 1780: "the worst passions of the worst men were thus working in the dark, and the mantle of religion, assumed to cover the ugliest deformities, threatened to become the shroud of all that was good and peaceful in society."[79] Tragically, at that time—and even to this day—many people came to think of religious passion, and an emphasis on dogma, as dangerous, because they believed that these things inevitably lead to violence. In fact, religious passion (with its related emphasis on the importance of "correct dogma") came to be seen as a serious danger to the survival of society, rather than as a virtue![80] Many looked for a way out of the intolerable conditions of the time for which religious passion was blamed. Tolerance,

79. Charles Dickens, *Barnaby Rudge* (Hertfordshire, Wordsworth Classics, 1998), p. 310.

80. It is a shame that people were not aware of the distinction made in the Orthodox spiritual tradition between "carnal zeal" and authentic religious zeal (for example, see St. Ignatius Brianchaninov, *The Arena*, Ch. 36, "Concerning Animal and Spiritual Zeal," pp. 140-144), as well as the traditional understanding of dogma—that it should be limited to only what is necessary to preserve the fullest spiritual experience for each.

rather than a Christ-inspired genuine love of God, neighbor, and even one's enemies, becomes the great virtue—an understanding that still prevails even more widely in much of western culture today.

One can certainly understand the appeal of an "objective" approach to interpreting Scripture in such a context: instead of killing one another over dogmas[81] which opposing sides claim are based on the same "self-interpreting" Scripture, let's forget dogma—and traditions—and instead, let's use a scientific method to carefully and thoroughly test any hypotheses and conclusions, considering all the evidence, and see "what is really there"—what all reasonable people will agree with.

The historical criticism has been seen by many as just such an objective, scientific approach that will lead to interpretations all "reasonable people" will have to agree with—thus ending strife ostensibly based on different interpretations of Scripture. Indeed, this approach came to dominate biblical studies for that reason. In the next chapter we will turn to a brief, more specifically focused history of the historical-critical method itself, and to the question of whether or not the dominance of this method is justified.

Before proceeding with this history, however, it is important to be clear that the basic *technical* premises of what is often generally referred to as the "historical-critical method" have been in use since the early days of Christianity—as indicated in the overview of the early history of Christian exegesis in Chapter 3. From the earliest times, for example, those interpreting Scripture have been aware of the value of knowing the historical setting of a text.[82] They would have realized that knowing that Jews and Samaritans would have nothing to do with each other at the time of Jesus significantly affects the impact on the reader of the parable of "The Good Samaritan" (Luke 10:30-35). Even in the New Testament itself, sometimes details are given to help provide the historical context for those from a different cultural/historical background—for example, the statement in the Gospel of John 4:9, the account of the Samaritan woman, that Jews and Samaritans have no dealings with one another.

Therefore, from any point of view, this kind of historical information is understood to be of value—sometimes of great value—in understanding the text of Scripture. In addition, the importance of careful linguistic analysis of the text (such as philological studies considering changing meanings of words, idioms, grammar, etc.), and of various other aspects of contemporary textual

---

81. Understood as authoritative propositional statements about truth as correct concepts that adequately express the truth believers must mentally assent to—statements more or less "containing" truth, rather than as authoritative statements needed to safeguard the fullness of experience of life in communion with Christ Who ultimately is Truth.

82. A few examples were given in Ch. 3.

criticism in a basic form, and other sorts of "technical" information, were recognized and valued within mainstream Christian hermeneutics, and are included in varying degrees in various patristic commentaries. The value of this kind of knowledge, found through what will be referred to as the TECH-NIQUES OF BIBLICAL CRITICISM—or just biblical criticism—in the context of traditional Christianity is not at issue here.

The historical-critical method, however, as will be demonstrated in the next chapter, involves the use, development, *and exclusive dominance* of these sorts of biblical critical techniques (and others) within the context of a very specific, secular, rationalistic world-view, radically different from traditional Christianity of any kind.[83] Such a world-view puts the Bible in a very different interpretive context, almost inevitably leading to interpretations radically different from those of traditional Christianity. This is especially the case when this methodology and its findings come to be seen as the only valid approach, and when they are given ultimate authority in determining the truths of the Christian Faith from Scripture. Looking in more detail into this method to see why it is "pseudo-science" will also enable us to continue to explore the two key issues of epistemology, and the role of science and the scientific method, in biblical studies.

---

83. Hans Frei calls this the world-view of "Scientific Realism." This world-view necessitates "a belief in the possibility of perceiving a language-neutral reality directly, or objectively, through the physical senses, thereby giving access to the truth about the world against which they could check or prove Scripture" (Mary Sanford, "'How Do You Read?': Theology and Hermeneutics in the Interpretation of New Testament Parables," unpublished doctoral dissertation, The University of Kent, Canterbury, UK, 1984, p. 64).

For false witnesses have risen against me, and
such as breathe out violence.
—PSALM 27:12

CHAPTER SIX

PSEUDO-SCIENCE AS UTOPIAN SOLUTION: A CRITICAL LOOK AT HISTORICAL CRITICISM

Let us flee from those who reject the patristic interpretations
and attempt by themselves to deduce the complete oppo-
site. While pretending to concern themselves with the lit-
eral sense of the passage, they reject its godly meaning.
—ST. GREGORY PALAMAS, 14TH C.[1]

The Father of the Method

What critic does not dream of a scientifically rigorous
way of characterizing the meaning of a text, of demon-
strating with tools of proven appropriateness that cer-
tain meanings are possible and others impossible?[2]

EVERY approach has its "fathers," though they are not always openly acknowledged. As we mentioned in Chapter One, the "father" of the first "scientific" method of interpreting Scripture is generally recognized to be the philosopher, Baruch Spinoza (1632-1677). He is the one credited with writing the first work advocating what we are calling "historical criticism," or

---

1. *The Homilies of St. Gregory Palamas,* ed. and trans. by Christopher Veniamin (Waymart, PA: Mount Tabor Publishing, 2009), Homily 34.2, p. 267.

2. Jonathan Culler, *Structuralist Poetics* (Ithaca, NY: Cornell University Press, 1976), p. 75.

the historical-critical method (as distinct from the TECHNIQUES OF BIBLICAL CRITICISM as used within traditional Christianity).

Spinoza was an ethnic Jew whose family was persecuted by Christians.[3] And he himself was excommunicated and "cursed with every curse of the Torah" by the Orthodox Jewish community in which he had been raised. It is not surprising, then, that his primary goal in life became to curb the dangers of religious passion, and "to find a new way to order society"[4] so that differing religious groups would be able to get along peacefully, and to have "civic equality and individual rights."[5] This could be done, Spinoza decided, through a new "scientific" method of interpretation based only on reason. Such an "objective" method, many came to hope, would result in interpretations which all reasonable people would have to agree with, thus ending strife over differing understandings of the Bible. Focusing on biblical interpretation allowed Spinoza to take advantage of the Bible's great authority at that time in order to achieve his political goal of tolerance.

In order to understand historical criticism accurately, why it is an "enemy of the Faith," it is very important to realize that Spinoza's new "scientific" method did not spring from a disinterested "objective" desire to find the truth through objective, scientific means. Rather, with his method, Spinoza hoped to reshape Christian (and Jewish) understanding of the Bible, and in the process, by-pass questions of ultimate truth which he viewed as unanswerable and only leading to strife. In other words, as will be evident from what follows, Spinoza's historical-critical method was not concerned with ultimate truths at all. Rather, it was inseparable from his utopian politics; it was really a covert vehicle for his very *subjective* beliefs and goals.

Spinoza's fundamental ideas were not new—he had his own "fathers," such as, the ancient Greeks Epicurus (341-270 BC) and Lucretius (94-55 BC). They had argued that the primary cause of all human unhappiness is fear of the gods, and that the "best happiness" in this life comes from overcoming this fear primarily through science, because it only concerns itself with *secondary* causes, using human reasoning alone. According to this view, then, religion, with its concern for *ultimate* causes, and science, with its concern for secondary causes, were considered to be such opposites that as one increases the other must decrease. Epicurean philosophy also presupposed that "the essence of institutional religion is the priestly manipulation of the fear of the gods by means of dogma and ritual." Building on tendencies in Reformation thought

---

3. The anti-Semitism of Spinoza's time was intense; even if a Jew became a Christian, he or she was just as vulnerable to being persecuted for his or her ethnic background.

4. Harrisville and Sundberg, op. cit., p. 38; second edition, p. 36.

5. Harrisville and Sundberg, op. cit., p. 265; second ed., p. 333.

sympathetic to this later idea, Spinoza and others "also claimed that traditional dogmatic exegesis of the Bible was driven by a nefarious purpose: to insure the political power of the ecclesiastical hierarchy."[6]

Actual history does not confirm this supposed opposition between religion and science. Often, quite the reverse is the case. Although science can be said to have had its beginning in ancient pagan Greece, there is ample evidence that *modern* science arose largely from the insights and efforts of pious Christians, especially within Western Christian culture, with significant input from pious Muslims.[7] Actual history also does not support the idea that dogmatic exegesis is usually "driven" by hunger for power, as demonstrated many times throughout history, such as the complete loss of "power" and exile of St. John Chrysostom (4th c.) for fearlessly exegeting the Gospel in a way that offended the reigning empress Eudoxia, or the cutting out of St. Maximus the Confessor's tongue (7th c.) for his fearless defense of dogmatic truths.

Beginning in the 17th century, partly as a result of the many successes of the natural sciences, and partly as a result of the Wars of Religion, as well as several influential theological errors,[8] many people came to have great faith—an almost blind faith—in the superior power of science, the scientific method, and reason[9] in *every* area of knowledge, over against the power of religion and

---

6. Harrisville and Sundberg, op. cit., p. 265; second ed., p. 332.

7. See, for instance, any of Stanley Jaki's works; and *God's Philosophers: How the Medieval World Laid the Foundations of Modern Science*, by James Hannam (London: Icon Books, 2010).

8. Including both the previously dominant Augustinian idea promoted by Luther that "the dark, predestinating will of God" controls everything, as well as the rejection of that dogma (Harrisville and Sundberg, p. 266; second ed., p. 333).

9. Here I am using the word "reason" as understood in the narrow Cartesian sense, the way in which we normally use the word today, in contrast to the earlier understanding of reason which included intuition, morality, etc. As David Bentley Hart has said, "Reason, in the classical and Christian sense, is a whole way of life, not the simple and narrow mastery of certain techniques of material manipulation, and certainly not the childish certitude that such mastery proves that only material realities exist. A rational life is one that integrates knowledge into a larger choreography of virtue, imagination, patience, prudence, humility, and restraint.

"Reason is not only knowledge, but knowledge perfected in wisdom. In Christian tradition, reason was praised as a high and precious thing, principally because it belonged intrinsically to the dignity of beings created in the divine image; and, this being so, it was assumed that reason is also always morality, and that charity is required for any mind to be fully rational. Even if one does not believe any of this, however, a rational life involves at least the ability to grasp what it is one does not know, and to recognize that what one does know may not be the only kind of genuine knowledge there is" (*Atheist Delusions: The Christian Revolution and Its Fashionable Enemies* [New Haven: Yale University Press, 2010]).

revelation. In a new version of the Epicurean view, it was also believed that it would be through reason, using the scientific method, that humanity would be enabled to control—or even dominate—nature,[10] overcome its problems, including bringing an end to warfare and all kinds of violence, and create an earthly paradise.

Spinoza's work extends this utopian hope of his day to biblical studies. It comes out of this great faith in human reason, and it increased in popularity at least partly because so many came to share this faith in reason alone and the premier method of reason alone: the scientific method. Many also came to accept the Epicurean view that science is necessarily opposed to any kind of revealed religion which claims access to ultimate truths and ultimate, or primary, causes, as well as the view that people should focus their scholarly attention exclusively on the less divisive secondary causes available to reason alone. It is not surprising that in this historical context, Spinoza's historical-critical method was developed and eventually came to be widely used.

As will be evident in the discussion of its defining principles below, the historical-critical method has a completely different focus and goals from those of traditional exegesis. These differences have allowed Spinoza's followers to have a great deal of success in reshaping the way many Christians' understand the Bible, and in doing so, thereby also reshaping the understanding of many aspects of their theology and dogma. It is important to emphasize again, however, that the fundamental differences between traditional exegesis and Spinoza's historical-critical method have little to do with the technical methods that are used in either, but a great deal to do with theology and dogma—*the interpretive context* within which the methods are used—especially Christology and epistemology. Tragically, this ignoring of ultimate theological truths has had a significant negative impact on the spiritual lives of the many people affected. And, of course, it has not succeeded in lessening violence among people; indeed, the effects of violence have become far worse with the technological "improvement" of weapons. Even without *any* religious zeal, people are still easily dominated by greed, envy, and lust, which are the negative passions that actually lead to violence, and which can only be truly overcome when the narrow path of virtue outlined in the Gospel of Christ and the Church's entire Tradition is practiced.

---

10. Throughout his book, *The Theological Origins of Modernity*, Gillespie makes an excellent case that reactions to the dark god of Nominalism largely motivated the huge push towards this way of thinking, including the idea that humanity should *dominate* nature. By contrast, in traditional Christianity mankind is seen as part of nature, or creation, which has an independent goodness in itself, since it was created by God. It was not good merely when it was useful to people. The ideas that people should "dominate" nature, and that nature is only good insofar as it is useful, are, in fact, later secular, non-Christian beliefs.

Defining Principles

It will be helpful to explain in more detail the principles of Spinoza's method, since those today who use the historical-critical method still subscribe to these *defining* principles. Underlying this system is the belief that God has never really revealed Himself, and thus that we cannot say He is "the good God Who loves mankind" as revealed by Jesus Christ and affirmed in traditional Christianity (or in Judaism, to some degree). Harrisville and Sundberg, authors of *The Bible in Modern Culture*, conveniently distill the fundamental principles of Spinoza's method. These, of course, reflect the secular, Enlightenment world-view of Spinoza, and can be summarized as follows:

1. "First, the Bible is treated like any other text. It is shorn of *a priori* religious authority."[11] The second principle is closely related:

2. "Spinoza rejects the dogmatic tradition of exegesis. The Bible must be understood . . . apart from the use made of it by synagogue and church."[12]

It is clear that "suspicion of the dogmatic tradition was a chief interpretive principle of the Reformation," and thus Harrisville and Sundberg, both Protestants, have no trouble recognizing that "Spinoza plants himself firmly in this Reformation tradition when he declares, 'all knowledge of Scripture must be sought from Scripture alone.'"[13] This approach was taken, of course, because it was assumed that the historic Church and her Tradition as expressed in the authorities of the past are not inspired or reliable, and thus there is no point in seeking a consensus of those authorities to determine if individual experiences and interpretations are authentic, or true.

It is this approach that also results, from the Reformation onwards, in an almost exclusive focus on the literal level, in the sense of the grammatical-historical meaning. Without a clear rule of faith provided by Tradition, allegorical interpretations come to be seen as dangerously subjective, and enabling the interpreter to make Scripture mean whatever he or she wants it to. And if allegorical interpretations have become very arbitrary (as they had by the late Middle Ages), and are even being used to try to define dogma—especially the doctrine of Papal supremacy—as they were in the medieval Roman Church, this negative assessment could be very accurate.[14] As is abundantly evident

---

11. Ibid., p. 44; second ed., p. 41.

12. Ibid.

13. Ibid.

14. A classic example would be Pope Innocent III writing in a letter to the nobles of Tuscany in 1198, saying that just as there were two lights in the heavens, there is both papal and royal

today, however, one can achieve this same negative effect quite easily while using the historical-critical method and focusing on the literal level—as some of the examples at the end of this chapter demonstrate.

3. Spinoza, however, radically narrows the meaning of the "literal" level, for he claims it must necessarily and *only* refer to a secular, temporal, and profane understanding. "The various books of the Bible are explained in relation to the mundane causes, historical conditions, and cultural presuppositions of the time in which they were written. . . . Central theological claims are neutralized by social context."[15] One could also say he assumes that God, and everything to do with the spiritual life, is only a matter of political power and control—a function of social systems, historical contexts, etc., and nothing to do with actual spiritual realities that transcend specific historical periods and social systems. Spinoza further arrogantly assumes that he, and those who use his "scientific" method, can be in relation to the Bible, rather like the omniscient author of a novel who can reveal hidden motives, and uncover for the reader the true thoughts of the characters—which may or may not correspond to what they say, and which they may not even be aware of themselves.

Thus, for him, the literal level of meaning of a statement such as "God said" cannot be that God really said whatever is stated, or even that God inspired the author. Rather, one must "go behind" the text to uncover why the human author would have used this expression. Indeed, Spinoza asserts that the Hebrews did not ever literally mean "God said" to indicate a direct revelation from God; it was just *a manner of speaking*, such as, "if they make money from some transaction, they say it has come to them from God."[16] But here Spinoza is clearly confusing secondary and primary/ultimate causes.[17]

The dogmatic tradition of exegesis is rejected so thoroughly that, as mentioned, it excludes even God Himself! Spinoza went so far as to insist that proper research into the meaning of Scripture must be undertaken "*'ut si Deus non daretur'*—as if there were no God."[18] It is hard to see how an interpretive approach to the Bible can rightly be considered "objective," or "scientific," when it rules out the existence of the Bible's main subject before any interpretation has begun! In any case, for Spinoza, God is an impersonal, necessary

power; and just as the moon derives its light from the sun, so royal power is derived from papal.

15. Ibid., pp. 44-47; second ed., pp. 41-44.

16. Ibid., p. 41; second ed., p. 38.

17. Spinoza seems to fail to understand that many things have *both* secondary and ultimate causes—it is not "either/or, but "both/and." See, for example, St. Dorotheus on his gout (*Discourses*, op. cit., p. 191).

18. Harrisville and Sundberg, op. cit., p. 44; second ed., p. 42. See Chapter One, above.

first cause, basically equivalent to the universe,[19] and not the personal, living God of Scripture. Of course, this means that he rejects both the personal God of the Jews and also the Holy Trinity—the God of the Christians. Surely he is a strange "father" for a method of interpreting *their* Holy Scriptures!

Influenced also by the "idea of Progress," which applied to all areas of human undertaking—not just discoveries in the natural sciences and technology—Spinoza's method assumes that people during his time were superior to those in the past. Earlier, in the Late Middle Ages and Renaissance, most people shared a very high view of the ancients as being the experts: indeed, they got into trouble at times by having such a high view of certain pagan ancients like Aristotle. However, this meant that they strongly believed that their contemporaries had much to learn from those of earlier times. Spinoza, and an increasing number of people in his time and after, had just the opposite view, so that the so-called *Enlightenment* of the 17th and 18th centuries—a name given to the period by those living in it—could more properly be called the Age of Arrogance.

Such beliefs reinforced and magnified the dismissive attitude of many of the Reformers and their followers towards the Church Fathers and the patristic heritage as a whole. Later on, this dismissive attitude was reinforced when the history of exegesis (now viewed as "scientific") was treated as comparable to that of the natural sciences. As Pope Benedict XVI points out, in

> natural science and technology, the *history* of their discoveries is not an essential part of themselves, but *only a prehistory*. Only the datum is significant, not how it came to be. In much the same way, the history of exegesis has degenerated for the [contemporary] exegetes into a prehistory with which their own efforts are not directly concerned.[20]

This has meant that once "scientific" historical criticism becomes the dominant method, rather than even considering the riches of the patristic heritage, rather than seeing themselves as *part of the communion of believers in all times and places,* and rather even than focusing primarily on the biblical text alone, many biblical scholars have been extensively concerned to interact primarily, or even exclusively, with their own academic contemporaries in biblical

---

19. As Harrrisville and Sundberg say, for Spinoza, "it is the pluralistic condition of reality that is itself divine" (p. 43; second ed., p. 41). Their entire discussion is very helpful.

20. Joseph Cardinal Ratzinger, *Principles of Catholic Theology: Building Stones for a Fundamental Theology* (San Francisco: Ignatius Press, 1987), Part 1, Section 2 E, p. 133 (my emphasis).

scholarship.[21] Unfortunately, in this way not only has much wisdom not been passed on, but also many serious errors have been perpetuated for decades, as will be seen in an example below.

4. "The 'truth' of Scripture is that which is recognizable to unaided human reason. The meaning of the Bible must fit the experience of reality as we know it [in a secular sense]. Its accessibility is determined by its correspondence to the 'everyday' of human life, particularly its moral sensibility."[22] Above all, it must be "reasonable." So again, for Spinoza—and his followers—there is a denial of any real *spiritual* knowledge, of any need for inner purification or other "training" to acquire it, or a need for prayer, or inspiration in any sense, as well as a denial of any need for the Church as a body to confirm, or authenticate in any way, interpretations and dogma. Instead, it is asserted that all the "truth" of Scripture is clear even to the unredeemed, unpurified, uninspired (but highly educated) person's mind—the very kind of person who would be most likely to deny that the primary kind of spiritual knowledge which Scripture was originally intended to communicate is even possible.

This can be seen as a new variation of what St. Symeon the New Theologian (late 10th and early 11th c.) called *falling into all the heresies at once*, by denying that all people have the possibility of being "both great contemplatives and see[ing] God by the illumination and reception of the Holy Spirit, through whom the Son is perceived together with the Father."[23] For those using the historical-critical method, direct knowledge of God or of the risen Christ is not even a remote possibility, and in any case would be considered irrelevant for proper, "scientific" exegesis. It would be difficult to imagine any position more alien to traditional Christianity. As St. Symeon says, "He who makes this claim subverts all the divine Scriptures."[24]

5. A key feature of Protestantism is the belief that all Christians can, and should, read the Bible. Yet, ironically, certain fundamental ideas from within

---

21. As Eta Linnemann explains: "Less concern is shown for the object of research than for—largely rhetorical—interaction with other hypotheses. *'Scientific knowledge' is seen as that which has become established in the interplay of opinions,* and not—as one might expect—that which has withstood earnest investigation subjecting a given hypothesis to searching light" (*Biblical Criticism on Trial: How Scientific is "Scientific" Theology?* Robert Yarbrugh, trans. [Grand Rapids, MI: Kregel Publications, 2001], pp. 184-185; my emphasis). "Scientific theology" in that book's title is essentially the same as the term "historical criticism" in this book.

22. Harrisville and Sundberg, op. cit., p. 44; second ed., p. 42.

23. St. Symeon the New Theologian, *The Discourses* (New York: Paulist Press, 1980), p. 312.

24. Ibid.

Protestantism itself (especially the key idea of "Scripture alone" which created the need for an alternative way of determining authoritative interpretations) led to Spinoza's last principle: "it is only an educated elite that is fit to judge what is and what is not reasonable. The true exposition of the Bible is confined exclusively to the intellectual class in society, not the masses. The masses will continue to be driven by their passions. They will be unable to absorb the knowledge engendered by scientific study of the Bible. But the intellectuals of society can use this knowledge to interpret Scripture for socially beneficial ends—above, all, the peaceful coexistence of differing religious sects."[25]

During the Middle Ages in the Roman Church, it was a hierarchical elite, the Church's priests and bishops—the teaching *magisterium*—who were considered to be the only ones who could properly understand the Scriptures. With Spinoza and his heirs, it is an academic elite—the intellectuals—who alone have all the scientific tools and knowledge now deemed essential for proper interpretation of Scripture. (Though as we've seen already, this elitist attitude was being held by some medieval intellectuals in the growing universities.) This elitist attitude continues to be held by many modern interpreters. The well-known 20th century biblical critic Norman Perrin, for example, explicitly says that those who "hear" Jesus "today need all the apparatus of historical-critical scholarship to be able to do so."[26]

A final, crucial aspect of this last principle to underline is the idea that only these "reasonable" interpretations, discovered by the academic elite through this "scientific" method, should/can be *authoritative*. This means, or comes to mean, that through this method *individual* academics can/should determine dogma authoritatively. That belief is based *solely* on the claim that this method is "scientific." This belief, as well as the method's elimination of any role for the Holy Spirit and for spiritual knowledge of any kind, are the most destructive elements of this approach, making it virtually the polar opposite of a traditional Christian approach.

In traditional Christianity—of the early centuries, and for the Eastern Orthodox still—*individuals* (even popes) cannot determine dogma authoritatively. For authoritative dogma, real spiritual knowledge through inspiration by the Holy Spirit, *and* being part of the communion with God and others in the Church (especially through a patristic consensus and the Church's Ecumenical Councils' interpretations of Holy Scripture), form the foundation. Because of this fact, it is very important to understand not only that the historical-critical method is not truly scientific, but also that even if it were, because of the kind of knowledge Scripture is primarily concerned with, and the kind of *reality*

---

25. Harrisville and Sundberg, op. cit., p. 45; second ed., p. 42.

26. Norman Perrin, *Rediscovering the Teaching of Jesus* (London: S.C.M. Press, 1967), p. 104.

that the Church which Jesus Christ founded is, this method could never be suitable for determining dogma (though again, most of the techniques used within it can be very helpful in understanding the meaning of the texts when used within the proper interpretive context).[27]

In addition to articulating these five basic principles, Spinoza very cleverly redefined other words. For example, he asserted that "true Christianity" consists only in its universal moral values, which are shared by all the world's major religions and by most "rational" people. Thus, in "true Christianity" there would be nothing to fight about, because there is nothing true that is unique to it or different from what any other religion teaches! Of course, this begs the question of who would decide which moral values were universal, which people were "rational," and which interpretations were "reasonable." False Christianity is, by implication, any and all forms of "dogmatic" Christianity, which he further characterizes as being a religion of "outward forms," prejudice, clerical greed, and superstitions. Ironically, he was applying to Protestantism itself things that the Protestant Reformers typically criticized the Roman Catholic Church for!

Spinoza went so far as to claim that virtually all interpretation of Scripture prior to his method had been largely a dishonest, purely subjective exercise by both clergy and believers. He says (and we can note the great irony), "We see nearly all men parade their own ideas as God's Word, their chief aim being to compel others to think as they do, while using religion as a pretext." This is, of course, precisely what he himself is doing! He goes on in even stronger terms, "We see, I say, that the chief concern of theologians on the whole has been to extort from Holy Scripture their own arbitrarily invented ideas, for which they claim divine authority."[28] (This is also very close to what Luther said about the Fathers as a whole—and now it is being applied to Luther himself, and to all interpreters of Scripture prior to Spinoza!) As Harrisville and Sundberg note, Spinoza in effect is saying, "Only a new form of biblical scholarship can free the bible from this yoke of oppression." Only this new form of biblical scholarship—the historical-critical method—studies Scripture dispassionately, looking at the historical context and taking "from it only what human reason can know."[29]

Spinoza's redefinition of "truth," and the distinction he made between "truth" and the "meaning" of the texts, indicated in principle 4 above, has further important implications which can be seen in the following summary of his thought:

---

27. See Ch. 8 for more on what makes for authoritative interpretation.

28. Quoted by Harrisville and Sundberg, ibid., p. 40; second edition, p. 38.

29. Harrisville and Sundberg, op. cit., p. 41; second edition, p. 38.

> Truth refers to matters of universal significance that reason is able to discern regardless of time and place. Meaning refers to the cultural expressions and artifacts of specific peoples bound to time and place. Miracles—that is, "stories of unusual occurrences in Nature"—and revelations, which appear in the Bible in the form of prophecies, are phenomena of meaning, not truth. They arise in specific cultural contexts and are bound to those contexts. Their significance is the historical function they played for the culture of their time.[30]

In other words, the miracles, prophecies, etc., found in the Bible are to be regarded as merely culturally conditioned idioms of the Hebrew people, not even possibly referring to real historical events.

So now, as Erasmus asked of Luther, one should certainly ask of Spinoza: On what basis should we trust your interpretations? What is the basis of your authority to redefine key Christian dogmas or key philosophical concepts—or to claim to reveal the hidden motives and meanings of ancient biblical authors and personages? How is it that you are elevated so far above all those great Christian men and women of the past who faithfully interpreted the Scriptures? Who do you think you are to summarily dismiss the possibility of miracles when multitudes of Christians in the past and present have affirmed their existence from their own experiences of them?

But of course, if one believes, as was common in the 17th and 18th centuries, that *everything always happens* according to universal *unbreakable* natural laws, then miracles are impossible, and one must come up with some explanation for their being described in Scripture other than that they actually happened. This understanding of natural laws being unbreakable, however, does not reflect 20th or 21st century science, or reality itself.

While at first it was only radical intellectuals of the 17th century, like Spinoza, who rejected the "search for ultimate causes . . . because it was seen as fruitless [not really even possible], and the chief cause of social chaos,"[31] this rejection later became dominant in academic, and other, circles.

Ironically, the initial Protestant attempt to reject any dogmatic tradition, and the attempt to use science, the scientific method, and the "laws of nature" as a substitute for Tradition and the rule of faith, helped lead to Spinoza's approach and its eventual acceptance. Indeed, as such ideas began to become pervasive, the historical-critical method itself came to dominate biblical studies almost exclusively in academic and mainline Protestant circles (and eventually in some other circles as well). And it came to dominate *precisely* and *only* because

---

30. Ibid., p. 41; second ed., p. 38.

31. Ibid., p. 46; second ed., p. 43.

it was believed to be a completely objective scientific approach quite comparable to that used in the natural sciences.[32]

It is important to note here that if one interprets Scripture within Spinoza's
framework, based on his Enlightenment worldview, one will *necessarily* get
radically different interpretations, at least of the fundamentals of the faith and
spiritual life, from those of someone interpreting within the framework of
traditional Christianity, *regardless of what techniques or methods are used.* As
Harrisville and Sundberg point out, "What we have in the Enlightenment tradition of criticism [i.e., historical criticism] is nothing less than *another religion*
that supplants biblical faith."[33]

In any case, as explained above, Spinoza's ultimate motive for inventing the
historical-critical method of interpreting the Bible was not to discover the true
interpretation of Scripture, or any kind of ultimate truth. Nor did it have anything to do with salvation, whether extrinsic or intrinsic. Nor did it have any
concern for the spiritual life—only for a vague, "universal" morality. Harrisville
and Sundberg can even say that Spinoza, Reimarus, and later, David Friedrich
Strauss, and those who followed them, understood historical criticism primarily to be "an agent of destruction whose purpose was to nullify the arbitrary
political power of those who used the Bible to legitimate their authority."[34] For
Spinoza and many of his heirs, "the Bible is an obstacle to progress that must
be gotten around."[35]

Spinoza's work was thus based on a fundamental deception (even if it might
have been self-deception): a pretense to be discovering the *true meaning* of
Scripture by means of a "scientific" and "objective" method focused exclusively
on the literal level. In actuality, his intention was to manipulate the "masses" in
order to change social attitudes—exactly what he accused those in the dogmatic tradition of interpretation of doing. Extreme interpreters, such as those
in the Jesus Seminar, are practicing exactly the same sort of deception today,
just as effectively—and no doubt for similar political ends (recall Chapter 1,
and see examples below). Ironically, such efforts, begun in the 17th century, are
usually heralded today as "startlingly new" and "cutting-edge."

Even though Spinoza's work was "the most vilified intellectual work of the
17th century" (next to Hobbes' *Leviathan*)—for instance, it was said to have

---

32. See Mary Sanford, "'How Do You Read?': Theology and Hermeneutics in the
Interpretation of the New Testament Parables," unpublished doctoral dissertation, Ch. 3, especially p. 64; and Hans Frei, *The Eclipse of Biblical Narrative*, e.g., p. 165.

33. Harrisville and Sundberg, op. cit., p. 268; second ed., p. 335; my emphasis.

34. Ibid., p. 266; second ed., p. 334.

35. Ibid., p. 47; second ed., p. 44.

been "forged in hell by a renegade Jew and the devil"[36]—it eventually increased in popularity because of the naive hope in science and reason characteristic of that historical period, *and* the absolute need of Protestantism to find a way to enable Scripture to be truly "alone authoritative."

As Sundberg and Harrisville further explain,

> What helped to make historical criticism of the Bible acceptable . . . was a fundamental feature of Protestant intellectual culture. From the time of the Reformation, Protestants had held the conviction that Roman Catholic Christianity was a false development of primitive Christian faith that distorted the clarity of the gospel. This simple, but revolutionary idea—the assertion that the church itself betrayed the divine intention—was like the opening of Pandora's box. . . . When taken to heart as a formal principle, it could easily be turned on the Protestant ecclesiastical establishment itself and used to undermine Protestantism's own dogmatic heritage.[37]

If one does not at some level trust the historic Church, at least on the major issues, and at least the Church of the early centuries, then nothing is sure. There is no solid rock to build authoritative interpretations on; and as has happened repeatedly, any set of ideas, no matter how alien to the Gospel of Jesus Christ and traditional Christianity, can end up being claimed to be "the true teachings of Jesus."

Spinoza's method has certainly encouraged doubt and weakened the religious passion of many. So in that sense, in terms of what he hoped to do, one would have to say that he, and those who continued to develop his method, have achieved a great deal of success. Tragically, however, his method not only weakened false religious zeal with its tendency towards violence,[38] but also true religious zeal with its profound dedication to self-sacrificial, Christlike love—love for God and neighbor, and even for one's enemies—while the violence he hoped to end continues, for a mulitude of reasons.

There is no need at this point to go into much more of the history of the historical-critical method in detail, because all the main, distinct ideas that have made this method radically different from simply using the techniques of biblical criticism within the Tradition as done in the past were brought together by Spinoza in the 17th century (though, of course, some had their origins in

---

36. Spinoza, "Biographical Note," *Ethics*, Great Books of the Western World Series, Vol. 31, p. 354.

37. Harrisville and Sundberg, op.cit., p. 52; second ed., p. 49.

38. For an excellent discussion on the topic of false zeal and true zeal, see "Concerning Carnal and Animal Zeal," in Ignatius Branchininov, *The Arena*, Ch. 36, pp. 140 ff.

the Middle Ages, some in the Reformation, and some in ancient Stoicism and Epicurean naturalism, i.e., pagan philosophy). In the centuries since Spinoza's time, his basic ideas and approach (at least as far as they affect the exegesis of Scripture) have simply been elaborated upon (for instance, by Immanuel Kant in the 19th century and Rudolph Bultmann in the 20th), and popularized in our own time (for example, by Robert Funk, Norman Perrin, Dominic Crossan, and Bart Ehrman) as various elements of the broader worldview have changed, so that Spinoza's once radical ideas have become quite mainstream.

To give one example that this is so, Pope Benedict XVI provides a helpful, brief summary of the crucial role which Kantian philosophy has had in contemporary exegesis:

> According to Kant, the voice of being in itself cannot be heard by human beings. Man can hear it only indirectly, in the postulates of practical reason. . . . thence comes the restriction to the . . . empirical, to the "exact" science, which by definition excludes the appearance of what is "wholly other," or the one who is wholly other.[39]

It should be clear how the result of this belief is the same as the second and third of Spinoza's five foundational principles. Both philosophers deny the key truth of Judaism—that God is a personal God Who has revealed Himself to His chosen people; and also the key truth of Christianity—that Jesus Christ, Who came to redeem all humanity, is the fullest possible revelation of this personal God, being Himself Divine. Both Spinoza and Kant are simply giving new expression to a view similar in its essentials to that of late medieval Nominalism (at least as it concerns exegesis), and to the thought of Barlaam the Calabrian (14th c.), St. Gregory Palamas' opponent. We recall that Barlaam's key disagreement with Palamas was exactly this point: is real, direct knowledge of God possible? In other words, does God really reveal Himself?

Pope Benedict XVI continues by explaining that the result for exegetes who accept Kant's philosophy is that everything in the text which speaks of God, the transcendent, the miraculous, has to be *by definition* ruled out as impossible to be known. Hence, all such passages have to be explained as something else. With this presupposition,

> What might otherwise seem like a direct proclamation of the divine, can only be myth, whose laws of development can be discovered. It is with this basic conviction that Bultmann [a prominent early 20th century

---

39. Cited in Mary Ford, "Seeing, But Not Perceiving: Crisis and Context in Biblical Studies," *St. Vladimir's Theological Quarterly*, Vol. 35, No. 23 (1991); my emphasis.

practitioner of the historical-critical method], with the majority of modern exegetes, reads the Bible. He is certain that it cannot be the way it is depicted in the Bible, and he looks for methods to prove the way it really had to be. To that extent there lies in modern exegesis a reduction of history into philosophy, *a revision of history by means of philosophy.*

The implications of this acceptance of Kant's philosophy—much the same as Spinoza's on this point—are profound:

The real question before us, then, is: can one read the Bible any other way? Or perhaps better, must one agree with the philosophy which requires this kind of reading? At its core, *the debate about modern exegesis is not a dispute among historians: it is rather a philosophical debate.* Only in this way can it be carried on correctly. Otherwise it is like a battle in a mist. The exegetical problem is identical in the main with the struggle for the foundations of our time.[40]

It is so little "a dispute among historians" that the well-known French scholar Louis Bouyer could say:

it is a fact that whenever professional historians venture into the maze of literature that gospel-criticism has produced, their judgment tends to be most severe in both methods used and the conclusions reached. Half a century ago, the German historian Edward Meyer observed that *if this critical approach were used in a study of the history of the Greco-Roman world, **nothing** would remain of the general agreement reached by ancient historians.*[41]

To summarize then, one can rightly say that the core debate in biblical studies is not about history, or about methodology. Rather, it is about *philosophy*—and more specifically, about *epistemology*, and thus ultimately about theological matters, especially *Christology*, for Christology and epistemology are inseparable (see above, Chapters 1 and 5). And the crucial questions are: Can we really know God? Has He, and does He, really reveal Himself to human beings?

What made it possible for the historical-critical method to become the dominant method of exegesis—a method presupposing the denial of the key facts

---

40. Ibid.

41. Louis Bouyer, *The Eternal Son*, 1st edition (Huntington, IN: Our Sunday Visitor, 1978), p.160 (my emphasis).

of the Judeo-Christian tradition, denying that it is possible for the intended purpose of Scripture as traditionally understood to be fulfilled? Its dominance came about both because of the key need of Protestantism to make "Scripture alone" work in practice, and an unquestioning faith in human reason and in science to provide not just knowledge of the physical world and practical benefits derived from that, but ultimately to provide any and all access to whatever truth is knowable by people. In other words, human reason and science come to be seen as the source of the only *real* knowledge, and thereby even of happiness, since science comes to be seen as the only, or at least the primary, kind of knowledge that can provide solutions to humanity's problems, and as the ultimate authority in all fields.[42]

The major problems with historical criticism (and its results) have largely to do with this anti-Judeo-Christian philosophy which denies that direct knowledge of God through the *nous* is real knowledge, or significant knowledge, or even possible; and the related naive 17th century view of science (still accepted by many today) which has led to historical criticism's being used as an ultimate authority in determining dogma (or what is true in, and crucial to, Christianity), and to its often being regarded as the only valid method of interpreting Scripture.

Not surprisingly, as previously mentioned, the dominance of this historical-critical method has led to a serious crisis in biblical studies. Beginning already in the 1970s, an increasing number of biblical scholars have come to recognize this crisis, and that the historical-critical method and the worldview it presupposes are at the root of it. Pope Benedict XVI could even say by 1988, "To speak of the crisis of the historical-critical method today is practically a truism.[43]

However, the crisis has not been caused simply by the use of most of the biblical critical techniques used in historical-criticism, but by the fact that these techniques are used *along with this outdated worldview* which Spinoza's principles and redefinitions imply. That is why many today feel the solution to this crisis lies in "a criticism of criticism." As Pope Benedict XVI, speaking for many biblical scholars, has said,

---

42. Although even in the realm of the natural sciences, while many have far more comfort and health as a result of modern science, there has also been unprecedented violence, with tens of millions killed in the 20th century by modern weaponry—hardly a utopia even on a secular, physical level.

43. Cited in Mary Ford, "Seeing, But Not Perceiving: Crisis and context in Biblical Studies," *St. Vladimir's Theological Quarterly*, Vol. 35, Nos. 2 & 3 (1991), p. 107. Some of the material in this article is included in what follows in a somewhat modified form, though much has been added to the original.

We must get beyond disputes over detail and press on to the foundations. . . . What we need now are not new hypotheses on the *Sitz im Leben*,
on possible sources or on the subsequent process of handing down the
material. What we *do* need is a critical look at the exegetical landscape we
now have, so that we may return to the text and distinguish between those
hypotheses which are helpful and those which are not. . . . only in this way
will exegesis be of real help in understanding the Bible.[44]

Now we will briefly take such a "critical look" at historical-criticism, using
two case studies, which bring out key points important for this discussion.

"Seeing and Not Perceiving" (Mark 4:12): A Closer Look

But when He was alone, those around Him with the twelve asked Him
about the parable. And He said to them, "To you it has been given to know
the mystery of the kingdom of God; but to those who are outside, all things
come in parables, so that

'Seeing they may see and not perceive,
    And hearing they may hear and not understand;
Lest they should turn,
    And their sins be forgiven them'" [Isaiah 6:9, 10].

And He said to them, "Do you not understand this parable? How will
you understand all the parables?" (Mark 4:10-13)

We will begin by looking at the interpretations of Mark 4:10-12 by two highly
respected biblical scholars, C. H. Dodd and Joachim Jeremias, whose works
have often been used as standard texts in university-level courses on Scripture.

The Mark 4:10-12 saying (or LOGION), since it follows the parable of the
Sower and introduces the allegorical explanation of this parable, was understood by many late 19th and 20th century biblical critics, such as Dodd and
Jeremias, to be a justification for the use of allegorical interpretation in general, especially in the light of Mark 4:13. They also held that this logion is a
saying implying that some people cannot and will not understand the parables *conceptually*—that they will not be able to translate or decode the "picture
part" (the story itself) into the deeper concepts which the parable is trying
to convey. Their own view was that everyone who heard the parables could

---

44. Ibid.

understand "immediately from the situation" what they truly meant, and they assume that this is in direct opposition to the understanding of the Evangelists as presented in the Gospel accounts, as well as the understanding of the early Church Fathers.

More importantly, Dodd and Jeremias claim that the Evangelists used this logion to support the belief that Jesus was giving secret teachings (in the form of allegories) to an elite elect—as was done in Gnostic circles—and that therefore the Evangelists believed Jesus did not *want* all to be saved, because He did not want all to conceptually understand the parables. With this in mind, Dodd claimed that Jesus never said this, while Jeremias asserted that though Jesus did say these words, the Evangelist misunderstood them and put them in the wrong place.

Clearly this logion is about interpretation and misinterpretation; we could loosely paraphrase it as "they will see, but they will not *interpret correctly*." Much light is shed on the subject of both exegesis and epistemology, therefore, if one simply studies this logion, along with examples of interpretation and especially misinterpretation in the chapters preceding the logion, as found in the Gospels of both St. Mark and St. Matthew.

In these and later chapters, one of the most striking things which the Evangelists describe is the large amount of *misinterpretation* of Jesus' words and actions on the part of those around Him. A typical pattern can be seen in the way most of Jesus' sayings are received:

1.   Jesus speaks;
2.   a misinterpretation of what He said is expressed;
3.   Jesus gives a correct interpretation; and
4.   all, including the disciples, continue ultimately to misunderstand (for example, Mark 8:14-21; Mark 8:31—9:10; Matthew 9:1ff).

A similar pattern can be seen in the description of many of Jesus' actions, especially the miracles of healing which He performs on the Sabbath. This is a pattern in all four Gospel accounts—even apart from the fact that quite a few of the same events are described in them. (A few of the many examples of both kinds of misinterpretation are found in Mark 2:5-12; Matt. 12:22ff.; Luke 7:36-50; Luke 11:14ff., and John 3 and 4.)

All of this misinterpretation, and how it is described, certainly has a bearing on the logion under discussion. If we actually look at how the Evangelists depict the way the parables in particular are heard, we find no indication at all that these are "secret teachings" given to an elite group of followers. The Evangelists depict Jesus speaking in parables frequently when the scribes and Pharisees are present. There is no hint in the Gospel accounts that these learned men had any difficulty conceptually understanding what His parables meant, at least by the end of the parable (sometimes explanations are even given, as in Matt. 21:28ff.). In fact, they usually understood all too well, and were angered, and/or struck silent, by His words, as in Mark 12:12 (KJV): "and they sought to lay hold on Him, but feared the people; for they knew that He had spoken the parable against them" (see also, for instance, Matt. 15:1-20, and 21:28-46). What sense would there be in "speaking a parable against them" if He knew they could not understand it! Clearly, they were angered and wanted to get rid of Him because they understood very well what He was saying on a conceptual level.

But the Evangelists do portray some people as not conceptually understanding the parables and other figures of speech that Jesus uses. They are not "the outsiders," but precisely His own disciples, and other simple, uneducated people who are open to Him (such as the Samaritan woman in John 4:7ff.). Yet, as is clearly portrayed in these accounts, Jesus explained what His sayings meant conceptually to these people (for example, in Mark 8:15-20). Thus, in the Gospel accounts in general, one sees Jesus needing to explain His parables to the simple among His own followers; while the educated people, who often oppose Him (many of the scribes and Pharisees), do understand conceptually what He is alluding to (or it is explained also to them).

Nevertheless, some do indeed "see and not perceive," and if one looks at the cases of misinterpretation preceding the Sower parable, it is quite clear what this means. It has nothing to do with simply being able to "decode" the story part of the parable and understand what the story refers to conceptually. Jesus' healings on the Sabbath, His forgiving sins, and His casting out demons are all interpreted by the scribes and Pharisees as indicating that Jesus is evil. When, for example, Jesus heals a blind and dumb demoniac, the Pharisees say, "It is only by Beelzebub . . . that this man casts out demons" (Matt. 12:24; also Mark 3:22). Jesus corrects their interpretation, saying, "How can Satan cast out Satan?" (Mark 3:23; Matt. 12:26). In the passage that follows in St. Matthew's account, Jesus indicates the way to discern which interpretation, His or that of the Pharisees, is correct: "the tree is known by its fruit" (Matt. 12:33).

Thus, all these and similar passages preceding the Sower parable show exactly how it is that the Pharisees and scribes "hear and do not understand," and "see and do not perceive." They hear Him ask, "Is it lawful to do good on the sabbath day, or to do evil?" (Mark 3:4), then they see Him heal the sick, and they conclude that He is evil. They see all His miraculous good works, they hear and conceptually understand His parables and teachings, they even recognize His wisdom (for instance, Matt. 22:22), yet they persist in interpreting all that He says and does as being evil. In biblical terms, their "eye is evil" because He is good (cf. Matt. 20:15).

In other words, they are misinterpreting His actions and refusing *truly* to hear because of their own spiritual state. They see evil in Him because of the evil in themselves, and hence they are unrepentant (see, e.g., Matt. 12:34). Thus, in its full context, the logion in question seems to be clearly *descriptive* of their state, and not *prescriptive*; for the Evangelists never portray Jesus/God as *causing* the scribes, the Pharisees, or others to fail to perceive and understand by speaking to them in allegorical parables, which only His followers who are already "in the know" can decode.

This is also exactly the interpretation one finds in the Tradition: those who "do not see and hear" are causing this failure *themselves* because of their own self-chosen hardness of heart.[45] They could turn and repent (in fact, some do so), but they *choose* not to, and in this way they fulfill the ancient prophecy of Isaiah. For example, St. John Chrysostom says of the logion in question,

> And this He says to draw them unto Himself, and to provoke them, and to signify that if they would convert He would heal them. . . . Even so, then, here too it is said, "lest at any time they should convert, and I should heal them"—implying both that their conversion was possible and that upon their repentance they might be saved.

And Chrysostom adds that "if it had not been His will that they should hear and be saved, He ought to have been silent, and not to have spoken in parables; but now by this very thing He stirs them up."[46]

What, then, can we conclude from looking at the context of this logion in the Gospel accounts? Jesus says, "The evil man out of his evil treasure brings forth evil"; and, "How can you speak good when you are evil? For out of the abundance of the heart the mouth speaks" (Matt. 12:35, 34). As mentioned also in Chapter Three above, there is clearly no sense here that one can be an objective observer and interpret Jesus' actions and words accurately from a detached position. How one interprets them *depends upon* one's spiritual state. One will only be able to interpret correctly if one's spiritual state is good—or at least, if one is open to repentance.

When seen in this context, it is obvious that this logion fits perfectly with the parable of the Sower, which is precisely about how the state of our hearts (what kind of soil *we* have made them) greatly affects whether or not we will truly hear the word of God and bear fruit. This theme is present in all the chapters preceding this parable, and the scribes and Pharisees provide example after example of "soil" which has "good seed" sown in it, yet bears no "fruit." In

---

45. See also Blessed Theophylact (12th c.) on John's similar passage, John 12:38-40: "Jesus . . . did everything He could to help them believe. . . . the prophecy was not the cause of the people's unbelief. . . . Rather, the people of their own will chose not to believe, with the result that the prophecy was fulfilled." The whole discussion is helpful.

46. NPNF, 1st series, Vol. X, p. 285.

fact, this parable, along with the Mark 4:10-12 logion, can be seen as a kind of interpretive summary of many of the events which happen in the preceding chapters. If one looks at more than one small passage at a time, one can see again and again how themes like this are brilliantly interwoven through many chapters in the work of each Evangelist.

In fact, it is most enlightening to look at much more of the context of this saying, beginning with the passage from Isaiah that the Lord is quoting here. Isaiah's text much more clearly has the sense the Fathers see in it in the Septuagint version, which the Evangelists were certainly very familiar with (often quoting from it), and which, of course, the Church Fathers were using. In the fuller context, Isaiah says that he "*saw* the Lord of Hosts, with my eyes," and as a result he is "*pierced to the heart*" (v. 5). He knows he is totally unworthy of such a vision, and after he confesses this, he is cleansed by the live coal from the altar. Then he says "I also *heard* the voice of the Lord, saying, 'Whom shall I send, and who will go to this people?'" And after Isaiah says, "Here I am, send me" (v. 8), the Lord says to him,

> "Go and tell this people, 'You shall hear indeed, but not understand; and you shall see indeed, but not perceive.' For the heart of this people has become insensitive [lit. "fat"], and their ears hear with difficulty. *They have closed their eyes*, lest they should see with their eyes, and hear with their ears, and understand with their heart, and return, and I should heal them" (vv. 9-10; my emphasis).

Surely it is not a coincidence that just before the verses 9 and 10 quoted by Christ, "seeing," "hearing," and the state of Isaiah's heart are all mentioned: Isaiah himself *sees* the Lord, *hears* His voice, and is "*pierced to the heart*"—thus expressing great humility and repentance. Then he is sent to the people who, because of the very different state of their hearts—arrogant and unrepentant—choose *not* to see or hear the Lord. And it is clear that they do not *want* to see or hear—"*they* have closed their eyes"—because their heart is hardened, or "fat." In other words, *they do not want* to change, to repent. But the Lord assures Isaiah that a remnant shall return and be healed (the name of his son in the next chapter is even "A remnant shall return").

Jesus Christ is also *sent* from God (as John's Gospel repeatedly emphasizes) first to the chosen people, many of whom will choose not to truly see or hear or repent. Given the whole context, however, it should be clear that the same assurance of a remnant "returning" and being healed is given in the New Testament, and the root of that remnant is "those around Him with the twelve" (Mark 4:10). Yet this is no elitist gnostic inner circle, but a band of witnesses who will begin to proclaim, as St. John says, "that which we have heard, which we have seen with our eyes, which we have looked upon,[47] and our hands have handled, concerning the Word of life" (1 John 1:1) to the whole world for its salvation.

The passage from Isaiah is referred to in all four Gospel accounts—and surely this is significant. Interestingly, in Matthew (13:14-15), after telling the parable of the Sower, Jesus quotes the Septuagint version of Isaiah more fully. As cited above, Jesus refers to this passage more briefly in Mark and very briefly in Luke (both of which quotations seem to be like prompts for those who could remember the rest, rather than exact quotes with the fuller context, as in Matthew). In John's account (John 12:39-40), the Evangelist himself applies the Isaiah passage to those Jews who reject Jesus, even though they had seen His many miracles, or signs, to indicate that this very rejection was a fulfillment of prophecy. For this message is what Isaiah prophesied, as St. John puts it, after "he saw His glory and spoke of Him" (John 12:41). That is, Isaiah was actually prophesying about what would happen to the Incarnate Christ.

Yet even though St. John says in John 12:39 that they "*could not believe*, because Isaiah said" (and then he quotes Is. 6:10, following the Hebrew version), he is very careful to make clear (as he does repeatedly) that their blindness is *self-chosen*, a result of their free-will and their refusal to repent.[48] John 12:42, just three verses later, explicitly says, "*Nevertheless*, even among the rulers *many believed* on Him." He then explains why, if they believed, they did not confess Him: "but because of the Pharisees they did not confess Him, lest they should be put out of the synagogue; for they loved the praise of men more than the praise of God" (vv. 42-43; my emphasis). Again, this is a spiritual, or "heart," problem, like the rocky ground where the weeds and thorns rise up and choke the good seed that is sown.

We also find the same understanding in the Book of Acts, which in its last chapter describes St. Paul speaking about Jesus to his fellow Jews in Rome "from morning till evening . . . trying to convince them about Jesus both from the law of Moses and from the Prophets. And some were convinced by what he said, while others disbelieved" (Acts 28:23-24). None of those arguments are reported, but Acts concludes dramatically by quoting this same passage from Isaiah. St. Luke explains that the disagreeing Jews "departed after St. Paul

---

47. The Greek word *etheasametha* used here only refers to things seen with the physical eyes. This emphasizes the point that *they really saw with their physical eyes* "the Word of Life," Jesus Christ (1 John 1:1). St. John gives this point even more emphasis in the next verse, stating that "the life was manifested, and we have *seen* and bear witness and declare to you that eternal life which was with the Father and was manifested to us" (1 John 1:2; my emphasis).

48. Dr. Edith Humphrey points out that for the ending of that verse St. John follows the Septuagint, which implies that God will heal them in the future (from personal correspondence).

had made one statement: 'The Holy Spirit was right in saying to your fathers through Isaiah the prophet'" (Acts 28:25); and then Paul quotes Isaiah 6:9-10, using the Septuagint translation with the verse "their eyes *they* have closed." He concludes, "Let it be known to you then that this salvation of God has been sent to the Gentiles; they will listen."

If one considers the complete context of this logion, then, it seems clear that the reason this passage from Isaiah is quoted in all four Gospel accounts, as well as in Acts, has nothing to do with explaining why allegorical interpretations of the parables are given (in any case, one does not usually explain what one does not have a problem with; and St. John and St. Paul do not even include the Sower parable or any other parable in connection with these verses). Rather, it has to do with the desire to help all repent, so that the Lord could heal them. It has also especially to do with the difficulty that St. Paul, and many other Jewish Christians, had: how could so many of the Jews have rejected their Messiah? Given all His miracles, His penetrating teachings, etc., how could it be that not all "perceived" and "understood" Who Jesus truly is? How could they ever "have crucified the Lord of Glory" (1 Cor. 2:8)?

Isaiah's prophecy confirms that this rejection by the Jews as a nation, and the "rulers of this world," was foretold, and thus encompassed by God's Providential care—His plan to bring salvation to the whole world. As St. Paul elsewhere explains about the Jews who reject Jesus, "have they stumbled that they should fall? Certainly not! But through their fall, to provoke them to jealousy, salvation has come to the Gentiles. . . . For God has committed them all to disobedience, that He might have mercy on all" (Rom. 11:11, cf. Rom. 10:19—11:32). Again, we recall the fundamental key of the entire *skopos* of the Scriptures: "Everything God does is for beneficence," because He "is the good God Who loves mankind."[49]

Now we can look specifically at the question of epistemology raised at the beginning of this section by examining the meaning of "hearing" and "seeing"—key terms in the logion. Throughout the New Testament, these terms are used to refer not only (or even primarily) to conceptual understanding, but to *living out* what has been heard and seen (for example, see Mark 4:20; John 6:60). In the New Testament, an intellectual understanding, while important, is never enough, since one *must* respond existentially, or else one has not *truly* understood "with the heart." Here we would do well to recall Christ's parable of the wise and foolish men who built their houses on rock and on sand:

---

49. As noted in Ch. 2 of this book, the first phrase/sentence quoted here is from St. John Chrysostom (see Ch. 2, fn. 7), and the latter is a phrase found in many hymns in the Orthodox Church; see Ch. 2, fn. 3, for some details.

"Everyone then who *hears* these words of mine *and does them* will be like a wise man who built his house upon the rock" (Matt. 7:24ff.; my emphasis).

This brings us to perhaps the most important reason why Jesus is commonly misunderstood—not only by those "outside," like the scribes and Pharisees, but also by His own disciples. This is because the spiritual truths at the heart of His message are not yet within the experience of His hearers; the implications of His words are often unimaginable to them with their current knowledge and experience. Probably the most striking example of this is the fact that Jesus's own disciples never really understood, until after Pentecost, His continual attempts to indicate to them the need for His death and Resurrection, and that His Kingdom was not of this world—as seen in Luke 18:31-34, to give but one of many examples.

In other words, even His closest disciples were not able to fully see and hear, in the sense of living out—or even in the sense of truly understanding conceptually—what He revealed (in other words, they could not understand solely on the basis of the teaching of the "historical" Jesus). Several times it is even stated that the full meaning of Jesus' words was "hidden from them" (e.g., Luke 18:34). Only gradually were their hearts softened and prepared. Only gradually were they able to see, hear, and understand the Kingdom accurately after they had begun to experience it—especially through their ongoing participation in the Holy Spirit beginning especially at Pentecost.

So, unless one has, like Isaiah, been "pierced to the heart" and filled with humility and repentance by a real encounter with God, everything about the spiritual life will inevitably be "in parables." But what Dodd, Jeremias, and other followers of Spinoza also do not seem to understand is that this is *not* a negative thing, for a biblical parable is a kind of light that enables one to see what one may not wish to see. In other words, it is an aid to repentance, a means of softening a hard, "fat," insensitive heart, an encouragement to return so that one can be healed by the Lord (we can recall here Nathan's parable spoken to King David, for example; 2 Sam. 12).

From the New Testament as a whole, we also can see that much more is at work here than merely conceptual knowledge, or understanding, of the teaching of the historical Jesus. The fuller context of 1 Corinthians 2:8 gives one example: "But we speak the wisdom of God in a mystery, the hidden wisdom which God ordained before the ages for our glory, which none of the rulers of this age knew, for had they known, they would not have crucified the Lord of glory" (1 Cor. 2:7-8). Indeed, as others have noted, there is nothing in the New Testament to indicate a primary focus on the *teachings* of Jesus; rather, the focus is on *a new life*, illumining and illumined by His teachings, which living His teachings leads to. It is a new life that is the result of real spiritual experience, of a real personal encounter, of being touched by the Holy Spirit—or at least, touched by those who have been. It is about eternal life, which is seen, and tasted, already in this life (cf. John 1, especially 1:14, 16; St. Stephen's defense in Acts 7, which is full of references to God's appearing, and ending with "You always resist the Holy Spirit"; 1 Peter 1; 1 John 1; and many, many others).

It is a commonplace among the Saints and Fathers of the Church, based on their experience, that one must live the Gospel commandments in order to truly understand the Gospel. From this vantage point, a method like Spinoza's (especially his 4th principle), which begins by assuming that any well-educated non-believer can "see" and "hear" Scripture fully and accurately in its most important points, is a method doomed to repeat the seeing that does not perceive, and the hearing that does not understand, because it reduces revelation to that individual's current fallen and unredeemed state. Such a reduction is necessarily a misunderstanding of the epistemology which the Bible assumes, in which true "seeing" and living out are inseparable from each other and from the experience of grace. For through this living of the Gospel, by God's grace, one's heart is softened and purified. Only then can one acquire knowledge of the spiritual realities of which the Scripture speaks—as we read in Isaiah, in St. Paul, or in many other biblical and patristic authors (though the faithful are often given glimpses even long before they may have reached an advanced spiritual state). When this is grasped, we can see once again why the holiness of the text demands a certain holiness of the interpreter to make possible a full and proper interpretation in terms of the crucial points and the *skopos* (though not necessarily in terms of the details).

This fact—that proper understanding of Scripture or any spiritual reality depends upon one's spiritual state, and therefore requires special preparation and help from God—is assumed throughout Scripture and the whole Church Tradition. As St. Paul says in 1 Corinthians 2:14, the "natural man" cannot know the things of the Spirit "because they are spiritually discerned." This is a key, fundamental principle that Spinoza and his followers deny; and the entire historical-critical method is essentially based on this denial. Yet spiritual discernment is essential if our reading of Scripture is to achieve its primary purpose.

As the well-known contemporary holy Egyptian monk, Matthew the Poor, says,

> Academic meditation alone, though useful in itself, without practical implementation leads . . . to a false intellectual devotion to the Gospel. . . . [Such academic meditation] on the Bible stimulates the mind but leaves the spirit unmoved. It makes the listener desire the truth without showing him how

to enter into it. It provides us with an image of God but cannot bring us face to face with Him.[50]

Or as Fr. Florovsky states, "it is the experience of all observers of spiritual things: no one profits by the Gospels unless he be first in love with Christ."[51] And as Christ says in the Gospel of St. John, speaking of the fruit of this love and the primary purpose of Scripture and all spiritual disciplines,

> If a man loves Me, he will keep My word, and My Father will love him, and We will come to him and make Our home with him. . . . If you keep My commandments, you will abide in My love. . . . These things I have spoken to you, that My joy may be in you, and that your joy may be full (John 14:23; 15:10-11).

The traditional approach to reading and interpreting Scripture is essential, then, because it alone enables an authentic understanding of the *primary* kind of knowledge which Scripture *intends* to communicate (i.e., spiritual knowledge, abiding in His love, a direct knowledge of and a real communion with the Holy Trinity, as indicated in the verses from John above). It alone can be the basis for an interpretation of Scripture which can help people to acquire this knowledge. It alone fulfills the primary purpose or goal that Scripture was written to fulfill. But, again, it is precisely this ultimate, primary goal, or purpose, that is deliberately ignored as irrelevant and even impossible by those using the historical-critical method.

The Nasrudin Approach: Nasrudin and the Key

> *A neighbor saw Nasrudin looking for something in the grass near his home and asked him what he was looking for. "My key," he replied, and the neighbor bent down to help him search. After looking a while without any luck, the neighbor asked, "Where exactly did you lose the key, Nasrudin?" "In my house," he replies. "Then why are you looking for it out here?" says the astonished neighbor. "There's more light out here," explains Nasrudin.[52]*

---

50. *The Communion of Love* (Crestwood, NY: St. Vladimir's Seminary Press, 1984), p. 23.

51. *Bible, Church, Tradition: An Eastern Orthodox View* (Belmont, MA: Nordland, 1972), p. 14. See also Appendix III, an excerpt by St. Theophan the Recluse on this topic.

52. Paraphrase of a traditional folk tale from a collection by Idries Shah, *Exploits of the Incredible Mullah Nasrudin* (Plume Publishers, 1972).

There is still more to learn from the example of Dodd and Jeremias. The primary reason the historical-critical method has been used as authoritative—the only reason these principles are being followed—is the claim that this method is "scientific" in a way parallel to that of the natural sciences. Therefore, that its results are as reliable as those of the natural sciences—or at least much more reliable than those found using a traditional approach. That was Spinoza's claim. But in what sense is this method, following Spinoza's principles, "scientific," and what really is its primary purpose?

According to the *Oxford Dictionary*, "scientific" means "according to rules laid down in exact science for performing observations and testing soundness of conclusions, systematic, accurate . . . assisted by expert knowledge (*a scientific boxer*)."[53] Obviously, no method of biblical interpretation can be scientific in the sense of testing by doing carefully controlled experiments, etc., but at least one should be able to expect "testing soundness of conclusions," being "systematic, accurate," and having "expert knowledge." Dodd and Jeremias do have expert knowledge in New Testament Greek and some other areas relevant for biblical studies, and also in exegesis using this supposedly scientific historical-critical method. But still, what do they actually base their understanding of this passage from Mark on *primarily*?

Clearly, from what has been pointed out above, they do not base their interpretation on the full context in the Gospel accounts. And although they claim that all those in the early Church incorrectly interpret the passage, "they do not give one example, not even one reference, citing a single patristic author who interprets and/or uses this logion the way Dodd and Jeremias say Mark," and those following him in the Tradition, do.[54]

As it happens, they cannot provide an example, because there is not one. Even Origen (3rd century), generally held to be the most extreme allegorizer of all, taught that Jesus spoke "obscurely"—in parables that are "hard to hear"—because "God in His goodness refrains from sending them the quicker help [in being able to understand easily] . . . since this course is *for their profit*."[55] Origen, like St. John Chrysostom some two centuries later, is saying that if the parable does prove to be difficult at first for some to understand, *this very difficulty* will be what is intended to prompt the hearers *towards*, rather than hinder them *from*, salvation. Obviously, this is the very opposite view from what Dodd and Jeremias claim that all those using allegorical interpretation always believe! Dodd and Jeremias have not, then, tested the "soundness of their conclusions," nor have they been systematic, or accurate—nor do they have expert

---

53. *Oxford English Dictionary* (Oxford: Oxford University Press, 1976), p. 1014.

54. Sanford, unpublished doctoral thesis, op. cit., p. 20.

55. Ibid., p. 22.

knowledge in the area of patristic exegesis, or else they could never have come to the obviously false conclusions they did.

The basic interpretation of both Origen and Chrysostom is the standard interpretation in the Fathers, no doubt coming from their looking at the full context, including Isaiah 6 in the Septuagint, and from their theology, their understanding of the *skopos* (see above, Chapter Two), which allows them to conclude that because God is the good God Who loves mankind, if He is making some things "hard to hear," it *must* be in order to help some of the hearers, so that they all *can* have the chance to be saved. It is hard to imagine an interpretation further from the idea that Jesus is giving secret teaching so that only an elite will be saved. In fact, Origen, the "arch-allegorizer," was even condemned—though long after his death—for teaching that everyone will ultimately be saved!

Furthermore, Dodd claims that this passage is not an authentic saying of Jesus since Jesus did not have the gnostic views Dodd thinks the logion implies, and Dodd gives linguistic (and other) evidence to "prove" his claim. Others, such as Jeremias, use other linguistic evidence to "prove" that Jesus did speak these words, but then they claim that obviously the Evangelists misunderstood them, and so put them in the wrong place.

So, what are these exegetes really basing their interpretations on? The many exegetes who insisted on some version of this interpretation could only ever have imagined it by first of all ignoring key elements of the *skopos* of Scripture, and "the dogmatic tradition of the Church" (Spinoza's principles 1 and 2)—specifically in this case, that "everything God does is for beneficence." Dodd, Jeremias, and many others also believed they did not need to look at the passage in its full context, in part because of erroneous ideas about the unreliability of the Gospel accounts (based partly on ignorance, common in their time, of how reliable oral traditions can be). There was also widespread, profound misunderstanding of first century Judaism in the 19th and first part of the 20th century among scholars that influenced their writings.[56] They were also far too quick to assume that the Evangelists and those in the early Church

---

56. One key aspect of this was the idea that Judaism and Hellenism were more or less opposites, and that it was only through the Church *after* the time of Christ that the Hellenistic influence came in. This even led some to claim that John's Gospel must have been written in the 2nd century. However, as more and more was discovered about first century Judaism, scholars also began to realize that there were strong Hellenistic influences already well-established *within Judaism* at the time of Christ and even before. This meant that using allegorical interpretation no longer seemed to be the result of a later, foreign influence.

misunderstood Jesus, and His "true teachings," and far too quick to assume that they themselves, 1900 and more years later, understood Jesus much better.[57]

These various false ideas, as well as misunderstandings about how language works, justified in their minds ignoring the multiple contexts for the passage—instead of using them to help clarify the meaning, as one would normally expect in a careful, systematic study of any text. Their epistemology misleads them in several ways, including leading them to overlook how the terms "hearing" and "seeing" are often used throughout the New Testament, and the reality expressed in 1 Corinthians 2:14—the need for spiritual discernment for knowledge of spiritual things. Thus, core presuppositions of the historical-critical method, and the Enlightenment world-view it presupposes, are what led these exegetes to believe that not only was their approach an acceptable manner of interpreting this ancient, sacred text, but that it was preferable, a better way to determine the "real meaning," and the "true teaching," of Jesus.

It turns out, however, that their approach merely left them more open to mistaken ideas of their own era. For the immediate source of the exegetes' misunderstanding of the logion is actually a false belief popular among literary critics in the 19th century: that the genre of allegory *always* implies secret teachings for an elite, as it did in Gnostic circles. It is no coincidence, then, that this misunderstanding of allegory was first proposed in biblical studies in the 19th century by the German scholar Adolph Julicher. This false idea was discarded in literary circles in the early 20th century, once literary critics realized that the "Gnostic" model of allegory is only one of many—and that it was not the kind of allegorizing used in the Christian Tradition before the Middle Ages. But this false 19th century view continued unexamined by biblical critics for many decades after literary critics had corrected their own view, and one still comes across it in popular level writings of certain contemporary biblical critics.

So, the problem is not that Dodd and Jeremias used biblical critical techniques, such as linguistic analysis, but first of all, that they did not have the proper interpretive context, or Tradition—including the proper epistemology—to guide them. Additionally, they were not systematic enough in their study, nor did they have expert knowledge in two keys areas: patristic exegesis, and literary genres, especially that of allegory. And, just as harmful, they were so confident that the presuppositions about allegory which they brought to the text were correct that they were not thorough and "objective" enough in their research. It is a further irony that when Jeremias, after all his research, finally "reveals" the true meaning of the Sower parable—which he says has

---

57. For an excellent discussion of just how absurd such claims are, see C. S. Lewis' essay, "Fern-Seed and Elephants."

been hidden for centuries and was unknown even to the Evangelists—what he says is virtually identical to what St. John Chrysostom said in the late 4th century. It should be evident from the discussion above that Dodd's and Jeremias's interpretation of the passage in context is false, and that one cannot rightly call their approach "scientific" in any meaningful sense.

Dodd and Jeremias are attempting to discover Jesus' understanding of the Kingdom of Heaven in order to determine proper dogma concerning this for Christians—something absolutely fundamental. Yet they do not carefully check the major assumptions of a fellow scholar, Julicher, or go back and check even a few prominent early patristic authors (which would be simple enough to do, even using the indices of translations of their works—a minimal knowledge is all that's necessary) before making their sweeping claims which go against traditional interpretations and the acceptance of the basic reliability of the Gospel accounts. We can also see how even something as seemingly neutral and factual as linguistic evidence cannot provide "objective proof" for any interpretation *by itself*, for even linguistic evidence is influenced by the interpreter's own presuppositions. And even two scholars like Dodd and Jeremias, who share so many presuppositions, can interpret the evidence in opposing ways. So it seems that confidence that their "objective" methodology will prevent such blindness has in fact blinded them to many of their own presuppositions, and has contributed to their misunderstanding the text, even on the conceptual level.

This case study also provides a striking example of how unexamined assumptions, such as those about allegory, can lead to false ideas that can become academic commonplaces in biblical studies accepted for decades without question—in this case, from Julicher to Dodd some decades later, and then a few decades after Dodd, to Jeremias, among many others. This, and other such false ideas, have dramatically influenced the exegesis done at even the highest academic levels by those using the historical-critical method as their ultimate authority.[58]

Eta Linnemann (a personal disciple and ardent follower of Rudolph Bultmann until she had a dramatic spiritual experience) eventually came to see the serious problems with the historical-critical method which Bultmann was a champion of. As she points out,

> In the natural sciences, a hypothesis is the foundation for research. It is tested either through experiments or through methodologically arrayed, wide-ranging observation. If it fails this testing, it is rejected. In so-called

---

58. For a thorough discussion of all the above, see my doctoral dissertation (Mary Sanford, op. cit.).

"scientific" theology [she means the historical-critical method here], however, there seems to be widespread ignorance of the fact that a hypothesis—a supposition that something is so—is nothing more than an assertion, for which one must . . . first clarify the presupposition and adduce the proof. Instead, hypotheses that have found acceptance [usually, because they fit well with the interpreter's theology, and/or politics] are treated like scientific results and circulated like facts. Certainly, experimental confirmation is not often possible in the realm of the humanities; still, particularly when one claims to do scientific work, one should feel obligated to adduce data that will furnish at least some broad evidential coverage of one's claims. Instead of this, many are content to make isolated observations in support of a hypothesis, treating contrary considerations as if they simply did not exist.[59]

The critical mistake of Dodd and Jeremias outlined above is certainly an example of what Linnemann is writing about. But perhaps the key example of an often unexamined, yet highly influential, assumption would be the core belief of historical criticism that an exegetical method can be "scientific" in anything like a scientific approach in the natural sciences, as well as the related idea that an interpreter of Scripture can, and should, be completely objective—beliefs implying that it is irrelevant *who* is interpreting, and what interpretive context they bring to their interpretations.

While an increasing number of exegetes have recognized that these are indeed very problematic views, many still hold that the best method of biblical exegesis will involve actively ignoring all possible influence from one's personal faith and from the Tradition as a whole. This is partly because of the ongoing need that many Protestants still feel to assert "Scripture alone," and partly because of a 17th century understanding of science that still prevails in many quarters.

This 17th century view is, briefly, that a "presupposition-less" person does experiments, observes results, and comes to an objective conclusion based solely on experimental observations—and that this provides the most reliable kind of knowledge in all fields, because there is no real knowledge that must be "spiritually discerned."[60] Yet much of this legacy of the Enlightenment was

---

59. Linnemann, op. cit., p. 184. See Linnemann's book for many examples of what she is describing above.

60. This presupposition about the necessity to be "completely objective"—to "let the text speak for itself"—was very much strengthened by the 17th century Cartesian "rule of doubt," according to which nothing can be accepted as certain which can in any way be doubted, and the way to achieve certainty is to be completely disinterested/objective, giving objective, scientific

abandoned long ago in scientific circles, where it is now generally understood that one must begin with a hypothesis—a theory based on one's presuppositions—and then check it by means of careful experiments; and if the evidence does not support the hypothesis, one must recognize that a new one must be developed which *is* supported by all, or the majority of, the evidence.[61]

As mentioned above, the Enlightenment era beliefs, combined with the Reformation rejection of the dogmatic tradition of the Church as an interpretive principle, gave great support to the first and second of Spinoza's exegetical principles: that the Bible should have no *a priori* religious authority, and that it must be understood apart from the Church's or Synagogue's understanding—in other words, the dogmatic tradition must be ignored. With these two ideas becoming dominant, it was a relatively small step to the widespread acceptance of the idea that not only *can* one interpret completely objectively, but in fact, one will be able to interpret *more* accurately without any "presuppositions" influenced by one's faith.

However, as Roy Harrisville explains, for example, in his introduction to Peter Stuhlmacher's book on the crisis in biblical studies caused by historical criticism,

> The expectation that the scholar was able in some fashion to hold himself aloof from the objects of his research and thus allow them to speak for themselves has lain unfulfilled. . . . This vaunted "functionalism". . . in historical-criticism has resulted in *a mammoth misinterpretation of scripture,*

---

methods ultimate authority. This was first proposed by René Descartes and transmitted by the Enlightenment tradition (we can note that the idea that one can be "traditionless" is also a kind of "tradition"!). This rule stands behind many aspects of historical-criticism (especially most of redaction criticism; see below). This "Cartesian confidence has sanctioned our imposition of an unacknowledged Enlightenment tradition upon the text of Scripture" (Roger Lundin; cited in my article, "Seeing Not Perceiving," p. 111).

After much linguistic and other kinds of research, there is now a consensus that the Cartesian "rule of doubt" cannot be realistically applied: "Because of the nature of language and the nature of our actions, there is not and cannot be a Cartesian, completely disinterested reading of any text" (ibid.).

61. In addition to the fact that one cannot do repeatable experiments with texts, it should also be remembered that even in science one's beliefs can determine and/or limit which experiments are done, and which are accepted—at least in the short-term. For example, shortly after the discovery of disease-causing bacteria, one researcher found that eating brown rice prevented beri-beri, yet his evidence was dismissed as impossible for some time, only because it contradicted the latest prevailing view: everyone "up to date" should know that all disease is caused only by germs!

since once faith was reckoned to be disadvantageous to the descriptive [i.e., saying what the text meant originally, as distinguished from its application—how it applies to us today], seven devils worse than the first assumed its place.[62]

From the perspective of more contemporary linguistics and other sciences that would inform a truly contemporary hermeneutical theory, it is recognized that "there is no such thing as an isolated, presupposition-less reading of a text. . . . All readings take place within communities and start from presuppositions which inform but do not determine the course of each reading."[63] This also means that no method of interpretation *by itself* can reveal what the author had in mind, or free the interpreter from his or her own presuppositions. There is no magical "correct method" that will always give the same interpretations to all reasonable people who use it properly, as many have imagined the historical-critical method to be.

This does not mean, however, that everything is reduced to pure subjectivity, or that we cannot know what Jesus taught as surely as—or more surely than—we can know what others in the past taught even on a purely secular level. It does mean, however, that proper interpretation necessarily involves a "mediating force," or Tradition—the proper interpretive context, ideally including the living community to which one should belong. This sounds strangely close to the patristic dictum: "One must have the true faith in order to interpret Scripture truly." And what is more, this traditional idea not only is supported by modern linguistic theories, but also is being supported in recent times by quite a few contemporary Protestant biblical scholars. What the Tradition, properly understood, can provide is precisely the living context in which the true intention can alone be seen and understood. It provides, equally importantly, a link of lived spiritual knowledge going back to the beginning—a version of "apostolic succession" in terms of personal holiness (which must always ultimately be confirmed by the Church).

---

62. Cited in "Seeing, But Not Perceiving," pp. 110-111 (my emphasis).

63. Ibid, p. 111. Because of misunderstandings about language, among other things, it was erroneously believed that although the task may require a lot of time, there are no great difficulties in determining exactly what an author intended, in decoding the text and finding the original, historical meaning—since all statements were assumed to have only one original meaning. In a truly modern hermeneutical theory, however, such assumptions have no place. A contemporary view in many respects reads like the exact opposite of the Enlightenment one upon which the historical-critical method is founded (for further details see, e.g., Mary Sanford, "An Orthodox View of Biblical Criticism," *Sourozh*, vol. 26 [November 1986], especially pp. 30-31).

Hence, from a contemporary worldview (rather than a 17th or 18th century one), as well as a patristic one, it is clear that to interpret properly—as accurately as possible, especially in terms of the ultimate goal of Scripture—an interpreter does not need to be *without* presuppositions. Rather, he or she needs the *correct* presuppositions. And in the case of Scripture, it has been held by those in the Church in all times and places that the correct presuppositions are acquired most effectively through living the Gospel, and also from the Church's Tradition (though the Tradition cannot automatically convey its truths, either—one cannot avoid the need to have living, spiritual knowledge). All this means that accurate interpretation may be difficult, and if one does not in some way have access to the meaning system of the author, it may be impossible.

The historical-critical method often ends up being what we could call the Nasrudin approach: looking for what would be easier to find in a "place," or with a method, that is easier to use, that has more "light" of human reason—in this case, the "scientific" method. Then, the attempt is made to try and convince people that these findings are more important/valuable and reliable, because they are "scientific," than what it is the *real purpose* of Scripture to communicate—something beyond the reach of science, something much harder to discern.

Indeed, as Roy A. Harrisville and Walter Sundberg say of this method, "The momentous consequence . . . has been to turn the energy of biblical scholarship from the study of the message of the Bible to theologically marginal matters of context and authorship."[64] With the Reformers insisting on no authority outside of Scripture, and conflicting interpretations of that Scripture encouraging division and even violence, a desire for certainty grew and grew. Lured by the shimmering mirage of certainty offered by mathematics[65] in science, many have been wandering in the desert of historical criticism for generations—never finding or offering real water, never mind a source that would be what Jesus speaks of, for example, to the Samaritan woman in John 4. And many of those using this method seem to have little or no concern for the practical implementation of the Gospel commandments and teachings in order to be transformed, to have a purified heart so that one might truly "see" God (cf. Matt. 5:8), or even with discerning on an intellectual level what an authentic theology is that truly leads to fullness of life.

---

64. Harrisville and Sundberg, op. cit., p. 45 (2nd edition).

65. However, in 1931, Kurt Godel proved his "incompleteness theorems," demonstrating that even in mathematics, no system is capable of proving all the truths within it, and no system is capable of demonstrating its own consistency.

Just as one can easily misinterpret a particular logion, like that of Mark 4:10-12, by ignoring its context and projecting false presuppositions onto the Evangelists' words (and in the case above, even in the name of an "objective" scientific method), so this can happen with Scripture as a whole. Thus, the crisis in biblical studies is largely the result of ignoring the primary and ultimate intended purpose of Scripture, and taking Scripture out of the context in which it was intended to be interpreted: the living Tradition of the Church. This Tradition includes the entire Bible, the liturgical context, the patristic consensus, the context of the entire believing community (especially reflected in the Church's great Ecumenical Councils), and the context of authentic spiritual experience—of the martyr/*martus*—the personal witness of those who are closest to reaching the ultimate goal, or who have reached it, as far as this is possible in this life—meaning the Saints, always as confirmed by the Church (see Ch. 8). The scholarly study of Scripture will be most effective within this broad context, especially in terms of discerning true interpretations that will be both inspiring and spiritually helpful.[66]

Back to the Beginning

Happily, however, an increasing number of biblical scholars are taking much of the above into account. There is an increasing number of good, scholarly studies using the techniques of biblical criticism within a broadly traditional Christian worldview—rather than using the historical-critical method with its outdated, unChristian world-view—a trend that hopefully will only increase. (A few examples of these will be given in the next chapter.) Such scholars are also writing to expose the most heavily promoted false claims of less careful scholars—which perhaps thrive mainly because of the "publish or perish" approach that many universities have, or because the sensational often sells better (not usually two distinct reasons!).

Unfortunately, such refutations are still necessary. There are still many other biblical scholars who ignore the realities discussed above. Some of them, such as members of the Jesus Seminar, take advantage of popular-level ignorance about the nature of science, language, and the limitations of "complete

---

66. As Dr. Edith Humphrey has pointed out, a more "neutral" approach can also be of value in some contexts, because more people "can gather around the text and discuss it, without being tempted immediately to dismiss the exegesis of someone because they have different presuppositions. . . . there is a place for public discussion of the text that does not foreground assumptions and presuppositions, but that of course is not naïve in thinking that we are presuppositionless" (private correspondence).

objectivity" to try to overthrow traditional interpretations with their suppos-edly highly scientific methods. Often the most popular-level and widely known biblical critics are the most "unscientific," and the most lacking in even basic scholarly "dispassion," or objectivity, in the broad sense. Of course, in this these exegetes are following their "father," Spinoza.[67]

As our final "case study" it will be instructive to go back to the work quoted in Chapter One. Looking even briefly at one penetrating critique of the Jesus Seminar's *The Five Gospels: What Did Jesus Really Say? The Search for the Authentic Words of Jesus*[68] will bring out other very important implications of this Spinozan approach.

Richard Hays, a biblical scholar teaching at Duke Divinity School for many years, lists four ways the Jesus Seminar's basic methodology is extremely prob-lematic; we will look briefly at two of these. The first has to do with the selec-tion and dating of sources which become the basis for the group's deciding which sayings of Jesus are authentic and which are not. The editor of *The Five Gospels*, Robert Funk, states:

> The first written gospels were Sayings Q and *possibly an early version of the Gospel of Thomas*. The gospel of Mark was not composed until about 70 AD. For these reasons alone, it is understandable that double attestation in the early independent sources Thomas and Q constitutes strong *documen-tary* evidence.[69]

As Hays notes,

> this valuing of Thomas as an early and independent source [it is the 5th "gospel" of the title] is, however, a highly controversial claim. The tradi-tional opinion among New Testament scholars has been that the Gospel of Thomas . . . was composed in the second century . . . [and was] heavily shaped by Gnostic teachings.[70]

---

67. Again, for many more such examples see, e.g., Linnemann, op. cit.

68. Edited by Robert W. Funk, Roy W. Hoover, and the Jesus Seminar (New York: Macmillan, 2004). In 2005, Robert Funk, who founded the Jesus Seminar group in 1985, died. In 2006, some of the Jesus Seminar members formed a new group called "The Jesus Seminar on Christian Origins" to study "Jesus traditions" in the first two centuries using the same methodology of the original Jesus Seminar.

69. Richard B. Hays, "The Corrected Jesus," a book review of *The Five Gospels: The Search for the Authentic Words of Jesus*, in *First Things*, No. 43 (May, 1994), p. 44 (Hays's emphasis).

70. Ibid.

This would mean that the Gospel of Thomas is significantly later than the Gospel of Mark, which many scholars now believe to have been written well before 70 AD.[71] Hayes continues concerning the Gospel of Thomas,

> Many scholars regard it as literarily dependent on the canonical gospels, though this remains a debated issue. No hint of these debates, however, is allowed to appear in the pages of *The Five Gospels*, which unhesitatingly treats the hypothetical Q and a hypothetical "early version of Thomas" as the crucial sources for locating authentic Jesus tradition. Here *some suspicion begins to arise concerning the candor of the editors of this book*. They claim that they want to make the results of the best critical scholarship available to the public, but *their working method trades upon a controversial and implausible early dating of Thomas, without offering the reader any clue that this is a shaky element in their methodological foundation.*[72]

One could add that it hardly seems reasonable for these authors to describe their "early version of Thomas" as "strong documentary evidence" when they themselves refer to it as only "possibly" existing. Even Q is merely supposed to exist in order to explain both the similarities and differences among the Synoptic accounts. What a tragedy that on the basis of such highly promoted, but extremely shaky—and misrepresented—evidence, the faith of some is weakened whenever these sorts of works appear.

Hays then notes that

> by drawing heavily upon the Gospel of Thomas and by packaging its results in a more user-friendly format than the abstruse hermeneutical musings of the "New Quest" [an approach to finding the "historical" Jesus which was popular in the 1960s], the Seminar has updated this approach.
>
> Whether it has thereby discovered anything that ought to be classified as historical knowledge is exceedingly doubtful. What the members of the Jesus Seminar have done, in effect, is merely to offer us an anthology of their favorite Jesus-sayings. . . .
>
> The difficulty with the work of the Jesus Seminar . . . is that *so much of the evidence must be thrown away* in order to save the hypothesis.[73]

---

71. Especially after a fragment of it dating from around 70 AD was found. But it takes time for manuscripts to get copied and circulated, which would indicate a significantly earlier date than 70 AD.

72. Ibid., pp. 44-45 (my emphasis).

73. Ibid., pp. 46-47 (my emphasis).

That is, of course, the direct opposite of the scientific approach they claim to be using!

Chapter 1 of this book begins with a quotation from this essay by Hays. It is worth giving the fuller context at this point:

> The Seminar's disingenuous self-representation[74] stands in service of a larger agenda: the deliberate creation of a new gospel. *The Five Gospels* is the realization of a vision clearly articulated by Funk in his keynote address at the opening meeting of the Jesus Seminar in 1985, subsequently published in *Forum*, the Westar Institute's journal. "The religious establishment has not allowed the intelligence of high scholarship to pass through pastors and priests to a hungry laity," and television preachers have "played on the ignorance of the uninformed." Thus, the Jesus Seminar rides to the rescue: "Our work . . . will spell liberty for . . . millions."

---

74. Another problem which Hays discusses is the deceptive way the members of the Jesus Seminar represent themselves—the crucial question of *who* is doing the interpreting: "Who are the scholars that make up the membership of the Jesus Seminar? The group's publicity creates the impression that they represent a broad cross-section of this country's leading critical scholars. It is asserted that "the scholarship represented by the Fellows of the Jesus Seminar is the kind that has come to prevail in all the great universities of the world." Though the Seminar expects to encounter hostile criticism, its work is said to be under attack principally "by conservative Christian groups" and by "those who lack academic credentials." The casual reader of the introduction to *The Five Gospels* might suppose that no serious New Testament scholar would differ materially from the consensus represented by this book, were it not for the single telltale polemical reference to anonymous "elitist academic critics who deplored the public face of the seminar." In fact—let it be said clearly—*most professional biblical scholars are profoundly skeptical of the methods and conclusions of this academic splinter group.* The membership of the Jesus Seminar does not include the overwhelming majority of the New Testament scholars who teach at the major graduate institutions in the United States. . . . Nor are there in it any major scholars from England or the Continent.

"This is not to say that the Seminar participants are without credentials. They hold doctorates from reputable institutions, with Claremont and Harvard being the most heavily represented, in that order. The point is simply that this imaginative book has been produced by a self-selected body of scholars who hold a set of unconventional views about Jesus and the gospels. They are of course free to publish these views; however, *their attempt to present these views as "the assured results of critical scholarship" is—one must say it—reprehensible deception"* (ibid., p. 47 [my emphasis]).

More recently, the Jesus Seminar has been criticized for having quite a few members either with no credentials in biblical studies, and/or no publications, or anything to indicate a serious academic level of training or work.

It is hard to imagine, given the communication technologies of even the 20th century, and the "anything goes" approaches of so many churches, how the "religious establishment"—whoever they may be—could possibly prevent "the intelligence of high scholarship" reaching anyone interested in learning about it. The real issue is that Funk, et al., no longer accept any form of traditional Christianity. As Hays says, "For him [Funk], the Bible's story of the world's history and destiny is a narrative fiction that has lost its credibility and usefulness in late modernity."

For Funk, the Bible as traditionally understood is clearly not true, and also is not able to inspire modern, scientifically knowledgable people. That's why Funk said in his speech,

> What we need is *a new fiction* that takes as its starting point the central event in the Judeo-Christian drama and reconciles that middle with a new story that reaches beyond old beginnings and endings. In sum, we need a new narrative of Jesus, a new gospel, if you will, that places Jesus differently in the grand scheme, the epic story.[75]

This is the "high scholarship" that has not reached the "hungry laity." However, as Hays points out concerning the overall driving vision for this and other works by this group,

> The pathos—bathos—of the project resides in the incongruity between Funk's epic pretensions and the actual findings of the Seminar. Does the passive, politically correct, laconic sage who speaks in the red type [that is, the words most likely, in their estimation, to be authentic] of *The Five Gospels* have the capacity to remake our imaginative world and provide a new fiction within which millions might find meaning for their lives? Surely not.[76]

In any case, a fiction can only inspire if it actually reflects the truth, and it is only truth that will help nourish the "hungry laity." In his in-house speech, Funk claims that "we need a fiction that we recognize to be fictive," and that this is what his group will provide. However, as Hays points out, "*The Five Gospels* purports to offer precisely the opposite: a factual Jesus discovered by scientific methods and disentangled from the fictive Jesus rendered in the Gospel narratives. Truth in advertising would be served if Funk's 1985 essay

---

75. Ibid., pp. 47-48.

76. Ibid., p. 48.

were published in place of the book's present introduction."[77] If what you really are after is a "new fiction," why pretend what you are doing is uncovering the "facts" through a scientific method, unless you intend to deceive? The image of misunderstanding, falsification, and deception which such scholars hold up as if this were true of the Evangelists and those in the early Church is actually a mirror in which we find reflected *exactly the kind of misunderstanding and deception they practice themselves.*

Hays' remarks below should be kept in mind when encountering *any* such sensational efforts that attempt to show how what Jesus "really taught" is quite different from what the Church has been teaching for twenty centuries:

> But even if the grand design of liberating millions through a new gospel should fail to pan out, Funk also has a more modest and realistic aim: "If we are to survive as scholars of the humanities, as well as theologians, we must quit the academic closet. And we must begin *to sell a product that has some utilitarian value to someone—or which at least appears to have utilitarian value to someone.*" Presumably, in the commercial realm, *The Five Gospels* will fulfill this hope. . . .

This example demonstrates that those in the Jesus Seminar are fully in the tradition of Spinoza: they seek to take advantage of the Bible's authority and people's interest in it, while also seeking to "get around" the Bible by attempting first, through pretended "scientific" study, to discredit the Gospel accounts as being largely falsified. They then put forward a new "Jesus"—based firmly on the "real history" they've supposedly uncovered—although, of course, this Jesus is, in fact, nothing more than a new fiction. This is something they surely know, but would never say in their popular-level works, because if they did so, very few people would even consider reading their books, let alone buying and being influenced by them. This is, by the way, just what the Devil in C. S. Lewis's insightful novel, *Screwtape Letters*, tells his devil nephew that he plans to inspire to happen: a new "historical Jesus" "every thirty years or so."[78]

---

77. Ibid.

78. *The Screwtape Letters* (New York: MacMillan Publishing Co., 1977), 25th printing, p. 106. In context, Lewis makes the Devil say, "The advantages of these constructions . . . are manifold. In the first place they all tend to direct men's devotion to something which does not exist, for each 'historical Jesus' is unhistorical. . . . each new 'historical Jesus' . . . has to be gotten out of them [the biblical accounts] by suppression at one point and exaggeration at another, and by that sort of guessing (*brilliant* is the adjective we teach humans to apply to it) on which no one would risk ten shillings in ordinary life" (pp. 106-107).

From Spinoza on, we see over and over an extreme elitism, and the manipulation of supposed science for political ends—a pretense of objectivity—to persuade people to accept highly speculative theories as "facts," and to accept ideas that they would reject immediately if they actually knew all the facts. It seems that most people never imagine or suspect the level of deliberate deception that these extreme, and sometimes highly placed, scholars are willing to engage in.[79]

Worse Than "Manifest Nonsense": The New Gnosticism

What Hays says about *The Five Gospels* of the Jesus Seminar holds true for the more recent claims about *The Gospel of Judas* (2006), and will no doubt hold true for *all* similar products of the historical-critical method. The well-known scholar N. T. Wright, for example, exposes the false claims made for the "gospel" of Judas in *Judas and the Gospel of Jesus* (2006), showing how this "gospel" from a 3rd or 4th century manuscript that was touted with much fanfare in the media to reveal, once again, the "real truth" about Jesus, in fact, does not tell anything about Jesus or Judas, but a lot about Gnosticism and why traditional Christians

---

79. A classic example would be John Boswell's books, *Christianity, Social Tolerance, and Homosexuality* (Chicago: University of Chicago Press, 1980), and *Same-Sex Unions in Pre-Modern Europe* (New York: Villard, 1994), in which he claims, for example, that the Russian Orthodox Church used to have a "same-sex" marriage service. However, what he describes is a service for making someone your brother (for inheritance rights, etc.) as if that were a marriage service, completely misrepresenting Orthodox liturgical practices, and even more significantly, the extremely harsh penalties in the Church canons of that same time for people actively engaging in any homosexual practices (as explained to me orally by the late Fr. John Meyendorff of St. Vladimir's Seminary)—among other problems with this idea. The falseness of these claims is explained, e.g., in an article by Archimandrite Ephrem, in *Sourozh* (Quarterly Journal of the Russian patriarchal Diocese of Sourozh) 59 (February, 1995), pp. 50-55, and in Edith Humphrey's "Same-Sex Eroticism and the Church: Classical Approaches and Responses," *The Homosexuality Debate: Faith Seeking Understanding*, ed. Catherine Hamilton (ABC Publishing, 2003), pp. 37ff.

But how many people would be able to check up on what he said—or would even think to question the research of a professor at Yale? Yet his false claims dramatically impacted many people's views—especially those of Christians—causing many of them to regard an active homosexual lifestyle much more favorably, because they imagined he was correct in claiming that it used to be viewed favorably by Christians! One need only read Athenagoras' letter to Emperor Marcus Aurelius (later 2nd century) to see that early Christians *and* many pagans not only were not accepting of an active homosexual lifestyle, but that even the pagan empire had laws against such practices at this early date.

were so opposed to it. Wright say that the current "fashion for favoring gnostic texts, even admittedly very bizarre ones, over against the canonical Scriptures has a great deal more to do with social and religious (or indeed anti-religious) fashions in North America than with actual historical research."[80]

In a very insightful discussion Wright explains why Bart Ehrman, Marvin Meyer, Elaine Pagels, and other such high profile authors (including those like Dominic Crossan who are still in the Jesus Seminar) so eagerly promote Gnostic works like this, and why they are "eager to teach and believe, even at the cost of writing what most historians will regard as *manifest nonsense*," what he calls "the New Myth of Christian Origins"[81]—in addition to the utilitarian fact that such sensational works sell well. For example, Wright points out that in Elaine Pagels's

> famous book *The Gnostic Gospels* she continually draws parallels between facets of ancient gnostic belief and telltale aspects of our contemporary self-help culture such as [some forms of] Buddhism, existentialism and the psychotherapy movement. . . . In particular . . . the new Myth wants us to believe that if we want genuine, liberating religion we shall find it in the gnostic vision rather than the mainline Christian one.[82]

Wright cogently argues that this "new Myth" has partly been so popular because, as Philip J. Lee powerfully demonstrated in his book *Against the Protestant Gnostics*,[83] "a kind of Gnosticism has been deeply entrenched in North American Protestant Christianity, and . . . has generated all kinds of ills not only in the church but in the wider society."[84] This "contemporary American Gnosticism" is characterized by a quest for finding "god in oneself"; since one finds god within oneself, the quest for "the divine" becomes actually a "quest for self-discovery." Self-discovery, then, becomes the primary obligation of this religion, leading to "the secondary obligation of 'being true to who I am'—even if that means being false to all sorts of other things."[85]

Added to this is "a relentless and culturally mandated 'pursuit of happiness' in terms of the kind of material and emotional well-being which would have

80. N. T. Wright, *Judas and the Gospel of Jesus: Have We Missed the Truth about Christianity?* (Grand Rapids, MI: Baker Book House, 2006), pp. 123-124.

81. Ibid., p. 120 (my emphasis).

82. Ibid., pp. 123-124.

83. (New York: Oxford, 1987/1993).

84. Wright, op. cit., p. 125.

85. Ibid., pp. 129-130.

appalled the hard-line ancient Gnostic."[86] It is no wonder that this American Gnosticism is often "both escapist, withdrawing from the world of politics and society, and narcissistic,"[87] favoring "the self-knowing individual over the believing community"[88] and promoting "'selective syncretism' over against the particularity of actual religious traditions"[89] which are generally found to be too restrictive. With this approach, your

> own deepest feelings and desires can be legitimized because, after all, if you have looked within your own innermost being, what you have glimpsed is the self-authenticating spark of the divine.[90] You don't need, after all, rescuing [or redeeming] —except from the wicked world around you. . . . Unlike the challenge of Jesus . . . this message doesn't tell you to deny yourself and take up your cross, but to discover yourself and follow your star. . . . Unlike the promise of Jesus, however, this message doesn't offer you a world renewed and filled with the justice and joy of the God who made it, but a world rejected and scorned by those who have found a way of escaping it.[91]

Adding to this mix, Wright points out that Western Protestantism since the Enlightenment tends to foster "the possibility of conspiracy theories."[92] Just as Harrisville and Sundberg pointed out, once you believe that the historic Church is "a false development of primitive Christian faith that distorted the clarity of the gospel, . . . the assertion that the church itself betrayed the divine intention was like the opening of Pandora's box." Hence, actually from the beginning, as Wright explains, Protestantism creates a culture particularly vulnerable to falling for 'conspiracy theories': whoever is in power must have "suppressed the 'real truth'" and "the 'real religion' that Jesus is supposed to have taught

---

86. Ibid., p. 130.

87. Ibid., pp. 125-126.

88. Ibid., p. 125.

89. Ibid.

90. Hence Wright connects this new Gnosticism with trends emphasizing everyone's "right" to give full expression to their own sexual "identity"/impulses. He explains that approach as asserting: "if my innermost 'experience' is the ultimate test of religious or spiritual validity, and my innermost 'identity' is the ultimate goal of my religious or spiritual quest, then discovering my own sexual identity, and giving it full expression, takes precedence over the restrictive and externally applied moral codes culled from ancient texts which may, after all, have less validity than we used to think" (ibid., p. 132).

91. Ibid., p. 144.

92. Ibid., p. 126.

and exemplified."[93] As Rowan Williams, former Archbishop of Canterbury, has tellingly said, "We treat them [biblical texts] as if they were unconvincing press releases from some official source, whose intention is to conceal the real story; and that the real story waits for the intrepid investigator to uncover and share with the waiting world. Anything that looks like the official version is automatically suspect. . . . It all makes a good and characteristically 'modern' story—about resisting authority, bringing secrets to light, exposing corruption and deception."[94]

Herbert Krosney, who wrote *The Lost Gospel: the Quest for the Gospel of Judas,* is not a biblical scholar, but a writer and film maker, so perhaps he can be excused for the ignorance his summary of the teaching in the Gospel of Judas betrays: "Following our own star is an idea that is as relevant today as it was back then. Rather than cast out the betrayer [Judas], perhaps we should look more deeply for the goodness inside ourselves."[95]

Just as legalism was a problem for the Pharisees in Jesus' time, the medieval Roman Church, and many other people in many times and places, so a temptation towards Gnosticism would also seem to be a common temptation for fallen humanity. It would seem that we are back to the very beginning with the serpent in Eden—the first Gnostic?—whispering that God is not a good God Who loves mankind, and that Eve (and Adam) can attain deification without Him. In fact, the serpent whispers that God is actually preventing people from attaining fulfillment, with all of His commandments and restrictions. This counterfeit gospel always proclaims, "Discover yourself, follow your own star, follow your own desires"—even though so often this results in merely being enslaved to one's passionate impulses in a self-centered rejection of real love for others, including God and His good creation.

It is hard not to hear playing in the background strains of the late medieval Nominalists' dark view of God, and/or of Lutheranism's and Calvinism's lies about total depravity (that the image of God in people is completely shattered, so that all they can do on their own is sin), and about double predestination. And then there are the over-reactions to these oppressive lies, updated in a "New Age-y" sort of way: we don't need God's help at all—He doesn't respond to us anyway, for God is not a good God Who loves mankind, doing everything to save us. We don't need redeeming, or forgiveness, or atonement—we especially don't need to repent! We just need to find our "true selves" on our own, and express ourselves, fulfill our desires, and realize our own goodness/

---

93. Ibid., pp. 126-127.

94. Quoted by Wright, ibid., p. 127. A classic example of this would the Bauer theory explained in Ch. 1, footnote 10.

95. Quoted by Wright, ibid., p. 133.

divinity. Those accepting and promoting such views probably believe they are choosing this "path" autonomously; but who have they actually been listening to? Would they really accept these ideas if they understood who the actual "fathers" of these ideas are, and their full implications? Who will they actually be in communion with in accepting these ideas? What real claim do these interpretations about reality have to being authoritative?

We can see from all the above that no matter how much one may claim to be "objective and scientific," to be simply revealing "what the text says" apart from the dogmatic Tradition of the Church—which is viewed as only blinding our good vision, rather than enabling us to see correctly—every person will always have "fathers," will always look at the text with some kind of "tradition" or presuppositions, and these will always be connected to their spiritual lives. Even the very issues and passages one chooses to look at (or avoid), the methods chosen to look at them with, as well as the conclusions drawn, will all reflect in a very profound way one's understanding and experience of spiritual life, one's understanding of what it means to be a human being, Who God is, as well as if and how people can relate to and know Him.

Who is interpreting, and the whole theology and spirituality of the interpreters, no matter what methods they use, or how much they insist they are being impartial, objective, scientific, etc., will profoundly affect the understanding of any text—especially one like Holy Scripture. To imagine it can be otherwise is a great illusion—going back to the serpent's deception of Eve. So it is critical that the interpreters we choose to listen have a true understanding of theology and spiritual life—or at least are honest about their presuppositions, and their reasons for writing.

The members of the Jesus Seminar, or those involved with the "new Myth of Christian Origins," are not just promoting "manifest nonsense" from a historical point of view: they are promoting spiritually deadly ideas, harmful lies about reality that are radically different from authentic Christianity. Actually, from an Eastern Orthodox point of view, it does not seem that exegetes like those of the Jesus Seminar have any idea what traditional Christianity even is; for they seem to think it is basically Calvinism, or perhaps some of the worst elements of mid to late Medieval Roman Catholicism, mixed with contemporary TV evangelism, such as the various "name it and claim it" groups.

When Krosney says "rather than cast out the betrayer," he seems to forget that it was not Jesus or His disciples who cast out Judas, but the Pharisees and Scribes who had just had Jesus crucified. And Judas was not simply a cast out victim; he "went and hanged himself," *choosing* death over repentance. When Krosney recommends "looking more deeply for the goodness inside ourselves," then like Judas, he also seems to forget—or probably doesn't agree with—Jesus, Who in crystal clear words begins His ministry with the call to all to "repent."

This avoidance of repentance is based on a deadly delusion. The rampant self-hate and depression in our culture that "looking for the goodness inside ourselves" is no doubt meant to be a remedy for, will not be cured by that method, but only through the healing offered by traditional Christianity based on the actual teachings of Jesus, beginning with the need to repent—the need to be honest, humble, to seek the Truth, Who ultimately is Christ Himself. And there is always the need to accept forgiveness; but if one cannot first admit that one has done wrong, then one cannot accept being forgiven, or feel the liberating power of forgiveness. Perhaps, deep down, people cannot bear to admit their sins, because they do not believe God truly is the good God Who loves mankind and does everything for our benefit.

Wright concludes,

> Has the "Gospel of Judas" betrayed the dark secret of Gnosticism ancient and modern, that it believes that the god who made this world is a stupid, wicked sub-deity bent on mischief? And how many people, faced head on with that god on the one hand and the Father of Jesus Christ on the other—the latter being, by definition, the God who created the world out of pure self-giving love and who has redeemed it by that same pure self-giving love, the God who reveals his glory taking the weight of the world's evils on to his own shoulders in the person of his suffering son, the God who unveils his future plans for the created order in raising that son from the dead as the start of his new creation—how many people will seriously say that they don't much like the Christian God and prefer the gnostic one instead? If people really read and study the 'Gospel of Judas,' might we not predict that quite a number of them will conclude that Gnosticism is not, after all, for them?[96]

Tragically, few people will actually do the research and come to see this head-to-head comparison. Instead, the effect of causing doubt about the truth and reliability of the Bible is achieved simply by widely publishing the headlines about the "new gospel" that will "revolutionize" the thinking about what Jesus really taught, etc. It does not matter what "manifest nonsense" it all is, because few will have the desire or resources to check up on it—and undoubtedly, those involved in making such headlines are well aware of this.

Anyone making a "gnostic" sort of appeal by claiming to be revealing the "true" or "secret" teachings, or "hidden gospels," or anything of this sort, is probably a member of this group of "unscholarly" scholars, who, like Spinoza, seem quite willing to deceive in order to achieve whatever their own agenda is.

---

96. Ibid., pp. 143-144.

As Wright says, "Anything will do, it seems, as long as it is not classic Judaism or Christianity."[97] Since these "new gospels" and "new revelations" are always similar (and thus, never actually new), once you see through one, you can see through them all. But once you have seen through one, you are unlikely to have any interest in looking at another—unless you feel called to expose it for the deception it is.

There are many fine books available today dedicated to debunking the shoddy scholarship and/or plain old deception for "political" reasons of these more extreme and sensational biblical scholars—the ones who are on TV and quoted in popular magazines like *Time*, such as numerous members of the Jesus Seminar, Bart Ehrman, Elaine Pagels, etc. Some good examples are *Jesus and the Eyewitnesses: the Gospels as Eyewitness Testimony*, and *The Testimony of the Beloved Disciple*, both by Richard Bauckham (Professor Emeritus at the University of St. Andrews), which detail evidence for the trustworthiness of the Gospel accounts; *Sanctified Vision: An Introduction to Early Christian Interpretation of the Bible*, by John J. O'Keefe and R. R. Reno; as well as the books by N. T. Wright, to mention a few. And as more and more scholars have become aware of the limitations of the historical-critical method, more and more genuinely scholarly—and helpful—books are being published by those using the *techniques* of biblical criticism, but without the false, out-dated, and anti-traditional Christian worldview that the historical-critical method presupposes. These are very positive steps in the right direction, even though they are still lacking from a traditional Orthodox Christian point of view.

In any case, from all this history, and the above "case studies," hopefully it is clear how important it is to understand the ultimate goals, or purposes, of any methodology being used, as well as the interpretive context within which it is being used. In the historical-critical—and other modern "critical"—approaches, interpretation is usually understood to involve primarily getting the "facts" correct: being clear about what the original words are, what the meaning of each word in the original is, the historical context, the allusions to first century Jewish practices or ideas, etc. The goal of the method is to find such information in order to discover what the Bible "really means"—or most often, what the historical Jesus "really" said and taught (too often implying that this must be different from what traditional Christianity has always affirmed).

All such "facts"—when they are accurate—are certainly valuable to know. But this is not what is understood to be the primary focus of Scriptural inter-pretation in the historic Tradition. There, interpreting truly means understand-ing the *skopos* well enough to live the Gospel and be personally transformed

---

97. Ibid., p. 123.

by it. It is the same as the primary purpose of the Christian life, which St. Seraphim of Sarov (19th c.), for example, summarized as being "to acquire the Holy Spirit"—to become holy, to attain to *theosis*. St. Seraphim read the entire New Testament every week. He had no training as a biblical scholar, did not know New Testament Greek, and no doubt lacked knowledge of much other pertinent information. Yet, through his living the Gospel and his extensive personal experience of the spiritual realities spoken of, through his being inspired by the Holy Spirit, he was able to interpret the Bible in such a way that he could dramatically help many others grow spiritually, drawing them closer to Christ—to be renewed and transformed, and thus to fulfill the ultimate purpose which the Bible was written and preserved to fulfill. And his powerful influence for good did not end when his earthly life did.

Especially if one has a living connection to the Tradition preserved in the Church, it is not necessary to know even the techniques of biblical criticism to understand the text well enough existentially to live the Gospel, to be redeemed, and to become holy, which is the ultimate purpose of every aspect of traditional Christianity. But the information gained through these techniques *is* necessary to understand the literal meaning of the text in terms of the meaning of the words, etc., as fully as possible. Properly done, using this critical approach can also be a way of meditating on and deepening our appreciation of Scripture, of holding it before our minds, of pondering its depths—just as Fr. Louth suggests for allegorical interpretation. It can be a means of continuing the ongoing process of articulating the Gospel to the surrounding society in our own time. It is also important apologetically to correct the wrong ideas that others may have.

For far too long, too many biblical critics have taken advantage of a claim to be scientific and objective that is largely without substance. In fact, it seems very misleading, if not downright deceptive, to call any methods or techniques involved in interpreting any texts "scientific," for even something like textual criticism involves many subjective decisions, and must be based on many presuppositions that cannot definitively be proved by experiments that others can perform, as in the physical sciences (for example, that the simpler will always be earlier, or that the more specific will be).

Although there certainly have been real gains in knowledge, and much helpful information found over the decades by serious biblical scholars, using valuable tools such as those of philological criticism even within the historical-critical method, when one takes the long view, one sees how often the "assured results" of biblical studies undertaken with the presuppositions of the historical-critical method are proved wrong, and how many studies are not even done in a thoroughly scholarly manner, let alone in a manner that could properly be called "scientific." Then one will realize that one cannot be too cautious regarding any findings that challenge a traditional understanding of Scripture. Again and again, as in the case with Dodd's and Jeremias's ideas about Mark 4:10-12, it turns out that the Tradition is correct after all, and the "scientific" method has led biblical exegetes astray.

Serious work on Scripture would be better served, it certainly seems, if this pretense of being "scientific" in the popular sense (meaning like in the natural sciences) were dropped altogether, and if scholars simply attempted to do thorough, fair-minded research—"testing soundness of conclusions," being "systematic, accurate," and having all the appropriate "expert knowledge" needed. Although such research, which thankfully is being done by some, could be called "scientific" in the less common meaning of the term, it seems far more helpful to call it simply "scholarly" in the best sense. This kind of research could also truly be called "dispassionate"—the term Spinoza misapplied to his own work.

In light of all the above, one might wonder: is there a way to keep all that is good in biblical studies from the past 400 years or so, and to recover, as far as we appropriately can, what has too often been lost from the first 500 years or so of the Christian era? What might such exegesis look like? A small attempt will be given in the next chapter.

One thing I have desired of the Lord, that will I seek: that I
may dwell in the house of the Lord all the days of my life, to
behold the beauty of the Lord, and to inquire in His temple.
—PSALM 27:4

CHAPTER SEVEN

THE BRIDEGROOM AND THE CHILDREN OF GOD

TODAY we are on the other side of all this history, for ours is not the culture of the early Church, nor that of Spinoza and his followers, with their very naïve view of science. Nevertheless, the most serious question today is the same as in St. John the Evangelist's time in the first century, or in St. Gregory Palamas' time in the 14th century, or in any other time—some form of the key question we raised in Chapter 1: Can we "see" God? And related to that: What kind of light do we need for such seeing, and how can we acquire it? Or we could express it: Has God really revealed Himself? Who is Jesus Christ? If God has, or has not, most fully revealed Himself in Jesus Christ, what does this mean for humanity?

Following the answers found in the Gospel accounts, the Fathers, and traditional Christianity, we will focus on the phrase "we beheld His glory" (from John 1:14) for this necessarily brief sample exegesis. In order to examine this phrase more fully (though far from exhaustively), we will also look at it in its immediate context (especially John 1:12 and 16), and then in its broader context within the first eight chapters of John (where some dimension of the Bridegroom theme is repeatedly found), along with drawing out helpful connections with other parts of Scripture.

All this biblical material will be illuminated by insights from the Fathers and Saints (both past and present), as well as from contemporary biblical scholars, in order to offer an interpretation in the light of the rule of faith understood within the context of the Orthodox Church's theology and liturgical life. In this way, additionally, the biblical roots of Orthodox Christology, epistemology, and the understanding of sanctification as deification[1]—a transformation of one's whole being through real, direct communion with the uncreated energies, or grace of God, and sharing in immortal, divine life—will be demonstrated.

Clearly then, the approach taken here will be in many ways the opposite of Spinoza's and that of the historical-critical method (though it will benefit from the techniques of biblical criticism). If all the resources mentioned above are used within the Church's interpretive context, they can contribute very positively to an edifying, accurate exegesis, especially when the text is treated respectfully. St. John's Gospel is so densely and brilliantly written, however, that it is impossible to follow all the threads that even such a short phrase interweaves; we can only begin to indicate some of the most important ones.

* * * * *

*And the Word became flesh and dwelt among us, and **we beheld His glory**, the glory as of the only begotten of the Father, full of grace and truth. . . . and of His fulness we have all received, and grace for grace.*
—JOHN 1:14, 16.

Packed into these two incredibly rich verses (John 1:14 and 16)—probably the most extraordinary sentences ever composed—we can find in summary the whole Christian Tradition. Even just looking at the phrase "we beheld His glory," we can find the core answer to the most fundamental question there is—the ultimate question with which we began this book and this chapter, the question which came to be answered so falsely by, for example, the Nominalists in the late Middle Ages: Can we really know God, and if so, what He is really like? (We recall that the Nominalists said, "No, we can't know Him; all we can know is that He is omnipotent.") How we answer this question will dramatically affect how we answer other fundamental questions, including: What is a person? What is the goal of our spiritual life, of human life as a whole? How can we attain what we most desire? How can we achieve true happiness? And even, how should we go about interpreting Scripture—what is a proper biblical hermeneutic?

---

1. "Although the language of deification is less prominent in Western theology, it remained in liturgical prayers and in the teaching of the mystics. . . . The patristic revival in the Oxford movement led to a recovery of the concept of deification" in some non-Orthodox Churches (*The Oxford Dictionary of the Christian Church*, third ed., Cross and Livingstone, eds. [Oxford: Oxford University Press, 2005], pp. 467-468).

"His Glory"

Let's begin with the word "glory." Many people today probably do not realize the full meaning of the word "glory" as used by St. John in verse 14. However, in the context of early Christianity, which was so directly connected to the Judaism of that time, this word has incredibly powerful, clear connotations. To the Jews at the time of Jesus, and to the early Christians, the glory or *doxa* of God (from the Hebrew *kabod*) had a twofold meaning, both referring to ways God reveals Himself.[2] First, "it is the visible manifestation of His majesty in *acts of power*." For example, Moses says of the miracle of the manna, "In the morning you shall see the glory of God" (Ex. 16:7-10). St. John very much intends his reader to understand that the divine glory of Jesus is revealed in part by what John calls His "signs"—the mighty, miraculous acts of power Jesus does—only a few of which St. John describes in his account. He makes this explicit in Chapter 2, verse 11, after the miracle of changing the water into wine: "This beginning of signs Jesus did in Cana of Galilee, and manifested His glory; and His disciples believed in Him." Also, at John 11:40, just before He raises Lazarus who was four days dead, He says to Martha, "'Did I not say to you that if you would believe you would see the glory of God?'"

So "glory" here

> includes all the manifestations of the divine majesty and power. . . . To assert that the glory of God has been seen in the incarnate Word is thus to claim that in the deeds and teaching [and Person] of Jesus Christ, and perhaps most of all at the moment of His sacrifice, God has manifested Himself to His people; and that in meeting with Him those who had eyes to see knew, as did their fathers of old, that God was dwelling in the midst of His people. . . . John means us to understand that in Jesus Christ, the incarnate Word, that future hope has already taken historical form. This is brought out in many ways in the Gospel.[3]

This glory, then, reveals both His power and His presence.

God's glory is also in the "cloud" whereby His presence, or glory, becomes *visible* to the Israelites in their desert wanderings (Ex. 16:10), and also in the

---

2. Glory/*doxa* does have other meanings in different contexts: triumph (glory over Pharaoh), praise—to give God glory, etc.

3. John Marsh, *Saint John*, in the *Pelican New Testament Commentaries* series (London: Penguin Books, 1968), p. 109.

"pillar of fire" (Ex. 24:17).[4] Even Moses' face was so radiant from his contact with God's glory that he had to be veiled so the Israelites could look at him. St. John himself mentions Isaiah seeing the Lord's glory (John 12:41; cf. Is. 6:1); and Ezekiel ends the first chapter of his book by saying: "I saw as it were the appearance of fire with brightness round about. Like the appearance of a rainbow in a cloud on a rainy day, so was the condition of the surrounding brightness. This was the vision of the likeness of the Lord's glory. I saw it, and I fell on my face" (Ezek. 1:27-28).

So "glory" also means *a powerful, visible, awe-inspiring manifestation* of the invisible God as *radiant*—and to use a later term, *uncreated light*. A clear New Testament example of this usage of "glory" as uncreated light would be Christ's Transfiguration (Luke 9:28-32), as the hymns for this feast make clear. For example:

> "The nature that knows no change, being mingled with the mortal nature, shone forth ineffably, unveiling in some small measure to the apostles the light of the immaterial Godhead."[5]

His glory as *light* is also a theme found elsewhere in the New Testament—for instance, at Luke 2:9: "The glory of the Lord shone around them, and they were greatly afraid"; and at Hebrews 1:3: "Who being the brightness of His [God's] glory, and the express image of His person." Many people, including St. Paul (Acts 9:3, 22:6, 26:13), both in the past and up to the present day, have literally seen this brilliant glory of the Lord.

But St. John gathers up these and even more of the rich Old Testament implications of this word "glory" in a brilliant, subtle way that those only using an English translation would completely miss. He makes it very clear that he has in mind both meanings of glory (not just the "signs") by his use of the word usually translated so inadequately as "dwelt." When John makes his astounding statement that the eternal, uncreated Logos or Word of God Who created all things became "flesh," actually participating "in man's creaturely weakness,"[6] the next word in the Greek is *eskēnosen* (from *skēnē* = tent, booth, or tabernacle, lodging, dwelling), meaning literally "pitched His tent," or "tabernacled

---

4. See Raymond E. Brown, *The Gospel according to John I-XII*, in *The Anchor Bible* series (New York: Doubleday, 1966), pp. 503-504.

5. Canticle Five, First Canon for Matins for the Transfiguration of Our Lord (*The Festal Menaion*, p. 487).

6. George R. Beasley-Murray, *Word Biblical Commentary: John* (Waco, TX: Word Books, 1987), p. 14.

among us." So we could better translate this verse as, "And the Logos became flesh and *tabernacled* among us, and we beheld His glory."

This word for "tabernacled" or "dwelt" brings up many powerful Old Testament associations, such as the Glory of God (*kabod*) *dwelling* in the Ark of the Covenant. Indeed, the word "tabernacled" or "pitched His tent" is *directly* linked to the second meaning of "glory" as light, since it was at the Tent [or tabernacle] of Meeting that the bright cloud of God's glory was seen, especially at the time of sacrifice. For example,

> "This is the thing the Lord commanded you to do, and the glory of the Lord will appear among you." . . . Then the glory of the Lord appeared to all the people; and fire came out from the Lord and consumed the things on the altar. . . . when all the people saw this, they were amazed and fell on their faces" (Lev. 9:6, 23-24).

A few other examples include Exodus 40:34-35:

> Then a cloud covered the tent of the congregation, and the glory[7] of the LORD filled the tabernacle. And Moses was not able to enter into the tent of the congregation, because the cloud abode thereon, and the glory of the LORD filled the tabernacle.

And also in 1 Kings 8:10-11, in speaking about Solomon's newly built Temple: "the glory of the Lord filled the house of the Lord" (repeated in 2 Chron. 5:13).

Thus St. John, by using the word "tabernacled," explicitly makes this connection between the Word/Logos and the Glory as brilliant uncreated light in the phrase we're considering: "And the Word became flesh, and dwelt/tabernacled among us, and we beheld His glory." Recalling the overwhelming visions of the Lord's glory from the Old Testament, St. John Chrysostom explains,

> we could not have beheld [His glory], had it not been shown to us, by means of a body like our own. For if the men of old time could not even bear to look upon the glorified countenance of Moses, who partook of the same nature with us, . . . how could we creatures of clay and earth have endured the unveiled Godhead, which is unapproachable even by the powers above? Wherefore He tabernacled among us, that we might

---

7. It is interesting that the Hebrew word "shekinah" used here, a later word for God's glory, is derived from *skēnē* (tent, or tabernacle), so the connection between these two words is very strong.

be able with much fearlessness to approach Him, speak to, and converse
with Him.[8]

By connecting the divine glory of Jesus with the word "tabernacled," as
Chrysostom notes, St. John the Evangelist already introduces the important
theme of Jesus as the *new* tabernacle/temple, the new special place of the
Presence of God, which will result in a new kind of worship (see John 2:13-
16; and 4:21-24). Likewise, St. Cyril of Alexandria (5th century) writes, "The
tabernacle was to them of old a type of Christ"; and again, "The Law brings in
the tabernacle, for a *figure of the true*: the Savior bears up to Heaven itself and
brings in the truer *tabernacle, which the Lord pitched and not man.*"[9]

The well-known patristic scholar Thomas Torrance points out a fascinating
connection in the Israelite priestly tradition between the Tabernacle and the
Word (*dabar*) of the Lord (YHWH):

> The Hebrew term for word, *dabar* . . . appears to derive from a Semitic
> *dbr* meaning 'backside' or 'hinterground,' which is apparent in the expres-
> sion for the Holy of Holies just mentioned, the *debir* [cf. II Kings 6:5, 16,
> 19-23, 30), which was lodged at the very back of the Tabernacle or Temple.
> This is one of the dominant understandings behind the Old Testament
> understanding of the cult, and indeed it looks as if the whole Tabernacle
> or Temple were constructed around the significance of *dabar*. In the very
> back of the Tabernacle or the Holy of Holies, the *debir*, there are lodged
> the ten Words or *debarim*. All through Israel's history the Word enshrined
> in the form of the *debarim* was hidden in the *debir*, but was again and
> again made manifest when God made bare His mighty arm and showed
> His glory.[10]

As another scholar, Fr. Matthew Baker, further observes of John 1:14,

> Jesus is depicted here as the true Tabernacle of Witness, in whom the glory
> of God is revealed, and as the Holy of Holies, in whom the *rimata tou*
> *Theou* [the spoken words of God] (John 3:34 ["For he whom God has sent
> *speaks the words of God*"]; also 5:47; 6:63, 68; 8:47; 12:47-48; 14:10; 15:7;
> 17:8) are hidden and revealed, as the ten *debarim* of the Law had once

8. Homily XII.1 on St. John (NPNF, first series, vol. XIV, p. 40).

9. *Commentary on John*, Book 4, Chapter 4; and Book I, Chapter 9; my emphasis.

10. T. F. Torrance, *Royal Priesthood* (Edinburgh: 1955), pp. 1-2; cited in Matthew Baker's
paper, "The Priesthood and Mediation of Christ in the Fourth Gospel," written in 2007 in fulfillment of the Johannine Writings course at St. Tikhon's Orthodox Seminary, South Canaan, PA.

been kept hidden in the *debir* into which only the high priest could enter. In John 2:19-21, this typology is extended by Jesus Himself to include also the Temple: "But He was speaking of the temple of His body" (John 2:21).[11]

These connections are also clear in the hymns for the Feast of Transfiguration. For example: "The Glory that once overshadowed the tabernacle and spoke with Thy servant Moses [Ex. 33:9], O Master, was a figure of Thy Transfiguration that ineffably shone forth as lightning upon Tabor."[12] This deep connection between the "glory" and the tabernacle is no doubt why Peter, upon seeing "the glory of the Lord" at the Transfiguration of Jesus, wanted to build three "tabernacles" (or booths/tents). Commenting about this, St. Gregory Palamas notes, "As Peter spoke these words, without realizing what he was saying, 'Behold a bright cloud overshadowed them' (Matt. 17:5), interrupting his words and making clear what sort of tabernacle was appropriate for Christ. But what was this Cloud . . . ? Was it not the unapproachable light in which God dwells . . . ?"[13]

Christ as the true Tabernacle/Temple of God also connects with the theme of the *topos theou*—the place of God. Moses, in Deuteronomy 12:5 and 11, and elsewhere in that chapter, says that Israel must only offer worship in *the place the Lord chooses for His name to dwell*. The *topos theou* is, then, a dwelling for the Lord's Name. Clearly Jesus is the ultimate form of dwelling place for the Lord's Name—of which the Hebrews' tabernacle and temple were only types.

---

11. Baker, op. cit. As Fr. Baker further notes in this paper, "Implied in this Tabernacle/Temple identification is also *sacrifice*." Origen further interprets the use of the term *sarx* (flesh) in John 1:14 in sacrificial terms, linking it with the statement of Leviticus: "Everyone who touches the holy flesh will be sanctified" (Lev. 6:8). Already, in the "flesh" spoken of in John's prologue, there is an intimation of "the one and perfect sacrifice," which all the sacrifices of the Old Testament "had anticipated in type and figure" (Origen, pp. 81-83; cited in ibid.).

Baker also notes: "The Pentateuch refers repeatedly to the Tabernacle as the *skēnē tou martyriou* (LXX: Ex. 38:21; 40:34; Num. 1:50; 9:15, 10:11; 17:7-8; 18:2); and the Ark of the Covenant as the *kiboton tou martyriou* (LXX: Ex. 25:16; 25:22; 26:33-34; 30:6, 26; 31:7; 39:35; 40:3, 5; Num. 4:5; 7:89; also Josh. 4:16)."

In view of the Tabernacle background of John 1:14, it is possible that these Mosaic associations of the Tabernacle with *martyria* form a priestly background to the important Johannine theme of "witness" or "testimony" (John 1:7-8; 1:15; 3:11; 3:26; 3:28; 3:32-33; 5:31-34; 5:36; 5:37; 8:17-18; 10:25; 15:27; 18:23; 18:37).

12. Canticle Three, Second Canon for Matins for the Transfiguration of Our Lord (*Festal Menaion*, p. 484).

13. Homily 35.9; Saint Gregory Palamas, *The Homilies*, Christopher Veniamin, ed. and trans. (Waymart, PA: Mount Thabor Publishing, 2009), p. 277.

Not only John 1:14, speaking of Jesus "tabernacling among us," is significant in this respect. In John 1:51 Jesus refers to Jacob's vision of the ladder uniting heaven and earth—and Jacob called that place "Bethel," meaning "house," or "dwelling place," of God (Gen. 28:19). Jesus then says that Nathanael will see that He, the Son of Man, *is* that ladder connecting heaven and earth, and that dwelling place of God, and/or His Name. And in John 2, of course, Jesus explicitly speaks of His body as the true temple—which is where the Name of the Lord dwells—to mention a few of the close connections.[14] This also connects with Jesus "coming in the name of the Lord," as the crowd in John 11:13 cries out: since He is the place where the name of the Lord dwells, He comes bearing the Lord's name Himself, the *egō eimi*, the "I AM," the name for Himself that God reveals to Moses (Ex. 3:14). Hence, all the "I AM" statements ("I am the Light of the world," etc.) that Jesus makes about Himself in John's Gospel.

Furthermore, this language in John 1:14 also "is evocative of the revelation of God's glory in the Exodus—by the Red Sea, on Mount Sinai, and at the tent of meeting by Israel's camp . . . (Ex. 33:7-11; . . . Ex. 40:34-38). The Exodus associations are intentional, and are part of the theme of the revelation and redemption of the Logos-Christ as fulfilling the hope of a *second* Exodus."[15] The first Exodus is clearly a type fulfilled in Christ's own Passover and Exodus, which is the second Exodus—as John later emphasizes, showing that Jesus is the Paschal Lamb, Who enables us to *cross* from death to life as He did in His death and Resurrection (John 1:29 and 36; 19:33-37).

We can see the same understanding of a second Exodus fulfilling the first in St. Luke's account of the Transfiguration. When Christ appears shining with uncreated light, the evangelist describes Moses and Elijah being with Him, and speaking of His "exodus" which He was to accomplish in Jerusalem (i.e., His death; Luke 9:30-31).[16]

Jesus as "tabernacling" among us is also a foretaste, or actually the inauguration, of the Last Day—on which the eschatological vision will be fulfilled, as it is spoken of near the end of the Revelation of John. In the vision of the New Jerusalem, or heaven, St. John writes: "Behold, the tabernacle [dwelling]

---

14. For further insights into the topic of the "place of God," see Bishop Alexander Golitzen's "*Topos Theou*: The Monastic Elder as Theologian and as Theology," in *Mount Athos the Sacred Bridge: The Spirituality of the Holy Mountain*, Dimitri Conomos and Graham Speake, eds. (Amsterdam: Peter Lang, 2005).

15. George R. Beasley-Murray, *John*, in the *Word Biblical Commentary* (Waco, TX: Word Books, 1987), p. 14 (his emphasis).

16. Alfred Edersheim, *The Life and Times of Jesus the Messiah* (Peabody, MA: Hendrickson Publishers, 1993, reprint), p. 541.

of God is with men, and He will [tabernacle] dwell with them, and they shall be His people, and God Himself shall be with them, and be their God" (Rev. 21:3).

So, in summary, the mention of the Logos *tabernacling* among us, and "we" "beholding His glory," would immediately bring to the Jewish-Christian mind of His original audience the Exodus and the Sinai experiences, the Tabernacle, the Temple, the visions of the Prophets—all the places of God's special appearances, the places "for His name to dwell"—and all the major ways God revealed Himself in Israel's past. The emphasis is clearly on *the experience* of those in both Old and New Israel, that it *is* possible to know God, because He does truly reveal Himself (most fully in Jesus Christ), enabling us at times to consciously perceive His presence—and even, at times, to see with our physical eyes a manifestation of His presence.

Applying this term "glory" to Jesus in the context of St. John's Prologue also testifies clearly to the belief that not only is Jesus the new "temple" or special place of God's presence, but more: He fulfills that type, *because He is divine.* They behold "*His* glory"—the glory of Jesus, which is so clearly linked to God's glory that John can only intend that it is one and the same. As St. Theophylact (11th century) writes, "'*We beheld His glory*,' but not such glory as Moses' face reflected, not as the cherubim and seraphim manifested to the prophet Ezekiel [see Ezek. 10:4], but such glory as befits the Only-begotten Son of the Father: the glory belonging to Him *by nature.*"[17]

In any case, this is something John makes clear from the first verse in his Gospel account: Jesus is God Incarnate, the Logos or Word of God made flesh, and *that* is the reason why He can uniquely make God manifest in the fullest, truest way possible for those of us also in the flesh—indeed, for all of humanity. Much of John's Gospel is dedicated to showing that Jesus Christ is the most perfect revealer of God, Who reveals Him most perfectly, because He Himself is divine. He is "in the bosom of the Father" (John 1:18), face to face with Him.

Simply by using the term "Logos" or Word of God, a term with a long history in Hebrew Scripture and thought (as well as in Greek thought), John brings in, from the first verse onwards, this major theme. Even for us, the words we speak reveal something of who we are. But of course, God's Word, being a word of power, does so supremely. Saying that the life of the Logos "was the light of men" (John 1:4) in part conveys the same thing—for light reveals, enabling us to see. Over and over again, St. John emphasizes that because Jesus Christ is the God-man, He reveals most perfectly what God is like *and* what people are created and called to be like. In and through the God-man, theology, Christology, and anthropology are inseparable.

---

17. *Commentary on John* (House Springs, MO: Chrysostom Press, 2007), pp. 22-23 (my emphasis).

As mentioned, Jesus even witnesses to His divinity by using the Old Testament name of God for Himself, the *egō eimi*, the "I AM," including when He says in John 8:12, "I AM (*egō eimi*) the Light of the world; he that follows Me shall not walk in darkness, but shall have the light of Life." Christ as Light connects to the theme of "glory" again. His Light is a guiding light, showing the way out of the darkness of ignorance, unbelief, and all other kinds of darkness. As physical light allows us to see things, this Light does so even more, simply by its presence; and it also reveals all things as they truly are, both the good and the bad. Hence it is linked to judgment as well. We see this, for example, in John 3:19: "the light has come into the world," but some prefer darkness "because their deeds are evil."

As Thomas Torrance points out, modern physics reveals yet another profound reason why this God-given analogy of Christ as the Light of the world is so apt:

> Light has a unique metaphysical and physical status, an absolutely singular place in the universe. Light is the one ultimate *Constant* upon which everything else both in nature itself and in our knowledge of it depends. If the speed of light were to vary, the whole universe would be disorderly and chaotic and would not be rationally or scientifically apprehensible. It is thus ultimately by reference to the mathematical properties of light that all our knowledge of the universe is gained; for light signals, the fastest messengers in the universe, are laden with information, so that all we know about the universe microphysically or macrophysically is gained through deciphering the mathematical patterns of light. Thus *singularity* has been found to belong to the fundamental structure of the created universe, and the *concept of singularity* has become inalienably lodged in the foundation and rational structure of scientific knowledge."[18]

How wonderful that only in recent times have people been able to appreciate the deep appropriateness of calling Jesus Christ the Light of the world in the fact that just as physical light is effectively the only means of access to our scientific knowledge of the universe, so also Jesus is uniquely the revealer of God—the only sure means of access to knowledge of God, and also of what it means to be a human being—what we are capable, in and through God, of becoming. As physical light holds an "absolutely singular place in the universe

---

18. T. F. Torrance, "The Atonement: the Singularity of Christ and the Finality of the Cross: the Atonement and the Moral Order," in *Universalism and the Doctrine of Hell: Papers presented at the 4th Edinburgh Conference in Christian Dogmatics, 1991* (UK: Paternoster Press, 1992), p. 228 (emphasis in the original).

... upon which everything else both in nature itself and in our knowledge of it depends," so Jesus Christ has an *absolutely singular place in the universe upon which everything else depends.*"

The hymns for the Feast of the Transfiguration make clear that this glory reveals the divinity of Jesus, that He is divine by nature. They also affirm that by assuming flesh in the Incarnation, He has transformed human nature itself, cleansing it, so that it shines with its original beauty:

> "for a short time He concealed the flesh He had assumed, and was transfigured before them, making manifest the excellence of the original beauty."[19]

> "Thou wast transfigured and hast made the nature that had grown dark in Adam to shine again as lightning, transforming it into the glory and splendour of Thine own divinity."[20]

> "Thou, O Christ, with invisible hands hast fashioned man in Thine image; and Thou has now displayed the original beauty in this same human body formed by Thee, revealing it, not as in an image, but as Thou art in Thine own self according to Thine essence, being both God and man."[21]

And St. John Chrysostom says of this word "dwelt" or "tabernacled":

> What then was the tabernacle in which He dwelt? Hear the prophet say, "I will raise up the tabernacle of David that is fallen" (Amos 9:11). It was fallen indeed; our nature had fallen an incurable fall, and needed only that mighty Hand. There was no possibility of raising it again, had not He who fashioned it at first stretched forth to it His Hand, and stamped it anew with His Image, by the regeneration of water and the Spirit."[22]

St. John Chrysostom brings in yet another aspect of "His glory" from the words of Jesus Himself:

---

19. Hymn at the lity for Great Vespers for the Transfiguration of Our Lord (*Festal Menaion*, p. 475).

20. Apostikhon at Great Vespers for the Transfiguration of Our Lord (*Festal Menaion*, p. 477).

21. Canticle Five, Second Canon, at Matins for the Transfiguration of Our Lord (*Festal Menaion*, p. 487).

22. Homily XI.2 on St. John (NPNF 1, vol. XIV, p. 39).

For we admire Him not only on account of the miracles, but also by reason of the sufferings—as that He was nailed upon the Cross, that He was scourged, that He was buffeted, that He was spit upon, that He received blows from those to whom He had done good. For even of those very things which seem to be shameful, it is proper to repeat the same expression, since He Himself called that action "glory."[23] For what then took place was (proof) not only of kindness and love, but also of unspeakable power. At that time death was abolished, the curse was loosed, devils were shamed and led in triumph and made a show of, and the handwriting of our sins was nailed to the Cross. And then, since these wonders were done invisibly, others took place visibly, showing that He was of a truth the Only-Begotten Son of God, the Lord of all Creation. For while yet that blessed Body hung upon the tree, the sun turned away his rays, the whole earth was troubled and became dark, the graves were opened, the ground quaked, and an innumerable multitude of dead leaped forth, and went into the city. And while the stones of His tomb were fastened upon the vault, and seals yet upon them, the Dead One arose, the Crucified, the nail-pierced One. And, having filled His eleven disciples with His mighty power, He sent them to men throughout all the world, to be the common healers of all their kind.[24]

We remember that in the Old Testament, the glory of the Lord appeared especially at the time of sacrifice. And Jesus' glory is also revealed especially in His voluntary death for all mankind, "while we were yet sinners" (Rom. 5:8). He seeks to save even those whose deeds are evil—those who, like Adam, are fearful of having their "nakedness" and disobedience exposed, those who "love the darkness" and hate the Light "because their deeds are evil," those who do not want to be rebuked, or to repent and change their ways (cf. John 3:19-20).

"Beheld"

Like St. Gregory Palamas and many others before him, John Marsh points out that in John 1:14, "the Greek word for 'beheld,' *etheasametha*, is used [only] of physical sight, and is in the historic tense. . . . The evangelist does not shrink from using the word 'beheld', which [in the Greek] implies that what is believed about the incarnate Word is not derived solely from spiritual insight, but is

---

23. As Christ Himself said of His approaching Crucifixion, "Now is the Son of Man *glorified*" (John 13:31; my emphasis).

24. Homily XII.3 on St. John (NPNF 1, XIV, p. 42).

rooted also in ordinary sense perception."[25] So the Greek word used for "beheld" emphasizes that Jesus' glory was truly manifested in history, and literally seen.

As previously quoted, St. John Chrysostom explains that

> we could not have beheld [His glory], had it not been shown to us, by means of a body like to our own. For if the men of old time could not even bear to look upon the glorified countenance of Moses, who partook of the same nature with us, if that just man needed a veil which might shade over the purity of his glory, . . . how could we creatures of clay and earth have endured the unveiled Godhead, which is unapproachable even by the powers above? Wherefore, He tabernacled among us, that we might be able with much fearlessness to approach Him, speak to, and converse with Him.[26]

Archimandrite Aimilianos, a contemporary holy elder, observes that in the Gospel accounts, "Christ is always presented as being seen, looked upon, and beheld." He gives this example:

> when Luke tells us that Christ was seen by them for forty days [Acts 1:3], you know what this means: perfection, completion, a fullness that cannot be surpassed. It designates a perfect period of time during which the One from beyond time revealed Himself perfectly. And He chose to do this, not simply through the medium of time, *but through sight, by means of vision, by being seen,* because seeing is the most powerful of our senses, and the one which provides us with the clearest and most enduring impressions. . . . what really makes an impression on me, what is unforgettable, is what I see. . . . That is why Christ is always presented as being seen, . . . and beheld. . . .
>
> This is why God is light: so that He can be seen. Thus the phrase, "He was seen by them for forty days," means that during a perfect interval of time, Christ revealed Himself to the most powerful, most gripping, of human senses, thereby providing us with the most compelling and permanent experience of God.[27]

Yet, during the earthly ministry of Jesus Christ, there were many who "saw and did not perceive" His glory. As John says in 1:11, "He came unto His own [literally, "His own things," "His own property"] and His own did not receive

---

25. Marsh, op. cit., p. 109.

26. Homily XII.1 on St. John (NPNF 1, XIV, p. 40).

27. *The Way of the Spirit*, p. 181 (my emphasis).

Him." The Pharisees and other Jewish leaders literally physically saw His glory in the sense of many miracles, but they did not perceive or understand what they were seeing; they always had some other explanation or interpretation for the miracles. A prime example would be when Jesus healed a demoniac, and they interpreted this to mean that He was in league with the devil (Matt. 9:32-34). In John 11:40, Jesus Himself indicates that physical sight alone is not enough, when just before raising Lazarus He tells Martha, "*If you believe*, you will behold the glory of God."[28]

Though at times, "ordinary sense perception" was involved, simply having eyes that work, and being physically present, was not enough to recognize that the Old Testamental longing to see "the face of God" (denied even to the great Moses)[29] was not merely a figurative expression indicating being in the presence of the personal God, but it also was a kind of messianic prophecy. This desire was fulfilled for those who saw the face of Jesus Christ, as John reports Jesus saying: "He who has seen Me has seen the Father" (John 14:9). And as Chrysostom says, "this is possible because His glory is veiled by His flesh"; yet that is also at least partly why, like the light of His glory, or His miraculous works, it was not evident to all. Even at least some of the chosen twelve disciples did not "see" in the sense of truly "perceiving" this before the Resurrection—that is why Jesus had to tell them (as recounted in John 14:9).

In speaking of the three disciples seeing the glory of the Lord on Mount Tabor at the Transfiguration of Jesus, the hymns for the Feast of the Transfiguration

---

28. My emphasis.

29. The great Moses was allowed to see the glory of God, but he was not allowed to see "His face" (Ex. 33:23). In spite of this, the Old Testament has many prayers expressing longing to see "the face of God." For example:

"When You said, 'Seek My face,' my heart said to You, 'Your face, Lord, will I seek'" (Ps. 27:8); "Restore us, O God; let Your face shine, that we may be saved!" (Ps. 80:3); "My soul thirsts for God, for the living God. When shall I come and behold the face of God?" (Ps. 42:2); "Seek the Lord and His strength, Seek His face evermore" (Ps. 105:5). And there is Aaron's blessing (which the Lord told Moses to convey to him): "The Lord bless you and keep you: the Lord make His face to shine upon you, and be gracious to you. The Lord lift up His countenance upon you, and give you peace" (Num. 6:24-26). And I Chron. 16:11 says, "Seek the Lord and His strength, seek His face continually!"

Seeking His *face* is partly an important way to speak of God's Presence that makes it clear that God is not some impersonal force, or energy, but a personal God Who allows, indeed Who welcomes, people to be in His presence. But we see in Christ that it is more than this, for St. John reports that Jesus told the apostles, "He who has seen Me has seen the Father" (John 14:9). Thus, at last, in Jesus, the Old Testamental longing to see God's face has been fulfilled in the face of the Logos Incarnate.

say, for example, "Now the invisible has become visible to the apostles: on Mount Tabor the Godhead has shone forth before them in the flesh."[30] St. Gregory Palamas makes it clear that "ordinary sense perception" alone was certainly not enough to make the invisible visible: "Take note that eyes with natural vision are blind to that light. It is invisible, and those who behold it do so not simply with their bodily eyes, but with eyes transformed by the power of the Holy Spirit."[31]

When St. John speaks of beholding the Lord's glory, he means literally seeing, but not *only* physically seeing. For as mentioned in the case of seeing His glory as uncreated light, eyes transformed by the Holy Spirit were needed. It is clear from Scripture itself, as well as from the whole Tradition, that there is such a thing as spiritual vision that truly sees more than can be seen with the physical eyes. In the case of understanding His glory in the sense of the miraculous events, the work of the Holy Spirit transforming the heart was, and is, also necessary. A heart open to the inspiration of the Holy Spirit was necessary to understand that these are not simply miracles wrought by a man sent from God, or to grasp that He is the Messiah—but not the Messiah most Jews were expecting: a political leader to free them from the Romans and set up a new nation. Such a heart was, and is, necessary in order to understand Who Jesus actually is: He is the *divine* Messiah, Who, in order to renew human nature and to offer redemption and eternal life to all mankind, voluntarily "tramples down death by death,"[32] rises from the dead, ascends into Heaven, and sends the Holy Spirit in fullness at Pentecost. Even the apostles did not really understand that entirely until after Pentecost, when they had received the Holy Spirit, the Spirit of Truth, Who enlightened their hearts and minds.

So, again, if one desires, like Spinoza and his followers, to restrict one's study of Scripture to "that which is recognizable to unaided human reason," to "ordinary sense perception," the experience of "reality as we know it," one will automatically exclude all that is most significant—what the Bible exists primarily to communicate, including access to the primary goal of reading Scripture—why it was written and passed down in the first place. One will be excluding the Holy Spirit, and the possibility of real personal spiritual transformation in Christ. One will not behold His glory in any sense, or recognize His face. "Beholding" in the Johannine—and traditional Christian—sense, necessarily involves more than "ordinary sense perception," but it usually does include it, just as the traditional allegorical approach includes the literal sense, but also much more.

---

30. Canticle Seven, Second Canon at Matins for the Transfiguration of Our Lord (*Festal Menaion*, p. 490).

31. Homily 34.13 (Veniamin, op. cit., p. 272).

32. From the main troparion for the Paschal services in the Orthodox Church.

This brings us to the last word in our main phrase: *Who* was beholding His glory? Who does the "we" refer to in the phrase "*we* beheld His glory," what was the result of their beholding, and why is this so important?

"*We*"

Since the verb "beheld" is in the past tense, the immediate short answer to the question of who exactly saw His glory in the sense of the uncreated light is, as far as we know, probably only Saints Peter, James, and John, the disciples closest to Jesus, who were with Him when He was transfigured on the Mount of Transfiguration, as the hymns for the Feast make clear: "Thou hast shown them, upon the holy mountain, the hidden and blinding light of Thy nature and of Thy divine beauty beneath the flesh."[33] (And their response was similar to those in the Old Testament who beheld His theophanies: they fell to the ground, unable to bear the awe-inspiring sight.) But given John's use of both meanings of "glory," the "we" would also have to include all those living at the time of Jesus who saw the "signs" or wonders that He worked, and recognized them as miracles from God (for example, the man born blind in John 9)—including the hundreds who witnessed Him after His Resurrection.

The "we" in our phrase seems also to be clearly connected to those mentioned in John 1:12, which reads: "But as many as *received* Him, He gave power to become children of God, to those who *believe* in His name: who were born, not of blood, nor of the will of the flesh, nor of the will of man, but of God."[34] In this verse, we read of a possibility offered of something that is greater even than beholding His glory: being "born of God," becoming a child of God. Actually, "beholding His glory" and becoming "children of God" are closely related, as the hymns for the Feast of the Transfiguration make clear, for by assuming flesh in the Incarnation, Jesus has transformed human nature, cleansing it so that it shines with its original beauty; and this is the foundation of why it is potentially possible for all human beings to become "children of God," being "changed into His [Christ's] likeness" (2 Cor. 3:18).

Notice that "received" is in the past tense, indicating that this group of God's children directly contrasts with "His own" people, literally His own possession or property, meaning the Jews as a nation, who as a body did not receive Him (v. 11)—though, of course, many individual Jews, like all the apostles, as well as some Jewish leaders, did accept Him. And according to Acts 6:7, "a great

---

33. A sessional hymn at Matins for the Transfiguration of Our Lord (*Festal Menaion*, pp. 479-480).

34. The "we" and the "children of God" are overlapping, rather than identical, terms.

many of the priests were obedient to the faith"—meaning Jewish priests who became Christians.[35] (Instead of seeing v. 11 as being more specific than v. 10, one could also understand it to be basically repeating v. 10 by translating "His own" to be "His own domain," referring to the whole world, which is His since He created it.)[36]

In one sense, all people are "children of God," because every single human being is created by God in His image. This was also a common term for the Israelites of the Old Covenant. It is clear from John 1:12, however, that there is now, in the New Covenant, a new requirement in order to become a child of God. This no longer happens automatically by being born as a human being, or by being born as a Jew, but by receiving the Logos Incarnate through faith and baptism (cf. John 3:5). And so the Church becomes the *New Israel*, and the New Israel is a new humanity, because of the new, "*zōē*" life—the eternal, divine life that Christ brings—which is open to all people who receive Him and believe on His name.

This phrase "believe on" has a dynamic, strong sense of being faithful to the nature of the One Whose name it is, living a life in communion with the One being named—like being "obedient to the faith" (Acts 6:7). It especially implies believing that Jesus bears the Divine Name[37]—in other words, that He is Divine and can apply the name of God, *O ōn*, the "I AM," to Himself.

"Believe," however, is in the present tense, indicating that such belief is possible to people in all times. It is not restricted only to those living at the time and place of the historical Jesus. John 17 confirms this interpretation. In John 17:24 Jesus prays for the eleven disciples, "that they also whom You gave Me may be with Me where I am, that *they may behold My glory* which You have given Me."[38]

---

35. One can also note that if in the Old Covenant the Jews are His possession, in the New Covenant, He gives all who choose it the power or "authority" to become not just God's own possession, but His very own children (cf. 1 John 3:1-2)—with inheritance rights, etc., which would be a powerful contrast.

This verse is the chiastic center of the Prologue according to Peter F. Ellis, indicating that this is the key point of the passage; see *The Genius of John* (Collegeville, MN: The Liturgical Press, 1984), p. 20. This makes sense, because it is the purpose John gives later for writing these things: "that ye might believe that Jesus is the Christ, the son of God; and that believing ye might have life through His name" (John 20:31). See also footnote 49 in this chapter. We note also that these priests mentioned were "obedient to the faith"—i.e., living the faith, not simply believing in only a mental way.

36. As, e.g., Rudolph Schnackenburg does, in *The Gospel According to John*, vol. 1 (New York: Crossroad, 1990), p. 259.

37. See Brown, op. cit., p. 11.

38. My emphasis.

But it is clear that He is not praying only for those present, for in 17:20 He says explicitly, "I do not pray for these [the apostles] alone, but also for those who will believe in Me through their word."

Also, in John 1:14, as mentioned, the verb for "beheld" in the Greek can only be used of physical sight. The same verb is used in 1 John 1:1[39]—in fact, two verbs of seeing are used there, to emphasize the crucial *eyewitness testimony* of the first apostles: they have really physically seen, and touched, the Lord Jesus Christ, and they have "perceived" and "understood." But in John 17:24, a different verb is used: when Jesus prays that they may "behold My glory," He does not use the verb *etheasametha* which refers to physical sight. Rather, he uses *theōrōsin* (from which we get the word "theoria," which can have the sense of spiritual perception), because He is speaking of all believers, all who will become children of God. He prays that they will be with Him, and that they will behold His glory not with their earthly eyes during His earthly life, because that time will have passed. But through the Holy Spirit, all can be with Him; and with their noetic eyes, the eyes of their hearts, all can potentially behold His glory. In this way, all believers have the possibility to become part of the "we" in John 1:12 and 14 who have become children of God, and to behold the Lord's glory.

It is worth noting, too, that immediately after St. John speaks of believers being able to be "children of God" and "born of God," he says that the Logos "became flesh" (1:14; became = *egeneto*, meaning a concrete historical event), thus emphasizing by his choice of words the historical physicality of the Incarnation. As St. John Chrysostom explains,

> Having declared that they who received Him were "born of God," and had become "children of God," he adds the cause and reason of this unspeakable honor. It is that "the Word became flesh," that the Master took on Him the form of a servant. For He became Son of Man, who was God's own Son, in order that He might make the sons of men to be children of God."[40]

Children are in many ways like their parents: Jesus is called the "Son" of God in order to make it clear that He is divine Himself—He has the same *nature* as God the Father. When St. John says that those who received and believe are given the power to become children[41] of God, he means that *by grace* they can

---

39. "that which we have heard, which we have seen with our eyes, which we have looked upon [or beheld], and our hands have handled, concerning the Word of life."

40. Homily XI.1 on St. John (NPNF 1, vol. XIV, p. 38).

41. To highlight Jesus' uniqueness as "the Son of God" and the difference in the relationship to God between Jesus and believers, St. John never calls believers "sons" of God, always "children"

become like Jesus Christ. He says explicitly in 1 John 3:1-2, "Behold what manner of love the Father has bestowed on us, that we should be called *children of God*. Beloved, now we are *children of God*, and it has not yet been revealed what we shall be like, but *we know that when He is revealed, we shall be like Him*, for we shall see Him as He is."[42]

The same idea is found in other places in the New Testament—for example, in Galatians 3:26-27: "in Christ Jesus you are all sons of God, for as many as have been baptized into Christ, have put on Christ." Or even more dramatically, in 2 Corinthians 3:18: "And *we all*, with unveiled faces, *beholding the glory* of the Lord, are being *changed into His likeness* from glory to glory."[43]

This sheds light on St. John's thought in John 1:12 as well, for we become children of God by being "changed into the likeness" of Christ. St. Gregory Palamas explains that when St. John

> says that we were born not of the flesh but of God, he proclaims regeneration and adoption through holy baptism; and when he says in his epistle, "Now are we sons of God," he means by baptism. On the other hand, when he says that God gave us power to become sons of God, as though we were not yet sons, he is referring to the perfection of adoption. A new-born babe has the natural ability to become wise, and is potentially wise; then when he grows older, if he earnestly pursues wisdom, he will actually be wise. In the same way, someone who has been born again through holy baptism has received the ability to be fashioned like the glorious body of the Son of God (cf. Phil. 3:21).[44]

The "we" who beheld His glory, then, are not only Peter, James, and John, who witnessed the Transfiguration, but also all the true children of God transformed by their encounter with Jesus during His earthly life—those who saw and perceived, who heard and understood, to paraphrase St. Mark's and St. Matthew's Gospel accounts, quoting Isaiah. And as both St. Paul and St. John

---

of God (see Brown, op. cit., pp. 13-14).

42. My emphasis. As St. Gregory Palamas says, "Then shall we be children of God, seeing and experiencing God's radiance, with the rays of Christ's glory shining around us, and ourselves, shining, as Moses and Elijah proved to us when they appeared with Him in glory on Mount Tabor (Matt. 17:3; Luke 9:30). 'The righteous,' it says, 'shall shine forth as the sun in the kingdom of their Father' (Matt. 13:43)" (Homily 57.16 [Veniamin, op. cit., p. 475]).

43. The King James Version renders 2 Corinthians 3:18 as "But we all, with unveiled face, beholding as in a mirror the glory of the Lord, are being transformed into the same image from glory to glory, just as by the Spirit of the Lord."

44. Homily 16.38 (Veniamin, op. cit., p. 132). See also Homily 57.16 (Veniamin, p. 475).

in his first epistle make clear, it is possible to become part of this "we" in a very real sense in any time or place. Thus, those coming after the time of the historical Jesus need not feel too deprived, and we can see how true are Jesus' words to Thomas after His Resurrection: "Thomas, because you have seen Me, you have believed. Blessed *are* those who have not seen and *yet* have believed" (John 20:29, NKJV).

Like Saints Peter, James, John, and Paul, however, there have been some in every time who have also literally "beheld His glory" in the sense of seeing the uncreated light, or even the risen Christ Himself—for example, St. Stephen the Protodeacon (1st century; Acts 7:55), St. Basil the Great (4th century), St. Symeon the New Theologian (10th century), St. Gregory Palamas (14th century), St. Seraphim of Sarov (19th century), and St. Silouan, Fr. Sophrony, and Fr. Aimilianos (20th century), and many, many others, both widely known, and unknown. So, there is always, potentially, a possibility for this kind of beholding in all times as well. Many more people have beheld the glory of the Lord in the countless miracles, both small and great, which He continually works for the faithful, and which He works for those outside His Church in order to bring them into the Faith.

This reality of becoming children of God, beginning with baptism, thus also includes those who come after the time of Jesus' earthly life, all of whom are called to be transformed into the likeness of Christ, to fulfill their potential to become "children of God." And they will surely "behold His glory" in the countless miracles both small and great that He continues to work, whether or not they "behold His glory" in the sense of seeing the uncreated light.

St. John further clarifies a little of what is meant by this likeness to Christ, this being a child of God, and how one may acquire it, when he says in John 1:16, "And of His fullness we have all received, and grace for grace." St. John links 1:14 to verse 16 by using the word "full" (*plērēs*): "we beheld His glory, the glory as of the only begotten of the Father, **full** of grace and truth" (v. 14); "And of His **fullness** (*plērōmatos*) we have all received, and grace for [*anti* = instead of] grace" (v. 16; my emphasis).

The Greek word for "fullness"—*plērōmatos*—is a very rich word. It has the sense of filling up, completing, even perfecting, as in Colossians 2:9: "the fullness (plērōma) of the Godhead dwelt in Him bodily." St. John Chrysostom describes this fullness as follows:

> He does not possess, says He, the gift by participation, but is Himself the very Fountain and very Root of all good, very Life, and very Light, and very Truth, not retaining within Himself the riches of His good things, but overflowing with them unto all others, and after the overflowing remaining full, in nothing diminished by supplying others, but streaming ever forth; and imparting to others a share of these blessings, He remains in this

sameness of perfection. . . . But of that Fountain, . . . however much a man may draw, It continues undiminished . . .

Let us suppose that there is a fountain of fire, and that from that fountain ten thousand lamps are kindled, or twice as many, thrice as many, or many times as many; does not the fire remain at the same degree of fullness even after its imparting of its virtue to such members? It is plain to every man that it does.[45]

Chrysostom indicates who the "we" includes as he introduces his explanation of the next phrase, "grace for grace":

all *we*—the twelve, the three hundred, the three thousand, the five thousand, the many myriads of Jews, all the fullness of the faithful who *then were, and now are, and hereafter shall be*—have "received of His fullness." What have we received? "Grace for grace," saith he. What grace, for what? For the old, the new.[46]

The phrase "grace for grace" could mean that grace is not given just once, but continually.[47] It could also reflect a Semitic expression which would mean abundant grace. But the Greek Fathers took it more literally as one grace *instead of* another. Chrysostom, for example, explains that the first grace is the Old Testament *type*, while the second grace is its New Testament *fulfillment*—just as there is also a new law, a new covenant, a new circumcision, a new adoption, a new baptism, a new service, a new glory, a new temple, and a new Sacrifice.[48]

One grace *instead* of another grace can also have the sense of fulfilling, completing, and even perfecting what was lacking in the Old Testament covenant (a recurrent theme in the Gospel accounts). This would then contrast the Old Testament gifts of God with the much greater gifts through Christ. This point is made in the next verse, which indicates that, as great as Moses the lawgiver was, Jesus, the giver of grace and truth, God's Only-Begotten, is far greater.[49]

All the Christians of St. John's time, by "receiving of His fullness," the "grace for grace," actually shared in what the Logos incarnate is—not just seeing and hearing Him.[50] This is a very powerful reminder to Christians of all times

---

45. Homily XIV.1 on St. John (NPNF 1, vol. XIV, p. 47).

46. Homily XIV.1 on St. John (NPNF 1, XIV, p. 48); my emphasis.

47. John Marsh, op. cit., p. 11.

48. Homily XIV.1, op. cit., p. 48.

49. The phrase "grace for grace" probably can be taken in all these ways. I follow the principle: whatever works with the text, and is in accord with the true Faith and is edifying, we can use.

50. Marsh, op. cit., p. 110.

that even though we cannot see and hear Him as many of the first Christians did, we *can* still receive of His fullness—that this grace is not only completing and perfecting what was given in the Old Covenant, but also completing and perfecting what is lacking in us (if we cooperate!). Through this grace we can receive life in abundance—"*zōē*," eternal life—which will be imaged in various ways later in John's Gospel, including drinking and eating, along with other links to the Eucharist. All of this is a very powerful reminder of our exceedingly high calling of deification.

The Bridegroom and the Children of God

There are many references to deification found in the writings of John and in the rest of the New Testament, such as "having life in His name," "receiving of His fullness," "putting on Christ," eternal life, entering the Kingdom of Heaven, etc. But in the Prologue of his Gospel, St. John carefully chooses the phrase becoming "children of God"; and, as mentioned, he indicates the centrality of this idea by placing it in the middle of the Prologue's chiastic structure.[51] It would seem that John chose this analogy partly to prepare the reader to understand more completely the Bridegroom analogy for Christ, and the marriage theme which he uses explicitly beginning in John 2:1ff. It is assumed in Scripture that marriage will normally precede having children, that children are normally the fruit of marriage and one of the main reasons explicitly given in Scripture for marriage ("Be fruitful and multiply" [Gen. 1:28]). Hence, to more fully appreciate what John means by saying that believers can become "children of God," it will be helpful to examine the analogy of marriage, and of Christ as the Bridegroom.

Much in the Old Covenant is fulfilled by being transformed in the New—the understanding of the Messiah, of the Forerunner, etc. This is also true for the imagery of God as the Husband of Israel (cf. Is. 54:5-6, KJV). Jesus is never spoken of as the "husband," but as the Bridegroom. The image of children is also used: Jesus is both the Bridegroom and a Child, the Son of God; and the people of God, as a whole, are both His children and His betrothed—His future "Bride." We will see that what marriage images is indicated with more intensity later on in other analogies in John's Gospel. Through multiple images

---

51. Chiasm, or chiastic parallelism, was a common literary form in the ancient Semitic world of writing, with a repeating pattern such as abcb'a'—where each letter stands for a section of the text with a particular theme or emphasis. This is helpful for memorizing, and for interpreting, as well as being an elegant literary form to use. See *The Genius of John: A Composition-Critical Commentary on the Fourth Gospel*, by Peter Ellis, for further details.

or analogies used in multiple contexts and seen from multiple angles, St. John helps the reader come to a deeper understanding of the great mystery of our salvation. Multiple analogies also help prevent the reader from taking any one analogy too literally.

Using the analogies of children and marriage allows John to tie both sets of imagery together with what was for the Jews the most important question concerning Jesus: His origin, and hence the source of His authority. In other words, who was the true, authoritative interpreter of God's revelation?—Jesus, or the Pharisees and other Jewish leaders of the time. Jesus presents some radically different interpretations of the Torah, and of the whole Jewish self-understanding of His time, which challenge that of many of the Pharisees and other leaders. Thus, from the beginning of His ministry, Jesus is calling the Jewish leaders' authority into question in significant ways. This goes far beyond simply the question of who should be in charge, to include who most truly reveals Who God is, which leads to the revelation of who we are, and how we should live. The question could also be phrased: Who speaks for God about ultimate truth?

The theme of origins and children occurs in almost every chapter in John's Gospel in some form. There are many angles to this, such as: Whose child are you? Who is your father? Are you a faithful son or a rebellious one? What family and ethnic group do you come from? Who are your ancestors? The question of *who* speaks for God, Jesus or the other Jewish leaders, is also inseparable from the question of who are the true *people* of God, who can be part of the *true Israel*, the ones who can become God's "Bride," following the Old Testament analogy (emphasizing the communion of faithfulness and love). Or following more the New Testament analogy, who can become His child (emphasizing likeness to Him, both in *how* we live, and ontologically in the sense of living with His "*zōē*," or eternal life—that is, deification)? In other words, how can one be purified so that it is possible to enter into the presence of the All-Holy God, living in a communion of love with Him?

This constellation of questions about who has the ultimate authority to reveal God could also be described as questions about interpretation: How do we know what is true? Whose interpretation can we trust? Who is your ultimate authority, and what is their authority based on? Who has the ultimate authority to give the best interpretation of Scripture *and reality*. For as Douglas Knight has said, "Scripture is exegesis of the world," and is "part of the effort that renews creation."[52] Scripture itself reflects the understanding that *who* is doing the interpreting is all-important.

---

52. *The Eschatological Economy: Time and the Hospitality of God* (Grand Rapids, MI: Eerdmans, 2006), p. 212.

So, what do we see in John's Gospel account about children, marriage, and Who Jesus really is—Who His Father really is, what His origin is, and what the source of His authority is? Jocelyn McWhirter has a very helpful study on Jesus as the Bridegroom and the marriage theme in John's Gospel. She notes that a number of passages from the Old Testament about marriage are prominent for John because he interprets them as messianic prophecies"[53] that "testify to Jesus." These include Jeremiah 33:10-11; Psalm 45, on the king's marriage; Genesis 29:1-20; and several verses in the Song of Songs. Showing that Jesus fulfills these prophecies helps people, especially John's fellow Jews, to understand and believe that Jesus is the Christ, the Messiah, which John gives as part of his purpose in writing his account.

As McWhirter explains, it is a "fundamental assumption of messianic exegesis that all Scripture presents the same unified theological message."[54] This leads to what has been called "the intertextual practice characteristic of biblical narrative"[55]—also characteristic of early Jewish biblical commentary. In other words, this was the common practice of seeing and indicating all kinds of connections between various passages from all over the Scriptures—something typically done by the writers of the New Testament as well.[56] Hence, there are many connections and references that a contemporary reader schooled in a later way of thinking about texts (and not nearly so familiar with the text of Scripture!) would probably never think of, but which would have been evident, or even obvious, to early interpreters. This is also the approach commonly used by both the early and later Christian Fathers. And an increasing number of biblical scholars today are realizing the importance of looking at the text of Scripture as the original authors, such as John, did, in order to more fully appreciate the richness of his intended meanings, and to more accurately interpret his words.

----

53. Jocelyn McWhirter, *The Bridegroom Messiah and the People of God: Marriage in the Fourth Gospel* (Cambridge: Society for New Testament Studies Monograph Series, 2008), pp. 106-107, 115, 120, 123, 143. Her insights in this book helped with much of this discussion.

54. Ibid., p. 19.

55. Ibid., p. 9.

56. Some tip-offs that a connection is being indicated are:

1. details that seem out of place "signal an allusion to another text where they are more at home."

2. One can determine the "evoked text by examining its verbal and thematic similarities with the originating text."

3. "Once the evoked text is recognized, it changes the content of the originating text such that all elements of both texts begin to interact" (McWhirter, p. 9).

If one assumes that Scripture is in any sense inspired by God, and that it thus speaks of true realities, and that its goal is to lead you to a life-transforming experience of God, then you will assume that John, and Paul, or even Moses, for that matter, are each speaking about essentially the same realities and experiences, though from the perspective of their different cultures and contexts. Thus, it is natural and not only completely legitimate, but even desirable, to make intertextual connections. This is why the New Testament authors did this—not because it was merely some sort of cultural convention.

But if you remove that level of spiritual reality and interpret the Scriptures "as if there is no God," then each author's work becomes an isolated text, and even passages become isolated "bits," and lots of ink is spilled in trying to show where the authors got their ideas from, and other secondary matters largely irrelevant to those in both the New Testament and patristic traditions. These questions may need to be answered by some in order to address those in the culture who have them, but they should be primarily of apologetic interest. They are usually irrelevant for spiritual life and the personal transformation called for in the Gospel accounts.

Bearing all of the above in mind, we will consider briefly the first eight chapters of St. John's Gospel.[57] These eight have been selected in part because of the need to limit the length of this chapter, and more importantly, because it is in these chapters that the main topics we are considering, all relating to Jesus' authority (hence, origins) and our deification, are imaged in terms of marriage and children, and connect most directly to the Bridegroom analogy first brought in with the myth of Psyche and Cupid in Chapter 1.

It will be helpful first, however, to consider what marriage symbolizes in the Old Testament, for this is what St. John is building upon. Genesis 2:24 says, "the two shall become one flesh." Since marriage is the closest possible physical relationship in all of human existence, and is assumed to be a loving union of persons leading to new life through the conceiving, bearing, and raising of children, it easily serves as an effective analogy, or symbol, of the closest possible real, personal relationship with God. Marriage is a loving communion of persons leading to new life in God—or at least, foreshadowing this. In

---

57. While we refer to the standard chapters, it is important to remember that these divisions are not original—the numbered chapters were only added in the thirteenth century. Also, although the passage concerning the woman caught in adultery is not found in the manuscripts of any Eastern Fathers until around the 10th century, it is found in many early Western manuscripts, and is commented on by a number of Western Church Fathers, most notably Saints Ambrose, Augustine, and Jerome, and is accepted by all Churches today as part of canonical Scripture, located in this place in St. John's Gospel. That is why we are considering it here, especially since the broader theme of marriage in John sheds interesting light on this episode.

the context of the Old Testament it requires purity, or purification, before this can happen. It requires faithfulness and obedience to continue—and all these are related: we keep ourselves pure because we are faithful to our spouse. In the Old Testament, idolatry—the worship of pagan gods—was understood as breaking faithfulness to God and one's purity before Him. And it is spoken of as *adultery*—breaking faithfulness to one's spouse.

This is also what marriage symbolizes in John: the closest possible communion in love between God and His people,[58] leading to new life—becoming children of God. In order for this union to be actualized and continued, purification/purity is required, as well as faithfulness/obedience to His commandments (see, for instance, John 14:15-16, 21, 23; 15:10). Jesus, the Logos Incarnate, is called God's "Only-begotten," or especially beloved Son, to emphasize His uniqueness in His oneness with God—His being of the same nature with God the Father. But through Jesus, as mentioned, each believer can also acquire the right, or the power or authority, to become a child of God. More of what this means we will now consider below.

Chapter 1

We have already mentioned the image of "children of God" in the Prologue, and from the first verse of chapter 1, John makes clear the true origin of Jesus, Whose child *He* truly is, and thus why He is the ultimate authority. This is stated very emphatically in 1:1, where the Logos is not only "with God," but also "was God"; and in John 1:18: "No one has seen God at any time; the only begotten Son, Who is in the bosom of the Father, He has declared (*exēgēsato*) Him." The root of the word *exēgēsato* is the word from which we get the English word "exegesis." So we could also say, "the Word has made the Father known," or "revealed Him," or even, "the Word has *interpreted* the Father." Jesus is the ultimate authority because, and only because, of His divine origin.

Chapter 1 ends with a reference to Jacob's dream in Genesis (cf. Gen. 28:10-19) of the ladder to Heaven. Jacob has this dream/vision on his way to seek a pure bride from among his kinsmen (and he was blessed by his father to do this; see Gen. 28:1-4). From this union (or actually, his unions with Leah

---

58. As Fr. Aimilianos says, Christian "Marriage, then, like monasticism, is a longing for the infinite; it is not the satisfaction of a biological drive, but an orientation of the self toward the eschaton. Marriage is a journey, an ascent toward the perfection of paradise" (*The Way of the Spirit: Reflections on Life in God* [Athens: Indiktos, 2009], p. 355); and also, "Thus the creation of Eve was a sacred rite, a mystical act, a rite of initiation, because marriage is a passage to fullness of life in Christ. To marry is to enter paradise" (ibid., p. 353).

and Rachel, and their handmaids), the twelve patriarchs are born, and their children become the twelve tribes forming Israel, God's chosen people. And after the dream Jacob says in Genesis 28:16-17, "surely the Lord is in this place. . . . this is the House of God, this is the gate of heaven." Hence he names the place *Bethel*, which means "house of God."

The words of Jesus to Nathaniel in John 1:51, especially as they bring to mind the whole context of the original image in Genesis 28, thus announce in a preliminary, summary way all that the disciples will eventually learn about Who Jesus is: He, too, is blessed by His Father to go and seek a pure bride who will be the Church, the New Israel. This New Israel, founded on the twelve apostles, however, is not limited to family or ethnic kinship, but is open to all. Jesus, like Jacob when he has his dream, is starting out on that journey at this point in the account of His public ministry. But Jesus is "greater than our father Jacob" (John 4:12), and fulfills what Jacob only dreamed: He is Himself the "place of God's presence," the new "house of God" tabernacling among us.

The "angels ascending and descending" (in John 1:51) partly indicates Jesus' two-way ministry; as St. Athanasius writes, "Our Lord, being Word and Son of God, bore a body, and became Son of Man , so that . . . He might minister the things of God to us, and ours to God."[59] For "the mediation of divine life and revelation is proper to God, and the priestly ministrations of intercession, atonement, and reconciliation are proper to man." Christ the God-Man fulfills both. John 1:14, in identifying Jesus with the Old Testament tabernacle or tent of meeting, establishes "the *flesh* of Christ as the *locus* [place] of divine mediation. *Like the "tent of meeting" in the Pentateuch, the Word-made-flesh is the* *"place" not only of divine life and revelation, but also of the priestly ministrations* *of intercession, atonement and reconciliation.*"[60] So this image even points indirectly towards His saving sacrifice on the cross.

The "angels ascending and descending" also refers to Jesus's constant communion with God the Father. Hence, the means of communion between heaven and earth is no longer a ladder for angels but for Jesus Himself, the son

---

59. Four Discourses Against the Arians, Discourse IV.6 (NPNF, second series, vol. IV, p. 435).

60. And, as Fr. Baker explains, this "does not take place in a way extrinsic to His person, but is ontologically rooted in the hypostatic unity of the Word-made-flesh." For early Christian exegesis, the presence of priesthood follows naturally from the identification of Christ's Body as Tabernacle or Temple. As the 4th century Latin apologist Lactantius writes, "This is the faithful house, this is the everlasting temple; and if any one has not sacrificed in this, he will not have the reward of immortality. *And since Christ was the builder of this great and eternal temple, He* *must also have an everlasting priesthood in it*" (Lactantius, *Divine Institutes*, Chap. XIV, "Of the Priesthood of Jesus Foretold by the Prophets"; cited in Fr. Matthew Baker's unpublished paper, op. cit.).

of Man—the true Messiah coming to save the world by making it possible for all people to become truly "children of God."

Chapter 2

The nuptial scene for Christ's first miracle in John's Gospel is very significant, recalling all the nuptial imagery of the Old Testament of God's marriage with His people (especially Hos. 2:16-25—"I will betroth you to Me forever"; Is. 54:4-8 and 62:4-5—"The Lord has taken you like a wife," which emphasizes that God is the God of all).

There are seven miracles before the Resurrection which John has selected to write about at some length, which he calls "signs" (*sēmeia* in Greek). In all these miracles, the focus is not so much on the mighty works of God as on what these works *signify*—what they mean. He selected so few because with each one he wants to emphasize much more than Christ's miracle-working power. The eighth miracle is the Resurrection itself. All the signs point to Jesus as the *divine* Messiah, and are "written that you may believe that Jesus is the Christ, the Son of God, and that believing you may have life in His name" (John 20:31).

This incident is the climax of the first calling of the disciples, bringing them to a deeper belief, for at the end of the account of the wedding it is stated that "His disciples believed on Him" (2:11). We see later in the Gospel that just because one sees a miracle does not mean one will truly believe on Him; as mentioned above, some reject Him after seeing the miracles, while others misunderstand and remain at a superficial level of having their stomachs filled, etc. It is a gift from God to truly "see and perceive," to see and believe.

Jesus' first sign in St. John's Gospel involves changing the water used for purification into an abundance of wine. Providing the wine at a wedding feast was the bridegroom's responsibility—that is why the governor of the feast, who tastes it first, exclaims to the bridegroom how unusual it is that he has saved the best wine for last, when most of the guests would not even notice (wedding feasts usually lasted for several days).

Abundant wine was a standard sign of the End Times (see, for instance, Is. 25:6-9), or the Last Day, in Jewish thought of the time. So, the disciples, and later Christian readers, realize that Jesus' miraculous provision of abundant wine reveals Him to be the true Bridegroom, fulfilling messianic prophecy (especially Jeremiah 33:10-15; but in the LXX, e.g., 7:33) and signaling the beginning of the Last Days. As St. Augustine says, "what wonder if He came to that house to a marriage, having come into this world to a marriage?"[61] Jesus'

---

61. Commentary on John, VIII.4; NPNF, first series, vol. VII, p. 58.

changing the Jewish water of purification into the best wine points toward what will truly enable the purification necessary to enable us to become "children of God": His death and Resurrection. And many Saints see here also an indication of the need for ongoing purification in our lives, which our participation in the Eucharist, the memorial (*anamnēsis* [Luke 22:19]) of His death and Resurrection, helps make possible.[62]

Additionally, this sign takes place in a largely Gentile area, which also fulfills Isaiah's prophecy that this abundant wine and feast will be for "all the nations"—i.e., for all the non-Jews (Gentiles), and not just for the Jews (as many Jews at the time of Jesus believed).

In v. 11, tremendous significance is given to this event: it is the beginning (*archēn*) of the "signs" when Jesus "manifested His glory." Of course, this glory is only fully revealed in the cross and what follows, but this is the beginning of that process: the triumph of the true Bridegroom, the true Messiah, in and through His death and Resurrection. At this point, John says only Jesus' disciples know what has happened, and they "believed in Him." (Here, the word for "in" [*eis*] is very emphatic.) His disciples believed not simply that He had power to change water into wine, but they began to realize in an ever deepening way that He was the true Bridegroom Who will provide the possibility of a real communion (marriage) with God by His sacrificial death for all. Some (such as John Marsh) have said that the real wonder here is not that water was turned into wine, but that the true Bridegroom of Israel comes to a marriage ceremony among the people of God and transforms the whole event.[63]

The cleansing of the temple (2:13-16) prophetically indicates the new temple of Jesus' body, and the new worship Jesus makes possible for all peoples.

---

62. The Old Testament refers to wine as the "blood of the grape" (e.g., Deut. 32:14—"they drank the pure blood of the grape"—showing how God cares for them and has abundantly provided for them). Hence, there might be here the idea that the Jewish rites of purification, which the jars of water were used for, do not really purify man, since they cannot cleanse him from sin. Only the blood of Christ can do this—so there is much powerful symbolism here, with clear Eucharistic overtones.

In fact, Clement of Alexandria (late 2nd c.), St. Cyprian of Carthage (3rd c.), St. Cyril of Jerusalem (4th c.), and many others see the turning of water into the best wine as prefiguring the Holy Eucharist, where wine becomes Christ's blood. Both Chrysostom briefly, and Augustine at length, say that this miracle is basically just a shortened version of what happens each year, when rain is turned into grapes. Augustine says we are so used to this that we do not see the wonder of it, so Christ had to do something to wake us up, so we could see the wonder that is really there all the time. He ends, "let us not therefore wonder that God did it, but love Him because He did it in our midst, and for the purpose of our restoration" (ibid.).

63. Marsh, op. cit., p. 142.

It clearly continues the purification theme as well. After this cleansing, Jesus alludes to what will be His last sign more directly: "destroy this temple and in three days I will raise it" (2:19). Here the crucifixion and Resurrection are brought in again explicitly. Through them He purifies us and enables us to have an even closer communion/oneness with God than was possible in the Old Testament.

Chapter 3

Becoming a child of God, being born of God by being purified and renewed, is the clear theme this chapter opens with, as Jesus instructs Nicodemus, one of the leaders of the Jews, who has come to Him "by night." He tells Nicodemus that in order to "see the kingdom of God" (v. 3), and in order to "enter the kingdom of God" (v. 5), one must be "born *again*"; but in the Greek, the adverb *anōthen* means "from above" as well as "again." Jesus sheds a bit more light on what this means in v. 4 when He says, "unless one is born of water and the Spirit, he cannot enter the kingdom of God"—with the water and Spirit being a clear reference to baptism. In 3:14 His eighth miracle is indicated again: Moses *lifting up* (*upsōsen*) the serpent in the wilderness is a clear sign of the crucifixion, which will lead to the Resurrection. The language John uses to describe Moses' action is also points toward Jesus' Ascension into heaven.[64] Verse 16 speaks of God's great love—the giving of His Child, His Son, unto death—so that all people can potentially have eternal life.

That baptism is being referred to here by "of water and the Spirit" is made clear also by St. John's juxtaposing this discussion with Nicodemus about the need to be "born again/from above," "born of water and the Spirit," with a scene about baptism. For next we see John the Baptist baptizing people in the Jordan River, and some of his disciples are concerned because now "all men" are coming to Jesus (3:26). This is echoed near the end of Jesus's public ministry by the Pharisees, another group who do not understand, when they are distressed that "the world has gone after Him" (John 12:19).

In St. John the Baptist's words which close chapter 3, we find the Bridegroom theme explicitly appearing again as the Forerunner emphasizes that he is "not the Christ" (v. 28); rather, he describes himself as the "friend of the *bridegroom* who stands and hears him, [and] rejoices greatly because of the bridegroom's

---

64. *Upsosev* in the Greek means lifted, or raised up; it is used also several times in the New Testament when the Ascension is spoken of—e.g., Acts 2:33 and 5:31, where this same word is translated "having been exalted" (to the right hand of God).

voice" (my emphasis). He concludes by declaring, "Therefore, this joy of mine is fulfilled" (3:29).

The analogy of the Messiah as the Bridegroom used by the Forerunner echoes an important messianic prophecy in Jeremiah to which Jesus seems to allude several times: Jeremiah 33:10-11 (KJV), which occurs just before Jeremiah mentions the "righteous Branch to spring forth from David," which is another prophecy of Christ:[65]

> "Again there shall be heard in this place . . . the voice of joy, and the voice of gladness, the voice of the bridegroom and the voice of the bride, the voice of them that shall say, 'Praise the Lord of hosts: for the Lord is good; for His mercy endureth for ever'; and of them that shall bring the sacrifice of praise into the house of the Lord. For I will cause to return the captivity of the land, as at the first," saith the Lord.

In Jeremiah 16, the Lord tells Jeremiah that because "your fathers have forsaken Me and have walked after other gods, and have served them, and have worshiped them, and have forsaken Me, and have not kept My law" (v. 11); and because "ye have done worse than your fathers," He says He will "cast them out" and "not show them favor." One key way He will do this is stated in verse 9: "Behold, I will cause to cease out of this place in your eyes, and in your days, the voice of mirth, and the voice of gladness, the voice of the bridegroom and the voice of the bride" (Baruch 2:23 in the LXX).[66]

So joy at the bridegroom's voice has strong echoes of this judgment being revoked—the Lord has forgiven His people, and they turn to Him and worship Him in truth once again. Jeremiah 33:10 says, "I will cleanse them from all their iniquity, . . . I will pardon all their iniquities." Jesus, then, is that Bridegroom Who not only signifies that the Lord has forgiven His people and is reconciled to them once more, but He also is the one Who *makes possible* this forgiveness, purification, and reconciliation through His voluntary death and Resurrection, which leads to this joy being fulfilled.

The connection here is much stronger than some might suppose, since this phrase "the bridegroom's voice" is found nowhere else in the LXX.[67] "John

---

65. Along with "a branch" from the root of Jesse (Is. 11:1-5), and the "Branch" (Zech. 6:12). These were all "undoubtedly accepted as messianic prophecy" (McWhirter, op. cit., p. 116). And McWhirter asserts that the messianic significance of the bridegroom in Jeremiah 33 is very clear through association with Psalm 45, as well as with the Song of Songs (ibid.).

66. Note that Jer. 7:34 is the same as 16:9; and in the Septuagint (or LXX), this is found in Jer. 7:33. Baruch was Jeremiah's scribe.

67. McWhirter, op. cit., p. 55.

reiterates important words from Jeremiah's prophecy in order to indicate its fulfillment."[68] The Forerunner is the first to rejoice at the coming of the Bridegroom Messiah. Actually, in Luke's Gospel account he is even more the first, for when the Virgin Mary greets Elizabeth, the Forerunner's mother, she tells Mary that her baby, John, "leaped in my womb for joy" (Luke 1:44)—and the word used for "joy" (*aggaliasei*) is a special term for joy at the coming of the Messiah![69] The emphasis is on the joy the Bridegroom inspires, *and* His increase (John 3:30)—that the number of His children, or disciples, will be multiplied. (These themes will be further developed in John's next chapter.)

This theme of joy at the Messiah's coming will recur later when Abraham will be described as "rejoicing in My day" (John 8:56)—with *day* having here the clear meaning of the Last Day, when the Messiah was believed to be coming.[70] It recurs again in John 20:20, when the disciples rejoiced (*echarisan*) when they recognize their risen Lord. Jesus also speaks several times of fulfilling the disciples' joy in the Last Discourse (John chs. 14—17).

Chapter 4

This chapter takes place at Jacob's well. This is the same Jacob who dreamed of the ladder, as mentioned in Chapter 1. In Old Testament times, wells were considered an ideal place to find a bride. Jacob finds his beloved Rachel at a well (Rebekah is also found for Isaac at a well, and Moses finds Zipporah at a well), so the well at least indirectly brings up an association with marriage. Jocelyn McWhirter makes a strong case that there are here deliberate allusions to Genesis 29, the story of Jacob meeting Rachel at a well. These allusions in this chapter of John shed light on important themes through comparing and contrasting the two accounts. The Samaritan woman even directly compares Jesus to Jacob in John 4:12.

Christ as the Bridegroom was just mentioned a few verses previous, and Jesus will ask about the Samaritan woman's husband during their dialogue. So talking with a woman at a well is sandwiched between two references to marriage, making it not a stretch at all to see here the new Bridegroom going to the well to find a new bride. McWhirter makes the interesting point: while Jacob's meeting Rebekah at a well ends in a marriage of two members of the same

---

68. Ibid., p. 56.

69. Andrew Louth, *Discerning the Mystery* (Oxford: Clarendon Press, 1983), p. 129.

70. McWhirter, op. cit., p. 58.

extended family,[71] eventually resulting in the birth of the twelve patriarchs and the foundation of ethnic Israel, Jesus' meeting the Samaritan woman does not result in a literal marriage with offspring, but in a new kind of family of faith that is not based on ethnic or family background.[72] The Samaritans believe in Him—and receive Him—thus becoming *children of God*, indicating again that the Messiah has not come just for the ethnic Jews, but for everyone. "As prophesied by John the Baptist, Jesus the bridegroom continues to increase (3:30). His encounter with a Samaritan woman produces spiritual offspring."[73]

There is also the theme of water for new, eternal life: "Whoever drinks of the water I give shall never thirst, but it shall be a fountain/spring (*pēgē*) springing up to eternal life" (4:14). So we see here a new step: a much greater bridegroom than Jacob or any of the Old Testament patriarchs is here. As John wrote earlier, "For the law was given through Moses, but grace and truth came through Jesus Christ" (1:14). There is something greater in the New Covenant that Jesus makes possible which is hinted at here. Jeremiah 2:13, for example, says, "for My people have committed two evils; they have forsaken Me, the fountain of living waters, and hewed out cisterns for themselves, broken cisterns, that can hold no water." God is compared to "living water" in John 4:14; and in John 7:39, John explains that when Jesus speaks of water "springing up," He is speaking of the Holy Spirit.

The Old Testament image for the people's relationship with God was a marriage, but now with Christ it is possible to have even closer communion with Him, which is imaged by *drinking* this living water which images the Holy Spirit. When we drink, the water becomes physically part of us, so this is a closer kind of "union" than is possible even in marriage.

Then we find out that this woman is a Samaritan—from a people who were not faithful to Yahweh—and that she is not living a faithful, pure life, since she has had five husbands, and her current "boyfriend" is not really her husband. So not only is communion with the God of Israel extended by Jesus to those of other "families or religions"—not only are *they* also "called"—but *even sinners* can now be purified, since Jesus is calling all people, even sinners, to be His Bride (cf. Hosea 2).

The Samaritan woman immediately goes from this revelation about her personal life to assuming (by implication) that Jesus is the Prophet like Moses, prophesied in Deuteronomy 18:15 and 18. So she asks Him where the true place of worship is (we recall Jesus as Jacob's ladder, and His body as the new

---

71. "The children of Israel must not have a Canaanite mother" (cf. Gen. 24:3; see McWhirter, p. 61).

72. Ibid., p. 65.

73. Ibid., p. 76.

temple). This is another way of asking the key question: How can we be part of Israel, the "Bride" of God? In other words, how can we be in the closest possible communion with God and have eternal life? Surely this is the ultimate reason why we worship the true God.

Jesus explains that "the hour is coming" (the "hour" always refers to the crucifixion and the Resurrection) "when true worshipers will worship the Father in spirit and truth" (v. 24). In other words, the key thing is not a particular place, but being in communion with God through the Holy Spirit, Who guides believers into all Truth.

The woman mentions the Messiah, the Christ, and "Jesus said to her, 'I who speak to you am He'" (lit. 'I AM [ego eimi] Who speak to you'; v. 26). This is what some call one of the "absolute" I AM's (seven "I AM" sayings without a predicate, in addition to the seven with a predicate, such as "I AM the Light of the world" [John 8:12]).[74] Using this language, Jesus is powerfully indicating that He is much more than the prophet like unto Moses (cf. Deut. 18:15, 18). He is God Incarnate as well as perfect man, revealing God and humanity in the fullest possible way.

In John 4:34 Jesus says, "My food is to do the will of Him Who sent Me," which connects the themes of food and His origin. Jesus repeatedly emphasizes that He is an obedient Son—not a rebellious one: He always does the will of His divine Father. And this is why He is the ultimate authority, the One Who most truly reveals God. He is even *nourished* by doing His Father's will.

Many Samaritans believe in Christ because of the woman's "testimony" (*martyrousēs*; v. 39), and then many more believe "because of His own word" (John 4:41) that He is the Christ, the Savior of the world.

Next, Jesus goes back to Cana in Galilee, the Gentile area (the evangelist repeats "where He made the water wine," because this is so important). And the second sign—or miracle—occurs, since, as Jesus says, "except ye see signs and wonders, you will not believe" (v. 48; this is in contrast to the Samaritans). The nobleman's son is at the point of death, and Jesus heals Him from afar, showing that He gives new life even to those physically distant from Him—which could perhaps be included partly as an encouragement to believers in later times and places. After the first sign at Cana, His disciples believed in Him; and here, after the second sign, indicating that He is truly from God (hence, His authority), the royal official (probably a Gentile) and his household all believe, indicating that Gentiles are also invited to the marriage feast of the Kingdom of Heaven.

---

74. Richard Bauckham, *The Testimony of the Beloved Disciple: Narrative, History, and Theology in the Gospel of John* (Grand Rapids, MI: Baker Academic, 2007), p. 244.

Chapter 5

In chapter 5 Jesus challenges the Jewish leaders' interpretation of the Law when on the Sabbath He heals the man paralyzed for 38 years. Following this miracle, the third "sign," there are many statements emphasizing Jesus' divine origin and His oneness with God—hence the source and legitimacy of His authority. For example, verse 17—"My Father works and I work"; and verse 19—"The Son does nothing of Himself but what He sees the Father do." All of this makes the Jewish leaders[75] want to stone Jesus to death—both for breaking the Sabbath (that was the punishment under the Mosaic Law), and especially for saying that "God was His Father, making Himself equal with God" (5:18)—and if His claim were not true, what He said would be terrible blasphemy, and another offense punishable by death.

Then Jesus speaks of His ability to give eternal life because of His oneness with God, His Father, and also of the witnesses who authenticate His divine origin, and that His revelation is true: "The Father Himself, Who has sent Me, has borne witness of Me. *You* have neither heard His voice at any time, nor seen His shape" (v. 37; my emphasis). Yet we know that Jesus, in contrast, is "in the bosom of the Father," "seeing His Father" (v. 19), doing only what the Father does, and this is why Jesus can truly make God known. All of this indicates that Jesus is the ultimate authority, rather than the Pharisees or other Jewish leaders, who do not even claim to have such direct knowledge of God.

Chapter 6

Chapter 6 begins with the feeding of the 5000. The people are told literally to "recline" on the grass: Jews at that time ate Roman-style, that is, reclining, for the feast of Passover, and also for wedding feasts. Hence this event images the wedding feast of the Kingdom of Heaven which will be inaugurated through the New Passover of Jesus, of which the Old Testament Passover was a type. By the time St. John wrote his Gospel, a number of expressions he used would have been clear Eucharistic terminology, such as verse 11—"He took the loaves" (*elaben tous artous*), "He gave thanks" (*eucharistēsas*; the word "Eucharist" derives from this), and "He distributed the loaves" (*diedōken*). In St. Luke's account of the Last Supper (Luke 22:17, 19), the same Greek words are used, as also in a prayer after Communion given in the Didache from the

---

75. It is very clear that when John says "the Jews" he usually means only the Jewish leaders, such as in 7:13: "no man spoke openly of him for fear of the Jews." Since everyone there was Jewish, attending a major feast, he has to mean only the leaders!

end of the first century (this prayer even includes the same words for "gathered" and "fragments").

Jesus then says that we must *eat* His flesh and *drink* His blood in order to have the new, eternal life in ourselves (John 6:53-54). This is strongly sacrificial language, indicating a new kind of sacrifice, thus hinting at a new kind of worship. This command opens the way for an even closer communion with Christ than the one imaged by marriage (John 2), and more dramatic than the image of drinking water (John 4). For this more intense and intimate communion is now being imaged by *eating* first the bread from heaven, the true manna, and then by eating His own Body!

In marriage, "the two become one flesh"; but eating His flesh makes us "one flesh" with Christ in a much more profound way. For by eating His flesh, He becomes literally part of us. As St. John Chrysostom says, "we become one Body, . . . blended into that flesh. This is effected by the food which He has freely given us. On this account He has mixed up Himself with us; He has kneaded up His body with ours, that we might be a certain One Thing, like a body joined to a head."[76] This is a crucial part of how we receive the new, eternal life already in this life. In this way, Christ has taken us far beyond the Old Testament understanding of our relationship with God in His heavenly Kingdom as being like attending a marriage feast. (This also prevents us from taking the marriage imagery too literally.)

The theme of Jesus' origins is also brought out in this chapter, for the true bread from heaven is He Who *comes down from heaven* and gives life to the world: "I am the bread of life that has come down from heaven" (v. 51)—the bread from heaven which alone has life in itself (since only God has life in Himself; this again indicates Jesus' divinity). By eating it we have the new, eternal life—to live with and in the life of God.

So Christ is the source of new life in God, fulfilling all that Judaism was attempting—especially to be able to enter into the presence of the All-Holy God, Creator of the universe, to be in a loving communion with that God, and even more, to become "like" Him, being "changed into the likeness," and becoming a child by adoption, by grace. And this is possible only because of Jesus' divine origin: He has "come down from heaven"—a phrase repeated in the Nicene Creed. As we have just observed, now in Jesus we can see that our union with Him is a much closer one than what is imaged by marriage.

The people ask Jesus to perform a sign "that we may see it, and believe You" (v. 30). The sign He gives is always some reference to His Crucifixion and Resurrection; here the "bread from heaven" indicates the Eucharist, the memorial of His death (Luke 22:19).

---

76. St. John Chrysostom, Homily XLVI.3 on St. John (NPNF 1, XIV, p. 166).

Chapter 7

We see that the Jewish leaders, who pride themselves on being the authorities on how to interpret the Law, are not obedient to the Law, since they unjustly seek to kill Jesus. He chastises them by saying, "Moses gave you the Law and yet none of you keeps it" (v. 19). He knows they want to kill Him because He healed on the Sabbath—yet, He reminds them, "You circumcise a man on the Sabbath" (v. 22). Then He asks them, "Are you angry with Me because I made a man completely well on the Sabbath?" (v. 23). So the Jewish leaders are not obedient sons, while Jesus is. Jesus again emphasizes that He is sent from God, and that what He teaches is not His, but from God. And He says that the people can tell if His teaching is from God if they live it (vv. 16-18).

In verse 27, the theme of His origin is explicitly brought up again: "We know this man whence he is, but when Christ comes, no man knows whence he is"; and again, in verse 41: "Will Christ come out of Galilee?" Of course, they only *think* they know His origins, and as St. John Chrysostom points out, they never actually ask Him. When it suits their agenda, they assume they know where He is from (Galilee), and who His parents are (Joseph and Mary). But when it does not (as in John 9:29), they say they do not know His origin—and speak of Him as a rebellious son, a lawbreaker, Who could not have any legitimate authority.

Trying to open the Jewish leaders to the truth, Nicodemus, who is one of them, asks: "Does our law judge any man before it hears him?" (v. 51). But they silence him, saying that no prophet arises from Galilee (v. 52). Again, they are the ones breaking the law, by judging before hearing Jesus or asking Him directly where He is from, as Nicodemus points out.

Verses 37 and 38 say, "If any one thirst let him come to Me and drink. He that believes on Me as Scripture has said: out of his belly shall flow rivers of living [zōntos, from zōē = divine life] water"—the water of eternal life. And then St. John says that Jesus was speaking "of the Spirit, which those who believe on Him will receive" (v. 39). Again, this is a deeper, closer union or communion than in marriage.

People always seem to be thinking too literally, and Jesus is always moving them from the literal to the spiritual level—to seeing deeper—a movement continued in the patristic tradition.

Chapter 8

It is very helpful to think about the marriage theme in connection with the woman taken in adultery,[77] when the Jews confront Jesus saying, "Now Moses in the law commanded that such should be stoned; but what do you say?" (v. 5). This was a trap, of course, as they wanted to accuse Him of being a lawbreaker if He said not to stone her (though this was no longer usually done); or to turn the people against Him if He said to fulfill the law and stone her, thus demonstrating that He was not as compassionate to sinners as the common people had thought.

He writes on the ground as if He does not hear, and the Jews do not seem to catch the significance at first. They keep asking, so He stands up and says, "the one of you who is without sin, cast the first stone at her" (v. 7).[78] Then He stoops down and writes again. This also demonstrates how He does not judge, for the accusers are then convicted by their own consciences and they all leave. Even more significantly, this passage shows that instead of trapping Jesus, they end up recognizing His authority, that He has gotten to the truth of the matter, that He is right and they are wrong.

From ancient times a connection has been seen between Jesus' writing in the dust and Jeremiah 17:13—"Those who turn away from you will be written in the dust, because they have forsaken the Lord, the spring of living water." This is very powerful in light of all that has been said previously: this writing on the ground seems to be a parabolic action; and the Jewish leaders realize, at least the second time Jesus does this, that although they perhaps have not literally committed adultery, they definitely *have* done so in the Old Testamental sense of being unfaithful to God, not keeping His Law, being bad shepherds (one example of this recurring theme would be 7:49-51; see also John 10). They did not really care about this woman at all—they were happy to sacrifice her life simply to try to get the better of Jesus in a low and deceptive way.[79]

---

77. As mentioned, though few if any question the authenticity of this passage, it may well not have been at this place in John's Gospel originally (it interrupts what comes before and after, and it is skipped over in the Orthodox lectionary). As mentioned, it does not appear in the biblical manuscripts in the East until, some say, the 10th century (though others say the 14th century), so there are no early Eastern Fathers commenting on it. But it does appear in many Western manuscripts, so several Western Fathers comment on it, and it is accepted in this place by all the Churches.

78. It was apparently the custom in such cases for the witnesses of the crime to cast the first stone (see Beasley-Murray, op. cit., p. 146).

79. Several modern scholars even speculate that the woman was deliberately trapped, since getting two witnesses to catch someone in adultery would seem to involve a planned trap, maybe

It seems very probable, therefore, that Jesus was acting out the passage from Jeremiah. He may have been leaving each one present free to think of ways he had been unfaithful to God, or as St. Jerome said, He wrote "the sins . . . of those who were making the accusations, as well as the sins of all mortal beings."[80] And He has just said that *He* is the source of the spring of living water—the means of communion with God and of new life in Him. For those reading this passage later, it should certainly be clear that the scribes and Pharisees are turning away on many levels from the "spring of living water"—that is, from Jesus, Who is God Incarnate.

Jesus is left alone with the woman, whom He asks, "Has no one condemned you?" "No one, Lord." "Neither do I, go and sin no more" (vv. 10-11). This could also speak profoundly to the Jews of St. John's time who had not yet become Christians, or not openly, as well as to everyone. For we all commit adultery in the Old Testamental sense every time we sin, every time we are not faithful to God, not doing His will. But He does not condemn us: Jesus forgave her, and He will forgive us—though He also asks *us* to "sin no more." If we are really going to receive the oneness with God that Christ offers, we must be faithful marriage partners: we cannot be deliberately sinning, and especially we cannot be choosing a path of darkness/sin.

In the rest of John 8 we find several verses that make reference to Jesus' divine identity:

8:12—"I am the light of the world: he who follows Me shall not walk in darkness, but shall have the light of life" (*phōs tēs zōēs*, which refers to life eternal). After Jesus says that His Father Who sent Him bears witness of Him (v. 18), the Pharisees ask Him, "Where is Your Father?" But Jesus only replies, "If you had known Me, you would have known My Father also" (v. 19).
8:23-24 —"Ye are from beneath; I am from above; ye are of this world; I am not of this world. . . . if ye believe not that I am He [*egō eimi*], ye shall die in your sins."

---

even involving the husband. See, e.g., Fr. Lawrence R. Farley, *The Gospel of John: Beholding the Glory* (Ben Lomond, CA: Conciliar Press, 2006), pp. 146-147.

80. Then Jerome quotes Jer. 17:13 (ACCS on John, p. 274). St. Augustine has several much more general interpretations: He wrote "as if indicating that the names of people like these men were to be written in the earth, not in heaven. . . . Or perhaps he meant to convey the idea of humility . . . or the time had arrived when his law should be written on soil that would bear fruit and not on sterile stone" (ibid.). Some much later interpreters speculate on specific sins that Jesus wrote the second time, as a logical (but not inevitable) next step from the connection with Jeremiah 17:13.

These statements provide strong further indications of Jesus' oneness with God the Father, and again, that He is an obedient Son, not a rebellious law-breaker—that His authority comes from God.

He repeats His divine origin and oneness with God the Father in 8:28-29: "When you lift up the Son of Man, then you will know that I am He [*egō eimi*], and that I do nothing of Myself; but as My Father taught Me, I speak these things. And He Who sent Me is with Me. The Father has not left Me alone, for I always do those things that please Him."

Next, beginning with John 8:31 comes a discussion revealing a very important dimension of the question of origins: "If you abide in My word, you are My disciples indeed. And you shall know the truth, and the truth shall make you free."[81] When His hearers respond that they are "children of Abraham" and have "never been in bondage to anyone" (v. 33), Jesus reveals that it is sin that puts a person in the kind of bondage He is speaking of (v. 34). And He tells them the key point: "If you were Abraham's children, *you would do the works of Abraham*" (v. 39).

In chapter 1 of St. John's Gospel, we saw that all those who believe and receive can, through Jesus, become "children of God." In chapter 3, He adds, one must be "born from above/again," of water and the Spirit, to become a child of God. In chapter 4, He reveals that sinners and those outside ethnic Israel can receive and believe and be "born of God." In John 5:24 it is necessary to "hear" His word, and believe "on Him Who sent Me" to have "everlasting life." In chapter 6 it is necessary to "labor for the food which endures to everlasting life which the Son of Man will give you" (6:27); and "believe on Him Whom He [God] sent" (6:29); and "Whoever eats My flesh and drinks My blood has eternal life" (6:54).

Here in John 8:31-59 is another step. Not only is it is no longer necessary to be born Jewish to be a child of God, but it is not even necessary to be ethnically Jewish to be a true *child of Abraham*. What is necessary is to "do his works," because the most important thing that makes one a true child is to be *like* one's Father *in one's life*, in what one does. Jesus explains that the Jews He is speaking with do not automatically have even God as their Father: "If God were your Father, you would love Me, for I proceeded forth and come from God. . . . You are of your father the devil" (vv. 42-44). He says this because the devil is a liar and murderer (v. 44), and they want to kill Him (v. 40). Jesus is, then, explaining that now in the New Israel which He is establishing, the key to being a son is likeness to the Father through how one lives, one's actions—that belief in Him *must result* in a life lived "according to His word," or commandments—what He calls in v. 51 "keeping" His word, living the Gospel life, in order for that belief to lead to eternal life.

---

81. *Knowing* the truth leads to, and necessarily includes, *doing* the truth (cf. John 3:21).

As St. Nikolai of Zicha (20th century) says about John 8:51,

> And what, my brethren, does it mean to keep the word of Christ in one-self? It means, first, to keep it in one's mind, thinking of it; then to keep it in one's heart, loving it; thirdly, to keep it in one's will, fulfilling it in action; and fourthly, to keep it on one's tongue, freely witnessing to it when necessity arises. In brief, to keep the word of Christ means to be filled with it and to fulfill it. He who thus keeps the word of Christ will indeed never taste of death.[82]

It is interesting to consider how parallel the situation of Abraham and these Jewish leaders actually was. Abraham was convinced that God's covenant with him would be fulfilled through Isaac, the son of promise—that through Isaac, "all the nations/tribes of the earth would be blessed" (Gen. 12:2-3). Yet when God commands that Isaac be sacrificed, Abraham has such faith in God that he is open to accepting this startling change in what he expected. He had such faith in the goodness of God that he was sure that if God commanded him to sacrifice Isaac, He would even raise Isaac from the dead and in that way fulfill His promise (Gen. 22:1-8).

The Pharisees, and the other Jewish leaders, also had in mind that God would fulfill His promise to His chosen people in a particular way, with a certain kind of Messiah—a political one. Yet unlike Abraham, when God revealed a different plan and a different kind of Messiah, so different from the earthly ruler they expected, they were not open to this startling change in what they expected. They could not reconcile what Jesus said and did with their preconceived ideas; so even in the face of many miracles and other evidence, they clung to their own "agenda." Truly, they were not children of Abraham.

It is also interesting to contrast the Samaritan woman with these Jewish leaders. After asking Jesus if He is greater than "our father Jacob," and when she is told that He can give her "a fountain of water springing up into everlasting life," she *immediately asks* for that water (John 4:12-15). These Jewish leaders, when they are told that "if any man keep My word, he shall never see death" (John 8:51), do not then ask how this can happen for them. Rather, they respond, "Now we know that You have a demon! Abraham is dead . . . Are You greater than our father Abraham? . . . Who do You make yourself out to be?" (vv. 52-53).

---

82. St. Nikolai (Velimirovich), *The Prologue from Ochrid*, vol. 1, p. 155.

Jesus then tells them, "Your father[83] Abraham rejoiced to see My day" (v. 56).[84] This is intended to mean that Abraham also recognized Jesus as the Messiah, Who would thus be ushering in the Last Days, even if only in type (as Chrysostom says); and that Abraham rejoiced at the Bridegroom's voice, as did John the Forerunner. Rejoicing at the coming of the Bridegroom Messiah is a crucial part of becoming part of the "Bride," the New Israel; and this is a crucial part of doing the works of Abraham, becoming truly one of his children.

We then find what many consider to be the most emphatic declaration recorded in the New Testament that Jesus ever makes about His divinity, as He appropriates for Himself the Divine Name revealed to Moses at the Burning Bush (Ex. 3:6): "Truly, truly [amēn, amēn; this is used for great emphasis], I say to you, before Abraham was, I AM" (egō eimi; v. 57). This would have been blasphemous in the extreme if it were not true, and the penalty for blasphemy was being stoned to death. That is why upon hearing this statement, the Jewish leaders did try to stone Jesus. Ironically, under the influence of Jesus, they did not stone the guilty woman caught in adultery, but here they try to stone the sinless Christ. His hour had not yet come, however, and so He slipped away (v. 58).

After this dramatic statement in 8:57, one could say that in the rest of John's Gospel, Jesus' being the *divine* Messiah, His oneness with God, is emphasized even more explicitly than in the earlier chapters. There is clearly a crescendo in the miracles recounted, the last two of the seven before the Resurrection (in chs. 9 and 11) being much more dramatic than the earlier ones. Indeed, though people knew of miraculous healings, and even of those who had been dead a short time being raised to life, these last two miracles were completely unheard of, and very much emphasize Jesus' own divinity. The miracle of the healing of the man born blind in chapter 9 was understood from very early times to imply that new eyes were created for the man, which could only have been done by the original Creator. Even more dramatically, no one had ever heard of a person being raised to life who had been dead *four* days, and had started to decay (ch. 11).

Jesus' oneness with God is also clearly emphasized by Jesus demonstrating (in healing and seeking out the man born blind, ch. 9), and then asserting, that He is THE Good Shepherd (ch. 10), just as God the Father is The Good Shepherd (e.g., in Ezekiel 34, especially 34:15-16). Jesus' being the Messiah (the Christ, the Anointed One) is also clearly emphasized, for example, in chapter

---

83. While they are not truly Abraham's children in the most important sense of doing works as he did, Jesus acknowledges that Abraham is their father in the ethnic sense.

84. It was a common idea in Jewish circles at the time that Abraham was allowed by God to see the future, including the time ("day") of the Messiah (see Beasley-Murray, op. cit., p. 138).

12 with His being anointed by Mary of Bethany (v. 3), and His triumphal entry into Jerusalem, fulfilling Old Testament prophecies about the Messiah.

The possibility for Christians to experience real, ontological communion with God in Christ through the Holy Spirit is also spoken of more directly in these later chapters. In the Last Discourse, chapters 13-17, our deification through communion with the Holy Trinity is spoken of explicitly (for example, 14:15-18, 21; 17:21-24). One also finds an analogy indicating the closest possible relationship between Jesus and believers—one that is much closer than the marriage union, or even food or water that we consume: that of the vine and the branches which can only live with the life of the Vine, the vine's actual sap, running through them (15:1-8). Finally, of course, Jesus' divinity is revealed in His conquering death through His Resurrection (ch. 20) and His sending the Holy Spirit, the Spirit Who will guide His followers into all truth (14:17, 26) and enable them to become holy, to truly participate in God.

Thus, Who Jesus Christ is—the divine Messiah; Whose Child He is—the Son of God; where He is from—He has "come down from heaven"; why He has come—to enable us to live with His life, for our deification; why He has ultimate authority and can most fully reveal God—because He is One with God—all this is made very clear in the Gospel of John, as well as elsewhere in the New Testament, in spite of what certain highly publicized biblical critics might claim. And it is clear in large part because "we beheld His glory" in all the senses these words can bear. Jesus has also made it abundantly clear that *all* peoples are invited to the Wedding Feast in the Kingdom of Heaven, celebrating the marriage of the Bridegroom Messiah with His Bride, the Church, the New Israel. All are invited to become children of God by THE Child of God, Who, because He is God's unique Son, has the authority to make the invitation, and to grant eternal life through communion with the Holy Trinity.

Christology is fundamental to the most basic concerns of biblical interpretation, and will shape one's epistemology (one's understanding of how we know), which in turn will shape what methods one chooses to use and the interpretive context within which one will use them, as well as why one is doing biblical exegesis in the first place. And all of this will inevitably have a profound impact on spiritual life. This is a primary reason why so much time has been spent on the question of Jesus' origin and authority in this chapter.

But more specifically, what does all this mean for exegesis today, especially the question of what makes an interpretation both inspiring and authoritative? This will be the theme of the final chapter.

*I would have lost heart, unless I had believed that I would
see the goodness of the Lord in the land of the living.*
—PSALM 27:13

CHAPTER EIGHT

WITNESS AND AUTHORITY: "TO BEHOLD THE BEAUTY OF THE LORD"

*One thing have I asked of the Lord, that will I seek: that I
may dwell in the house of the Lord all the days of my life,* **to
behold the beauty of the Lord** *and* **to inquire** *in His temple.*
—PSALM 27:4

I N the preceding chapters, fundamental theological and spiritual principles
have been brought out and a historical overview given, to indicate how
such principles determine one's approach to interpreting Scripture: what
methods and techniques one will use, why one uses them, as well as the whole
context within which they will be used. In other words, one's approach to interpreting the Bible will reflect one's understanding of reality, and one's reading
will depend upon what one believes the primary *purpose* of Scripture to be.
And that will be closely related to how one answers the questions considered
in the exegesis just covered in Chapter 7: "Who is Jesus?" and "Why did He
come?"—"What does His coming mean for humanity?" One's answers to these
questions, even if unacknowledged, will be the foundation for how one answers
the question about how to determine whose interpretations are authoritative,
beginning with: "How can we best know what *Jesus'* interpretations and *His*
teachings really are?"

The approach of Spinoza's historical-critical method, discussed in Chapter
6, insists on the reality of a secular world-view—that God, if He exists, has not
and does not reveal Himself, and that there are no spiritual realities that affect
people in this world, since only the material realm exists, or at least only it can
be known. Hence the Bible must be treated like any other text. Church doctrine and personal beliefs must be ignored, while the literal level of meaning is
only allowed to refer to secular, historical, or sociological facts and causes. In

effect, interpreters must only take into account, and look for, information comprehensible by, and acceptable to, any "reasonable," educated atheist. And it is only the highly educated specialists, having the knowledge and tools to extract such information, who can give authoritative interpretations.

In sharp contrast, we have also seen how a traditional Christian approach insists on the reality of the traditional Christian—and biblical—world-view: God, the "good God Who loves mankind," has and does reveal Himself, most fully in Jesus Christ. Spiritual realities do affect people in this world, spiritual realities can be known, and they cannot be understood by the reasonable atheist (unless he, or she, has a change of heart!). In fact, one's spiritual state *determines* one's ability even to perceive, let alone understand, spiritual realities, including many aspects of the Bible that concern such realities. Therefore, it is not only the highly educated who can potentially benefit from reading the Bible, but especially all those with spiritual discernment. This does not mean that historical, linguistic, and other such kinds of information are ignored; for information found through the techniques of biblical criticism can take its proper, useful place to clarify the literal level of meaning, while not usurping a role which such kinds of information do not have the authority to bear.

This brings us back to the main concern of this chapter: for when we come now to consider how to determine which interpretations are authoritative, and the related question of how we can interpret in a way that will truly be inspiring, we cannot so easily sum up what all traditional Christians believe about this, as we could do for those embracing historical criticism. There is, unfortunately, significant divergence on these issues among traditional Christians, especially since the time of the late Middle Ages and the Reformation. Indeed, as indicated previously, the *sola scriptura* approach of many Protestants since the Reformation has dramatically increased this divergence.

One thing this book hopes to accomplish, through giving the history it does, is to correct some common misunderstandings held by many who follow the Reformers—for example, whether or not the reading and study of Scripture was "officially" encouraged before the Reformation, and whether or not vernacular translations were used (the short answer to both being "yes"). With at least some misunderstandings cleared up, hopefully, a broader way is opened to consider this critical matter of authoritative interpretations. Indeed, the witness of Christians generally is seriously hindered in the modern secular world by the great variety of voices that all claim to speak authoritatively for Christianity.

All traditional Christians can surely at least agree that in considering this key matter of how to determine whose interpretations of Scripture are authoritative, it will be important to begin with Scripture itself—and that is what will be done in this final chapter. We will first consider what is written in Scripture itself about what is needed to be an ideal interpreter. The Gospel of John will again be the focus for this necessarily brief look. The Book of Acts is also consulted for the light it sheds on what the Apostles did when significant conflicting interpretations arose in the earliest days of the Church. Following that, how the Church has handled this question of determining authoritative interpretations in the early centuries after the time of the New Testament will be considered.

It will be most helpful to look at this question of how to determine authoritative interpretations before examining the third of the four important issues in hermeneutics today (mentioned in Chapter 1) which will conclude this study. That third issue raised by some of those using the historical-critical method and reflecting their world-view, is: "Can the Bible as traditionally understood inspire people today powerfully enough that it truly shapes their world-view and enables them to flourish?" They might also ask more directly, "Is a traditional understanding of the Bible still credible and effective in a post-modern culture?"

This question will be answered by looking at four contemporary Christian witnesses whose lives and works demonstrate dramatically that the answer is certainly, "Yes!" And as the quotation above, chosen from Psalm 27, hints, in the final sections a strong connection will be shown between being able "to behold the beauty of the Lord" and being able to effectively, inspiringly, and authoritatively "inquire" into and interpret Scripture. In this way, we will return once again to the myth of Psyche and Cupid, that rich analogy helping to illuminate our subject.

Authoritative Interpretation in Scripture: The Ideal Exegete

Let us turn now to St. John's Gospel for the insight it provides into the traditional understanding of these questions, as well as for the models it provides. St. John presents Jesus as the ideal and best, most authoritative "exegete" of God—revealing God most fully and truly, because He is Himself God: "He who has seen Me has seen the Father" (John 14:9). He is "in the bosom of the Father" (John 1:18)—in the place of greatest intimacy and love. He is "from above" (John 8:23), "from heaven" (John 6:38), "sent" by the Father (John 5:36-37). He is the Divine Logos "tabernacling" among us (John 1:14). Therefore, *He knows from direct experience.*

But even in His case, Jesus does not indicate that personal experience alone is all that is needed for authoritative interpretations, nor does He expect that those among whom He is living should accept His teaching for that reason alone. Jesus reveals that He came from God, and is the most perfect revealer of God—revealing His glory, His real presence—through His own "works" (see John 10:38 and 14:11), indeed, His whole life: His miracles, His teaching,

His relationships with other people—for example, the unconditional love He shows to sinners as well as to the righteous—as well as through His very being.

At the same time, Christ emphasizes repeatedly that He *only* speaks the words of God (e.g., John 8:28; 12:49-50), and He *only* does what He sees the Father do (John 5:19). Showing us the Way, He models being a humble, obedient, loving son, one Who is not asserting his own autonomous interpretations or views. Thus He corrects the mistake of Eve and Adam, and shows the serpent's lie for what it is. For there are no "autonomous" interpretations; all interpretations come from and lead to communion with someone. Acting as if there are interpretations that are independent of persons/authorities/"Fathers" is the way leading to deception and ultimately, death.

But that is not all. The fact that Jesus is Who He says He is—the divine Bridegroom Messiah, the Christ fulfilling the prophecies of old, which is why His interpretations are authoritative—was also confirmed by the greatest of the prophets under the Old Covenant, the holiest *living witness* of Jesus' day from that Covenant. That prophet was St. John the Forerunner (cf. Matt. 11:11; Luke 7:28; also John 5:33). And as Jesus Himself says, the truth of His revelation was also supported/confirmed by *witnesses from the past*, i.e., Moses, the other prophets, and the Hebrew Scriptures as a whole (cf. Luke 24:27, 44; John 5:39, 46). So *Scripture itself* is a witness to this truth (as we saw in Chapter 3).

This truth is also witnessed to later on by the New Testament as a whole, and especially by *the fruits* which this truth has borne in the lives of countless numbers of people in the past roughly 2000 years, in many radically different cultures and places, including many places around the world today. Clearly, this traditional understanding was able to "capture the imaginations and inspire the wills" of all of these incredibly diverse holy men and women, shaping their world-views and lives to such an extent that they became "vessels of the Holy Spirit," "partakers of the divine nature" (2 Pet. 1:4). They thereby dramatically shaped multiple cultures, again, in a variety of times and places, inspiring large numbers of others at least to attempt to live life inspired by the Gospel revealed by Jesus Christ.

The truth of Jesus' revelation, then, is supported in the interpretive context of the witness of His own life and teachings (in Rev. 3:14, He is called "the faithful and true witness/martyr"; see also Rev. 1:5). And it is supported by the fruits of His life and teachings as preserved in the interpretive context of the Church which He founded. And in addition, it is experienced by many who became living, holy witnesses in their own times and places.

The purpose of this revelation which Jesus gives—or better, *is*—is to give all of humanity an opportunity once again to be purified, to become holy, to become "partakers of the divine nature." This means that we can not only come into the presence of the Triune God, the Creator of the universe—an awesome enough experience— but also that we may even live with and in His divine, eternal life, a life of loving communion/union with Him and all believers—ultimately, so that we may inherit eternal life. As Jesus says, "My sheep hear My voice and I know them, and they follow Me. And I give them eternal life, and they shall never perish" (John 10:27-28). The purpose of His revelation is, then, emphatically *soteriological*—for our salvation.

In his Gospel account, St. John presents *himself* in a parallel way—though, of course, on a far different level. Thus, St. John is an ideal, authoritative exegete to reveal Who Jesus is, for he is in a parallel position of intimacy and love to that of Jesus and the Father: "Now there was leaning [literally, *reclining*] on Jesus' bosom one of His disciples, whom Jesus loved" (John 13:23). The Jews at the time of Jesus ate the Passover meal, as well as certain other special meals, in the Roman style—lying on their left sides and elbows, and eating with their right hands. This means that the beloved disciple[1] is reclining on Jesus' right side (the place of honor, showing that he is, indeed, specially loved), so that if he leans back to quietly ask Jesus something, he would be leaning on His chest.

Thus the image of the ideal, most authoritative interpreter is one who has a very close, loving, personal relationship with the one whose teachings he is interpreting. He knows from personal experience.

But St. John is the ideal interpreter not only because of his great love for and closeness to the Lord, and his profound understanding of His teachings. He also is a witness to Jesus's glory—both in the sense of His miracles and His life as a whole, and in the sense that John was one of the three disciples who witnessed Jesus' glory on the Mount of Transfiguration (Matt. 17:1-8).

St. John also witnessed in his own writings and life to the reality of the new life that Christ came to give. And *the Church confirmed* that his witness is inspired, that it is in line with and supported by the rest of Scripture and by the community of the Church, by preserving and passing down his Gospel account—as well as his other writings—and including these writings in what became canonical Scripture, the New Testament as we have it today. As we saw in Chapter 3, this was not inevitable, or automatic, but it was the result not only of divine inspiration but also of careful, informed consideration by those in the Church in the early centuries. So, the ideal interpreter's interpretations are in line with the rest of Scripture as confirmed within the interpretive context of the Church and further living witnesses.

And *why* does St. John tell us that he wrote his "revelation" of Who Jesus is? What does he say is the purpose of his account? He tells us explicitly: "these things are written that you may believe that Jesus is the Christ, the Son of God, and that believing you may have life in His name" (John 20:31).

---

1. "Specially loved" is another meaning of *monogenēs* in John 1:18 and 3:16. Often translated "only begotten," more literally it means "one of a kind, unique."

The fuller meaning of the phrase "have life in His name" may not be readily apparent. First of all, the word used for life, *zōē*, never refers to merely physical life in John's Gospel (*psychē* is used for that, as in John 10:11). "*Zōē*" always means spiritual, or eternal, divine life, as in John 10:28.[2]

What about the phrase "in His name"?[3] John 12:13 describes the crowd quoting Psalm 118:26—"Blessed is he that comes in the name of Lord"—as Jesus enters Jerusalem just before Passover and His crucifixion. The crowd does not realize, however, that Jesus "comes in the name of the Lord" in a very unique way: He actually is the *bearer* of the Name. He can rightfully say "*egō eimi*," "I AM." For after Moses asks God for His name (Ex. 3:13), "*egō eimi*" is the name which God gives for Himself (Ex. 3:14).[4] God is the only existing One—that is, He is the only One Who has being or life *in Himself*. That's why He is the "I AM." Hence, He is the *only One* Who can give life—any kind of life, including eternal, or divine life (all living beings, as created by Him, have their animate life from Him). As one contemporary scholar explains, "Unless Jesus is the true Son of God, Jesus has no divine life to give. Unless he bears God's name, he cannot fulfill toward men the divine function of giving life."[5]

The phrase "in His Name" is essentially the same as "on and in His person" (cf. John 3:18; 1 John 3:23; 5:13).[6] Thus, having life "in His Name" means having life in Him. So, John is indicating many things in John 20:31, including, we could say, that the purpose of his writing his Gospel account is so that people may understand Who Jesus truly is—the most authentic and authoritative revealer or interpreter of God, since He is divine Himself—in order that through such a correct understanding about Christ (i.e., having the correct *Christology*), they may believe in such a way as to live in Him, sharing in the new, divine, eternal life He offers. Again, the goal is clearly soteriological: a real, transforming, saving experience of God in Christ through the Holy Spirit.

There is one final model from Scripture we will consider which more closely reflects the situation of those living after the time of Jesus' Ascension. This is found in the Book of Acts (or as it is traditionally known, the Acts of the

2. See, e.g., Raymond E. Brown, *The Gospel according to John, XIII—XXII*, in the *Anchor Bible Commentary* (New York: Doubleday, 1966), pp. 7, 506.

3. We recall here what was said in Chapter 7 about Jesus being the "*topos theou*"—the place of God, the place where the Name of the Lord dwells.

4. All the Old Testament theophanies, such as the voice in the burning bush, are seen by the Church Fathers as manifestations of the pre-incarnate Christ—He is the Angel, or Messenger (both these words are *angelos* in Greek), of the Lord.

5. Brown, op. cit., p. 1061.

6. Rudolf Schnackenburg, *The Gospel According to St. John* (New York: Crossroad, 1990), vol. 3, p. 339.

Apostles). There we see that God did not *separately inspire* even the twelve Apostles, never mind all the rest of the believers in the early Church, to clearly understand *all* the important aspects of the Faith (though they all did share the same understanding of the core truths). Even among the Twelve, whose lives had been so radically transformed by the Holy Spirit, there were disagreements, controversies, problems in how to interpret. So what do we see in Acts about how such differences in interpretation—when they became significant—were handled?

For instance, what about the much disputed question of whether Jewish converts to Christianity needed to continue keeping the Mosaic Law, especially the requirement for males to be circumcised? After "no small dissension and dispute" (Acts 15:2), a council was held in Jerusalem, with all "the apostles and elders" attending (v. 6). Then, after "there had been much dispute" (v. 7), Peter, Barnabas, and Paul—living, holy witnesses to the key spiritual realities—spoke of the work of the Holy Spirit that had already been accomplished among the Gentiles. Then James, in his role as the first bishop of Jerusalem, gave the final summation, considering all the discussion and the testimony of the witnesses, and quoting the Hebrew Scriptures in support of his conclusion. He then gives the decision that all agree with—they come to a *consensus*. Next they decide to send out a letter from the Council to be shared with all the communities where this question was a problem, explaining the Council's decision. In that letter they introduce their decision by saying, "For it seemed good to the Holy Spirit and to us" (v. 28).

This first Church council, known as the Council of Jerusalem, set the pattern for solving serious disputes, for determining whose interpretation is authoritative in the Church, and this has continued without interruption in the Orthodox Church up to the present day—even after the schism with the Roman Church in 1054. There have been many other councils held in various regions that are considered local, such as this first council.

The Orthodox also recognize seven great "Ecumenical Councils"—councils that concerned matters of such great importance that they affected *the whole world* (which is what the word "ecumenical" means in Greek). These councils, made up largely of bishops who all had proper standing by virtue of apostolic succession, each one representing the voice of his portion of the entire Church, received their final authority through being accepted by the Christian people as a whole. Indeed, a few councils which were intended to be ecumenical—since their decisions were accepted by most of the bishops in attendance—ended up being rejected by the Church community as a whole. So we see that the accepted Ecumenical Councils truly reflect the will of the whole Church—the clergy and the laity together—and not only the will of the bishops.[7] All of the Ecumenical Councils ultimately were concerned with Christology, and thus they continue to be vitally important in safeguarding the fullness of the experience of the new life in Christ.

The contemporary holy elder, newly canonized St. Porphyrios of Kafsokalyvia, a living witness in our own time, speaks of this new life as follows:

> Christ is joy, the true light, happiness. . . . He is a joy that transforms you into a different person. . . . Fast as much as you can . . . attend as many vigils as you like, but be joyful. Have Christ's joy. It is the joy that lasts forever, that brings eternal happiness. It is the joy of our Lord that gives assured serenity, serene delight, and full happiness. . . .
>
> Christ desires and delights in scattering joy, in enriching the faithful with joy. I pray that your joy may be full (John 16:24). . . . This is what our religion is. What is Paradise? It is Christ. Paradise begins here and now. . . . those who experience Christ here on earth, experience paradise. . . . Our task is to attempt to find a way to enter into the light of Christ. . . .
>
> The essence of the matter is for us to be with Christ—for our soul to wake up and love Christ and become holy. . . . That is what Christ wants most of all, to fill us with joy, because He is the well-spring of joy. This joy is a gift of Christ. In this joy we will come to know Christ. . . . These are the things our soul desires to acquire. If we prepare ourselves appropriately, grace will bestow them on us.[8]

This new, joy-filled life in Christ is the goal of the Gospel, and so it should be the goal, the ultimate purpose, of Scriptural exegesis. Christian exegesis of Scripture is not meant to be merely a question of this intellectual idea or that, this particular phraseology or that, this particular detail or that—let alone a question of which "fiction" is more inspiring. As St. Gregory Palamas said,

---

7. The Eastern Orthodox Tradition has never accepted that individual interpreters are able to determine dogma. No one, not even a pope or the greatest biblical critic, can alter or validate the dogmas of the Church on his own. Hence, from a traditional Christian point of view, it is absurd to consider individual academics, who may even deny the existence of God, to be the authorities in validating Scriptural interpretation and dogma, rather than the Saints and the Ecumenical Councils (representing the whole Church as a community guided by the Holy Spirit).

8. Elder Porphyrios, *Wounded by Love: The Life and Wisdom of Elder Porphyrios* (Limni, Evia, Greece: Denise Harvey, Publisher, 2005), pp. 96-97.

"Our religion is not a question of words, but of realities."[9] Thus it is fundamentally a question of: How do we safeguard, and give people access to, this *reality*, this new life in Christ, in our own time?

Because Christianity and its Scripture deals with "realities"—real experiential knowledge of God and spiritual things, real spiritual experiences—Scriptural exegesis and spiritual life cannot be separated. Nor can either one of these be separated from theology—especially Christology—if they are to be properly understood, and lived as intended. The attempt to separate spiritual life from theology and Scriptural exegesis comes from, and certainly results in, a "different gospel"—one which those who seek the Truth and the authentic Christianity of the living God must avoid (as St. Paul already warned long ago; for example, see Gal. 1:6-9). The very attempt to divide this necessary unity into isolated parts already reflects a non-traditional theology, in particular a false Christology and epistemology.

Many of those currently seeking a solution to the crisis in biblical interpretation, who realize that the naive view of "objectivity" held in the Enlightenment era is no longer tenable, are placing great emphasis upon interpreting the canon of Scripture as we have it. They are also realizing the need for an interpretive tradition to rely on, and the need to interpret Scripture responsibly (i.e, ethically, considering the purposes of our interpretation),[10] within and for the Church community.

But there still needs to be much more awareness that the crisis is essentially a spiritual one. And this means that one further aspect needs to be emphasized, one which is still often neglected: that is, the implications for exegesis of the real possibility of *knowing God directly—that God can and has and continues to reveal Himself*—that such spiritual experience provides real knowledge, indeed, the highest, most certain kind of knowledge, which is the very foundation and heart of traditional Christianity. As St. Paul so beautifully indicates in 2 Corinthians 4:6, "For it is the God Who commanded light to shine out of darkness, Who has shone in our hearts to give the light of the *knowledge* of the glory of God in the face of Jesus Christ" (my emphasis). (This is, of course, the opposite of Kant's and Spinoza's views.) But this will only happen when exegetes are open to the transcendent and the miraculous, rather than

---

9. Quoted by Fr. John Meyendorff, *A Study of St. Gregory Palamas* (London: The Faith Press, 1964), p. 239.

10. For emphasis on the canon of Scripture, and interpreting it as we have it, see, e.g., the work of Brevard Childs; on realizing the need for an interpretive tradition to rely on, see, e.g., the work of Hans Gadamer; on the need to interpret Scripture responsibly (i.e., ethically, considering the purposes of our interpretation), see, e.g., *The Responsibility of Hermeneutics*, by Roger Lundin, et al.

dismissing these realms because of *a priori* philosophical assumptions; when they are willing to make a personal change—to repent, and to begin trying to live the Gospel life; and finally, when they become aware of which version of "traditional" Christianity is indeed most authentic.

Authoritative Interpretations After the Time of the New Testament

Because Scripture is concerned with persons and their lives, and not simply with ideas, as we pointed out in Chapter 2, *who* is doing the interpreting makes all the difference. This is the first thing we should be paying attention to in our own exegetical work. If the ideal interpreter after the time of the Ascension is one who has direct, personal experience of the new, eternal life here and now that Christ came to give and that the Gospel accounts were written to encourage and support, and if this personal experience must also be in line with the rest of Scripture, and confirmed by the community of the Church, including living holy witnesses, then clearly the Church Fathers, along with other Saints, are the ones who best fit this model. Indeed, the Church provides "a cloud of witnesses" (cf. Heb. 12:1) stretching through time—throughout the roughly 2000 years of Christian history, and through space—across most of this planet.

All the Saints attest, and reflect in their faces and lives, the reality that God honors our love and efforts, our humanly impossible ascetic struggle to achieve likeness to Christ, by granting many believers a real taste of communion with the Father, in the Son, through the Holy Spirit—a real taste of the joy of the new Paradise, the heavenly kingdom, as St. Porphyrios described above. Partly this happens through the Lord granting to some in this life the transforming vision of God's glory as both dramatic miracles and as uncreated light (as St. Paul and others describe). Many of the Saints have borne witness to the realities of the Faith in their writings, with the greatest of these theologians becoming known as *Church Fathers*. Such writers have been active in many places and in many very different cultures, from the time of the Gospels until today. Surely, these Fathers, and their writings which make them known, taken collectively, will be the most trustworthy guides to gaining access to the fullest experience of the life Jesus came to give. Hence, following them will be the surest path to the ultimate goal of Scripture itself.

Any interpretations based primarily on technical information—such as historical or linguistic data—which do not concern dogma, the "*skopos*," or require knowledge of a practical spiritual kind, should be open to change if and when more accurate information becomes available. It should be noted, however, that this kind of information more or less concerns "details." As Fr. Thomas Hopko writes, "it may certainly enlighten, but it never conclusively determines."[11] Thus, any relatively fair-minded academic may provide help with such things. Such information—for example, about Jewish customs at the time of Jesus—has been very worthwhile in illuminating the text, explaining difficulties, etc.[12] But interpretations that affect fundamental dogmas, or the *skopos* of Scripture, or that require knowledge of spiritual realities that can only be acquired through grace and living the spiritual life, must remain only the province of the true experts in *those* areas—the Fathers and Saints recognized by the Church, who speak with the Church's voice, because they have acquired "the mind of Christ" (1 Cor. 2:16). If you do not maintain the same dogma, the same *skopos* of Scripture, the same understanding of spiritual life and practices that the Church has held through the ages to support growing in the new life in Christ, how can you expect to get the same spiritual result?

To use a crude analogy, if you want to make a delicious chocolate cake you have read or heard about, the more closely you follow the original recipe, the better your result will be. If you take out the chocolate and sugar, you will not have a cake, but something else. If you take out the rising agent and add 1/3 cup of salt instead of the sugar, what you make will not even be edible. Of course, a more apt analogy would be the recipe for an antidote to slow poison. The unbroken link of living witnesses, going back to the apostles and their successors, confirmed by the Church, helps us keep as close as possible to the original "recipe" that is truly life-giving.

This is why the settled Tradition of the Orthodox Church is that the surest guide to authentic interpretations of Scripture in its most important elements, what is important for sanctification and salvation, will indeed be a *consensus* of these Fathers and Saints through the ages. As St. Photius the Great (9th century) taught, "The safe criterion of Orthodoxy is the majority"[13]—referring to the majority of the Fathers recognized by the Church. And these Fathers are also the ideal interpreters because they have witnessed to this new life in their

---

11. Fr. Thomas Hopko, *All the Fulness of God* (Crestwood, NY: SVS Press, 1982), p. 74, fn. 52.

12. This does not mean that spiritually helpful points based on an inaccurate technical detail should be ignored, or "corrected"! See also Fr. John McGuckin, "The Traditions of Orthodoxy," in *Sacred Text and Interpretation*, p. 308. But by the same token, Fr. McGuckin also says, "It would be ridiculous in the name of authenticity to patristic tradition, for example, to resurrect some of the patristic biblical homilies that . . .[might] prove a barrier to the comprehension of the core biblical message of salvation. Some element of falling out of memory, and falling out of favor, in the life of the Church is an important aspect of the self-renewal of the tradition of the saints" (p. 309).

13. As summarized by Christos A. Arabatzis, *Patristic Hermeneutics: 4-14th Century* (Columbia, MO: Newrome Press, 2013), p. 91. See this book for a summary of hermeneutical rules for interpreting the Fathers.

lives as well as in their writings. In other words, what they write about is not just theoretical for them, but based on what they have actually experienced in their own lives.

It is necessary to have a consensus, because the validity of any author's individual interpretation is not *necessarily* guaranteed even by the holiness of that person, even if he is a miracle-worker,[14] as Leontius of Jerusalem (6th century), among others, points out. Along similar lines, Anastasius of Sinai points out that something which is said only once, or rarely, or that contradicts other statements, is not valid.[15] Christos Arabatzis summarizes St. Photius the Great explaining that "it is possible that Fathers can be found who, by reason of their humanity, made mistakes, without however, having their sanctity and honor being reduced within the Church."[16]

Again, the personal experience of an individual (or even of a group of individuals), even those recognized to have a high level of holiness, is not enough *by itself*. The way to safely discern if the personal witness is accurate on any particular topic is whether it is confirmed by a consensus of a majority of other witnesses—including witnesses living in the same period of time—as confirmed in the interpretive context of the Church (through her long history of Scripture interpretation), which simply means again, a consensus of Churchly witnesses, both past and present. "The attempt to construct formal principles of exegesis by which the certain understanding of the scriptures is automatically guaranteed, without reference to the total life, wisdom and experience of the Church, is a hopeless one."[17] This statement by Fr. Hopko applies both to those who would attempt to use the experience of any individual (including themselves!) no matter how holy, as a kind of "secure, automatic," infallible criterion of truth, as well as to those who attempt to use the historical-critical method, a "scientific" approach, in a similar way.

What if a recognized Father disagrees with other Fathers, or is unclear, about a specific point? In the exceptional cases when a passage in the writings of a Father actually does express a different theology from the patristic consensus, then, as Innocent of Maronia—one of the participants at an important theological consultation in 532—wisely says, "we neither condemn, nor do we receive them as the others, because we find even in the Acts of the holy Apostles that the blessed Paul circumcised Timothy by way of economy (condescension), but the same one wrote plainly to the Galatians, 'if you become

---

14. Ibid., p. 44 (though it would be very rare that such a person would be in error on a major point).

15. Ibid., p. 57.

16. Ibid., p. 89.

17. Hopko, op. cit., p. 90.

circumcised, Christ will be of no benefit to you' (Gal. 5:2)." Then he gives other similar examples, concluding with Acts 15:28-29 and saying, "From that time onwards what was written *by common consensus* and was *confirmed by the Holy Spirit* was accepted by us as ecclesiastical law; however, what was done by way of economy [i.e., as an exception] by each of them privately (separately) is not accepted, or hated, or condemned."[18] (It is understood that there may be an exception made in a individual case, or that an individual statement may be exaggerated in the midst of a debate, etc.)

For these and other reasons, Holy Scripture, and truths approved by councils of the Church, especially Ecumenical Councils, carry more weight than, and even "override," the statements of any individual Fathers in their writings.[19] When there is a question, the Church in council, following the pattern in Acts, decides what the patristic consensus is.[20] As Nilus Cabasilas (14th century) also explains, "Generally, it is the Church and the Ecumenical Councils that define matters relating to the faith, and it is to this rule that the doctrines of the Fathers are aligned."[21]

For any topic, then, one should consider as being valid what the majority of Fathers say, especially if it is explicitly supported by an Ecumenical Council. Fr. McGuckin has a very apt term for this basic approach: "a hermeneutic of familial trust," as opposed to a "hermeneutic of suspicion."[22] In the rare times that a Father might say something different from this, such a text should be rejected, as Arabatzis says, "without affecting the sanctity of the author, since what is rare cannot constitute a law for the Church, nor can it guide it correctly."[23] Again, as we quoted above, "The safe criterion of Orthodoxy is the majority."

In any case, the Fathers can only be understood properly as faithful members of the Church, whose primary concern is soteriological, and not personal power, fame, or any individualistic goal, as their sacrificial lives generally make clear. Christos Arabatzis summarizes St. Maximus the Confessor, who had his tongue cut off for defending the correct Christology, explaining that the Fathers teach "out of love for humanity," inspired by the Holy Spirit,[24] supplementing

---

18. Arabatzis, op. cit., p. 36, n. 47 (my emphasis). All this is in the spirit of "covering your father's nakedness"—which Noah's sons were condemned for not doing. It is done out of love and respect, because the Church is supposed to be a communion of love. And indeed, none of the Fathers is considered to be infallible.

19. Ibid., pp. 25-27, 155.

20. Ibid., p. 99.

21. As paraphrased by Arabatzis, ibid., p. 147.

22. McGuckin, *Sacred Text and Interpretation*, op. cit., p. 308.

23. Arabatzis, op. cit., p. 84.

24. Ibid., p. 61.

what was insufficiently said by the Councils. Further, the Fathers "are those that continue the synodical work within the historical Church, correcting, approving and assisting in the *soteriological* understanding of the dogmas," giving "an ongoing validation and confirmation."[25]

Because "a patristic word does not house the true faith (piety) by means of the word but by means of the purpose," all Scripture, and all interpretations of it, should be considered from a soteriological perspective—again, with the understanding that Scripture and the Fathers are trying to communicate "realities" in language that can only point to these realities. They are not merely concerned with ideas, concepts, speculative academic questions, or merely theoretical knowledge. They are trying especially to express a common experience in and through the Holy Spirit.[26] The "common illumination" of the Fathers "is confirmed in the identity of their lived experience," and the texts they wrote are "integrated within this broader spirituality."[27] This understanding, of course, assumes that "the personal experience of grace" has a "specific cognitive role." It "agrees, follows, and certifies the preceding experience of the Church."[28]

As one contemporary Orthodox theologian, Archimandrite Vasileios, eloquently explains,

> In all the Fathers one can find the same guiding line. All lead to the same end, to the land of the liberty of the Spirit. Each one speaks in his own way, expresses his own experience, stresses what he has understood. And from the whole of this Spirit-filled multitude, who have lived in various places and in different centuries, there arises a harmonious and single voice, which sings one hymn before the throne of the Lamb.[29]

What is crucial is the underlying meaning, the common mindset, the realities, the experiences, "the inner tradition of the Church,"[30] that the Fathers have and continue to witness to in their lives, and are trying to speak of or write about in their works, because this is what safeguards **"the reality of salvation in Christ."**[31] What is not crucial are technical details, or mere verbal

---

25. Ibid., p. 62 (my emphasis).

26. Ibid., pp. 60, 70.

27. Ibid., p. 152.

28. Ibid., p. 110.

29. Archimandrite Vasileios, *Hymn of Entry* (Crestwood, NY: St. Vladimir's Seminary Press, 1984), p. 121.

30. McGuckin, *Standing in God's Holy Fire* (Maryknoll, NY: Orbis Books, 2001), p. 151.

31. Arabatzis, op. cit., p. 38 (my emphasis).

agreement, for the same words can mean different things in different contexts.[32] Happily, one can get many details wrong and still get right "the one thing needful," and accomplish the goal, the purpose for which Scripture was written and preserved and passed down, for which Christ became incarnate. Not that there is anything wrong in wanting to get the details correct—that can be valuable as well, especially in defending the Faith. It is only problematic if this is done at the expense of "the one thing needful"—which has so often been the case in biblical studies dominated by historical criticism which rejects the primary kind of knowledge that Scripture has been preserved to provide.

Since the primary concern of Scripture and the Fathers is soteriological, when we look at Scripture with the help of the Fathers we should try to discern how they attempted to make this experience of new life in Christ accessible through their exegesis. Indeed, truly "following the Fathers," who "follow the meaning [and pattern] of Scripture," requires much more even than this often neglected dimension, as Archimandrite Vasileios explains so eloquently:

> What the Fathers require and give is the change which comes from the Spirit. . . . Communication of the patristic word, the word of the Holy Fathers, is not a matter of applying their sayings to this or that topic with the help of a concordance. It is a process whereby nourishment is taken up by living organisms, assimilated by them, and turned into blood, life and strength. . . . it means passing on the joy . . .
>
> Thus the living patristic word is not conveyed mechanically, nor preserved archaeologically. . . . It is conveyed whole, full of life, as it passes from generation to generation through living organisms, altering them, creating "fathers" who make it their personal word, a new possession, a miracle, a wealth which increases as it is given away. . . . Offering the words of the Fathers to others means that I myself live, that I am changed by them. . . .[33]
>
> Worldly knowledge, which sees things from a human point of view and mechanically, is sterile and lifeless. Knowledge in the Holy Spirit . . . is the

---

32. Ibid., p. 37. In contrast, heretics tend to insist on literal, verbal identity of key terms. In addition to insisting on absolutizing particular language (literal, verbal agreement), heretics also tend to give too much weight to just one or two Fathers—"the isolation of a Saint from the entire company of Saints" (ibid., pp. 154-155). They also tend not to consider the whole of a Father's works; they "steal little sayings and fragments" (p. 55), and detach works of the Fathers "from their historical and theological interconnection" (p. 154). They also tend to approach things from the perspective of speculative/theoretical philosophical premises rather than spiritual experience—being too rationalistic, and not having a soteriological perspective.

33. Archimandrite Vasileios, op. cit., p. 35.

only knowledge which is communicable . . . When it is offered, it gives
life.[34]

Archimandrite Vasileios adds, "And if *our* theology does not assume *us*, if it does
not change our life, it will leave our life outside the taste of the new creation, in
the darkness of ignorance, and so outside the mystery of theology which is the
manifestation of the struggle for and the fact of salvation in Christ."[35]

It is also crucial to take into account that the study of Scripture was only one
part of the Fathers' overall effort to safeguard access to this new life in Christ.
It would be wrong to ignore the central role of liturgical/corporate worship[36]
from the very beginning of the Church with its proclamation of the Gospel
not only in sermons, but eventually also in theologically rich hymns, icons,
architecture, and gestures, as well as the invaluable spiritual help of participation in the sacraments. With proper preparation and attention, all of this
provides a powerful interpretive context for understanding the Scriptures and
for enabling the believer to enter more fully into the new life in Christ. As
Archimandrite Vasileios explains about some of the hymnography, "the Old
Testament readings intersect with the readings from the New Testament. This
is mediated by the hymns, in which the melodists provide a commentary on
all the truth of the Old and New Testament through the music and words of
their poems."[37]

In addition to other spiritual disciplines like fasting, almsgiving, and other
concrete expressions of love and help for others, as well as other elements of
the Gospel life, maintaining an active personal prayer-life is crucial. So as Fr.
McGuckin says,

---

34. Ibid., p. 39.

35. Ibid., p. 23 (my emphasis).

36. Those who choose to follow the Fathers will also realize that, at least in the Orthodox
Church, the liturgical hymns (many from the 9th century onwards, some from well before)—especially for the major feasts of the Lord—provide a beautiful interpretive context for understanding the key aspects of Scripture. Very biblically based, these hymns sometimes provide profound
insight even into "details."

For example, many modern biblical scholars have puzzled over Jesus' saying in Luke 9:27,
"But I tell you of a truth, there be some standing here, who shall not taste of death, till they see the
kingdom of God." Matthew's Gospel says, "till they see the son of Man coming in His kingdom."
And Mark's Gospel says, "till they see the kingdom of God coming in power." But the hymns for
the Feast of the Transfiguration—the account of which occurs immediately after these sayings
in these three Gospel accounts—make clear that Jesus was referring to the revelation of His own
divinity, that God's kingdom is His, and can be experienced in communion with Him.

37. Ibid., p. 105.

by a recurring cycle of liturgical celebrations and daily prayers, under-
lined by regular practices of fasting and the customs of bowing, venerating
the icons, and frequently making the sign of the cross during prayer, the
Byzantine tradition fosters the abiding sense of Christ's sanctification of
ordinary life. It is as if the life of prayer is an invocation, a state of read-
iness, in accordance with those words of the Lord: "So I say it to all of
you. Stay awake, for you know not the hour of the Bridegroom's coming"
(Matt. 25:13).[38]

Archimandrite Vasileios goes on to explain,

> Today . . . we often take theology out of the theanthropic mystery of the
> Church in which it was sung by the Fathers. We transfer it to the field of
> mere academic discussions, where each person, remaining an individual,
> an isolated authority, states his opinion and goes his way. The resultant
> "theology," however, is not the very theology of the Church. . . .
>
> In philosophy, in the field of theories, systems and hypotheses, each
> person can say anything and maintain whatever he likes. . . . In theology
> this cannot happen. Orthodox theology is a different matter from begin-
> ning to end. *It does not assert a proposition; it bears witness.*[39]

He then gives a model of what he is talking about from Scripture itself:

> How frequently the Lord would stop people who wanted to start a "theo-
> logical" conversation with Him. They would ask, "Will those who are saved
> be few?" and the Lord replies, "Strive to enter by the narrow door" (Luke
> 13:23-24). . . . In a moment He leads the conversation into the field of per-
> sonal life, of true theology. In every case, He is interested in the person, not
> in theological discussion as an isolated occupation remaining out of touch
> with life and with the very person who is speaking. . . . theology seeks the
> person and his salvation. . . . He did not come to discuss, He came to seek
> out and save the one who had gone astray (Matt. 18:11). He came and took
> on our whole nature. He entered into us, into the shadow of death where
> we are, and drew us to the light. We passed into His life: we live in Him.
>
> This life which is in Christ, and the expression of it, constitutes the true
> theology which is the one truth, because it speaks of and brings us to the
> one eternal life. . . . The material offered to each person to struggle with, to

---

38. McGuckin, *Standing in God's Holy Fire*, op. cit., p. 149.

39. *Hymn of Entry*, p. 32 (my emphasis).

write theology with, and to speak about to the Church, is none other than his own self, his very being, hidden and unknown.[40]

Sadly, most of modern biblical criticism has not been concerned with "the one truth," "the one thing needful"; nor have most biblical critics been interested in following the pattern of the ideal exegete found in Scripture itself and followed by the Fathers; nor do most of them seem to be aware of a traditional Christian approach, at least as understood by those in the Eastern Orthodox Church. Sadly, one could theoretically get all the details right (though that has been far from happening!), and still miss the main point. Because even if the historical-critical method could have succeeded in the impossible task of providing unquestionably authoritative interpretations for all of Scripture, this method would still be inadequate, because it is based on a false understanding of the primary purpose of Scripture.

As a methodology, the historical-critical method implies (and was indeed founded upon the belief) that the purpose of interpreting Scripture is *to provide information*—in the case of the New Testament, information about the historical Jesus and what He taught. Jesus becomes simply a great teacher (yet one Whose immediate followers often did not understand what He was teaching, according to the same people!). This approach comes out of a profound distrust of the Church—and in fact, a distrust also of the Scriptures she collected and preserved. It promotes a hermeneutic of suspicion: too often the implication is—"What did Jesus *really* say or mean? Surely not what traditional Christianity has claimed." Even the positive reasons for wanting to discern the true teachings of the "historical Jesus" are not always evident, and are no doubt varied. But it would too often seem to be either a largely academic exercise, or at best, an attempt to determine an ethic, a manner of living, in order merely to be a "good" person.

Ultimately, as already discussed, the historical-critical approach seems to come out of a faulty Christology which led to an extrinsic and juridical view of salvation (with divine justice essentially the same as human justice), or for some, no kind of salvation at all. And it is linked to a search for an externally guaranteed infallible criterion of truth such as science was thought to provide, a search that occurred at least partly because the people involved no longer truly believed that "God is the good God Who loves mankind."

One can even legitimately describe the attitude that comes to prevail with the so-called Enlightenment—the historical context for the historical-critical method—as being *negative*, or *pessimistic*, towards God, Scripture, nature (i.e., asserting that things are randomly arranged by impersonal, natural forces

---

40. Ibid., pp. 32-33.

according to impersonal, natural laws), and all kinds of difficulties, whether in one's life, or in Scripture. In this view, nature is not how it should be, so it is held that people should, and are capable of, *conquering* nature and forcing the establishment of some kind of *utopia*. If there is a God, he is so far removed and indifferent that it makes no practical difference. So in this view there is no possibility of synergy, of deification/sanctification, or of experiencing the heavenly Kingdom now—even if there is such a thing as an after life, which there most probably is not. If there is any happiness possible in this life, it is all up to humanity to make it.[41]

At first, this view does not lead to despair, because the people having an "Enlightenment" world-view were extremely optimistic about fallen humanity—at least the humanity of their own period of history. They believed that human reason was at such a high level, including human language, that there should be no problems in correctly interpreting Scripture, deciphering and taming nature, and forging humanity into a utopian state.[42]

The attitude towards difficulties is completely negative—there can never be a good reason for them, and they should always be avoided, if possible. For

---

41. What Fr. Alexis Trader explains about "meaning assignment," or "the meaning we assign to what we experience" (p. 51) is very interesting in light of the very negative perception of reality characteristic of the Enlightenment as noted in this section. He writes, "meaning assignment *determines perception*" and also *"depends on one's spiritual state"* (p. 52). Furthermore, he states that "our perceptions are channeled through our interpretations of our situation, interpretations that are often influenced more by our imagination than by objectively measurable external reality. Interpretations in the form of thoughts and images shape our views of others and ourselves. Good thoughts bring us joy, increased insight, and wisdom, whereas bad thoughts [i.e., a negative way of interpreting] can throw us into a state of melancholy, confusion, or even folly. . . . thoughts not only give rise to emotional reactions, but also coalesce over time into character traits. If we alter our way of interpreting, we can bring about changes in mood and character. The patristic consensus also views *our soul's orientation to God and things eternal as decisive in the way we interpret reality"* (p. 55).

Even from a secular point of view, "healthy meaning assignment is of utmost importance for successful human functioning," while from that of the Tradition "meaning assignment [also] plays a crucial role in the faithful's efforts to lead a virtuous life and in their relationship with God" (*Ancient Christian Wisdom and Aaron Beck's Cognitive Therapy* [New York: Peter Lang, 2011], p. 253).

42. Of course, after the so-called Enlightenment era of the 18th century, the negative attitude towards God, Scripture, nature, and difficulties continued, but the high opinion of human reason, and the naïve views about human language, etc., did not, leading many to despair, or at least depression, especially in the 20th century.

example, those holding Enlightenment views imagined that language should always be as clear and straightforward as a math problem. So, when something is difficult, or unclear, in Scripture, the attitude is that something must be wrong with Scripture: the text was not well-written, or poorly edited, etc. And this means Scripture is far from perfect, in their definition, so it cannot be God's inspired word. Therefore, it must be culturally conditioned, and merely historically interesting—though perhaps morally inspiring—material. There is an implicit suspicion that the authors of Scripture were not as intelligent or as knowledgable as those in the current era. Thus, not much is expected of them or of what they wrote, and many things are misunderstood as well as interesting points overlooked (such as the chiastic structure of many biblical texts, until fairly recently).

One main problem for such interpreters was that Scripture did not give them the information they wanted. So they had to try to force the text to yield what they were looking for by going *behind* it, to retrieve the most original "pieces"—words, passages, etc. It never seemed to occur to them that they might have been looking for the wrong thing—that they should first have tried to determine what the Bible was primarily trying to convey. In spite of all their problems in interpreting Scripture, they believed that through reason, and using the right tools, there should be no serious difficulties in interpretation—no existential or other fundamental difficulties. With the right methods and tools, though it might take some time, one could without much difficulty find the right interpretation of any particular text. Here we find a general attitude of arrogance.

As previously discussed, for example, in Chapter 3, we see the opposite understanding in traditional Christianity, where we find a very positive attitude toward difficulties in Scripture, in biblical interpretation, as well as in life in general, which comes out of that key fundamental Christian experience which we see everywhere in the Fathers and Saints: that God, as Love, does everything to benefit, to help, mankind spiritually. So the attitude toward Scripture is that there really are difficulties, which is not surprising in light of the fact that the economy of salvation is an ascetic one, and so the difficulties must be there for a good reason. One should therefore try to discern the benefits, through asking, How can we as interpreters engage the difficulties in any particular text (and in life) in order to make them spiritually beneficial? There is a very positive expectation of a depth of meanings, of great richness, and of powerful benefits to be had in studying Scripture, and these are found.

This approach also reflects an attitude of complete faith and trust in God; it is completely optimistic toward God, Scripture, and nature/reality, for God is the good God, Who out of His infinite and all-encompassing Love has arranged everything for our spiritual benefit. At the same time, this approach realizes the many limitations of fallen humanity, including human reason, freely recognizing that the finite cannot understand, or even approach, the infinite. We can only know what God Himself chooses to reveal to us, and that will be what is compatible with our limited nature. This approach is clear about the inadequacy of human language—that it can never fully convey reality, especially spiritual realities. Rather, it can only point to such realities; and it can only communicate effectively if God gives assistance through His grace. It is also clear that our means of transmitting language, especially hand-copied manuscripts, have possibilities for scribal errors, etc. Therefore, there is no way to by-pass the need for God, and the Church. Thus, the general attitude is one of humility.

Just about the only point of agreement between the traditional patristic and the Enlightenment approaches is that both recognize the inadequacy of the means of transmission—i.e., hand-copied manuscripts. But while the Fathers expect God's grace to overcome this inadequacy, those accepting an Enlightenment world-view expect to overcome this inadequacy with scientific methods. The level of their faith in science is truly amazing at this point in time. They assumed that they could get back to the original text, and then that they could rather easily work out all the answers which were to be found by determining what the single original historical meaning of the human author was.[43] After several hundred years of failed attempts at this enterprise *as a whole*, it should be obvious that the assumptions this overall undertaking was built on were false. By now, it should be clear why. This is also not to say that nothing has been learned—much useful information has been gathered—but the positive results are far more modest than expected.

In the Tradition, however, because God is a good God Who loves us and does everything for our benefit, through His grace all the inadequacies mentioned above can become very adequate to help us towards sanctification. So, if we cooperate with God—through synergy—we can reach the highest possible reality, which is true life in Christ. And we can even experience the greatest joy in this life—we can really begin to experience paradise, the heavenly kingdom now—so there is no need to force the creation of some kind of utopia. This means that Scripture, with its human imperfections, is actually, through grace, God's perfect Word just as it is, including with the inadequate means of its transmission, because it is just what people in all times and places need

---

43. See David Laird Dungan, *A History of the Synoptic Problem* (New York: Doubleday, 1999), especially Part Two, for a history of the attempts to ascertain the original text of the Gospels. Those in the Tradition are not so concerned to try to find the exact original words, because they have the authentic Tradition, and they trust God's grace to be guiding the entire process of preservation and transmission. Also the printing press, which could guarantee copies exactly alike, made such attempts more imperative.

to guide us to a life of communion with Him. It continually reminds us by its very form and content, *and* by the way it has been transmitted, of our need for others—for the Church, and most especially, for God Himself, if we have the ears to hear.

Capturing the Imagination and Inspiring the Will: The Fathers' Children

When that "one thing needful" is understood and lived properly, then the answer to the third concern mentioned in Chapter 1 and above—"Is a traditional understanding of the Bible still credible and effective in a post-modern culture?"—will be a resounding "Yes!" And the crisis in biblical studies caused by historical criticism will begin to take care of itself.

How this may be so can be seen from the lives of a few of the highly influential holy witnesses living in our own day, some of whose theological writings we have been quoting from—two of whom this author has known personally, and two of whom are still alive. Although none of them wrote biblical commentaries as such, they all have powerfully preached the Gospel "in deeds and words,"[44] and reveal the fundamentals essential for truly authoritative and inspiring biblical exegesis. They fit the model for the ideal exegete, partly because it can rightly be said of each of them that "his mission is not to effect something by his thoughts or to organize something by his own capacities, but by his life to give his witness to the conquest of death."[45]

The first of these figures, whom we have quoted above, is Archimandrite Vasileios of Iveron (one of the monasteries on Mt. Athos, Greece[46]), who was born on the island of Crete in 1936. He studied theology both in Athens and in Lyons, France. He says that after visiting Mt. Athos, the ancient center of monastic life for the Orthodox Church, he "felt at home" and decided to stay. Later on, inspired by his influence, and that of several other holy spiritual fathers, such as Elder Joseph the Hesychast, a totally unexpected—even amazing—thing occurred on Mt. Athos beginning in the early 1960s: "Monasteries that were in a critical state, virtually deserted, with only a small group of elderly members, have in the course of a few years been totally transformed: they are now full of young monks, under the guidance of abbots and spiritual fathers

---

44. Hymn for St. Herman of Alaska.

45. Archimandrite Vasileios, *Hymn of Entry*, op. cit., p. 119.

46. Mt. Athos is the ancient center for Eastern Orthodox monasticism that has for centuries included monasteries and monks from many nations around the world. Both the monastics and the thousands of visitors come not only from many nations, but also from many walks of life.

who have a word of life not for Athos only but for the Christian world as a whole."[47]

Hence, Fr. Vasileios has been described as "the pioneer" of "the striking revival and renewal of monastic life on the Holy Mountain."[48] In this capacity, he has strongly impacted many thousands of lives internationally in various ways; but that is not all. For more than 30 years, he has been invited to speak at many theological meetings and other gatherings, being especially popular with the youth. He is also the author of a number of inspiring books. The well-known theologian, Metropolitan Kallistos (Ware), a former professor at the University of Oxford in England and also an author of many widely read books, says in his Foreword to the first of Archimandrite Vasileios's books to appear in English, *Hymn of Entry*, "if we are to write theology, it can only be in such a way as this."[49]

Our second witness, Metropolitan Anthony of Sourozh (Anthony Bloom; 1914-2003), was from a very different world. He was the son of a Russian diplomat, whose childhood was spent largely in Persia. After the Russian Revolution, the family fled to France, where they lived at first in a state of poverty and serious hardship. Metr. Anthony always considered himself "a man of science," and was a practicing medical doctor for many years, serving in the French Medical Corps in WWII, as well as being a member of the French Resistance, before he became a priest monk, and then a bishop.

From 1950, Metr. Anthony lived in Britain as the Moscow Patriarchate's ruling bishop there. He was also a widely respected man of prayer, and a powerful speaker who also had great revitalizing influence—capturing the imagination and inspiring the will of many hundreds of thousands, especially in the former Soviet Union, as well as Great Britain.[50] According to his obituary, during the time Metr. Anthony was making a lot of radio broadcasts (and some television

---

47. METROPOLITAN Kallistos of Diokleia, in his Foreword to Abbot Vasileios's *Hymn of Entry*, op. cit., p. 7.

48. Ibid.

49. Ibid., p. 10.

50. For many years he made radio broadcasts, including broadcasts of Church services, into the Soviet Union, and no doubt impacted hundreds of thousands in this way, as well as during his visits there as one of the only free hierarchs of the Moscow Patriarchate. I had the great blessing to know him personally, and to observe how, when he was invited to give the spiritual talks at the Lambeth Conference in Canterbury, UK, in 1978, many Anglican bishops came up to thank him, with great emotion, for his work, saying how much it had helped them and many they knew. For a more detailed description of his conversion to Christ, see, for example, the Introduction of his excellent book, *Beginning to Pray* (also published as *School for Prayer*).

ones as well), Gerald Priestland, a well-known BBC religious correspondent, called him "the single most powerful Christian voice in the land."

The source of his powerful preaching is clear from the account of his conversion from atheism as a teenager. In an unusual way, he was compelled to read one of the Gospel accounts, so he chose Mark, since it was the shortest. Then, as he has written,

> While I was reading the beginning of St. Mark's gospel, before I reached the third chapter, I suddenly became aware that on the other side of my desk there was a presence. And the certainty was so strong that it was Christ standing there that it has never left me. This was the real turning point. Because Christ was alive and I had been in his presence I could say with certainty that what the gospel said about the crucifixion of the prophet of Galilee was true, and the centurion was right when he said, "Truly he is the Son of God." It was in the light of the Resurrection that I could read with certainty the story of the Gospel, knowing that everything was true in it because the impossible event of the Resurrection was to me more certain than any event of history. History I had to believe; the Resurrection I knew for a fact.[51]

The following excerpt from the speech he gave after accepting an honorary doctorate from the Moscow Theological Academy gives a further glimpse into why his writings and talks were so powerful. These words of his are also indicative of the true answer to the crisis in biblical studies:

> this diploma will testify before the Churches of the West that my word is an Orthodox word, not a personal view, but the voice of the whole Church. About ten years ago the Presbyterian Theological Faculty of the University of Aberdeen granted me a similar Doctorate of Divinity "for the preaching of the Word of God and the renewal of the spiritual life in Great Britain," and I rejoice that I can say now that the Russian Church recognizes my word as a word of truth, of the Church's truth.

Notice that he did not wish to be "cutting-edge," or "original," but that he twice emphasizes his joy that the Russian Church has affirmed that in his preaching of the Gospel, his word is "a word of truth, of the Church's truth." He continues,

---

51. Metr. Anthony Bloom, *School for Prayer* (London: Dartman, Longman & Todd, 1970), p. xii.

From my very early years, from the moment when as a boy of fourteen I read the Gospel, I felt that there could be no other task in life but to share with others that joy which can transfigure life and which disclosed itself to me in the knowledge of God and of Christ. And then, still a youth, I started speaking of Christ, "in time and out of time," at school, in the underground, in children's camps; of Christ as he had revealed himself to me: as Life, as Joy, as Meaning, as something so new that it made all things new; and if it were not out of place to apply to oneself words of Holy Scripture, I could say together with the Apostle Paul, 'Woe unto me if I do not preach' (1 Cor. 9:16). Woe! because not to share such a miracle would be a crime before God who had worked this miracle, and a crime before men who through- out the world are athirst, ATHIRST for a living word about God, about man, about life: not about the life which we experience day by day, which is so dull at times and at times so frightening, and again at times so tender; not the life of the earth, but a life of exulting plenitude, about Life Eternal gushing like a torrent in our souls, in our hearts, enlightening our minds, making us not only heralds but witnesses of the Kingdom of God already come with power, deeply penetrating our soul, pervading our life.[52]

With this in mind, it is not surprising that he would also say in an interview with seminarians:

We should understand that the Christian Church, the believers, should be believers not only on account of their view of the world but also in their lives, through their inner experience, and that our part consists in bring- ing light into this world where it is so dark and at times so frightening . . . There is no point in saying that a man errs in his view of the world when we fail to provide him with the living experience of the Living God.[53]

Another such witness is the contemporary Greek bishop, Metropolitan Meletios of Preveza and Nikopolis, who was born in a small village in Greece in 1933 to very pious parents. As a bishop, he dramatically revitalized a diocese that had been nearly destroyed by the scandalous ways of his predecessor—an impossible situation from the point of view of human reason. In words similar to those of Metr. Antony, Metr. Meletios says,

---

52. http://www.mitras.ru/eng/eng_12.htm, accessed Feb. 27, 2014 (his emphasis). Whether or not all of his, or anyone else's, speculations actually express "the voice of the whole Church" will be determined in time by the whole Church.

53. Metr. Anthony Bloom, *Encounter*, trans. Tatiana Wolff (London: Dartman, Longman, and Todd, 2005), p. 161.

> Once a glowing ember of men [the apostles] played an active role unrivaled in the world. They re-created the inhabited world, beginning without any support from anyone. Because they had within them the power of imperishable life. . . . Institutionally, we can hardly do anything. . . . Spiritually, however—that is, with the power of the imperishable life of Jesus—if we have it, if we feel it, if we experience it, we can achieve all things."[54]

His own life and work are a witness to the truth of what he says. He is described in the book about him as a "church leader who applied his ancient faith in a modern context to inspire social and religious change."[55]

Tragically, many exegetes, and even Christian leaders, do not have this *living spiritual experience* to offer. Indeed, many do not even believe it is possible, nor do they have the "ancient faith" of the holy Metropolitan. They do not speak with "the Church's voice," or even desire to. This is partly because of the faulty hermeneutic that had its unintended beginning in the Reformation and sprang, essentially fully formed, out of the heady arrogance and ignorance of the Enlightenment. That is a hermeneutic that separates exegesis from spiritual life, because those developing it attempted to reject completely the Church and her Tradition in an over-reaction to the corruption of the Roman Catholic Church of their day, rather than trying to recover the authentic Tradition of the Church which is focused on giving access to the new, imperishable life in Christ. Nor, following the pattern in Scripture itself, did they seek a consensus of the Fathers and Saints (including contemporary living, holy witnesses) in line with Scripture, and with the long history of the Church.

Many such exegetes of the Scriptures wanted an infallible, *external* criterion of truth that all reasonable people would be "forced" to accept, ultimately because these exegetes did not believe that God is the good God Who loves mankind, and that He became incarnate in Jesus of Nazareth. They did not know Him, and they did not understand His ways, or those of His Church. They did not understand that corruption in the Church is the result of fallen, sinful people who can repent and change, and that such corruption can be—and has often been in the past—cleansed and the Church renewed by the grace of the Holy Spirit.

God has never offered, and did not create the universe to provide, an infallible external criterion of truth—a short-cut way involving bypassing God and other people, not unlike what Eve so foolishly thought she could obtain by following the serpent's interpretation of God's words. God did not offer such an

---

54. Stephen R. Lloyd-Moffett, *Beauty from Ashes: The Spiritual Transformation of a Modern Greek Community* (Crestwood, NY: St. Vladimir's Seminary Press, 2009), p. 151.

55. Ibid., back cover.

easy way to Adam and Eve, or to Abraham, or to anyone else. What everyone has always been offered is much harder, but far better, because it cannot be separated from our actual lives, and it cannot be separated from love—God's infinite divine love for us, and our love, or lack thereof, for Him and one another, since He Himself is Love, and He created us out of His love in order first of all that we would freely love Him and others in return.

Metropolitan Anthony explains the loving approach of this God Who is Love, by saying that God

> calls us and reveals the beauty and truth of things, but . . . does not force them upon us and, like our conscience, prompts us with the truth but leaves us free either to listen to the truth and the beauty or to deny them.

And Metr. Anthony adds, "It seems to me that the church must be just like that."[56] Hence, he also says, much like the Greek bishop quoted above,

> We need to become Christians—Christians in the manner of Christ and his disciples, and only then will the Church acquire not power—that is, the ability to coerce people—but authority—that is, the ability to speak such words that once any soul [at least many souls!] hears them it will shudder and will open itself to the eternal depths.[57]

Archimandrite Sophrony (Sakharov), our last witness, was born in Russia in 1896, and lived until 1993. As a young man he was a successful artist in Paris in the early 1920s, captivated by non-Christian religious traditions. After having a dramatic conversion to Christ in 1924, realizing that God is love and must be *personal*—and can be related to only by total love—he went to be a monk on Mount Athos. While there, he became a disciple of the great contemporary Saint, Silouan of Mount Athos (1866-1938), who was a simple Russian peasant. Fr. Sophrony is perhaps best known himself for making St. Silouan, and his writings, known to the world.

Silouan was a Saint who emphasized prayer for the whole world, the immeasurable love of God for us, and the importance of acquiring the Holy Spirit. St. Silouan says, for example, "The Lord is love, and He sent the Holy Spirit on earth, Who teaches the soul to love her enemies and pray for them, that they too may find salvation. That is true love."[58] And "no man can conceive of this

---

56. *Encounter*, op. cit., p. 160.

57. Ibid., p. 161.

58. Archimandrite Sophrony (Sakharov), *Wisdom from Mount Athos: The Writings of Staretz Silouan 1866-1938*, trans. Rosemary Edmonds (Crestwood, NY: St. Vladimir's Seminary Press,

great love [of the Lord] without the grace of the Holy Spirit. The Scriptures tell of this love, but neither are they to be understood by the mind, for in the Scriptures too speaks the same Holy Spirit."[59]

Making the life and works of St. Silouan known to the world would alone be enough to warrant including Fr. Sophrony as a highly influential contemporary witness, but he also left a number of powerful writings himself.[60] In addition, many thousands of people have benefited from visiting the monastery in England where he lived, preached, and liturgized for four decades. This monastery continues today in the same spirit as when he was alive. Some of his own spiritual children, such as Archimandrite Zacharias (Zachariou), who has visited the U.S. numerous times, have become living witnesses themselves, and are inspiring many by their lives, talks, and books. Here we see a contemporary example of spiritual apostolic succession, of which there are many others.

The following excerpts from Fr. Sophrony's writings give a little more insight into the question of knowledge of spiritual realities, or epistemology. He explains that

> where we encounter a deficiency of rational knowledge we should do well to remember that prayer, independently of man's intellectual capacity, can bring a higher form of cognition . . . of demonstrative argument; and there is the province where prayer is the passageway to direct contemplation of divine truth.[61]

He speaks further of mankind's "talent for cognition not only of the created world but also of the Divine world. Consumed with love, man feels himself joined with his beloved God. Through this union he knows God, and thus love and cognition merge into a single act. . . . This personal revelation makes the general revelation of the New Testament spiritually familiar."[62]

He goes on to explain that "This personal revelation may be granted suddenly" (as in the case of Metr. Anthony above):

1974), p. 35. I also had the great blessing of meeting with Fr. Sophrony many times, beginning in 1977.

59. Ibid., p. 28.

60. The Greek theologian, Anestis G. Keselopoulos, has even called him "the St. Symeon the New Theologian of our day."

61. Archimandrite Sophrony (Sakharov), *His Life Is Mine*, trans. Rosemary Edmonds (London: Mowbrays, 1977), p. 56.

62. Ibid., p. 44.

But though suddenly received man can only assimilate it by degrees, after long ascetic struggle. From the first instant the vital content of the revelation is clear, and the soul feels no impulse to explain in rational concepts the grace experienced. But as a matter of course she aspires to ever deeper knowledge.

Another important aspect of this spiritual knowledge is the awareness that it is impossible to adequately explain it in words. As Fr. Sophrony continues,

The divine nature of this personal vision is startlingly authentic, though words may fail to convey it. Yet the knowledge it offers has an objective *sui generis* character which we repeatedly observe down the centuries in the lives of many individuals largely identical in their experience, and self-determining.

And as he says further,

Only sin can stifle the Divine breath within us. God Who is Holy, does not blend with the darkness of sin. When we seek to justify a sinful action we *ipso facto* sever our alliance with God. God does not constrain us, but neither can He be coerced. He retires, leaving us bereft of His luminous presence. . . . man can avoid the consequences of sin—separation from God—through repentance.[63]

An infallible external criterion of truth, if it did exist, would have a kind of coercive power. But as Metr. Antony, Archim. Vasileios, Metr. Meletios, Archim. Sophrony, and many others demonstrate, what we have instead is *the authority of true witnesses* who radiate that living, personal experience of the Holy Spirit, confirmed by Scripture as a whole, and by the Church and her Tradition. And on these essentials, these witnesses speak with one voice, the "voice of the whole Church."

If we doubt that such experience of God, of the new, imperishable life in Christ through the Holy Spirit, is possible, to whom are we listening? Who are their sources, what are their lives like—where do their ideas lead? What basis do they have for claiming to be authoritative? Are they the people we really admire and wish to be like? Is what they offer going to fulfill our deepest longings and fill us with peace, love, and joy—not to mention eternal life, the new Paradise, that can be tasted already in this world?

---

63. Ibid., pp. 44-45.

In a final consideration of the ideal interpreter, here is one further thought-provoking statement by Archimandrite Vasileios:

> theology is a gift of the Spirit, a consecration of man and a text written by God, inscribed on his very existence. **It nourishes and renews the theologian and makes him a support and joy for the Church.**[64]

We should also ask ourselves, are the interpreters we are listening to "a support and joy for the Church" like the Holy Fathers of the past, and these four contemporary witnesses quoted above? Are they nourished and renewed by their own theology? And again, who are they—individual scholars sounding off their own opinions which are not life-giving, writing perhaps only in order to get academic tenure, or for some other personal benefit? Are their voices "a word of the Church's truth," in line with Scripture as a whole and with the majority of other holy witnesses throughout the Church's long history, and even today? What is their effect on the Church and the individual believer? Are they "passing on the joy" of life in Christ in a life-giving way?

Or do they sound like the serpent, casting doubt on the goodness and love of God? Another thing that the remarkably paradigmatic story of Adam and Eve shows us so truly is that we are always listening to *someone* concerning the fundamentals of life, and we are always free to choose whom we listen to. So it is crucial to ask these sorts of questions about the competing voices that claim to reveal the truth about Scripture, and the truth about reality.

There was never a time when everyone has been open to the Truth—not everyone was convinced even by God Incarnate Himself. But the offer of unlimited love, truth, and beauty were, and still are, there. And it is clear from the lives of these living witnesses—only a few out of many, many others—that there is nothing in contemporary culture that is an obstacle to people being deeply inspired and having their lives transformed by the Gospel as understood from within the context of the authentic Christian Tradition—at least as understood in the Orthodox Church—especially when made "flesh" in the life of a holy human being inspired by the Holy Spirit. Indeed, many people who think they know about Christianity and reject it, have no idea what that authentic Christian Tradition is—especially if they have never met a truly holy, grace-filled person. And most likely, then, they also have little or no experience of true grace themselves.

---

64. Archimandrite Vasileios, op. cit., p. 34 (my emphasis).

"That Beauty to Which We Are Called"

> "the Church does not give us Holy Scripture as a book to study and inter-
> pret on our own. Rather, it opens to us the door of that beauty to which we
> are called by the Bridegroom Himself" (Archimandrite Vasileios).[65]

According to the Cupid and Psyche myth, Cupid was so beautiful that seeing
him only once was enough to inspire such an intense love for him in Psyche as
to completely focus her desire and her life on finding him once again (before
she saw him, she already loved him for his kindness). Indeed, in that one
glimpse, he "captured her imagination," "inspired her will," and transformed
her life.

That ancient story provides us with a vivid analogy of a key way that
Christians have always become true witnesses, able to give authoritative interpretations of Scripture, especially through their lives, but also through scholarly exegesis. Simply having seen Jesus Christ, even His miracles, with one's
physical eyes did not, and could not, make one a true witness. It is not enough
only to see the surface, to "judge according to appearance" (cf. John 7:24). One
has to perceive the underlying reality. One has to perceive its beauty and goodness so profoundly that one's heart is filled with a life-transforming love, and
one is thus inspired, like Psyche, to do whatever is required to be in the presence of the beloved Bridegroom again.

This is the way that Christians have always been inspired and have inspired
others. Indeed, the connections between seeing, beauty, goodness, and desire,
and between inspiration, longing, love, delight, and joy, are very strong for
human beings. As the contemporary Greek theologian Christos Yannaras says,
at the most fundamental level people "are not interested in the validation of
concepts or legal guarantees of ultimate justification. Human beings seek the
love (*philia*) of the good and long for beauty (*kalos*)."[66]

This longing, this "lifelong nostalgia," C. S. Lewis identifies as a kind of
"proof" that we are made for eternal life—for, he argues, mankind as a whole
would not have an innate desire for something that does not exist. Lewis also
points out that we often call this "beauty and behave as if that had settled the

---

65. *Hymn of Dismissal*, op. cit., p. 105.

66. Christos Yannaras, *Orthodoxy and the West* (Brookline, MA: Holy Cross Orthodox Press,
2006), p. 125. See also on this topic an excerpt by St. Theophan the Recluse, given in Appendix
III below.

matter." The truth is, however, that the beautiful things that so move us are only "good images of what we really desire."[67] As Lewis explains,

> We do not want merely to *see* beauty, though, God knows, even that is bounty enough. We want something else which can hardly be put into words—to be united with the beauty we see, to pass into it, to receive it into ourselves, to bathe in it, to become part of it.[68]

Ultimately, what we are longing for is "the beauty of the Lord's Person." As Yannaras says, "Longing for the beauty of the Lord's Person is part of the personal relationship or communion that constitutes incorruptible, immortal, true life."[69] The longing that we associate with beauty and joy is ultimately, then, also a longing for eternal life, a union with God made possible by Jesus Christ in the Holy Spirit.

The well-known historian of the early Church, Robert Wilken, points out that actually, "Beauty is the corollary of seeing. In the Scriptures many of the key terms used of God's self-disclosure, words such as *glory, splendor, light, image* and *face*, have to do with the delight of the eye."[70] This connection in Scripture between God and seeing, beauty, desire, love, delight, and joy is continued by many Christian writers from the earliest times up to our own day.

For example, from early times Christians have understood Psalm 45 to be a messianic Psalm about the Bridegroom of the Church Who is "surpassing all in beauty"—or more literally, Who is "fairer than the sons of men." St. Clement of Rome, writing around 96 AD, speaks of the inexpressible "radiance of His beauty."[71] The ancient Christian writer Origen (3rd century) states in his *Commentary on the Song of Songs* that the "soul is moved by heavenly love and longing when it beholds the beauty and the comeliness of the Word of God."[72] A post-Communion prayer frequently used in the Orthodox Church speaks of "the everlasting rest, where the voice of those who feast is unceasing, and

---

67. C. S. Lewis, *The Weight of Glory and Other Addresses* (New York: HarperCollins, 2001), p. 30.

68. Ibid., p. 42 (his emphasis).

69. Yanneras, *Orthodoxy and the West,* p. 12.

70. Robert Wilken, *The Spirit of Early Christian Thought: Seeking the Face of God* (New Haven: Yale University Press, 2003), p. 20.

71. I Clement 49:2-3 (*The Epistles of St. Clement Rome and St. Ignatius of Antioch,* James A. Kleist, trans. [New York: Newman Press, 1946], p. 39). This is also sometimes translated: "Who can explain the bond of the love of God? Who can adequately describe the greatness of its beauty?"

72. Quoted by Wilken, op. cit., p. 20.

unending is the **delight** of those who **behold the beauty beyond all words of thy countenance**."[73] St. Basil the Great (4th century), after his dramatic experience of God's glory as uncreated light, exclaimed, "What is more marvelous, more worthy of love, than the beauty of God?"[74] St. Cyril of Alexandria (5th century) wrote that "God's only Son shows us his Father's beauty by presenting himself in his radiant image."[75] And St. John of Damascus (8th century) wrote, "Thou hast taken me captive with longing for Thee, O Christ, and hast transformed me with Thy divine love. Burn up my sins with the fire of the Spirit, and count me worthy to take my fill of delight in Thee, that dancing with joy I may magnify both Thy Comings, O Lord Who art good."[76] (These words the Orthodox Church still sings today.)

In the 19th century St. Theophan the Recluse wrote:

> How did St. John the Theologian attain such lofty love for the Lord and become a model of love for all of us? I think that he did this in the same way that people begin to love one another. They see the beauty and goodness of a person and become attracted to them with all their heart. In like manner St. John saw the beauty of the Lord and was attracted to Him. He sensed the Lord's special love for him and likewise was inflamed with love for Him.[77]

As a final example, St. Porphyrios of Kafsokalyvia (late 20th century), says, "Christ is everything. He is our love. He is the object of our desire. This passionate longing for Christ is a love that cannot be taken away. This is where joy flows from."[78] He goes on to speak of the Song of Songs 5:8, paraphrasing it: "the bride who is looking to find Christ the Bridegroom says, 'I am deeply wounded by my love for Him. How can I forget Him? How shall I live without Him?'"[79]

In light of all the above, it is easy to see why the contemporary Orthodox theologian and historian Fr. John McGuckin can say, "the Church's task is no

73. Author unknown; in Nicolas Zernov, ed. *A Manual of Eastern Orthodox Prayers* (Crestwood, NY: St. Vladimir's Seminary Press, 1983), pp. 78-79 (my emphasis).

74. St. Basil the Great, "Long Rules," cited by Archimandrite Aimilianos in *The Church at Prayer: The Mystical Liturgy of the Heart* (Athens: Indiktos, 2005), p. 130.

75. Quoted in *Road to Emmaus*, vol. XIV, no. 3 (Summer, 2013), p. 71.

76. Canticle Nine, Second Canon for Matins for Transfiguration (*Festal Menaion*, p. 494); also used as a prayer in preparation for Holy Communion.

77. Cited in *Road to Emmaus*, vol. XV, no. 2 (Spring, 2014), p. 41.

78. *Wounded by Love,* p. 96.

79. Ibid., pp. 120-121.

less than to show the way back to a renewed sense of the Beautiful."[80] And one can also see that this is not some vague love of a philosopher's abstract sense of "Beauty," but rather a personal love of Jesus Christ that is so strong it can only be compared to that strongest of desires and loves known to humanity—the intensity of the first falling in love that captures all our attention and focuses our will on the beloved, which is imaged in Scripture and Tradition by the Bridegroom and the Bride.

Indeed, Fr. McGuckin can even say, "the beauty of Christ which shines through centuries of the Eastern Church's tradition of prayer, and art, and intellectual culture; a beauty that always renews itself however much it is degraded by outrageous failures or incapacities on the part of Christians . . . and the sense of its healing qualities is . . . the dominant motif of the entire Byzantine spiritual tradition."[81] Thus, also, Wilken is right to conclude that in traditional Christianity, "God's revelation can be seen from the perspective of its ineffable beauty as well as its truth and goodness."[82]

That many people still long for this heavenly, inexpressible beauty, and even go to extreme lengths to try to find it, is just as true today as it was in the first, or the fourth, or any century after that. And this is so in spite of telescopes and far more modern technologies. This is so, even in spite of decades of militant atheist propaganda, as is demonstrated by this brief explanation from a group of talented, healthy, happy, successful young men who joined a monastery in very difficult times for the Church in the former Soviet Union: "for each of us, a new world had suddenly opened up, incomparable in its beauty."[83]

This being the case, then surely what will be authoritative, inspiring exegesis in the best sense is what will open "to us the door of that beauty to which we are called by the Bridegroom Himself," what by its beauty, *as well as its truth and goodness*, will enflame our desire and inspire our wills, what will "pass on the joy," so that we are moved to personal transformation in Christ, by the Holy Spirit.

For this to happen, it would also seem clear that, once again, what is needed are *living witnesses* to the beauty and truth of the new, imperishable life in Christ—witnesses who speak with an authority that is both personal *and* confirmed by the Church, such as those briefly described above. Or at the least, we need those who are willing to learn from, and depend primarily and first of all upon, such witnesses. Historical criticism has had as its goal discerning

---

80. *Standing in God's Holy Fire*, p. 35.

81. Ibid., p. 150.

82. Wilken, *The Spirit of Early Christian Thought*, op. cit., p. 20.

83. Archimandrite Tikhon (Shevkunov), *Everyday Saints and Other Stories* (Moscow: Pokrov Publications, 2012), p. 3.

accurate information, the "facts" that all reasonable people will have to agree with, in order to promote tolerance. But tolerance is a poor substitute for authentic Christian love, and mere "facts" are an even poorer substitute for the briefest real glimpse of the ineffable beauty of Christ.

Much more than facts or original historical meanings, and quite the opposite of "new fictions," inspiring exegesis for today—as for every time—will not only need to be connected to our present lives and our deepest desires. It will also need to reflect the reality of spiritual laws and knowledge—to reflect a fullness of truth including, but not limited to, "facts"—and first of all to be itself inspired by at least a glimpse of divine Beauty. What is needed is exegesis that reveals more than surface reality, exegesis that opens us to the "beauty beyond all words of Thy countenance"—a real encounter with God in Christ through the Holy Spirit, so that our desire can be directed towards a life-transforming love, which leads us, by God's grace, to true worship and the experience of eternal life in Christ—to a taste even here and now of the inexpressible joy of the new Paradise. But this is only possible if one, as a minimum, believes that authentic spiritual experience and knowledge are really possible, that they are inseparable from theology, and that they both must be a foundational part of biblical exegesis.

The "Flight From Beauty" Today

> "men loved darkness rather than light, because their deeds were evil" (John 3:19).

The reality of the ineffable beauty, truth, and goodness of God revealed in Christ is reflected in the analogies which those who have "seen" for themselves use when speaking about the experiential reality of God's Presence. St. Gregory of Nyssa (4th century), for example, says that just as one could never explain what sunshine looks like to one who has never seen it,

> so it is with the true light of the spirit. Each man needs his own eyes to see its beauty. And the soul that does see it by some divine gift and inspiration, retains his ecstasy unexpressed ... *But the man who has not seen it cannot even be made to realize his loss.* For how can you represent to him the supreme Good if it totally escapes him? How can anyone make him see what is indescribable? For we have not learnt the proper words to express this beauty. Nor is there any example of what we are looking for in the created world ... Who, for example, would compare the sun with a little spark, the endless expanse of the sea with a tiny drop? And that tiny drop, that little spark, bear the same relationship to the ocean and the sun as any

beautiful thing which men admire bears to the beauty that we contemplate in that supreme Good which surpasses all things.[84]

St. Gregory continues,

> For God is not dependent on anything for His beauty; His beauty is not limited to certain times or aspects; but He is beautiful by Himself, through Himself, and in Himself. He is eternal Beauty . . . For no one could be so blind as not to realize that the God of all things is the first, supreme, and unique Goodness, Beauty, and Purity.[85]

As is evident in one strand of modern culture and art, however, there are those in our contemporary society who *are* so blind, who instead of seeking to experience and/or create beauty, seek instead to destroy it. We will briefly explore this very important dimension of modern culture by looking primarily at some of the insights of the contemporary English philosopher, Roger Scruton, who has articulated some important general considerations about beauty in contemporary art and culture which are also, perhaps surprisingly, relevant to contemporary biblical studies and our spiritual lives, which take place in this culture and are certainly deeply affected by it.

Scruton sees two main strands in the modern arts: one seeks to restore lost tradition, and to make beautiful art—to *recover* true beauty—while the other seeks to destroy, or at least to reject, tradition, and is a flight *from* beauty. This second kind of modern art believes that art's main purpose is to shock and/or disturb us. Some in the Jesus Seminar have even claimed this was the *primary* purpose of Jesus' parables! Some even push that "flight from beauty" to an extreme and want to desecrate or ruin beauty, and then what such "artists" create borders on, or even is, pornographic and/or very violent.

Scruton suggests the reason for this rejection of beauty is that "beauty makes a claim on us: it is a call to renounce our narcissism and look with reverence on the world." He goes on to say that

> beauty also points us beyond this world, to a 'kingdom of ends' in which our immortal longings [what C. S. Lewis speaks of] and our desire for perfection are finally answered. As Plato and Kant both saw, therefore, the feeling for beauty is proximate to the religious frame of mind, arising from

---

84. St. Gregory of Nyssa, *From Glory to Glory: Texts from Gregory of Nyssa's Mystical Writings* (Crestwood, NY: St. Vladimir's Seminary Press, 1979), pp. 104-105 (my emphasis).

85. Ibid., p. 111.

a humble sense of living with imperfections, while aspiring towards the highest unity with the transcendental.[86]

Thus, Scruton continues, this "desecration," which we find in much of modern "art" and also in some modern historical criticism, "is *a kind of defense against the sacred, an attempt to destroy its claims.* In the presence of sacred things our lives are judged, and *in order to escape that judgement* we destroy the thing that seems to accuse us."[87] In other words, some people in our culture choose to try to destroy whatever is sacred, instead of "coming to the light" and repenting, "because their deeds were evil" (John 3:19). In this they follow the pattern seen in the choices of Adam, Eve, and their son, Cain, rather than that to which Christ calls us.

Scruton, in making an interesting connection between beauty and love, goes on to say,

> The willful desecration of the human form, either through the pornography of sex or the pornography of death and violence, has become, for many people, a kind of compulsion. And this desecration, which spoils the experience of freedom, is also a denial of love. It is an attempt to remake the world as though love were no longer a part of it.[88]

Postmodernism, then, is "a loveless culture, which is afraid of beauty because it is disturbed by love."[89] It is afraid of loving, perhaps because it does not believe that real love is possible, largely because it does not believe that there is a God Who is a "good God Who loves mankind." No wonder that Fr. McGuckin claims, "the Church's task is no less than to show the way back to a renewed sense of the Beautiful." For as a whole, McGuckin continues, the western world "has already declined far from its former and higher standards of religious civilisation, and now urgently needs catechising about the very nature of the simplest truths—what constitutes Beauty, and where lies the reconciliation of Aesthetics and Justice."[90]

Traditionally, Scruton explains, art has attempted "to present images and narratives of our humanity as a thing to live up to"[91]—not just bare "realism"

---

86. Roger Scruton, *Beauty: A Very Short Introduction* (Oxford: Oxford University Press, 2011), pp. 145-146.

87. Ibid., p. 147 (my emphasis).

88. Ibid., p. 148.

89. Ibid.

90. McGuckin, *Standing in God's Holy Fire*, op. cit., p. 35.

91. Scruton, op. cit., p. 152.

which attempts to depict things "as they really are," meaning all too often at their worst, or most banal. While such art may depict in a superficially accurate way how some things are at a certain moment, it fails to reveal *what they are capable of becoming*—and surely that is what is more important. Surely, what is needed are things that will encourage us to strive to be better—for we can all become better—and not things that merely leave us where we already are, or depress us towards a worse state! But this assumes a judgment that some ways are better, higher than others. And that judgment is precisely what underlies a goal of wanting to help, to serve others to improve themselves and/or their lives—a goal motivated by love of others, rather than some kind of narcissistic self-promotion ("expressing your [supposedly] true self," with no consideration as to how this may affect others) that we see reflected in the modern art that "desecrates" beauty.

So, whether it is the art of biblical exegesis as practiced by interpreters like those in the Jesus Seminar, or any other kind of art, the desecrating strand of modern art is against aesthetic values, and above all does not want to be judged.[92] It is often content with making something merely exciting, "cutting edge," provocative, or even revolting—something which requires comparatively little thought, which stirs superficial emotions, and which is unconcerned with truth or spiritual realities. This, then, takes the place of making art which is truly beautiful, which makes us think about how we are living, and which stirs us to long to be better than we currently are—or which at least points us to something higher.

In the light of this present study, Scruton makes the very interesting suggestion that a key reason for this rejection of beauty and love is that "Love and affection between people is real only to the extent that it prepares the way for sacrifice."[93] In other words, real love always follows the pattern Jesus Christ shows us. Scruton can even say, "Sacrifice is the core of virtue, the origin and meaning and the true theme of high art";[94] and, "this connection between sacrifice and love is presented in the rituals and stories of religion. It is also the recurring theme of art."[95]

Sacrifice finds its highest expression in Christianity. As Metr. Meletios says, "the salvation of the world does not happen by proclamation, but only with suffering and sacrifice. For this reason, Christ not only did not avoid the Cross but also he made it his desire, his aim, his glory. . . . only the one who bears it radiates virtue, which the Cross symbolizes and inspires, illumines and sanctifies;

---

92. Ibid., p. 153.

93. Ibid., p. 160.

94. Ibid., p. 161.

95. Ibid.

only when it has something from God and the inexpressible beauty of the virtues of our first and great priest, Christ."[96]

Scruton concludes by saying that "beauty is vanishing from our world because we live as though it did not matter; and we live that way because we have lost the habit of sacrifice and are striving always to avoid it. The false art of our time, mired in kitsch and desecration, is one sign of this."[97] Historical criticism, which we could call the false biblical criticism of our time, is surely another.

C. S. Lewis illuminates another important element to consider here (mentioned only briefly above), which provides a corrective for a possible misunderstanding of Scruton's ideas concerning beauty. He speaks of

> the secret we cannot hide and cannot tell . . . because it is a desire for something that [at first] has never actually appeared in our experience. We cannot hide it because our experience is constantly suggesting it. . . . Our commonest expedient is to call it beauty and behave as if that had settled the matter. . . . But all this is a cheat. . . . The books or the music in which we thought the beauty was located will betray us if we trust to them; it was not *in* them, it only came *through* them, and what came through them was longing. These things—the beauty, the memory of our own past—are good images of what we really desire [i.e., heaven, and eternal life in Christ]; but if they are mistaken for the thing itself, they turn into dumb idols, breaking the hearts of their worshippers.[98]

Lewis then indicates another source of this tragedy of the "flight from beauty" and all that this implies in our culture: "Almost our whole education has been directed to silencing this shy, persistent, inner voice [our longing for Heaven]; almost all our modern philosophies have been devised to convince us that the good of man is to be found on this earth."[99] Because Divine Beauty, the beauty of the Lord's Person, is ultimately inexpressible, and because God does not coerce, but leaves us free and only calls gently to us, offering us the Beauty, Truth, and Goodness we long for, it is important for our ability to hear this voice to be cultivated rather than silenced if we are to be able to respond to God's call. And biblical exegesis should play an important role in this cultivation—but it cannot if it operates with the assumptions of historical criticism, or within the framework of the desecrating strand of modern art.

---

96. Lloyd-Moffett, op. cit., pp. 191-192.

97. Scruton, op. cit., p. 161.

98. Lewis, *The Weight of Glory*, op. cit., pp. 30-31 (his emphasis).

99. Ibid., p. 31.

There is good news from Scruton in spite of all of this, for he points out that rational beings "have the freedom . . . to live in another way. The art, literature, and music of our civilization remind them of this, and also point to the path that lies always before them: the path out of desecration towards the sacred and the sacrificial."[100] There is also good news from Lewis, who asserts, "Do what they [the educators and philosophers] will, then, we remain conscious of a desire which no natural happiness will satisfy."[101]

"To Regain the Delights of Paradise"

Yet there is even better news from the "good news" of traditional Christianity and its living witnesses, who reveal the way not only to hear God's call, but even to behold the inexpressible beauty of the Divine Bridegroom and to taste "the delights of Paradise," the heavenly Kingdom, even now. As one of the Orthodox hymns during Holy Week says,

> O Bridegroom, surpassing all in beauty [cf. Ps. 45], Thou hast called us to the spiritual feast of Thy bridal chamber. Strip from me the disfigurement of sin, through participation in Thy sufferings; clothe me in the glorious robe of Thy beauty, and in Thy compassion make me feast with joy at Thy Kingdom.[102]

Jesus Christ, the beloved Bridegroom of the soul, desiring to adorn us with "the glorious robe" of His beauty, provides the way to the heavenly Kingdom, the new Paradise, if we allow Him to help us truly repent. We must also be willing, at least at times, to endure suffering, to sacrifice our own wants and comforts for love of Him and other people—our neighbors.

Yet in a consumer society, and perhaps especially in our society, what this repentance and sacrifice, and the asceticism they necessarily involve, actually means is generally very misunderstood. Yannaras explains the underlying truth as follows: "Within the tradition of the Church, asceticism is *philokalia,* love for the beauty of that 'uncompleted perfection' which is personal fulfillment, the restoration of God's darkened image in man to its original beauty."[103]

---

100. Scruton, op. cit., p. 161.

101. Lewis, op. cit., p. 32.

102. Apostichon for Canticle Nine, Matins, Great and Holy Tuesday (*Lenten Triodion*, p. 528); quoted by Archimandrite Vasileios in *Hymn of Dismissal*, p. 105.

103. *Freedom of Morality*. op. cit., p. 111.

It is clear from history as a whole, and especially from our consumer society today, that one fundamental aspect of human life is desire and pleasure-seeking: anything that captures our imaginations and inspires our wills will have to tap into our desires, our passions, and our thirst for pleasure or delight. Fr. Aimilianos of Mt. Athos, who has inspired hundreds of thousands of people, even says, "we were created for pleasure. God created Adam and Eve and placed them in a garden of 'delights,' for this is what the word 'Eden' means (cf. Gen 2.15). In seeking pleasure, they were seeking what God had instructed them to seek and experience."[104] Psalm 27:4, the key quotation for this book, is sometimes translated more literally so that the one thing the psalmist desires and seeks, in addition to dwelling in the house of the Lord all his days, is "to behold the 'delights' of the Lord"—hence, a return to Paradise, the door to which has been opened, so unexpectedly, by the cross of Christ.

Thus, according to traditional Christianity, in seeking pleasure—and in seeking to become like God—Adam and Eve were following the deep desire that God had given them, what He intended for them to seek and experience. "However, they sought wrongly [apart from God], and instead of pleasure, they found themselves caught in the grip of pain." Fr. Aimilianos continues, "Beginning, therefore, from the pain into which I have fallen, my aim is to find what I was seeking, to arrive at the place of true pleasure, to regain the enjoyment of the delights of paradise,"[105] a paradise that, as Archimandrite Vasileios says, "is beyond our powers or our expectations."[106]

This is why Christianity has always been so concerned with all aspects of human life that involve our desires—perhaps especially two of the most powerful desires: the desire for food, and sexual desire. Traditional Christianity does not seek to eliminate pleasure and desire; rather, as C. S. Lewis writes,

> if we consider the unblushing promises of reward and the staggering nature of the rewards promised in the Gospels, it would seem that Our Lord finds our desires not too strong, but too weak. We are half-hearted creatures, fooling about with drink and sex and ambition when infinite joy is offered us, like an ignorant child who wants to go on making mud pies in a slum because he cannot imagine what is meant by the offer of a holiday at the sea. We are far too easily pleased.[107]

Lewis says further,

---

104. *The Way of the Spirit*, p. 19.

105. Ibid.

106. Archimandrite Vasileios, *Hymn of Entry*, p. 103.

107. Lewis, op. cit., p. 26.

If a trans-temporal, trans-finite good is our real destiny, then any other good on which our desire fixes must be in some degree fallacious, must bear at best only a symbolical relation to what will truly satisfy."[108]

The clear goal of traditional Christianity is in fact to deepen and transform our desires through reorienting them towards Christ, in order to help us fulfill our *deepest* desires, which lead to the greatest pleasure—or the deepest joy—and give us a life full of meaning, enabling us to fulfill the primary vocation of every human being—to be, or to become, our authentically "true selves," something possible only in Christ, in Whose image we are made. As Archimandrite Vasileios explains, "man's vocation in life is one. It is love: an exodus, a departure from the narrow prison of self-love for the promised land, the land of the Other, of 'my brother, my God.'"[109] For it is only in a loving communion with God that a person can become "capable of loving all humankind and all things."[110]

And that vocation is linked with "a characteristic and fundamental truth about spiritual life that St. Symeon the New Theologian [early 11th century] expresses when he tells us: 'God requires nothing from us men save only that we do not sin; and this *is not a work of law but an inviolable safeguard of the image* [of God in man] and of the dignity we have from on high.'"[111] As confirmed by the experience of certainly hundreds of thousands—if not millions—of Christians through the ages, the only way to turn from sin, to repent, to seek to do the Father's will, is the path Christ showed: voluntary self-sacrificial love, the way of "seeking not His own" but only always doing the Father's will. As the Gospel accounts demonstrate, this has always included "retraining" of our wills, overcoming self-centered egotism, especially through ascetic efforts, such as prayer and fasting, as well as almsgiving, and other means of serving our neighbor and overcoming our own negative passions. And as Archimandrite Vasileios confirms, "in the end, in the midst of much labor, of ascesis and vigil . . . a shoot comes to birth, a shoot of new and unfading life which gives a fruit a hundredfold. And then you bless all pains and sufferings. You sacrifice all things, because the joy which has appeared is a gleam of the age to come, which gives light and life to both the present and the future."[112]

Actions or thoughts are considered sinful, therefore, when in some way they are going against authentic love, against our "true selves" as we were created

---

108. Ibid., p. 29.

109. *Hymn of Entry*, p. 109.

110. Ibid., p. 123.

111. Ibid., p. 101 (my emphasis).

112. Ibid., p. 123.

to be. They usually involve using, or abusing, others as if they were objects, and not persons made in the image of God. Or they can even result in self-destructive behavior, using oneself as an object—or making what should be only secondary into the ultimate aim of our life and desires, which would be a kind of idol worship. For when we choose a sinful path, we are turning away from Christ, Who is Love Incarnate, from God the Father Whose will is ultimately only that "all be saved and come to the knowledge of the truth" (1 Tim. 2:4). That is largely why He is the good God Who loves mankind.

Sinful deeds and thoughts also go against the spiritual laws underlying reality. As Archimandrite Vasileios writes,

> There is a power in the depths of man's earth. There is a power in the seed, in the word of God. . . . there is a power unimaginably greater than our power, our will and our expectation: a power which works spontaneously within us in a beneficial and amazing way *when we respect its laws.* This is the spring of water welling up to eternal life. A preparation is made, an action on man's part, an assent to the divine will. Following this, the Spirit of God undertakes to do what is beyond nature, to overcome the order of nature. For only in the area beyond the tyranny of natural laws and in the movement which is beyond our own physical or spiritual capacities can man rest and be saved in his full extent, and assuage his insatiable and unbounded yearning for life.[113]

We usually have no trouble being aware of the basic things we desire—various pleasures like nice food, a warm house, the approval of others, etc. However, our modern culture teaches us that people primarily, or even only, want and need the freedom to *indulge* in all that we want on this basic level, to satisfy as fully as possible all of these kinds of desires—and that traditional Christianity is wrong, or even bad, because it restricts that freedom. Yet, as one young man confessed about the time before his conversion to Christ, "Up until that time, I had felt bitterness, a lamentation inside me that I tried to cover up with wild, crazy rock music, by living it up, with wild antics, dancing, sex, and with any sensual pleasure I could find." But when at a very low point in his life he called out to Christ and said, "Come close to me, Lord," he explains that "Christ heard me and came instantly. I felt His presence near me, a living reality! From then on my life changed. It became enlightened. The darkness of my soul dissolved."[114]

---

113. Ibid., pp. 106-107 (my emphasis).

114. Lloyd-Moffett, op. cit., p. 200.

And he came to realize that "a man's deliverance from his passions is not like being skinned alive but like being set free."[115]

True freedom is described by Archimandrite Aimilianos as "the first, essential gift of God," as "*liberation from* passionate impulses and from every deception. It is, in other words, our emancipation from the unconscious, which to a certain extent has now been enlightened by divine grace."[116] And Metr. Antony explains further why our culture's teaching about what it means to be "free"—i.e., free to indulge every passionate impulse—is such a deception:

> we are never free; we are never free not because God enslaves us, not because He hunts us down. We are never free because He is ultimately, in the end, the only supreme longing of our whole being, because He is the fullness of life, the glory of life, the exultation of life for which we long and which we try to glean right and left [from other sources, by indulging in passionate impulses, etc.] in vain.[117]

There is no short-cut or substitute for acquiring true freedom—acquiring the imperishable life of Jesus—which only the Holy Spirit can bring through struggle, sacrifice, and repentance. That these can be avoided is only claimed by the "serpent" and those of his children desiring to have power over others, to desecrate in order to make "a denial of love," and "a kind of defense against the sacred, an attempt to destroy its claims." And they do this because, as quoted above, "In the presence of sacred things our lives are judged, and in order to escape that judgement we destroy the thing that seems to accuse us."[118]

Tragically, so often we do such things that deny love and avoid judgment because, having listened to the serpents of this world, we do not understand the way of Jesus Christ, and *His* judgment. We imagine only that "God is the God of judgment and righteousness," and that, as Archimandrite Aimilianos says, "Although God does not intrude upon our freedom, He will nevertheless call us to account for all that we have done in our lives. . . . We need, then, to add the truth of justice to the truth of what a moment ago we called patience and forbearance." But when people want to flee repentance because they imagine God's judgment to be merely an accusation that will destroy them, they do not understand what Archimandrite Aimilianos further describes so beautifully:

---

115. Ibid., p. 212.

116. *The Way of the Spirit*, p. 31 (my emphasis).

117. From a sermon on St. Mary of Egypt; http://www.pravoslavie.ru/english/60981.htm; accessed 3-30-14.

118. Scruton, op. cit., p. 147.

as the Psalmist says, *Thy throne, O God, is made up of justice. Justice is the preparation and the basis of Your throne* (Ps. 88:15; 96:2). But to this the Psalmist immediately adds: *Mercy and truth shall go before His face.* In His desire to save the world, God holds back His judgment, and gives us instead His *mercy and truth,* His serenity, love, and gentleness of heart. . . . *His mercy will hunt us down.* Wherever we may be, whatever we may be doing: sitting, sleeping, keeping vigil, sinning, thinking, talking, God sends out His mercy at that very moment.

And when will the judgment come? When the hunt is over. When God's mercy and grace have pursued us and taken us captive, softened our hearts, moved us deeply, and made us think of nothing but Him. We catch a glimpse of this in the iconography of the Second Coming of the Lord. Have you ever noticed that, within the very center of these images there is an empty throne? This is the throne of Christ, but Christ isn't there. The throne is either empty, or has the Gospel on it. That is a symbol of God's love. How? Christ is absent from the throne at which we will be judged, as if He's telling us: "I'm not finished with you. I'm not ready to sit on my throne, pick up my gavel, and pass sentence. I'm still roaming the streets, your houses, your hearts, hoping to find you, so that you are not lost forever." The *books*, as Daniel says, *are opened,* but God does not wish to close them until our names are inscribed therein, *for if anyone's name is not found written in the book of life, he will be thrown into the lake of fire* (Rev. 20:15).[119]

Tragically, too many people do not hear this voice of Jesus as the voice of Love Incarnate calling us to repent, to sacrifice, to have sacrificial love *in order to* have the greatest joy, to have our deepest desires fulfilled, to find our true selves, to fulfill our human vocation, and to experience eternal life—to have a taste of the new Paradise—both in this life and in the next.

In *Everyday Saints*, a book which sold over a million copies and several million electronic copies in less than a year, and was voted by far the most popular book in Russia in 2012, a book that has thus inspired millions, Archimandrite Tikhon concludes, in a sense, by describing his book's content in the following way:

One ascetic monk once told me that every Orthodox Christian could relate his own Gospels, his own Glad Tidings about coming to know God. Of course, no one would compare such testimony to the books of the Apostles, who saw the Son of God alive on earth with their own eyes. Yet

---

119. *The Way of the Spirit*, op. cit., pp. 327-328.

still, though we are frail and feeble sinners, we remain His disciples, and
**there is truly nothing more beautiful in this world than the contempla-
tion of the remarkable unfolding of the Providence of our Savior in His
divine will for the salvation of this world.**[120]

That Archimandrite Tikhon succeeded in describing this most beautiful reality of "the Providence of our Savior in His divine will for the salvation of this
world" is no doubt the cause of his book's great popularity, and shows that the
thirst for such beauty, and for an authentic life in Christ as understood in traditional Christianity, is far from disappearing.

* * * * *

In concluding this book, we can return to the title: the best known description
of what the soul truly longs for is found in Psalm 42: "As a hart longs for flowing streams, so longs my soul for thee, O God. My soul thirsts for God, for the
living God." Then, the psalmist—on behalf of humanity, we could say—asks,
"*When shall I come and behold the face of God?*" In answer, the witnesses of
Scripture have spoken and are pointing. The witnesses in the Church—the
Saints both canonized and not—are pointing with their words and their lives,
in which those who wish to can catch a glimpse of the "likeness of Christ," the
longed for "face of God."

Many Saints both past and present, as well as many who are still struggling
to become holy, have experienced in different degrees this reality—figured
by Psyche. And surely this is what today's interpreters of Scripture, whether
preachers or teachers, need themselves, and need to encourage in their hearers
and readers. The Prophet David, as single-minded as Psyche, shows us the way:

> "*One* thing I have desired of the Lord, that will I seek: that I may dwell in
> the house of the Lord all the days of my life, to behold the beauty of the
> Lord and to inquire in His temple" (Ps. 27:4).

Beholding the Lord's beauty in some way, in some degree, must be first. This
must come *before* our "inquiry," if the inquiry is to be truly inspiring and
fruitful.

Following all these witnesses, God helping us, our biblical interpretation
should attempt ultimately to give at least a glimpse of "the beauty beyond all
words" of the face of Christ, so that we, along with our hearers and readers,

---

120. Archimandrite Tikhon (Shevkunov), op. cit., p. 490 (my emphasis).

may also experience the "unending delight of those who behold . . . His countenance," as well as a taste in *this* life of the Paradise of "delights"—for "Christ, Our God," is truly "the very desire and joy beyond declaring of those that love Him."[121]

Yet only when we ourselves are willing to embrace sacrificial love for God and for others, to live ascetically, to see our sins, to repent, and therefore to be unafraid of coming to the Light and living in accordance with His life-giving precepts, can we "behold" at least a little of this beauty of the Lord—that He truly is the good God Who loves mankind and does everything for our benefit. And only when we listen to those who know this beauty best will our inquiry into His temple of words, the Holy Scriptures, fulfill our needs and bear the abundant, life-giving fruit that the Bible has always been intended to bear. As the Church prays,

> "Make straight the hearts of Thy servants towards Thine unapproachable Light, O thrice-resplendent Lord, and bestow the effulgence of Thy glory upon our souls, that we may behold Thine ineffable beauty" (Hymn from the *Parakletiki*).[122]

---

121. From a post-Communion prayer; quoted by Zernov, op. cit., p. 79.

122. Quoted in *Road to Emmaus*, vol. XIV, no. 3 (Summer, 2013), p. 71.

Glossary

apophatic and kataphatic—since God is beyond human understanding, even beyond being, all human language about God must be inexact. An apophatic theology thus does not try to describe God in words, but only to say what He is not. This does not mean we cannot know God; rather that He can best be known through mystical union with Him in prayer. Kataphatic theology does make positive, descriptive statements about God which are based on what God has revealed in Scripture and Tradition, which is the only basis for positive statements. Both approaches are important.

archimandrite—an honorary title given to a priest monk in the Orthodox Church.

biblical criticism—see **Techniques of biblical criticism**.

Church Fathers—theologians recognized by the Church as especially trust-worthy because of the general orthodoxy of their writings, and their personal holiness. They were usually highly educated bishops who wrote to defend the faith and to edify the faithful, though some like St. Maximus the Confessor were not bishops, or in his case, even ordained. Although in the Western churches this term is commonly only used for such people living before c. 750, so that St. John of Damascus (d. 749) is the last Church Father, the Orthodox consider that there can be, and have been, Church Fathers in every age.

deification/*theosis*—"participation in the divine nature" (2 Pet. 1:4); becoming through grace, what Christ is by nature. What St. Paul (2 Cor. 3:18) and St. John (1 John 3:2) refer to as likeness to Christ—"being transformed into the same image [or likeness]," as St. Paul says. This is not merely behaving in a holy way, or even sanctification as it is often understood by Christians in non-Orthodox traditions, but being united in both body and soul to God in Christ through the Holy Spirit; living with the *zōē*, divine life which it was the purpose of Christ to give us (John 20:31). It should not be imagined that people cease to be human in deification, but rather that in Christ, humanity is perfected and fulfilled, and that when *theosis*, or deification, is attained, the person is most perfectly human. Indeed, we only know what a fully human person is by looking at Christ.

divine economy/the salvation economy—God's providence for creation, especially His entire plan for the salvation of the human race and the restoration of creation.

divine energies and essence—While God is unknowable in His essence (you would have to be God in order to know Him in that way), we can know Him through our communion with His energies, which are not created, not simply a gift, "but a direct manifestation of the living God Himself, a personal encounter between creature and Creator . . . When we say that the saints have been transformed or 'deified' by the grace of God, what we mean is that they have a direct experience of God Himself" (Timothy Ware, *The Orthodox Church*, 4th ed. [Penguin Books, 1993], p. 68).

dogma/doctrine—truths of the Faith clarified in order to safeguard the fullness of the experience of the new life in Christ. These were generally clarified by the Church Fathers and confirmed in Ecumenical Councils.

Ecumenical Councils—assemblies primarily of bishops representing Christians from the whole Christian world ("ecumenical" is from the Greek word *oikumenē* meaning the whole world) who gathered to defend traditional beliefs crucial for salvation in the face of confusion over how to understand and speak of them, caused by various heretics. Their work assures the continuity of the unity/oneness of mind of the Church, through faithfulness to the Apostolic teaching and the whole ongoing life of the Church. In order for these councils to be truly "Ecumenical" they must afterwards be accepted by the people of God as a whole. The Eastern Orthodox recognize 7 Ecumenical Councils.

exegesis—interpretation.

filioque—the addition to the Nicene Creed of the words "and the Son" (in Latin) to the statement "And in the Holy Spirit, the giver of life, Who proceeds from the Father." This addition is strongly objected to by the Orthodox for theological reasons (it reflects a demoting of the Holy Spirit as a less than equal member of the Holy Trinity, with serious repercussions for spiritual life), as well as from the perspective of Church governance: the Creed was accepted by the whole Church at Ecumenical Councils, and no individual, including the pope of Rome, has the authority to change it.

grace—not simply an abstract unmerited favor of God, but the actual uncreated energies of God. There is no division between created and uncreated grace, as in Latin scholasticism, and no opposition between grace and nature, as in the Western Churches.

heart—the spiritual center of a person, not simply the physical organ. The "*nous*" is often called the "eye of the heart." See also *nous*/**noetic**.

hermeneutics—the study of interpretation; in the context of this book, how biblical texts are interpreted, both theoretically and actually, through history. It also involves determining methods, principles, and guidelines that will help in correctly interpreting especially sacred texts. Although the term arose in the 17th century, interpreters from ancient times right through till today have been aware of, and taken advantage of, various methods and principles of interpretation. For example, both Jesus and St. Paul clearly use rabbinic rules of interpretation.

historical-critical method, or sometimes simply **historical criticism**—the use of the standard techniques of biblical criticism, as well as more recent and more speculative ones, within the context of a secular materialist world-view that is usually extreme in its historical skepticism (little or nothing original was likely to have survived from the oral traditions about Jesus), and agnostic at best (interpret as if there is no God). The newer techniques are primarily **form criticism** (attempting to reconstruct pre-literary forms of the current text) and **redaction criticism** (attempting to discern how the special purposes of the final editors, or redactors, influenced the original traditional material—though the assumption in the 20th century has often been that the redactors have significantly changed the original material in a distorting way). Today, quite a few scholars question many of the assumptions of this method, asking, e.g., is the meaning of an event only what is objectively verifiable? How can it help Christians understand the Bible if one takes as a fundamental, initial working assumption that God is not active in history?

"historical Jesus"—this usually refers to the attempt to reconstruct what the historical person Jesus of Nazareth said and did completely apart from any churchly understanding, though it could be used simply to refer to Jesus during His life and ministry in the Holy Land.

"incarnational allegory"—allegory, or allegorical interpretation, that reflects the Incarnation by valuing both the literal sense and a deeper meaning communicated through that sense, similar to Christ's being both man and God. This term was coined by Graham Hough, a literary critic.

Latin Church/Roman Church—the Church in the West in the earlier centuries, before the Middle Ages, especially before the mid- to late Middles Ages, when that Church was still in communion with and sharing the heritage of the Greek Orthodox Churches and still part of the "one, holy, catholic [meaning simply universal], and apostolic Church" that the Nicene Creed speaks of. The new doctrines and spirituality that developed in Western Christianity, especially in the Middle Ages, are properly what would make this Church become the "Roman Catholic" Church that continues to this day.

logion—a short saying found in Scripture.

metropolitan—the title given to a senior bishop who usually is in charge of a large diocese (or even an entire country, in some cases). He may, or may not, have bishops under him.

nous/**noetic**—a person's highest faculty, through which, if it is purified, he or she can truly know God—through "direct apprehension," or "spiritual perception." This is a kind of knowledge that is experiential, not only "mental" based on abstractions developed by the reasoning mind. Through the *nous* one can also know about spiritual realities, or the inner essences, or *logoi*, of things, thus having an understanding of reality that fully takes into account the spiritual dimension. It is the innermost aspect of the **heart**, sometimes called the "eye of the heart," and sometimes it is translated "spiritual intellect," or even just "intellect," though it must be distinguished from the reasoning mind.

passions, or negative passions—impulses that dominate the soul, such as anger. Sometimes this is used only to refer to negative passions such as lust or anger. However, some Fathers and Saints, often writing more practically from the perspective of the ascetic struggle, speak of all the passions simply as negative. Others, often writing more theoretically and comprehensively, see them as essentially good, since they are created by God, but that they are often misused—hence they should be educated and transfigured, rather than eliminated or minimized. When properly used according to nature, or in accordance with how they were created to be used, they become the virtues such as love, love of beauty, dispassion—a state of spiritual freedom in which one is free from negative passions such as anger against other people (rather than against sin), or envy, and one has a completely unselfish love for all. See, e.g., the glossary in the *Philokalia* for more details.

repentance—not simply feeling sorry for wrongs done, or good actions not done, but a true change of mind (*metanoia* in Greek) that brings one to focus one's whole life towards God.

"rule of faith"—the truths, or essential beliefs, that the Church confesses and that Christians should believe in order to grow in likeness to Christ and experience the new divine life He came to offer. See also **dogma/doctrine**.

Saints—while there are many righteous Christians, the Saints are those who have an especially high level of holiness. Usually the canonized Saints have become widely known through their public role in life (royalty, hierarchs, abbots or spiritual fathers to many, etc.). This often, but not necessarily, includes working numerous miracles while they were alive and/or after their passing into the next life. They are officially named as Saints by the Church in a formal process known as glorification or canonization because of their widely recognized exemplary sanctity (this process is not nearly so clear-cut as in the Roman Catholic Church, but depends primarily on popular-level recognition). It is understood that there are also many Saints who are never formally canonized.

Septuagint (abbreviated as LXX)—the early Greek translation of the Hebrew Bible often quoted by New Testament authors, and considered the "official" version of the Church from the earliest times. It was not until the 5th century, with St. Jerome, that the Roman Church began to use largely the Hebrew version of the Christians' Old Testament instead of the Septuagint (St. Augustine, among others, was, however, very opposed to this, in part because he rightly feared it would create a division with the Greek-speaking Churches). Protestants have by and large continued this Roman practice.

sin—literally "missing the mark," failing to be fully who one is created to be; failure to achieve the purpose for which one is created. This broad sense is important to keep in mind, as well as the narrower sense that refers to specific sins, or vices. The vices are harmful because they either prevent one from being/becoming one's true self, fulfilling one's purpose, or they reflect the fact that one is "missing the mark."

skopos—overarching purpose or goal of a text, especially the Bible, to which all the parts are related. More literally a target, a mark, on which to fix the eye so that one can hit the target, or achieve one's goal.

salvation—this involves real ontological transformation, a real becoming holy, not "imputed righteousness"—merely having our sins being covered by the blood of Christ, etc.

techniques of biblical criticism—various scholarly methods used to better understand/interpret Scripture. The ones listed below were used in a basic form by various Fathers and ancient interpreters. These techniques/methodologies include, simply put, **textual criticism**, attempting to determine as accurate a text as possible from varying manuscripts (Origen and his *Hexapla* would be an early example); **philological criticism**, involving knowledge of and study of biblical languages, including their vocabulary and grammar (St. Basil the Great spends 13 chapters on prepositions in his work *On the Holy Spirit*); **literary criticism**—study of stylistic features, genres, etc. (Origen discusses stylistic differences between the Epistle to the Hebrews and the other Pauline epistles—he concludes the content of Hebrews is Paul's but written up by someone else); and **historical criticism**—taking the original historical setting, the culture, etc., into account (for example, St. John Chrysostom explaining about the "governor" of the feast at the wedding at Cana in John 2). The Church Fathers did not have nearly as much information of this type as we do today, nor was it deemed as important as it generally is today; but what information they did have, they used when appropriate.

theosis—see **Deification/*theosis***.

Tradition—in this book, when capitalized, the common heritage of East and West from the early centuries of Church history that the Orthodox Church has maintained overall, but a number of aspects of which were not continued in the later Latin (Roman Catholic) and Protestant Churches. When not capitalized, **tradition** refers usually to the common ethical tradition and other basic elements (belief in the divinity of Christ, the virgin birth, etc.) that have been kept by all traditional Christians, even if these may be understood in different ways. Within Orthodoxy, **Tradition** indicates those aspects of the Faith that can never be changed, such as the Nicene Creed, while **traditions**, such as the style of icons or music, can vary from place to place and time to time (though still remaining within certain limits).

uncreated light—the glory of the Lord as visible, uncreated light. There are many examples of Saints and others experiencing this. Perhaps the most famous account, apart from that of Sts. Stephen (Acts 7:55) and Paul in the Book of Acts (Acts 9:5; 22:6; 26:13), is that of St. Seraphim of Sarov with Nicholas Motovilov (a layman who was his spiritual child) in Russia around 1830.

Key Principles for a Patristic/ Orthodox Approach to the Interpretation of Scripture

THIS approach always presupposes that God is real and has become incarnate in Jesus Christ, revealing Himself to us in the Person of Christ most fully, as well as in the Scriptures, and in various other ways in the Church. These facts also imply that Christ is the center of the Bible on all levels. He is the key to understanding the Old Testament—at least all of it that is directly relevant for Christians—as well as the New.

1. You have to love Christ—which implies real knowledge of Him and communion with Him in the Holy Spirit, which, of course, includes prayer.

2. Christ Himself has to open our understanding for us to properly understand the *skopos* and the rule of faith, that is, to understand the most important things Scripture conveys. Hence, *the reader* has to be inspired to fully, properly understand the inspired text (Luke 24:45—"Then opened He their understanding, that they might understand the Scriptures"). As Archimandrite Justin Popovich says, "The bible is not a book, but life; because its words are 'spirit and life' (taken from John 6:63, where Christ says the 'words I have spoken to you are spirit and life'). Therefore, its words can be comprehended if we study them with the spirit of its spirit and life of its life."[1]

Or as Origen (3rd century) says of St. John's Gospel, "this work has been committed to the earthly treasure-house of speech, of writing which any

---

1. "How to Read the Bible," p. 2. This article is available many places online.

passer-by can read." But he then adds, one must "have the mind of Christ" to fully, correctly understand it.[2]

This also means that God can communicate directly through Scripture to those who are properly prepared, inspiring them in a way similar to the way He inspired the original authors—though they will not, of course, have the same authority (which comes from the Church's seal on the canon).

3. Because of the above, as is emphasized by all Saints in all times and places who say anything about interpreting Scripture, one's ability to interpret depends upon one's spiritual state (see, for example, Matt. 12:35). One will only be able to fully and correctly interpret the most important elements if one's spiritual state is good, or at least if one is open to repentance.

Related to this is the truth, also universally emphasized, that one must live the Gospel, the teachings of Scripture, in order to fully, properly understand it (especially the commandments and the general way of life that Christ revealed). Archimandrite St. Justin Popovich rightly calls this the fundamental rule, or principle, of Orthodox exegesis.

4. Because Scripture is inspired, it is one harmonious whole, a unity, even though it has many authors and was written in different times and within different cultures (we see this in the way the authors of the New Testament and the Fathers quote from it as a whole, as did Jewish interpreters before them).

5. Words and thoughts have a proper order, a proper harmony; therefore, one must interpret having the *skopos* in mind, that is, the goal or ultimate purpose which reflects that proper harmony and order, and which includes an overarching understanding according to the rule of faith—especially, of course, the key of Christ Himself. St. Ephrem the Syrian (4th century) describes this "rule" as "the keys of doctrine which unlock all of Scripture's books."[3]

St. Irenaeus (late 2nd century) is the one generally acknowledged to have first spoken of the "rule of truth," or "rule of faith," and he gives this classic example of why it is essential: you can take all the pieces of a beautiful mosaic depicting a king, and then rearrange them to be a "poorly executed" mosaic of a dog. All the pieces are identical, but the result is far different, depending on how the same pieces are arranged! Thus, it is not enough to have the right "pieces," because the pieces must be arranged according to the *proper intent*—or "rule." If they are arranged differently, one will not know what was originally

---

2. ANF, vol. X, p. 300.

3. Hymns on Paradise, Hymn VI (Sebastian Brock, trans. [Crestwood, NY: St. Vladimir's Semimary Press, 1990], p. 108).

intended, or be able to understand it. In the case of Scripture, one must interpret the "pieces" correctly, according to the overarching intent of its authors, in
order to have a proper understanding *and* the spiritual benefits that flow from
this.[4]

Another dimension of the *skopos*, we could say, is that the ultimate purpose
of interpreting Scripture must be the same as the ultimate purpose of life, as
understood within traditional Christianity—deification, or *theosis*: becoming in grace and by grace like God through a real communion with Christ in
the Holy Spirit, and in this way to have love for all. This is not to cease being
human, but to be *fully human*. This what is meant by entering the Kingdom of
Heaven, which is not of words, but of power. So the ultimate goal of biblical
interpretation has to be soteriological.

6. Only within the community of the true Faith, with the Church and her
Tradition, can Scripture be fully and correctly interpreted. This includes all
aspects of the life of the Church, including writings and Lives of Saints, and
involves a patristic consensus.

7. Scripture is a witness to the truth, not explicitly containing everything that
is important for the Church. This means, for example. that we do not eliminate
making the sign of the cross because it is not explicitly mentioned in Scripture
(as St. Paul says in 2 Thess. 2:15—"stand fast and hold the traditions which ye
have been taught, whether by word, or our epistle). Many things, such as having youth ministers, or monasteries, are not mentioned in Scripture, but are
natural extensions of Scriptural principles in certain situations.

It is very clear that it is important to understand the kind of writing Holy
Scripture was intended to be. For instance, it was never meant to be a detailed
explanation of everything those in the Church do. Thus, you will misinterpret
it if you treat it as if it were supposed to do this.

8. The primary emphasis must be on interpreting the Bible as we have it—the
canon is critically important. The main focus should not be on trying to find
original pieces behind the books as we have them, and then making a sort of
new canon; or on excluding certain books or passages because some scholars think they are written by someone other than who they are traditionally
attributed to. If the Church has accepted them as canonical, then they are, and
we must interpret them as we have them as our primary focus.

---

4. *Against Heresies*, Book I, Chapter 8; ANF, vol. I, p. 326.

9. As interpreters, we should follow the model of God's condescension, as St. John Chrysostom describes it in his sermon on the Magi: that God reaches out to people where they are, using what will help them, like God at first used a star to attract the Magi, but then later, used angels. In other words, use whatever will be helpful, always with discernment.

10. Interpreters should strive to have a similar attitude to that of St. Basil towards difficult texts when he says, for example, "This is my second attempt to attack the text. If anyone has a better interpretation to give, and can consistently with true religion amend what I say, let him speak and let him amend, and the Lord will reward him for me" (NPNF 2, vol. VIII, p. 119). In this quotation one can see that "true religion," or the rule of faith, is the context within which all interpretations of Scripture must be made. One can also see the recognition that some passages are very difficult to interpret, and that even the Church Fathers were not always certain about how to interpret every passage. St. Gregory of Nyssa says, for instance, "We shall leave what we say conjecturally and by supposition on the thought at hand to the judgment of our readers. Their critical intelligence must decide whether it should be rejected or accepted" (The Life of Moses, #173; p. 98).

11. St. Gregory's words also indicate that reason, and secondary types of knowledge/information, such as historical information, literary study of genres, archaeological studies, etc., all have an important place in interpreting Scripture. Generally speaking, this kind of knowledge is essential and most valuable as long as we realize that it is secondary in the sense that its function is to illuminate, and not to conclusively determine, anything to do with the rule of faith, or the interpretive context provided by "true religion," apart from the Church and other principles above.

Finally, we could say that Scripture is not primarily simply an object to look at, but should be used like glasses correcting our poor vision. Because we are fallen, sinful, far from God, we do not have 20/20 vision—we do not see reality clearly as it really is, so we need help. We need Scripture to give us a basic interpretive framework for understanding reality—and for knowing how to enter into authentic life. For example, from Scripture we learn that humanity has fallen—we are not living a natural life any more; and that in Christ we can once again live naturally—according to our true nature, and be godlike by grace, transcending death.

(This is the opposite understanding of most people in our culture since the time of the Enlightenment, which promoted the belief that people see reality clearly without any special spiritual purification or help, and that therefore one's pre-understanding, one's beliefs, get in the way, distorting one's vision. It is true that if you have good vision, glasses will distort it, but if you have bad vision, of course, they correct it.)

Furthermore, Scripture's perfection includes the difficulties involved in interpreting it. The difficulties are a positive and expected reality, part of the ascetic economy of the fallen world, designed to benefit us, helping us draw closer to God. In addition, the fact that there are difficulties compels us to look to the Church and her Saints for help in understanding.

An Orthodox/patristic hermeneutic approaches Scripture as if it were a key. The purpose of a key is to open a lock. One could do a history of the origin of the key, the key shapes, who has owned the key, etc., but the "key" thing is practical: does it open the lock and allow us to enter into this new life in Christ? Thus, the ultimate check on the validity of our interpretations of Scripture, and our interpretations of the Fathers (and their interpretations of Scripture), is this: do they work? Do they help to accomplish this ultimate goal of our sanctification? Do they at least in some way help us draw closer to Christ? If they do not, then something is wrong with them.

There are, of course, other checks as well, such as being in harmony with a patristic consensus, conforming to Scripture as a whole, with the rule of faith, as well as, at times, with other kinds of knowledge as far as we understand them (but because there is so much we do not understand about our physical world, we cannot rely too heavily on this kind of knowledge).

APPENDIX II

HERMENEUTICAL RULES FOR INTERPRETING THE FATHERS

Based on
Patristic Hermeneutics: 4th — 14th Century
by Christos Arabatzis[1]

1. Everything must be considered from a soteriological perspective, with the understanding that the Fathers are trying to express realities—not merely ideas, concepts, or speculative academic questions, not merely theoretical knowledge. Rather, they especially emphasize a common experience in and through the Holy Spirit (pp. 60, 70, 72). The "common illumination" of the Fathers "is confirmed in the identity of their lived experience," and the texts they wrote are "integrated within this broader spirituality" (p. 152). In this understanding, the "personal experience of grace" has a "specific cognitive role." It "agrees, follows and certifies the preceding experience of the Church" (p. 110).

2. Therefore, the Fathers "do not contradict themselves, nor do they oppose one another, because of the common source of their illumination" (pp. 14-15), "their common experience" (p. 81). They represent a unified Tradition (p. 132).

3. What is crucial is the underlying meaning, the common mindset, the realities, the experiences, that they are trying to speak or write about, and "**the safeguarding of that which they defend, that is, the reality of salvation in Christ**" (p. 38). Uniformity on specific terms, mere verbal agreement, is not crucial, for the same words can mean different things in different contexts (p. 37). (Heretics tend to insist on literal, verbal identity.)

---

1. Trans. and ed., Protopresbyter George D. Dragas (Columbia, MO: Newrome Press, 2013).

4. One must seek a patristic *consensus*, rather than focusing too much on one Father (or a few; p. 22).

This consensus is a result of sanctification; it's more than rational agreement on a human level (p. 81).

5. When dealing with wrong doctrine, the Fathers "have recourse to the biblical basis of Patristic theology," for "all the dogmas of the Church that have been formulated by the Fathers are based on Scriptural texts," even if these dogmas are not expressed with identical wording (p. 151).

6. One must consider all of a Father's works, and not "cherry-pick" isolated passages—just as with Holy Scripture (p. 13).

7. Any passage that's ambiguous should be interpreted in a way that's consistent with later texts which are clearer, or have even been corrected by the Fathers (p. 13).

8. Differences of terminology or expression were usually dealt with by "rigorous analysis of the terminology" (p. 22). In addition, for each text, one must consider the broader historical and theological context of the work, the reason why it was written—whether the Father is trying to heal, or to correct—and the specific challenges the Father was facing (p. 144). Fathers contemporary with the author, and later approved Fathers, "are the most credible witnesses for understanding" what a particular Saint meant in a passage that is in question (p. 89). In particular, one must consider if the Father is referring to the Incarnation and the salvation economy, or the Eternal Trinity. One must also bear in mind that how to speak about certain realities becomes clear gradually over time within the life of the Church. One must also consider the type of writing: is it polemical, dogmatic, etc. (p. 144).

9. One must consider if the manuscript is accurate, or if it is corrupt (p. 148).

10. If using a translation, one must be very careful not to ascribe too much weight to particular terms, unless these have been carefully checked with the original by someone who is very knowledgable, e.g., about the language of the time, and the ways the terms were used at the time of the writing.

11. In the exceptional cases when a passage actually does express a different theology from the patristic consensus, as Innocent of Maronia (6th century) says, "we neither condemn, nor do we receive them as the others, because we find even in the Acts of the holy Apostles, that the blessed Paul circumcised Timothy by way of economy (condescension), but the same one wrote plainly

to the Galatians: 'that if you become circumcised, Christ will be of no benefit to you' (Gal. 5:2)." Then he gives other similar examples, concluding with Acts 15:28-29, and saying, "From that time onwards what was written by common consensus and was confirmed by the Holy Spirit was accepted by us as ecclesiastical law; however, what was done by way of economy by each of them privately [separately] is not accepted, or hated, or condemned" (p. 36, n. 47). Anastasius II of Antioch, the Sinaite (7th century), further explains concerning any statements a Father has made that are incompatible with the faith, that they are due either to a corruption of the manuscript, or to the fact that they were "expressed 'exceptionally and innocently,' or 'were understood by way of honor'" (p. 50).

Arabatzis summarizes St. Photius the Great (9th century) saying, "it is possible that Fathers can be found who, by reason of their humanity, made mistakes, without however, having their sanctity and honor being reduced within the Church" (p. 89).

Related to this, the validity of a text is not guaranteed by the personal holiness of the author, even if he is a miracle-worker (though it would be rare that such a person would be in error; p. 44, referring to Leontius of Jerusalem); and something that is said once, or rarely, that contradicts other statements is not valid (p. 57).

12. For these and other reasons, Holy Scripture and truths approved by Councils of the Church (p. 25), especially Ecumenical Councils, carry more weight and even "override" the statements of any individual Fathers in their works (pp. 27, 155). When there is a question, the Church in Council, following the Book of Acts (ch. 15), decides what the patristic consensus is (p. 99; also p. 134, quoting St. Gregory Palamas [14th century]). "Generally, it is the church and the Ecumenical Councils that define matters relating to the faith, and it is to this rule that the doctrines of the Fathers are aligned" (paraphrasing Nilus Cabasilas [14th century], p. 147).

For any particular topic, one should consider what the majority of Fathers say as valid; and if a Father says something different, this text should be rejected "without affecting the sanctity of the author, since what is rare cannot constitute a law for the Church, nor can guide it correctly" (p. 84). "The safe criterion of Orthodoxy is the majority" (p. 91, quoting St. Photius; see also pp. 103, 125).

In any case, the Fathers can only properly be understood as faithful members of the Church, whose primary concern is soteriological, not personal power, fame, or any individualistic goal (e.g., pp. 36, 56-57). As St. Maximus the Confessor [7th century] says, they teach "out of love for humanity," inspired by the Holy Spirit (p. 61), supplementing what "was insufficiently said by the synods [Councils]. . . . They are those that continue the synodical work within the historical church, correcting, approving and assisting in the soteriological

understanding of the dogmas, . . . [giving] an ongoing validation and confirmation" (p. 62).

Heretics tend to insist on absolutizing particular language (literal, verbal
agreement); they tend to give too much weight to just one or two Fathers—iso-
lating "a Saint from the entire company of Saints" (p. 155); they do not consider
the whole of a Father's works (p. 49). They "steal little sayings and fragments" (p.
55); they detach works "from their historical and theological interconnection"
(p. 155); and they approach things from the perspective of speculative/theoret-
ical philosophical premises rather than from spiritual experience—being too
rationalistic, not having a soteriological perspective.

As Nilus Cabasilas, summed up by Arabatzis says, "The Fathers are content
with theologizing on the basis of the Scriptures, defending all that is contained
in the Scriptures and keeping it . . . *un-multiplied . . . undiminished, and . . .
undistorted*" (p. 141).

HOW TO LEARN TO LOVE
THE LORD

A Sermon by

St. Theophan the Recluse (Russia, 19th century)[1]

LAST week the Holy Myrrhbearers instructed us on love and today St. John the Theologian also instructs us concerning love. He loved the Lord more than anyone else and was loved by Him. Let us imprint in our minds this image of love, and let us begin to turn our feelings according to it and our attitude in relation to the Lord.

How did St. John the Theologian attain such lofty love for the Lord and become a model of love for all of us? I think that he did this in the same way that people begin to love one another. They see the beauty and goodness of a person and become attracted to them with all their heart. In like manner St. John saw the beauty of the Lord and was attracted to Him. He sensed the Lord's special love for him and likewise was inflamed with love for Him. He saw the great, wondrous, and fruitful works of the Lord and, moved by fervent piety, he became completely devoted to Him. He tasted the sweetness of love for Him and, immersed with his whole heart in this love, took rest in it. Here follows the path of assent in love for the Lord. Let us enter upon it, and in the end we will acquire it.

First: St. John saw the beauty of the Lord and was attracted to it. In the same manner love among people is born. They see someone's beauty, spiritual or physical, and begin to love one another. Let us lift up our mind to the

---

1. May 8, 1864, the feast of St. John the Apostle and Evangelist. Translated from the Russian original, *"Bogougodnaya zhizn voobshche,"* *Sermons of Bishop Theophan the Recluse*, pp. 75-81. Printed in *Road to Emmaus*, Vol. XV, No. 2, Spring 2014 (#57).

contemplation of the Lord's beauty, and surely we will not remain cold and indifferent towards Him. The Lord's beauty is the sum total of all His perfection. "Look and observe, what does the Lord lack?" says St. Tikhon of Zadonsk. Anything that you might desire can be found with the Lord in indescribable and unlimited fullness. Do you seek blessedness? He has eternal and true blessedness. Are you seeking beauty? "Comely art Thou in beauty more than the sons of men" (Ps. 44:3). Do you seek nobility? Who is more noble than the Son of God? Are you looking for honor? Who has more honor or is more elevated than the King of the heavens? Do you seek wisdom? He is the Person (Hypostasis) of God's Wisdom. Do you want gladness? He is the joy and gladness of blessed spirits and the chosen of God. Do you need comfort? Who can comfort you more than the Lord Jesus? Do you seek rest? Here is the eternal rest of those souls that love Him. Do you want life? He is the fountain of life. Are you afraid of being lost? He is the way. Do you fear deception? He is Truth. Are you in fear of death? He is life as He Himself assures us: "I am the Way, the Truth, and the Life." In short, all the perfection, beauty, and goodness that the human soul could love is found in Him. Force your mind to grasp this and, you will not be able to do otherwise than love the Lord. St. Catherine the Great Martyr promised to love the one in whom she would see the same wealth that she possessed, the same beauty, the same wisdom she boasted of, expecting that in the whole world she would not find such a person. But when she came to know the Lord, she saw that compared to His beauty, wisdom, and wealth her own was nothing and contemptible. She then gave herself completely to Him, clinging to Him and offering herself to Him as a sacrifice.

Secondly, St. John the Theologian, sensing the Lord's love for him, was inflamed with love for Him. Sincere and selfless love, when experienced from another, always inspires a corresponding feeling. Let us experience the Lord's love and kindle our love for Him. "What did the Son of God not do for us?" asks St. Tikhon. "What did He not attain for us? What did He not bear and suffer for the sake of our poor and needy souls? What labors and sufferings did He not take upon Himself in order to bring us, who had fallen away, to His Heavenly Father? He came down from Heaven in order to raise us, who had been cast out of Paradise, up to Heaven. For our sake He was born in the flesh in order to bring us unto Himself through spiritual regeneration. He humbled Himself for our sake, in order to lift us up. He became impoverished, in order to enrich us wretched ones. He suffered dishonor and wounds in order to heal and glorify us. He died for us in order to give life to us who were dead. Behold what condescension and humility His perfect love and sympathetic mercy brought Him to." Has not each one of us experienced this movement of God's love? How often have we fled from this love by sinning? Every time, because of one phrase, "I am guilty and will not do it again," have we been reunited through His mercy. How many times have we angered Him by giving into the temptation of the delights of this world. Then when we turned to Him again we were admitted to the Lord's Table, to partake of His Body and drink His Blood. Is this not the embrace of His merciful love? Christ is among us in our everyday life. Who among us has not experienced His caring nearness to us, in deliverance from misfortune, illness, sorrow, difficult circumstances, in all needs spiritual and physical? Is it possible not to respond to such great love and turn to One who so untiringly loves us? Is it possible because of distraction and inattention to forget about the Lord's love for us? Having known and remembered this love, it is then impossible not to experience a feeling of love for the Lord no matter how calloused one's heart might be. He who continually walks in the presence of God's love will always be kindled with love for Him. Such is the nature of love!

Thirdly: St. John tasted the sweetness of love for the Lord and with perfect peace rested on his breast. Love is in itself a gift which can be compared with no other. It brings a blessing which is higher than anything in heaven or on earth. The Lord says, "He that hath My commandments, and keepeth them, he it is that loveth Me: and he that loveth Me shall be loved of My Father, and I will love him, and will manifest Myself to him, and If a man love Me, he will keep My words: and My Father will love him, and We will come unto him, and make Our abode with him" (Jn. 14:21, 23). How comforting are these words! What great and exalted promises the Son of God offers to those who love Him—that the true lover of Christ will share in friendship with the Father and His Son! The human mind cannot fathom God's goodness. God Who is great, endless, and unattainable, desires to have friendship with man whom He created and who is His slave. He desires to have friendship as long as man does not reject it ...fellowship is with the Father, and with His Son Jesus Christ (I Jn. 13) writes St John. Where the Son and the Father are, there also the Holy Spirit is not excluded. Behold what the love of Christ attains! He who loves is worthy to be the dwelling and home of of the Most Holy Trinity. The Tri-Hypostatic God—Father, Son and Holy Spirit—is well disposed to dwell in man by Grace. God is love; and he that dwelleth in love dwelleth in God, and God in him. (I Jn. 4:16). Blessed indeed is such a heart! Even here on the earth it feels joy which is abundantly poured forth into the hearts of the chosen unto eternal life. The heart tastes the very essence of "how good the Lord is" and possesses that which is meant by the words, The Kingdom of God is within you.

For there where God is, is also all that belongs to Him. If God is within you because of your love, then you will have His justification for your sins, deliverance from your captivity, peace instead of your evil conscience, joy instead of your misery, comfort instead of your sorrow, justification at God's judgement, assistance against your enemies, wisdom and intelligence instead of confusion and ignorance, strength in your weakness. If the Lord dwells in you for the sake of your love, then who can be against you, what harm can befall you? If

He is your peace, then who can disturb you? If He is your joy and comfort, then who or what can cause you sorrow? If He is your strength, then who can overcome you? If He is your King, then who can subjugate you? "If God is with us then who can be against us," boldly exclaims St. Paul together with all those who love the Lord (Rom. 8:31). Such is love, and behold what it brings with it! Those who enter into the love of the Lord feel that they are more and more filled and perfected. For love is the bond of perfectness (Col. 3:14).

If you desire to love the Lord then strive to contemplate with your mind His beauty, or the fullness of His perfection, sense the warmth of His love and taste the sweetness of love itself with your heart. One cannot learn love, it takes place in the hidden places of the heart. It is sown in secret and ripens unobserved, like seed cast on the ground which sprouts without the knowledge of the sower, bringing forth a stem, an ear of grain and seed in the ear. Love is sown mysteriously, always, however, from the effect on the heart, the object of love. Turn your mind in your heart to the radiant, visage of the Lord, full of love and worthy of love, and from His eyes a spark will descend into your heart and kindle it with love for Him. He who stands by a fire is warmed by it, and he who turns to the Lord with his mind and heart is warmed by the fervor of His love, and himself begins to return a warm disposition towards Him. "...The love of God is shed abroad in our hearts..." (Rom. 5:5), the Apostle Paul teaches. Love is a gift, but a gift prepared for everyone who seeks it: only desire it and seek, and immediately you will receive it. Just as the Lord embraces everyone, so it is impossible not to love Him. However, since not everyone turns to Him and seeks Him, so not everyone loves Him. For indeed He loved us first, and therefore we should love Him [even after the fact].

As it is, we have loved something instead of Him, something not pleasing to Him and not blessed by Him—and are not capable of loving Him since we have but one heart and not two. Therefore we cannot work for God and mammon [the world]. Remember, brethren, that the friendship of the world is enmity with God (James 4:4). Enmity with God! This is terrible! But worse are the words, "If any man love not the Lord Jesus Christ, let him be Anathema, Maranatha" (I Cor. 16:22). Such was the expression of St. Paul's zealous love.

Let us dwell on these things brethren, and force ourselves to love the Lord with all our hearts, all our souls, and all our strength. Even better, let us arouse the love for Him sleeping in us and bring it out into action to be seen by us and everyone. Amen.